EROTIC CITY

EROTIC CITY

*Sexual Revolutions
and the Making of
Modern San Francisco*

JOSH SIDES

OXFORD
UNIVERSITY PRESS

2009

OXFORD
UNIVERSITY PRESS

Oxford University Press, Inc., publishes works that further
Oxford University's objective of excellence
in research, scholarship, and education.

Oxford   New York
Auckland   Cape Town   Dar es Salaam   Hong Kong   Karachi
Kuala Lumpur   Madrid   Melbourne   Mexico City   Nairobi
New Delhi   Shanghai   Taipei   Toronto

With offices in
Argentina   Austria   Brazil   Chile   Czech Republic   France   Greece
Guatemala   Hungary   Italy   Japan   Poland   Portugal   Singapore
South Korea   Switzerland   Thailand   Turkey   Ukraine   Vietnam

Copyright © 2009 by Oxford University Press, Inc.

Published by Oxford University Press, Inc.
198 Madison Avenue, New York, New York 10016

www.oup.com

Oxford is a registered trademark of Oxford University Press.

Library of Congress Cataloging-in-Publication Data
Sides, Josh, 1972–
Erotic city : sexual revolutions and the making of modern
San Francisco / Josh Sides.
    p.   cm.
Includes bibliographical references and index.
ISBN 978-0-19-537781-1
1. Sex customs—California—San Francisco—History.   I. Title.
HQ18.U5S543 2009
306.7709794'6109045—dc22   2009002743

9 8 7 6 5 4 3 2 1

Printed in the United States of America
on acid-free paper

For Rebecca

CONTENTS

EROTIC CITY

INTRODUCTION:
FRED METHNER'S
STREET

Beginning in the mid-1960s, the spectacle of sexuality appeared on the streets and in the public places of large cities throughout the United States in ways that had been unimaginable at any other moment in the nation's history. The increasingly public nature of sexuality—a critical dimension of a larger moment in history that we call the sexual revolution—was rapturous for sexual revolutionaries. It was empowering for gays, lesbians, and bisexuals who could finally express their affection, though never truly free from fear; it was liberating for unmarried women and men who "shacked up" before marriage, often to the wagging consternation of their older neighbors. It was ecstatic for the young men who crowded around—and even occasionally paid to enter—the thousands of strip clubs, sex shops, and massage parlors that dotted the urban landscape like a neon constellation. And it was profitable for the small armies of female and male prostitutes who swarmed from the hinterlands to the nation's big cities, recognizing that sexual freedom need not be free. Sharing their profits in the highly sexualized metropolis were legions of pornographers, whose wares, once relegated to the back rooms of only the seediest skid row stores before the sexual revolution, were now displayed prominently in storefront windows throughout the cities, and even in the suburbs. For so many, the sexual revolution was an extended engagement with, and celebration of, the human libido.[1]

But Fred Methner was definitely not celebrating. Since assuming the role of Secretary and official spokesman for the East & West of

Castro Street Improvement Club in 1962, Methner had developed a well-earned reputation as the busiest busybody and crankiest crank in San Francisco's Noe Valley district. And most of his neighbors loved him for it. They even honored him with the sobriquet "the Mayor of Twenty-fourth Street," in reference to his eminence on the main commercial thoroughfare of the district. Most of them, like him, were European immigrants—Germans, Czechs, Slovaks, Latvians, Poles, Irish, and Italians—who had landed on the docks of the city in the 1920s and 1930s, contributing their backbreaking labor and well-honed craft skills to the burgeoning metropolis, buying modest homes in its lowlands west of Guerrero Street, and developing a strong sense of both civic pride and proprietorship. Methner had emigrated from Germany by way of New York City and landed in the 1920s in San Francisco, where he soon apprenticed as a lithographer, a trade that he learned from his father and that suited his fastidious temperament well. He and his neighbors had spent their lives operating and patronizing the businesses on Twenty-fourth Street. Mostly Catholic, they had attended Sunday Mass under the daunting spires of St. Paul's Catholic Church and the more modest St. Philip's Church for years, and many of them sent their children to the St. Paul's school, one of the largest parochial schools in the western United States. And they had planted and tended hearty, fog-resistant gardens of jade, nasturtium, and California poppies, testament to the pride of Noe Valley's homeowners and to an abiding faith in their California dream.[2]

Since the early sixties, Methner had made regular excursions to meetings of the San Francisco Board of Supervisors and the City Planning Department to complain about small assaults to the character of Noe Valley. In fact, this parochial district—which had emerged in the late nineteenth century as a streetcar suburb tied to the downtown, waterfront, and South of Market areas—was largely unscathed by the sweeping economic and social transformations taking place in San Francisco during the 1960s and 1970s. But even small infractions warranted Methner's attention. He had lobbied the board to criminalize the posting of advertisements on telephone poles and, failing in that, went around tearing them down himself. He fought for, and won, a zoning ordinance forbidding the opening of any new liquor stores in Noe Valley, as well as a very sensible ordinance outlawing dog waste on sidewalks. In 1970, Methner rallied over five hundred Noe Valley residents in a protest against the San Francisco Department of Public Health (SFDPH), which sought to build a mental health clinic on Twenty-fourth Street near Church Street. He derided what he personally considered would be a glorified "drug center" catering to the weakness and lassitude of "hippie culture." Hippies, Methner insisted, were not only drug addicts but also "the ones who are

St. Paul's Catholic Church, Valley & Church St.
H. Blair

FIGURE I.I. St. Paul's Catholic Church, the spiritual and cultural heart of Fred Methner's Noe Valley neighborhood. Courtesy: San Francisco History Center, San Francisco Public Library.

causing the VD epidemic."[3] He and his supporters ultimately convinced the SFDPH to abandon the plan.

By the late seventies, Methner was a seasoned veteran of neighborhood defense, but few of his battles prepared him for what he saw one morning across the street from the St. Philip's school at Diamond and Twenty-fourth streets. On display in the window of a liquor store, and in plain view of the impressionable schoolchildren at St. Paul's, were pornographic magazines. After exchanging unpleasantries with the store owner, Methner marched down to a meeting of the City Planning Department to complain. This time, however, he was joined by his neighbors just down the hill in the Mission District, merchants and hoteliers in the more distant Tenderloin and Union Square areas, and property owners from other parts of town. They all complained about the profusion of pornography and prostitution in their neighborhoods, lending their support to a proposed ordinance restricting the display of pornography throughout the city. "I have been a resident of San Francisco for over fifty years now," Methner began. "I have seen my beloved adopted city degenerate from something lovely and beautiful to something vile, vicious and venomous. Rules and regulations which are the basis of any civilized society have been undermined till we have nothing left to be proud of." The display of pornography, Methner argued, was just one symptom of the recent and unbearable climate of "total permissiveness" plaguing the city.[4]

As he had so many times before, Methner won the battle: an extremely ambitious city supervisor named Dianne Feinstein had been working for almost a decade to reverse the visible cues of the sexual revolution in San Francisco, and she finally secured passage of an ordinance restricting "adult entertainment" businesses in 1978, shortly after Methner's heated protest at the Planning Department. But he was losing the war. Feinstein had conceded as much when she grudgingly admitted to a *New York Times* reporter in 1971 that San Francisco had become "a kind of smut capital of the United States."[5]

Methner and his neighbors were part of what was increasingly being called— often disparagingly—the "old" San Francisco. But there was absolutely no love lost: Methner and his embattled peers wanted nothing to do with the "new" San Francisco, a city whose skyline was being transformed by massive new skyscrapers, whose factories were closing, and whose neighborhoods were flooded with men and women who worked not with their hands but with their heads, others who seemed to work not at all, and still others who brazenly flaunted their unwholesome sexuality. Indeed, Methner and his neighbors likely saw themselves as victims of two simultaneous revolutions—one economic and one social. Once a city of roughnecks, craftsmen, and financiers, San Francisco was becoming a white collar corporate center par excellence. "Manhattanization"— as critics called it—brought thirty-one new skyscrapers to the downtown in the late 1960s, and a construction boom in downtown hotels and convention centers followed quickly in the 1970s.[6] Yet at the very same time—and much more famously—San Francisco also became the epicenter of the nation's countercultural and sexual revolution, and the signs of that transformation were no less jarring to folks like Methner than the giant skyscrapers piercing the city's once unobscured skyline. Gays and lesbians held hands and kissed in public; prostitutes, panderers, and pornographers flooded the streets with their filth; and a few free lovers literally danced naked in the street. As Herb Caen, the longtime columnist for the *San Francisco Chronicle,* observed in 1964: "The old-timers think the newcomers are ruining the city, and newcomers regard the old-timers as a bunch of fuddy-duddies intent only on preserving a distant dream."[7]

Although there were certainly exceptions to this rule, Caen had it about right. The results of a 1974 survey conducted by *San Francisco Focus* magazine, for example, revealed that 74% of respondents under thirty years of age felt that adults who wished to see pornographic films should be allowed to do so, while only 25% of respondents over sixty believed this. Similarly, 77% of respondents under thirty disagreed that homosexuality should be a crime, but only 29% of those over sixty did.[8] Though they must have felt outnumbered in increasingly libertine San Francisco, seniors could take comfort in knowing that their views were generally consistent with those of Americans nationwide. In a 1969 Gallup national survey, 71% of respondents said they found nude pictures objectionable, 73% wanted stricter state and local laws restricting the sale of obscene materials on newsstands, and 48% were willing to join a neighborhood group to protest the sale of pornographic material on newsstands.[9]

Fred Methner's crusade is an easy one to overlook when considering the cultural history of a city that became famous in the 1960s and 1970s for producing silicone-enhanced topless dancer Carol Doda, fratricidal pornography impresarios Jim and Artie Mitchell, and supervisor Harvey Milk, one of the nation's first openly gay politicians. Yet an understanding of the reactions of Methner and those like him illuminates essential dimensions of the history of both the sexual revolution and the postwar American metropolis that have been invisible in most accounts. The sexual revolution is remembered as an era in which the individual pursuit of higher consciousness and physical ecstasy became part of the zeitgeist, and a time in which millions of personal sexual revelations, as well as countless experiments in erotic communalism, permanently shattered sexual taboos in the United States. Famed participant-observer Todd Gitlin remembers that the "sex was ethereal" and that the point of the sixties' cultural revolution was "to open up a new space, an *inner* space, so that we could *space out,* live for the sheer exultant point of living."[10]

But as Fred Methner's humble and rather pedestrian crusade suggests—and this book demonstrates—some of the most important battles of the sexual revolution were fought not necessarily in the mind, around the dining room table, or in the nation's courtrooms but instead in the streets of America's cities. Furthermore, the outcome of this bitter contest about sexual expressions in public spaces—on streets, in parks, on newsstands, in bars, in nightclubs, and in steam baths—is the most enduring legacy of the sexual revolution in the United States.[11] In few cities were these battles more pitched, and the outcomes more transformative, than in San Francisco.[12] And San Francisco's street-level battles over prostitution, pornography, homosexuality, nudism, transgenderism, "social diseases," AIDS, and marriage have prefigured the nation's for almost half a century.

Yet, contrary to common lore, nothing in San Francisco's history destined it to become an internationally renowned bastion of sexual libertinism. Instead, sex radicals created it, despite fierce resistance from several generations of the city's residents. Before the sexual revolution, a very clear distinction between private and public sexuality existed in San Francisco—as it did in many American cities—and this distinction had clear geographic parameters. From the Gold Rush up to about 1915, both the Tenderloin district and the Barbary Coast were the sites of erotic entertainment and prostitution. Had the activities of the sexual revolution remained within these historic parameters, they would hardly have aroused the passions they did. But by normalizing the activities that occurred in these once well-contained districts, the sexual revolution allowed spectacles of sexuality to spread into residential and "family" neighborhoods and once-hallowed public spaces. Indeed, it could be said that Methner and his allies believed that cities functioned best when ordered by a kind of moralists' geography in which ostensibly reputable sexual practices were sharply segregated from unsavory ones. "I am the last one to deny those who are looking for a sexual thrill the right to have such," Methner told the commission, striking a cosmopolitan tone, but they should go "to an area specially set aside for that purpose."[13]

Sex radicals violently assailed the moralists' geography in San Francisco and elsewhere. Emboldened by the Supreme Court's historic 1957 decision in *Roth v. United Sates,* and subsequent rulings that continued to narrow the legal territory of "obscenity," sex radicals published and distributed a dizzying array of sexually explicit literature on street corners. Some swam nude at genteel Aquatic Park. Others stripped to their panties and made erotic dance history, while others became prostitutes. Some marched against homosexual discrimination on the steps of the Federal Building in 1966, and many of them marched again in 1969, not as homosexuals but as "gay-libbers." Countless "hippies" moved into communal apartments where clothing was optional and orgies were common. By the 1970s, gay men proudly walked the streets of the Castro District and claimed it as their own, and many others prowled the streets South of Market or the trails of Golden Gate Park for public sex encounters; long hidden from sight, lesbians claimed their own urban spaces in the Mission District in the 1970s, opening their own coffee shops and bars. In these ways and many others, sex radicals—those individuals who willfully violated the sexual taboos of their era—asserted both their real and perceived rights to express their sexuality as fully as they desired at any given moment and in any particular place. In many cases, the public spectacles of sex radicals were noble, even heroic, particularly when their aim was to expand the rights of individuals to live happy, sexually and emotionally fulfilling lives; in many other cases, they were purely provocative; and in still other cases, they were self-indulgent and tasteless. Whatever the nature of the spectacle, however, sex radicals transformed the ways Americans experienced and came to imagine their metropolises.

If sex radicals left an indelible mark on the urban landscape, so did the increasingly vocal and politically innovative sexual counterrevolutionaries, those individuals from across the political spectrum who shared a traditional view of the proper place of sex in society. As the charge of obscenity became legally untenable after the *Roth* decision in 1957—and politically untenable in increasingly libertine San Francisco—sexual counterrevolutionaries sought to reassert the moralists' geography by elevating the concept of "neighborhood character" to a sacrosanct position among planners and other civic officials. Bureaucratic, ostensibly nonjudgmental, and sufficiently vague, the "neighborhood character" doctrine became a repository for moralists' anxiety about the fate of their vision of civic life. This new strategy created the delicate balance— under which American urbanites today live—between on the one hand constitutionally guaranteed rights to free speech and expression and on the other hand people's rights, both statutory and perceived, to protection from uses of space in their neighborhoods that they deem noxious or offensive.

The manipulation of zoning laws, however, was only the high road. Most sexual counterrevolutionaries were not as disciplined as Methner and his City Hall and Planning Department allies. One of the forgotten legacies of the sexual revolution in San Francisco is the campaign of physical violence and repression it unleashed. The assassinations of Supervisor Milk and Mayor George Moscone in 1978 stunned San Franciscans and shook their faith in their city's fabled tolerance. But the assassinations were merely the most high-profile acts of violence in an era that was marked by shocking violence against sex radicals in general and homosexuals in particular. Throughout the late sixties and the seventies and across the city, young neighborhood toughs physically assaulted and sometimes killed free-loving hippies, gays, and lesbians to punish them for their unorthodox appearance and their "faggoty" behavior. Another group— hardened criminals, particularly rapists—exploited the naiveté of young hippies and other sex radicals by infiltrating their social milieu. In addition to the untold damage this nefarious brand of predation caused its victims, it had the unfortunate effect of contributing to the conflation of sex radicalism and violent crime in the minds of both sexual counterrevolutionaries and journalists—despite the fact that abhorrence of violence and the defense of personal liberties were the essential values of virtually all sex radicals.

The dramatic potential of this conflation was not lost on the engineers of American entertainment. In the late 1960s and 1970s, Hollywood directors released a spate of films that depicted respectable urbanites being victimized by violent pimps, transsexuals, gays, pornographers, and rapists and celebrated the heroism of the smut-busting, pervert-pulverizing vigilante. Trading on San Francisco's rising national notoriety as a repository of "fruits and nuts," and aggressively courted by the newly established Mayor's Film Production Office, Hollywood increasingly chose San Francisco over other, older film locales like New York. Today, Clint Eastwood's "Dirty" Harry Callahan is the best remembered San Francisco vigilante of that era, but he stood in a crowded field of Hollywood vigilantes who were determined to make the streets of San Francisco "once again safe" for "regular" Americans.

Wildly popular and profitable, the San Francisco vigilante films of the late 1960s and 1970s portrayed a city that spectacularly exceeded Americans' worst impressions of San Francisco. When the actual events of the sexual revolution in San Francisco melded, in the popular imagination, with the phantasmagoric San Francisco of the Hollywood studios, an eminently exploitable symbol of American moral decline was born. It became a particularly potent symbol for the Republican Party. In November 1969, President Richard Nixon transfixed conservatives, and transformed the history of conservatism, when he appealed to the "silent majority" of Americans to support the war in Vietnam in a nationally televised speech, in which he deftly used San Francisco as a foil. "In San Francisco," he said—and then came a pregnant pause—"a few weeks ago, I saw demonstrators carrying signs reading: 'Lose in Vietnam, bring the boys home.'" Fifteen years later, when President Ronald Reagan's United Nations Ambassador, Jeane Kirkpatrick, blasted "San Francisco Democrats" during her famous "Blame America First" speech at the 1984 Republican National Convention in Dallas, she was referring to the Democrats' alleged "softness" on communism. But the phrase—casually interchangeable with "San Francisco liberals"—worked precisely because it vindicated the worldview of social conservatives who loathed "countercultural" values as much as they did communism. Reagan traded on Dirty Harry's combativeness when he taunted congressional proponents of tax increases in 1985: "Go ahead, make my day!" mimicking Eastwood's line in the 1983 San Francisco vigilante film *Sudden Impact*. The line was not likely lost on Americans: a 1985 survey by *U.S. News & World Report* found that Eastwood was then ranked as the most "inspirational" public figure "living anywhere in the world" by Americans ages eighteen to twenty-four.[14]

When the AIDS epidemic arrived in the early 1980s, San Francisco was devastated. The prevalence of sex radicalism in the city virtually assured widespread transmission of the disease, and San Francisco had the highest annual rate of AIDS infection in any American city until 1995.[15] Yet despite the staggering toll of the disease in the city and the Reagan administration's callous response to the crisis, doctors at the University of California at San Francisco (UCSF), the SFDPH, community groups, individual sex educators, and one-time sex radicals responded with remarkable alacrity, creating a highly coordinated and compassionate network that became known in health-care circles nationally as "the San Francisco model." Outside the health-care community, however, the response to the crisis was highly uneven. Property owners throughout the city vigilantly "defended" their properties from AIDS-infected tenants, stimulating the creation of new civil rights laws. Sexual counterrevolutionaries exploited the crisis by repackaging their moralism in the discourse of public health. In the Tenderloin, persistent poverty and alienation among male-to-female transgenders led too many of them into the increasingly risky world of prostitution. And in Bayview–Hunters Point—the geographically isolated and resource-poor black community on the remote southeastern corner of the city—AIDS made a belated arrival in the 1990s, creating an entirely new wave of the epidemic, one that defied, and continues to defy, easy remedies. Ultimately, the AIDS crisis laid bare the savage inequalities plaguing San Francisco, many of which had been masked by the "good vibes" of the sexual revolution.

By the 1990s, many of the most radical manifestations of the sexual revolution had disappeared from the urban landscape of San Francisco. Driving this dynamic was the specter of AIDS, the explosion in consumption of home video and Internet pornography, and the in-migration of an affluent, consumer-oriented population. The declining visibility of sexual behavior in public, coupled with the curtailment of radical sex among many gay men and "swinging" straights, led to popular pronouncements that the sexual revolution was over. In fact, it was not; it continued under the leadership of lesbians and bisexual women. Skeptical about the rigid politics of the lesbian pioneers of the 1970s, knowledgeable about safe sex practices, and less affected by AIDS than gay men, lesbians in San Francisco created a second sexual revolution, occupying new neighborhoods, opening new businesses, publishing new magazines, and sometimes having group sex in sex clubs. In the process, they arguably expanded the scope of acceptable female sexual practices both locally and nationally.

This book explores the fertile nexus of geography, morality, sexual desire and behavior, and law enforcement that has so profoundly affected urban life in America. This nexus's manifestations and influences during the nineteenth and early twentieth centuries have been very well documented, but those during the late twentieth century have scarcely been considered.[16] By analyzing the contours of this nexus in the late twentieth century, I chart a new direction in the bourgeoning, dynamic literature on the fate of the postwar American metropolis. Since the early 1990s, scholars and historians in particular have explored the myriad ways race and racism, coupled with the vast expansion of suburban housing opportunities, fueled the postwar process of "white flight" and "urban decline." That process, historians have shown, was often accompanied by the simultaneous suburbanization and internationalization of industrial production, leaving behind cities whose populations were increasingly black, increasingly poor, and increasingly marginalized by an ascendant, suburban "New Right" that was as hostile to desegregation as it was to taxes.[17] In the West, this process was further complicated by regional variations in the racial composition and economic profiles of Seattle, Los Angeles, Oakland, and other metropolitan areas.[18]

In this book, I challenge the notion that race was always the prime mover in postwar urban history by arguing that it was the shifting *culture* of cities that more directly influenced their destiny. Cities' changing racial profiles represented one of the most important transformations in postwar America, but the case of San Francisco also suggests that these racial shifts—and the anxieties they produced—were part of a larger cultural shift that was frequently understood in moral and not strictly racial terms. The city, as the famed urbanist Lewis Mumford explained, is always a "theater of social action," and the "sociality" of the city informs its physical and economic structure.[19] The case of San Francisco reminds us that not simply human sociality but also the desire for sexual knowledge and stimulation, and the countless exchanges and transactions that desire has inspired, shapes cities as well.

Appreciating the influence of shifting culture on urban life allows us to better understand the diverging trajectories of postwar cities. With this appreciation, we can move beyond the trope of urban decline, which is ill equipped to capture the complexity of postwar urban development. As Bryant Simon has astutely observed regarding Atlantic City, "urban decline is not, and never was, a one-way street."[20] Indeed, in San Francisco, gays, lesbians, and straight sex radicals and bohemians often became both consumers and producers in a dynamic new economy, even as the city grappled with the consequences of white flight and the decline in manufacturing work, those ostensible indicators of urban decline. Sex radicals—recklessly experimental, fearless, and sometimes foolish—foisted their vision of a sexually liberated, creatively driven, and highly tolerant society onto San Francisco, and created one of the most dynamic metropolises of the twentieth century.

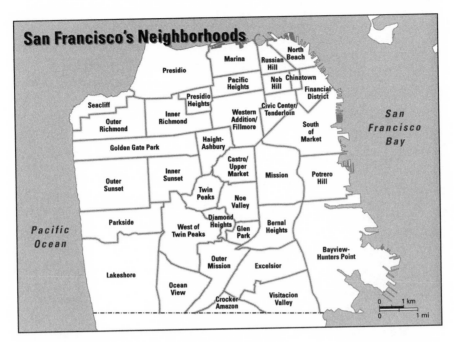

San Francisco's Neighborhoods

Presidio

Marina

Russian Hill

North Beach

Pacific Heights

Nob Hill

Chinatown

Seacliff

Presidio Heights

Civic Center/ Tenderloin

Financial District

Inner Richmond

Western Addition/ Fillmore

Outer Richmond

San Francisco Bay

South of Market

Golden Gate Park

Haight- Ashbury

Castro/ Upper Market

Outer Sunset

Inner Sunset

Mission

Potrero Hill

Twin Peaks

Noe Valley

Parkside

Diamond Heights

Bernal Heights

West of Twin Peaks

Glen Park

Pacific Ocean

Bayview- Hunters Point

Lakeshore

Outer Mission

Excelsior

Ocean View

Crocker Amazon

Visitacion Valley

0   1 km

0   1 mi

MAP 1. Map by David Deis, Dreamline Cartography.

1

WHAT'S BECOME OF THE PARIS OF THE WEST?

In June 1946, exotic dancer Sally Rand entered the stage at the Club Savoy near San Francisco's Union Square and yet again performed her world renowned "fan dance." As she had since unveiling the dance at the 1933 World's Fair in Chicago, Rand danced nude to Claude Debussy's "Clair de Lune" and Chopin's "Waltz in C Sharp Minor," while manipulating two giant, pink ostrich feathers to cover her breasts and genitalia, which themselves were covered with tiny flesh-tone patches of fabric that gave the illusion of complete nudity. It was an act she had performed literally thousands of times nationwide since 1933, and probably hundreds of times in San Francisco, first during a well-publicized trip in 1933, when she was welcomed by officials at City Hall, again during the Golden Gate International Exposition of 1939–1940, and yet again during an extended stint at the Music Box during the Exposition.

By 1946, Rand's routine was hardly new or even particularly risqué by contemporary standards. True, she had modified her act by adding a giant transparent bubble on and around which she performed gymnastic feats before disrobing. But the very need to add this gimmick was indicative of the simple fact that Rand's act was, by 1946, frankly passé. Forty-two years old and deeply in debt, she had been eclipsed by younger, more immodest dancers like Gypsy Rose Lee, and particularly Lili St. Cyr, who titillated crowds in the late 1940s by taking a nude bubble bath in a transparent glass tub. So Rand was stunned when the chief of the San Francisco Police Department (SFPD), Charles Dullea, arrested her

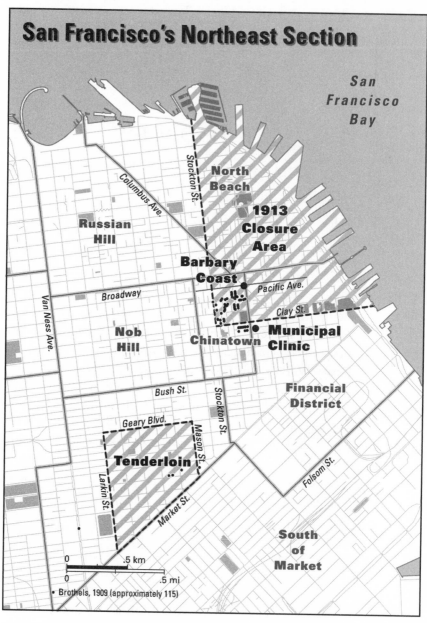

San Francisco's Northeast Section

San Francisco Bay

Stockton St.

Columbus Ave.

North Beach

1913 Closure Area

Russian Hill

Barbary Coast

Broadway

Pacific Ave.

Clay St.

Van Ness Ave.

Nob Hill

Chinatown

Municipal Clinic

Financial District

Bush St.

Stockton St.

Geary Blvd.

Mason St.

Tenderloin

Larkin St.

Folsom St.

Market St.

South of Market

0   .5 km

0   .5 mi

• Brothels, 1909 (approximately 115)

MAP 2. Map by David Deis, Dreamline Cartography.

FIGURE I.I. (*opposite page*) Sally Rand poses before her appearance in court on charges of lewdness in 1946. Courtesy: San Francisco History Center, San Francisco Public Library.

on charges of violating city and state ordinances against performing "obscene, immoral" shows "offensive to public decency." It also shocked her dashing, theatrical, attorney, Jake Ehrlich, who had successfully defended numerous burlesque dancers, San Francisco's Grande Madame, Sally Stanford, and later Billie Holiday when she was arrested on drug charges. "What's going on around here?" Ehrlich melodramatically demanded of the court shortly after Rand's arrest. "What's become of the Paris of the West?"[1]

There were a number of answers to Ehrlich's question. One was Chief Dullea himself. Having joined the SFPD in 1914 and quickly risen to the rank of lieutenant by 1923, this burly Irishman had a reputation as a "dogged copper" who had single-handedly taken down five armed suspects in one of his most publicized exploits. Impressed with Dullea's outstanding record as a homicide investigator—and probably his penchant for authoritarianism—Mayor Angelo Rossi had leaned on the San Francisco Police Commission to appoint Dullea as chief in 1940. In response to the wave of prostitutes, servicemen, and carousers that had descended on the bustling city during World War II, Dullea had taken the unprecedented step of ordering the closure of all brothels in the city, and he continued to aggressively pursue prostitution convictions after the war, even to the consternation of local judges and civil liberties advocates. More significantly, under the subsequent mayoral administration of shipping magnate Roger Lapham—known as "the business mayor"—the restoration of an inviting and morally uncompromised shopping area downtown had moved to the top of the civic agenda. Under the Rossi administration, the city had begun construction of one of the nation's first underground parking lots beneath Union Square, and during Lapham's administration, local business interests succeeded in luring Eastern retailers, including Sears-Roebuck, Woolworth, and Bullock-Magnin, to San Francisco. Most significant, the landmark O'Connor, Moffatt & Company Department Store building at Union Square was in the process of being renovated to accommodate an influential new tenant whose name would become synonymous with the square: Macy's. Once regarded as part of the downtrodden Tenderloin district, and sometimes called the Downtown Tenderloin, Union Square was in the process of being remade along more "respectable" and remunerative lines. It was a twist that Rand, a master of optical illusion, could surely have appreciated, if only grudgingly: her dance had not changed, but the tableau behind it had.[2]

The much more comprehensive answer to Ehrlich's question was that San Francisco had not, in fact, been the Paris of the West for at least two decades. Beginning in the 1850s, the mostly male town of San Francisco had hosted a staggering number of saloons, a dizzying array of erotic performances and prostitutes, and a few homosexual men and women. But by the early twentieth century, the "wide-open town" began to close. The rising female population diminished the market for prostitution and erotic dancing. More important, in the wake of the sensational graft prosecution of 1906, and the great earthquake of 1906, San Francisco's financial elite sought to project an image of the city as clean, orderly, morally reputable, and therefore worthy of financial investment. By the end of World War I, erotic entertainment, prostitution, and homosexuality were curtailed in San Francisco as thoroughly as in any other American city.

Between World War I and the late 1950s, representatives of the city's financial elite, municipal government, local law enforcement, and sundry cultural and religious leaders, like their counterparts in other large American cities, sought to suppress the ubiquitous and irrepressible human tendency to express sexual identities and desires. And when suppression was either impossible or unfeasible, they pursued an aggressive policy of geographic containment by sharply limiting the urban space in which that human tendency could flourish. From the perspective of most authorities and reformers, prostitution, erotic entertainments, and open expressions of homosexuality threatened the moral fiber of the American city, and there was general unanimity in officialdom's response to these activities: sexuality was a private affair, intended—by God and other respectable folk—to stay that way.

Gold Rush Legacies on the Barbary Coast

In addition to inspiring the first mass migration to California, the Gold Rush of 1849 also shook loose many of the social moorings of the Victorian era for the eager men crowding the mining camps. Prostitution was not only prevalent in the mines—it was often exotic: in addition to patronizing American prostitutes, miners could easily find Chilean, Chinese, Mexican, and particularly French ones—who outnumbered all others by most accounts—to fulfill their sexual desires. The sexual milieu of the camps was further complicated by the disproportionate gender ratio of the camps' populations, which created opportunities for an easier expression of same-sex desire than miners found in conventional society. Miner John Marshall Newton, for example, was not afraid to be "caught looking" at a tall Danish miner named Hans, "one of the most magnificent looking young men I ever saw," whose "massive shoulders and swelling muscles" left an indelible impression on Newton.[3] Commercial leisure in the camps offered yet more opportunities for sexual experimentation and gratification through saloons and "fandangos," Gold Rush–era dancehalls in which female dancers regularly concluded their performances by having sex with customers offstage.

San Francisco, about 140 miles southwest of the place where gold was first discovered, became the nexus of Gold Rush–era transportation, commerce, and finance virtually overnight. Its population grew from fewer than a thousand inhabitants in 1848 to more than fifty thousand by 1860. By 1900, the city that been just a sleepy Mexican village only fifty years earlier claimed more than 340,000 inhabitants, making it the ninth largest city in the nation.[4] Its early financial and political elite acquired most of their wealth and influence from speculation in large-scale industrial mining projects in the gold mines of California, and later in the silver mines at Nevada's Comstock Lode. The city's nascent political culture drew on and perpetuated the skullduggery of mining camp life. At least before the first prosecutions of graft, in 1906, San Francisco's government was a glorified plutocracy, and most city contracts, permits, utilities, and police protection came at an extraordinarily high price, one that was usually paid directly to the mayor's office. Finally, the imprint of the region's Gold Rush history was also evident in the built environment. Partially because the gender ratio remained skewed into the late nineteenth century, an unusually large proportion of men in San Francisco lived in residential hotels and lodging houses and ate in local restaurants. In both the Tenderloin and South of Market areas, residential hotels, large apartment buildings, and late night restaurants were landmarks of the bachelor culture that supported the city's carousing nightlife. That pattern persisted well into the early twentieth century, as the proportion of the population living in single-resident-occupancy hotels continued in San Francisco to exceed greatly that in older, eastern American cities.[5]

If early San Francisco's financial leadership, political culture, and residential arrangements were inheritances from the Gold Rush, so, too, was its culture of disreputable amusement and sexual license, notorious from its very inception. The Barbary Coast, as San Francisco's unplanned sexual entertainment district was known, was the principal site of that culture, the epicenter of San Francisco's licentiousness. Encompassing approximately one and a half square miles, concentrated predominantly on Pacific Street between Kearny and Montgomery streets, the Barbary Coast sat squarely between what would become the city's central downtown business district and the predominantly Italian community of North Beach. In his classic and colorful 1933 account of the Barbary Coast, journalist and amateur historian Herbert Asbury attributed its unique culture to the "influx of gold-seekers and the horde of gamblers, thieves, harlots, politicians and other felonious parasites who battened upon them" who created a "unique criminal district that for almost seventy years was the scene of more viciousness and depravity, but which at the same time possessed more glamour, than any other area of vice and iniquity on the American continent."[6]

FIGURE 1.2. Nightclubs and patrons line Pacific Street in the Barbary Coast, 1909. There were more than one hundred brothels in the blocks surrounding Pacific Street. Courtesy: San Francisco History Center, San Francisco Public Library.

If Asbury, writing in the 1930s, celebrated the historic bawdiness of San Francisco, earlier accounts were less flattering. The earliest published works on San Francisco helped popularize the notion that it had unique iniquities. Scotsman and argonaut J. D. Borthwick observed that the city was full of men "whose actions and conduct were totally unrestrained by the ordinary conventions of civilized life." A man "could follow his own course, for good or evil," Borthwick wrote, "with the utmost freedom." E. S. Capron, author of one of the earliest histories of California, was much more critical. The "excess of immorality," he wrote, "far exceeded that to be found in other cities." By far the most wrathful account appeared in B. E. Lloyd's 1876 *Lights and Shades in San Francisco:* "Like the malaria arising from a stagnant swamp and poisoning the air for miles around does this stagnant pool of human immorality and crime spread its contaminating vapors over the surrounding blocks on either side."[7]

Of course, one cannot easily quantify degrees of depravity, but regardless of its ranking, there is no question that between the Gold Rush and the early twentieth century, the Barbary Coast—so named because of its alleged similarity to the ignominious slave-trading coast of West Africa—sustained a greater variety of sexual commerce and entertainment than most people who arrived there had ever encountered, or, if they were only visitors, would likely ever encounter again. Though principally associated with female prostitution, Barbary Coast dives also offered crude burlesque performances, "leg-shows," belly dancing, and coin-operated "peep shows" that allowed patrons to watch prostitutes ply their trade. The women who worked the Coast and adjacent Chinatown, like those who had worked the mining camps, were an ethnically and racially diverse group that included African Americans and immigrants from eastern and western Europe, Mexico, Chile, China, and Japan. By the turn of the century, if not earlier, Pacific Street venues offered female impersonators who performed dances and, for the right price, sexual favors. Though there is very scarce evidence of commercialized homosexual activity on the Barbary Coast, there was, evidently, enough cross-dressing going on to alarm the Board of Supervisors, which added an ordinance to the Health Code in 1903 forbidding anyone to appear on "any public highway" in clothing "not belonging to or usually worn by his or her sex."[8]

The city's Christian leadership put up a determined fight against the city's deeply entrenched depravity. Most notable was Father Terence Caraher, pastor of the Roman Catholic Church of St. Francis, an Irishman who migrated to the United States in 1873 and whose hostility to public amusement extended beyond the indubitably salacious saloons of North Beach into the realm of roller-skating. "Some of the male skaters," Caraher complained, "speak to one another afterwards of their experiences and their conquests of young women in the rinks, and where do the skaters go after they leave the rinks? I answer, some of them go to perdition."[9] Donaldina Cameron, a Presbyterian missionary from New Zealand, offered a less flamboyant and more enduring challenge to the prevailing debauchery of the Coast and neighboring Chinatown. Assuming the directorship of the San Francisco Presbyterian Mission Home in Chinatown in 1895, Cameron crusaded against Chinese "slavery," inculcated Chinese prostitutes with Christian principles and Victorian habits, and selected proper partners—Christian Chinese men—for them to marry.[10]

Despite their efforts during the early twentieth century, San Francisco moralists made very little progress in a city where both sexual permissiveness and outright political corruption had always prevailed. Neither the SFPD nor any mayoral administration during this period seriously enforced the state and local ordinances outlawing prostitution or "lewd, indecent, or obscene acts." When the SFPD did crack down on prostitution, it merely discouraged prostitutes from plying their trade on specific streets or in certain neighborhoods, thereby relocating the industry while tacitly approving of it. "Protection" for the industry from enforcement lined the pockets of more than a few police officers and at least one mayor. In 1906, it was revealed that political boss Abe Ruef and Mayor Eugene Schmitz had personally collected up to one-quarter of the profits from a large brothel on Jackson and Kearny, appropriately known as the Municipal Brothel. Sex-related political corruption had reached a level in San Francisco that made even veteran carousers blush.[11]

When San Franciscans began the process of physically rebuilding the city in the wake of the devastating earthquake of 1906, the political reformers and the financial elite among them recognized an opportunity to simultaneously rebuild the city's political culture. Remarkably, the Board of Supervisors' response to the revelations of prostitution-related corruption in San Francisco was *not* a wholesale drive against prostitution. Instead, the board heeded the recommendations of Julius Rosenstirn, an influential doctor, and sought instead to regulate the industry. Rosenstirn was chief of staff at the city's prominent Mount Zion Hospital and chairman of the health committee of the Civic League of Improvement Clubs. While serving in the latter capacity, he learned that the venereal disease rate was escalating in the wake of the earthquake. After virtually all the city's brothels were destroyed in the quake, the prostitutes turned to "street trade"— lowly and usually unhygienic—to make their livings. Rosenstirn may not have learned that the brothel keepers actually rebuilt their houses quite quickly: by 1909 there were 108 known in San Francisco.[12] But the post-quake street trade phenomenon obviously left an indelible impression on Rosenstirn. Determined, like fellow Civic League members, to rebuild the city along more hygienic lines, he began an extensive correspondence with doctors in European cities where regulation was practiced and became convinced of its efficacy. Mayor P. H. McCarthy—whose interests were much more informed by political calculations than by health ones—heartily endorsed Rosenstirn's vision.[13]

Rosenstirn was certainly no libertine; he regarded prostitution as a "social malady," "the most ancient cancer of society," and one that brought germs from the "house of shame" to "the trusting helpmate of the home and to its innocent blessing in the cradle." But as a man of science, he was contemptuous of attempts to eradicate prostitution or to "legislate sex-virtue to mankind," and he loathed the prevailing attitudes toward sex education. "Instead of arming the young with the clean and sharp weapon of knowledge," he railed in 1913, "they are permitted to enter the battle of life with its temptations and pitfalls, ignorant of all its most vital constructive and destructive conditions, or they are at best merely provided with scraps of misinformation snatched from the gutter." After two years of lobbying, a plan for a clinic at 682 Commercial Street, between the Barbary Coast and the business district, was approved by the Board of Health. Opening in 1911, the San Francisco Municipal Clinic was an instant success, cutting the rate of venereal disease among known prostitutes by a staggering 66% and preventing an untold number of infections that would have been transmitted from these prostitutes to clients.[14]

The clinic succeeded for several reasons. First, it reconciled "the necessity of enforcing sanitary control" of diseases while exercising "the modern spirit of forbearance," as Rosenstirn described it. The atmosphere of the clinic was generally convivial, and prostitutes were neither chastised nor shamed, though the clinic staff did successfully discourage many novices from continuing down the risky path ahead of them. "Do not forget," a pamphlet distributed by the clinic read, "that the municipal clinic is your friend and for your own protection." The clinic also offered clear-eyed, unabashed medical information for prostitutes about how venereal diseases were transmitted and the proper techniques for identifying symptoms in themselves and in their male customers. A clinic pamphlet on gonorrhea, for example, spoke in unflinching terms about the disease:

> Gonorrhea, commonly called clap, does not simply mean a more or less creamy discharge from the vagina, with the attending burning and soreness in the private parts; and difficulty and pain urinating; but it may, and frequently does travel further up the vagina, into the womb and tubes, and into [the] urethra, bladder and kidneys, to set up inflammation and pus-formation there, or cause very painful swelling of the joints.[15]

Even this assertive educational campaign could not succeed, though, without an enforcement mechanism. Thus, the second element of its success was the support of the SFPD. Prostitutes who were registered with the clinic were given a booklet that identified their race and other physical characteristics, and they submitted to physical exams and blood tests every four days. Prostitutes who were in this way "clean" received a dated stamp that, when shown to police officers, freed them from harassment. Prostitutes without booklets, or with outdated medical inspection records, were charged with vagrancy. The program—whose medical results were unassailable—also received the strong support of the next mayor, future California governor James "Sunny Jim" Rolph, who took office in 1912. "I think it is one of the best institutions we have. It does great work of charity, as well as cleanliness," Rolph said in a published interview in March 1913. But a mere two months later, he ordered the SFPD to cease enforcing the booklet policy, effectively closing the clinic.[16]

Rosenstirn was outraged by the news and jumped to the erroneous conclusion that the "pious prudery" of "militant churchmen" had finally shamed the mayor into closing the clinic. To be sure, the city's Christian leaders regularly condemned the clinic as a municipal endorsement of sin, but Rolph had privately dismissed "anti-vice" crusaders as "self-advertising Pharisees" and "well meaning hysterics." However, he could not so easily brush aside the mounting pressure from local business interests to "clean up" San Francisco in advance of the Panama-Pacific International Exhibition of 1915. Officially a celebration of the opening of the Panama Canal, the exhibition was widely regarded as an opportunity for San Francisco to demonstrate its post-earthquake resilience and rehabilitation to the world. As early as 1910, San Francisco's business elite had already pledged $4 million to the exhibition. Most influential was California power broker and newspaper magnate William Randolph Hearst, whose *San Francisco Examiner* published a series of front-page articles detailing the licentiousness of the Barbary Coast in September 1913. Within a week, Rolph announced that the San Francisco Police Commission would enact new policies that would shut the Coast down.[17]

Applying to the historic Barbary Coast and most of North Beach, the order forbade prostitution, dancing in any saloon, and the presence of female employees or patrons in any saloon. The *Examiner,* reflecting the salience of business interests in this "clean up," opined: "the purpose" of the crusade "is to shut up the market of immoral and vulgar pleasure" and replace it with "a great market for the sale of wholesome and decent fun."[18] A few nightclubs limped along, but the following year the state legislature passed the Red Light Abatement Act, which shifted punishment for prostitution from the prostitutes to the property owners who permitted it, allowing for the seizure of the property by the state of California. In case the threat of real property seizure was an insufficient disincentive for would-be brothel keepers, the act also allowed the state to keep all furniture and musical instruments found on the property.[19]

Rosenstirn pleaded with Rolph to restore SFPD participation in the work of the clinic, providing Rolph with irrefutable proof of its efficacy. He invited several supervisors down to the clinic, where he introduced them to a "perfectly healthy looking woman" who had effectively hidden a syphilitic ulcer "about the size of a quarter dollar" on her soft palate. Because police participation had been withdrawn, Rosenstirn explained, the woman was now free to ply "her sad trade in the low dive she occupied . . . constituting a source of infection for every one of her fifteen or twenty daily visitors." Even after several influential supervisors presented Rolph with this parable, he refused to budge. The fact that Rolph went on to serve eighteen years as mayor before becoming California's governor was proof that despite his famed tolerance of "vice" he was above all a man of politics. From Rosenstirn's perspective, the closure of the clinic was an "unwarrantable wrong" that would cause the citizens of San Francisco incalculable sickness, pain, and suffering. He was prophetic, but too few recognized it at the time.[20]

Prostitution after the Barbary Coast

Mabel Busby, was poised to take advantage of the closure of the Barbary Coast. An affable but hard-nosed young woman who had been born into poverty on a carrot farm in rural Oregon, Busby had moved to California in the early 1920s in search of prosperity. She found it, briefly, in the serene seaside community of Santa Paula, where she mastered that famous craft of the prohibition era, bootlegging. After meeting and marrying—in the span of one week—an attorney from San Francisco, she abandoned her bathtub operation and moved to San Francisco in 1923. Again relying on her inclination toward illicit enterprise, she quickly corralled a stable of young women, paid off the "wonderful set of burglars" running San Francisco, and opened the first of her many houses of prostitution in the Tenderloin. She took the name Sally Stanford—adopting the family name of California's best known tycoon, Leland Stanford—and quickly became the city's best known madam.[21]

Stanford's quick and remarkable success was an indicator of the ineffectiveness of municipal efforts to eradicate prostitution by closing down the Barbary Coast. In fact, while the crusade succeeded in closing down most saloons, nightclubs, and other venues of commercial erotic entertainment, it scarcely put a dent in the prostitution market. Prostitutes simply took their business elsewhere.[22] Once confined almost exclusively to Chinatown and the Barbary Coast, prostitutes and brothels set up shop in the Tenderloin and the adjacent area just south of Market Street.

In 1966, Stanford published her ghost-written memoir *The Lady of the House,* which became a best seller. It was a saucy and shamelessly self-congratulatory romp through her twenty-plus years as San Francisco's leading madam. "One thing was certain in those days," Stanford said of the 1920s: "San Francisco was an open town and the people were happy about it."[23] She detailed her elaborate cat-and-mouse games with vice officers, the ebb and flow of campaigns to run her out of town, her eleventh-hour evasions of arrests and convictions, and the ultimate triumph of her quick wit and savvy over her many boorish opponents. Stanford's houses of prostitution thrived because of her meticulous management, her sensitivity to the needs of men, and her inexplicable intuition for impending trouble.

Although both the Great Depression and World War II had created booming business for Stanford, she marked the early 1940s as the beginning of the "end of the wide-open town as we'd known it."[24] She largely attributed the "decline" of the San Francisco "nightlife" to a few "silly, gabby," and daffy "twists" whose arrests brought the wrath of the SFPD and the local newspapers

FIGURE 1.3. Sally Stanford, San Francisco's leading brothel operator through the late 1940s, pictured in 1952. Courtesy: San Francisco History Center, San Francisco Public Library.

down on her and her peers in the prostitution business; but she must surely have recognized the larger forces at work in the city. Several years earlier, under the administration of Mayor Angelo J. Rossi, the SFPD had begun a new campaign against brothels in response to the release of the Atherton Report, which exposed widespread police corruption and chronicled "protection payoffs" for 135 well-known San Francisco brothels.[25]

Adding to the citywide pressure to eradicate prostitution were new mandates from the federal government on the eve of the nation's entry into World War II. Fearing the debilitative effects of venereal disease on members of the armed forces—and justifiably skeptical about the ability and willingness of local law enforcement agencies to suppress prostitution—Congress in July 1941 passed the May Act, making prostitution near military bases a federal crime. Although the act was rarely invoked nationally—and never invoked in California—the mere threat of it allowed agents from the FBI and the armed forces to secure quick compliance from local authorities. California governor Culbert Olson also weighed in, calling an emergency meeting with state and federal public health experts and urging vigilance on the part of California's local law enforcement agencies against the "sixth column" of venereal disease.[26] In San Francisco, Mayor Rossi coordinated with army and navy officials to "round up" all known prostitutes, raise the cost of bail, and establish a special women's court to streamline prosecutions. Most dramatically, Dullea closed down all known houses of prostitution in 1941.[27]

Like William Randolph Hearst's 1913 campaign to close the Barbary Coast, Dullea's 1941 brothel closure changed the geography of prostitution without diminishing it. Whereas the campaign of 1913 had the effect of shifting prostitutes into other districts, the 1941 brothel closure had the unintended effect of making prostitution more publicly visible than it had ever been by driving prostitutes into bars, a fact that the author of the plan, Chief Dullea, candidly admitted in the *San Francisco Police and Peace Officers' Journal*. "The prostitute transferred her activities to the bars and taverns or sought her customers on the streets," he wrote. "Teen age girls soon came into the picture as well as the class of women who follow the service men around the country." Despite the abysmal failure of this effort, Dullea did not conclude that brothel closure was the wrong approach. Quite the contrary; he believed it was essential to "repel any and all attempts to re-establish houses of prostitution."[28]

The most radical and enduring change in local prostitution policy came when Mayor Rossi empowered the SFPD with quarantine authority. Approved in 1944 as an emergency ordinance by the Board of Supervisors and the new district attorney and future California governor Edmund G. "Pat" Brown, this new policy broke sharply with tradition. With the exception of the years

1922–1932—when the SFPD had insisted on quarantine control—venereal disease control had been the sole domain of the SFDPH. The department had pursued a policy of voluntary quarantine for infected prostitutes since the short-lived Municipal Clinic had closed in 1913. When prostitutes sought the services of the health department and tested positive for venereal diseases— usually gonorrhea or syphilis—health department doctors tried to locate and inform their potentially infected clients or sexual partners and then insisted on the prostitutes' voluntary quarantine. The health department only notified the SFPD when it discovered that infected prostitutes had violated their quarantines and returned to work.

With the transfer of quarantine authority to the SFPD and the installation of Dullea as chief quarantine officer for the city, the nature of venereal disease control changed entirely. Dullea instituted a so-called preliminary quarantine policy, whereby suspected prostitutes or suspected venereal disease carriers were quarantined in jail for seventy-two hours, without bail, pending results of a mandatory medical exam. If found to be infected, women were sentenced to quarantine at the county jail. For supporters of the new policy, the results of venereal disease tests spoke for themselves. In 1947, for example, of the 1,440 women arrested on suspicion of prostitution or venereal disease infection, 303 (or about 21%) were found to be infected with venereal diseases (238 with gonorrhea, 57 with syphilis, 8 with other venereal diseases).[29]

While the quarantine was, and still is today, an essential component of any public health authority, the empowerment of the SFPD with quarantine authority invited a complete abridgement of civil liberties. The policy gave the SFPD a long-sought and highly effective way to deal with socially undesirable women—including prostitutes, well-known alcoholics, and women who were known to be promiscuous—under the guise of health enforcement. It gave the SFPD, in effect, greater power to regulate the behavior of women in public spaces. Although the ordinance stipulated that officers should determine the likelihood of infection *after* making an arrest, in practice, suspicion of infection became grounds for arrest. In the vast majority of cases, neither syphilis nor gonorrhea manifested any plainly visible symptoms, so the arresting officers' determination of the "likelihood of infection" was entirely subjective and depended on their personal judgment of "immoral behavior." One pair of suspected prostitutes, for example, was arrested and quarantined because they "carried on in such a manner it wasn't decent for people to look at." In another case, a woman was quarantined because she was seen getting drunk with sailors at a tavern South of Market.[30]

This policy also became an effective tool for maintaining what the SFPD considered racial order. When two white women named Naomi Barker and

Sheila Dought were arrested for "vagrancy" for hanging around in a Filipino restaurant, they were booked and quarantined. As Ernest Besig—the vigilant director of the ACLU—observed, "the officer had no evidence of promiscuity, and took the position simply that these women had no business hanging around in a place in which there were Filipinos."[31] In a particularly egregious case in April 1949 in Berkeley, where the same policy had gone into effect, Berkeley police stopped Annie Lee Harris, an African American, on the street as she was walking through a predominantly white neighborhood. Harris was a domestic worker, returning from a long day of cooking and cleaning for an affluent white family. "What have you been doing with your big black belly?" one officer reportedly asked. "When was the last time you saw a doctor?" the other asked, as he forced her into the police car. She was taken to jail, forced to take venereal disease tests—all of which were negative—and imprisoned for three days.[32]

The exclusive application of the preliminary quarantine to women underscored that a social, rather than medical, rationale was driving the SFPD's enforcement policy. If the protection of public health had been the chief concern of the SFPD, then the men arrested along with the suspected prostitutes would have been subjected to quarantine and medical inspection as well, since they were almost as likely to be vectors of sexually transmitted diseases. Instead, they were routinely released on bail. Although Besig received reassurances from the director of public health, Jacob Casson (J. C.) Geiger—a man who had learned all he needed to know about venereal disease from public health stints in New Orleans and Chicago in the 1920s, Besig's observations of sentencing patterns led him to the conclusion that "johns" suffered no penalties for their indiscretions.[33]

Naturally unpopular among prostitutes and other socially undesirable women who were swept up in the VD dragnet, the SFPD's preliminary quarantine policy was also deeply troubling to both public health officials and civil libertarians, and was entirely out of step with the policies of the United States Public Health Service. Edwin James Cooley, the regional representative of the Social Protection Division of the Office of Community War Services found the policy inherently problematic because of the likely authoritarian overreach of the SFPD. Referring to it as the "vicious quarantine detention practice," he found himself allied with Ernest Besig.[34] Nor did Eugene A. Gillis, the senior surgeon of the United States Public Health Service, support the sort of quarantine policy the SFPD adopted. At the 1946 meeting of the International Association of Police Chiefs in Miami, Gillis warned against the continuation of quarantine based on "reasonable suspicion of infection" in the postwar years. "If such policies were allowed to become the rule rather than the exception in postwar years, they likely would prove detrimental rather than helpful to the

cause of venereal disease control and detrimental to the cause of law enforcement in general." "Under our legal code," Gillis reminded the police chiefs,
"it is no crime to be infected or suspected of being infected with venereal disease." He concluded by quoting the findings of the National Advisory Police
Committee to the Federal Security Administration, which concluded that the
arrest of "prostitutes or detention of extremely promiscuous women" should
only happen in cases where there is a clear violation of statutes, "and not as
suspect of having a venereal disease." "There is no legal charge of this kind,"
the report concluded, "and without visible lesions not even a physician could,
at sight, suspect a man or woman of being infected. A police officer testifying
to his suspicion of the accused being venereally infected would be laughed out
of court."[35] And a San Francisco judge said of Dullea what Besig and federal
health officials had been too polite to say: "If the chief hasn't brains enough to
tell the difference between the medical and criminal aspects of prostitution, he
should resign."[36]

Despite these sound objections by legal and health professionals, the
SFPD's preliminary quarantine policy continued—until late 1975. This virtually
guaranteed that prostitutes, to a much greater extent than other criminals, were
subjected to erratic shifts in arrests, prosecutions, and sentencing. Preliminary
quarantine was just one piece of an expanding antiprostitution legal apparatus
in the postwar years. Pat Brown's ascent to the position of state attorney general further raised the stakes of the antiprostitution campaign. His Commission on Organized Crime published its findings in 1953: despite eradication
efforts, San Francisco still had a well-organized and well-protected prostitution ring. The San Francisco Chronicle simultaneously ran a sensational, week-
and-a-half-long exposé of police protection of prostitution in the Tenderloin
in April 1953.[37] The immediate effect of the commission's report was the state
legislature's passage of the "B-girl statute" in September, which empowered
the Division of Liquor Control and local police agencies to arrest "B-girls" who
received a "cut" of drink sales at bars where they enticed men to drink with
them with the implicit promise of sexual favors.[38]

More broadly, the state-level crusade against prostitution transformed
opposition to prostitution from a political liability into a political strength,
even in San Francisco. This proved the case for Republican George Christopher, president of the Board of Supervisors, who won a landslide victory in
the 1955 mayoral election on a probusiness and antivice platform. Christopher
overhauled the SFPD, successfully undermining the decades-old system of
payoffs for police protection of commercial sexual entertainment, prostitution,
and queer nightclubs in particular. According to former police chief Michael
Riordan, who served briefly after Dullea, Christopher "was the first mayor here

to say to the department, in unmistakable terms, 'I want gambling and vice laws enforced.'"[39] Christopher reformed the San Francisco Police Commission and appointed the famously incorruptible Frank Ahern as chief. These changes coincided with the state legislature's permanent, long-contemplated removal of liquor control responsibilities from the Board of Equalization and its subsequent creation of the Alcoholic Beverage Control Board (ABC). The creation of this new agency gave new state sanction to crusades against alleged immorality. In particular, it drove many otherwise tolerant tavern owners into the antiprostitution camp because they feared the revocation of their businesses' lifeblood, the liquor license.

Further intensifying the postwar crusade against prostitution in San Francisco was the ascendancy of a powerful coalition of progrowth business leaders, ambitious politicians, public administrators, and professional planners under the auspices of the San Francisco Redevelopment Agency (SFRA). In its efforts to stave off white suburbanization and create a postindustrial administrative and service center, the SFRA had set its sights on the redevelopment of the mostly black Western Addition, also known as "the Fillmore." From the end of the war to the mid-1960s, planners cited the Fillmore's "prostitution problem" as completely self-evident and irrefutable proof of the need for massive neighborhood rehabilitation.[40] One SFRA study described the neighborhoods in the Western Addition as "breeding grounds for crime and delinquency."[41] "It is only a step from home, in the Geary-Fillmore, to a store, a market, a bar, a gambling joint, or a house of prostitution," yet another report concluded.[42] "Children with no place to play...grow up on intimate geographic terms with bars, pool rooms, and the variety of places tagged as 'commercialized vice.'"[43] In short, antiprostitution efforts served not only the purposes of the moralist in San Francisco but also the advocate of urban renewal.

As for Sally Stanford, she appears to have again been saved by her "sixth sense; call it intuition, ESP, or a woman's whim."[44] Sensing the changing atmosphere and watching the Tenderloin "fall apart" as brothels and cafes closed their doors under the new regime, she abandoned her Tenderloin operations for the upscale neighborhoods of Nob Hill, Russian Hill, and Pacific Heights. The sumptuousness of these houses and their patrons' pedigrees gave Stanford's operation an air of gentility that kept the SFPD at an arm's length for most of the 1940s. Though her establishments were raided in 1949 and charges against her again dismissed, Stanford chose at that point to end her career as a grand madam, San Francisco's last and most accomplished. She moved to the picturesque town of Sausalito where she became a restaurateur, longtime city council aspirant, and finally mayor in 1976. "Food," she wrote of her restaurant career, "has the dubious advantage of being legitimate, and one's customers somehow manage to live longer without sex than food, if you call that living."[45]

Mildly Erotic Amusements

In 1930, a Chicagoan named Eddie Skolak came to San Francisco with a suitcase and a dream of pasties. He imagined he might become a West Coast Flo Ziegfeld or a Minsky, titillating capacity crowds with seminude burlesque shows in San Francisco as these impresarios had in New York and reaping a fortune in the process. Skolak quickly broke into the industry by managing a flagging downtown theater called the Capitol, where he launched *Capitol Follies,* a show he promoted as "spicy," "glamorous," and, of course, "Parisian." Playwright and poet Ettore Rella described Skolak's brand of burlesque as "little more than the inspection of a commodity in a commercial boudoir."[46] Skolak probably took it as a compliment.

Skolak soon discovered what his peers in San Francisco erotic entertainment already knew: San Francisco, in contrast to Chicago and New York, was simply not a burlesque town. It rarely had the audiences to fill the theater's three thousand seats. Productions like *Capitol Follies,* which featured almost eighty scantily clad women, were expensive, despite the dancers' meager wages. And if, as Sally Stanford put it, "it was easier to come by professional female company in San Francisco than it was to catch a rash in a leper colony," most men seeking erotic entertainment simply skipped the tedium of burlesque on their way to the brothel or the B-girl.[47] In 1941, Skolak closed down the *Capitol Follies* and moved to a much smaller, cheaper theater in a scrappier part of the Tenderloin. A far cry from the extravagance of *Ziegfeld's Follies,* Skolak's *President Follies* nonetheless had a good run into the early 1960s, outlasting the several other burlesque houses by more than a decade.

Skolak's fellow entertainment businessmen probably regarded his determination to promote the aging medium as quixotic if not foolhardy. Nor did they have the temerity or patience to remain vigilant against the threat of police action. Unlike moralists in New York, who exerted enough pressure on the mayor and the licensing commissioner to permanently shut down burlesque in 1942, opponents of San Francisco burlesque were few and fairly tame.[48] Arrests for "lewd theatrical performances" spiked in 1945 and 1946 as Dullea tried to restore order to the wartime and immediate postwar metropolis, and *President Follies* was shut down briefly in 1945. But this was an exception; between 1947 and 1957—when the U.S. Supreme Court radically transformed the legal boundaries of obscenity in *Roth v. United States*—arrests for lewd performances in San Francisco averaged fewer than three per year.[49] Nonetheless, few aspiring entertainment moguls thought the risk of staging a burlesque show was worth it, especially given the high cost and relatively low demand for burlesque in San Francisco.

The savviest among them pinned their hopes instead on "supper clubs," restaurants that featured live stage shows. Emphasizing female glamour and beauty and marketed largely to heterosexual couples, the supper club stage shows were more chaste than burlesque. Bimbo's, Sinaloa, Goman's Gay 90s, Monaco, Hurricane, the Lion's Den, the Chinese Sky Room, and the Forbidden City, among others, dotted North Beach and the edge of Chinatown. Here the lavish but small stage shows were easily subsidized by the sale of food and drink. Though nudity was unheard-of in these shows, they probably induced an erotic charge for some couples. In their book *Where to Sin in San Francisco,* Jack Lord and Jenn Shaw assured their readers that for the female patron of the supper club show, "seeing shows that sizzle is just as much her business as it is her guy's. So she nonchalantly watches the whole proceeding and tries to learn something she can use herself."[50]

One of the city's more "exotic" supper clubs was the Forbidden City, opened in 1938 by Charlie Low, a Chinese American businessman. Low hired dancer Noel Toy and began to successfully market Asian exoticism to predominantly white audiences. He created Chinese stage names for Japanese or mixed-race performers and promoted his club with slogans that exploited white curiosity about Chinese women. "Is it true," one read, "what they say about Chinese girls?" All the female performers began their acts clad in traditional Chinese clothing before changing into more modern, western costumes of leggings and bodices.

All of this was immoral enough to offend Chinatown's older population. "They wouldn't talk with us because they thought we were whores," one Forbidden City performer named Jadin Wong remembered. "Chinese people in San Francisco were ready to spit in our faces because we were nightclub performers."[51] But outside that community, Forbidden City was not just respectable but passé. The theater hosted celebrity actors, for example Ronald Reagan and his wife, Jane Wyman, and the staid mayor George Christopher even brought King Baudouin of Belgium for a visit, although the king did insist that no photographs be taken of him inside the club. *Collier's* even described the Forbidden City as a tepid club for "tourists."[52]

Rounding out these "exotic" and mildly erotic entertainments were San Francisco's several cross-dressing nightclubs. The best known was Finocchios's, which featured female impersonators and became a major local attraction after opening on Broadway in North Beach in 1936. Catering to tourists, couples, and visiting celebrities and billed as "America's Most Unusual Nightclub" in local tourist guides, Finocchios's was also home to a nascent community of gay performers and patrons. Nearby on Broadway was Mona's, a nightclub that featured female cross-dressing performers and drew tourists and a lesbian clientele. The Black Cat, a more low-key bohemian bar on the edge of North Beach, began hosting cross-dressing entertainment in the early 1950s. Only the Black Cat bore much resemblance to the solidly gay bar as gays and lesbians would come to understand that type of venue in the 1960s. But as historian Nan Boyd has demonstrated, these venues were essential social outlets for those gays and lesbians who were brave enough to recognize their sexuality in the years prior to the sexual revolution.

The ever-shifting legal definition of obscenity dramatically shaped San Francisco's prerevolutionary erotic nightlife. The arrest of Sally Rand clearly exemplified this dynamic. Club Savoy, where Rand was arrested in 1946, was an entirely unexceptional supper club. The circumstances of that arrest provide a window on the convoluted, unsettled nature of obscenity law in the United States at the time. Dullea maintained that Rand's dated act was "obscene and immoral" because his arresting officers could not, from the crowd, detect whether or not she was wearing a small patch over her pubic region, as she claimed. From their perspective, the alleged immorality of the act hinged solely on the question of nudity. At the time of the arrest, the officers were naturally acting under pressure from Dullea and largely on intuition rather than intimate knowledge of the California Penal Code. However, section 311 of that code—the one Rand was accused of violating—did not forbid nudity per se but rather "willfully and lewdly" exposing one's "private parts" anywhere in public.[53] Ehrlich denied that Rand had performed nude but also argued that even if she *had* been completely nude, she certainly was not lewd.

Because the U.S. Supreme Court had not yet rigorously defined obscenity or lewdness, and because lower court precedents were ambiguous, Ehrlich was largely at the mercy of the municipal judge, Daniel Shoemaker.[54] In *A Life in My Hands* (1965), Ehrlich recalled that during his arguments, he noticed that the judge "was paying more attention to the lower portions of Miss Rand than he was to my appeal." So Ehrlich asked the judge to allow Rand to perform her dance for the court to prove its decency. Shoemaker assented, and for perhaps the first time in the history of jurisprudence, a judge ordered a court to be convened at a nightclub. *Playboy* later recounted the scene:

> Ehrlich, the judge and Assistant District Attorney Frank Brown,
> brother of the district attorney, were ushered to the best ringside

table.... In due time Sally danced, using the same fans, war surplus
balloon, talcum and midnight blue spotlight she always used. The
applause at the end was deafening.

After witnessing Rand's performance, Shoemaker sided with Ehrlich's assertion that nudity, or near nudity, was not synonymous with lewdness. To the
judge's mind, "anyone who could find anything lewd in the dance must have a
perverted idea of morals." He pronounced Rand not guilty.[55]

The acquittal freed Rand to continue performing, which she did well into
her sixties, but did nothing to resolve the issue of what, exactly, constituted
obscenity in California or anywhere else. In fact, the issue only seemed to
get more muddled during the 1951 Los Angeles obscenity trial of Lili St. Cyr.
Though she was nude during her performance, St. Cyr and her celebrity attorney, Jerry Giesler, convinced the jury that she never made "bedroom gestures"
or any other motions that could be regarded as anything other than artistic.[56]

Dullea, who had served Mayor Lapham well in his efforts to rehabilitate the
postwar downtown shopping area, nonetheless felt himself a "Rossi man" and
never saw eye to eye with the "business mayor." Dullea retired from the SFPD
in 1947, and under Lapham's administration, and the subsequent administration of Elmer Robinson, the suppression of purportedly obscene behavior by
female dancers ceased to be a priority. Both Lapham and Robinson pinned
their legacies on large-scale infrastructural projects, including the consolida-
tion and modernization of the municipal railway network and the expansion
of the San Francisco international airport. Even if they had set their sights on
exotic female dancing, the larger American culture in which they governed
had changed. The "pinup girls" of the war years brought eroticism into the
patriotic mainstream, with profound postwar results. By the mid-1950s, magazine distributors were flooding newsstands in San Francisco and other cities
with so-called nudie magazines—though they rarely showed more than an
exposed breast—including *Scamp, Jem, Mr. Stag, Sir, Follies, Gent, Tan, Hit,
Rogue, Swank, The Dude, Revealing Romances, Uncensored, Vue, Male Life,* and,
of course, *Playboy.* Estimates of the annual gross income of these magazines
and lurid paperback books in the mid-1950s ranged from a few hundred million to one billion dollars.[57]

As Americans became more tolerant of mild erotica, the courts
responded. In *Adams Theatre Co. v. Keenan* (1953) the Supreme Court of the
State of New Jersey was the first to attempt to reconcile the ambiguities of
laws like California's section 311. In a six-to-one ruling, the court reversed
the decision Newark's public safety director had made to deny Harold Minsky a licensing permit for a performance at Newark's Adams Theater. In a

novel and victorious strategy that moved beyond the question of obscenity, Minsky's lawyers argued that Keenan's preemptive ban constituted a prior restraint on free speech. Future U.S. Supreme Court justice William Brennan wrote the opinion for the case, warning: "the standard 'lewd and indecent' is amorphous."

> There is ever present, too, the danger, that censorship upon that
> ground is merely the expression of the censor's own highly subjective
> view of morality unreasonably deviating from common notions of
> what is lewd and indecent, or may be a screen for reasons unrelated
> to moral standards.[58]

The Newark decision presaged the U.S. Supreme Court decision in *Roth v. United States* (1957) that significantly narrowed the legal domain of obscenity, in a six-to-three decision, for which Justice Brennan again wrote the majority opinion. While arguing that obscenity was not protected by the First Amendment, the Court ruled not only that for the material in question to be defined as obscene its "dominant theme" had to be "the prurient interest" but also that obscenity was to be defined by the viewpoint of the "average person, applying contemporary community standards."[59]

The SFPD responded to shifting cultural norms, and the *Roth* decision in particular, by largely abandoning its halfhearted pursuit of obscene performances and literature. With the high-profile exception of Dullea's arrest of Lawrence Ferlinghetti for distributing Allen Ginsberg's poem *Howl* in 1957, the SFPD did not engage in extensive antiobscenity work. As historian Christopher Agee has explained in his study of San Francisco policing, rank-and-file officers had little incentive to pursue obscenity cases. "Beat cops," Agee writes, "earned the respect of their peers through a physical control of the streets and regulating dirty magazines did not qualify as corporal policing."[60] Consequently, even the Catholic-led campaigns against obscenity like the San Francisco Citizens for Decent Literature failed to gain much traction among beat cops, whose daily lives involved the street more than the pulpit.[61]

A landmark decision, *Roth* is justly credited with further expanding the market for erotic performances, books, magazines, and films. But the ruling left many questions unanswered. How, precisely, were community standards to be determined? Precisely where was the line to be drawn between public and private exposure of potentially offensive materials? And if performing partially nude was not regarded as obscene, was it nonetheless a violation of other laws against indecent exposure? In short, *Roth* was unsatisfying to both purveyors of erotic entertainment and their opponents. It was also unsatisfying to Eddie Skolak, the success of whose follies depended on larger societal taboos and legal codes against female nudity. "Nudity," he lamented shortly before his death in 1959, "has become respectable."[62]

Silencing Birth Controllers

While the legal definition of obscenity was significantly reformulated on the eve of the sexual revolution, long-standing laws regarding abortion and the dissemination of birth control information remained largely unchanged, and that was a boon for the well-known abortionist Inez Burns. When SFPD homicide detective Frank Ahern raided her Fillmore Street apartment in 1948, he expected to find some money, but not so much of it. In the years since her first arrest for performing an abortion in 1924, Burns had recruited a one-time city autopsy surgeon named Dr. Adolphus A. Berger to perform the abortions, and by 1948 the pair were thought to have conducted from five thousand to ten thousand abortions. Burns's business worked because abortion was illegal, there was always a demand for abortions, and, most significant, there were always policemen "on the take." But Ahern was not one of them. When his officers raided her apartment, Burns showed him a pile of cash worth more than $300,000. "Don't be a fool," she apparently said; "put it in your pocket." "You've got the wrong guy," Ahern replied, before carting Burns off to jail.[63]

Before the landmark *Roe v. Wade* decision in 1973, abortion mills like Burns's were a common feature of the urban underground throughout the country. And they were wildly profitable; one 1941 study concluded that an abortion specialist could easily earn $25,000 annually, and doctors with wealthier patients earned between $150,000 and $200,000. In order to conduct more abortions and maximize profits, operators usually forwent elementary aseptic techniques. Anesthetics were rarely used because they carried an unacceptable liability risk for the operator, and they prolonged recovery times, slowing down "the mill." Patients were usually ushered out of the recovery room after about thirty minutes to make room for new ones; professional gynecologists of the era recommended complete bed rest for seven to ten days.[64]

Alarmed by the horrific medicine of the abortion mill and frustrated by watching low-income patients struggle with multiple, unplanned children, several female doctors brought birth control advocacy to the Bay Area at considerable personal and professional risk. Inspired by American birth control crusader Margaret Sanger, Dr. Adelaide Brown and Dr. Florence Holsclaw opened the Maternal Health Center, San Francisco's first family planning center, on Oak Street in 1929. The forerunner of Planned Parenthood in San Francisco, the center saw thousands of clients in its first years, a testament to women's intense hunger for practical knowledge about family planning, particularly during the Great Depression.[65]

But disseminating such knowledge in San Francisco was enormously challenging. First, there was the law. Until 1965, it was a felony for anyone—even public health providers—to publish or distribute any literature about abortion or the "prevention of conception."[66] Thus Brown and Holsclaw operated in a legal grey zone that made them highly vulnerable to periodic harassment by the SFPD, though they managed to avoid arrest during their careers. Less fortunate was birth control agitator Carl Rave, who was arrested in the nearby suburb of Redwood City for selling a pamphlet on "family limitation" and served three months in jail. "I think that to keep this information out of the hands of the workers," Rave defiantly wrote, "is one of the greatest social crimes of today, because it causes needless, untold suffering and degradation."[67] Sanger's Birth Control Review recognized the unique risks taken by Rave, Brown, and Holsclaw: "Owing to the ambiguities of State law, the Maternal Health Clinic, as well as other clinics in California, do not publish their addresses; neither do they seek publicity. On the contrary, they endeavor to avoid it."[68]

In addition to the legal challenges of disseminating information, birth control advocates in San Francisco faced strong opposition from local religious interests. The Women's Christian Temperance Union of California used the occasion of its 1929 annual convention in San Francisco to denounce the "birth controllers": "Our aim is to educate the public, from its youth, to pure monogamous marriage for procreation only. Birth control and illegitimacy are spreading alarmingly and will be the main targets for the organization's activities during the coming year."[69] Similarly, at a national Catholic convention hosted by San Francisco archbishop Edward Joseph Hanna, the keynote speaker advocated the suppression of birth control information, arguing that it contributed to the "robbing" of "American womanhood."[70] Several San Francisco landlords expressed their disdain for birth control advocacy by denying tenancy to the Maternal Health Clinic, and the local phone company rounded out the conspiracy of silence by refusing to list "birth control clinic" in the phone book. Consequently, the vast majority of women who patronized the services of the Maternal Health Clinic only learned about it via word of mouth.[71]

The greatest challenge Brown, Holsclaw, and other birth control advocates faced came not from the law, the police, or even the influential local Catholics but from the San Francisco medical community generally and from the SFDPH in particular. Most troubling, from the perspective of birth control advocates, was the policy of San Francisco General Hospital, the main intake hospital for the city's lower income groups who would ostensibly benefit most from more self-conscious family planning. San Francisco General refused to allow birth control advocates to talk with patients or even to distribute literature in waiting rooms.[72] And through the early 1960s, the hospital's superintendent recruited operating room nurses to be vigilant in reporting any "funny stuff" in the Department of Obstetrics and Gynecology, especially any attempts at either tubal ligations or therapeutic abortions. In short, the most authoritative medical voice in the lives of working women in the city—its health department— was deeply invested in concealing and suppressing knowledge of birth control. Consequently, birth control knowledge and contraceptive devices were largely accessible to only the well-informed or well-connected before the sweeping social and legal changes of the 1960s.

San Francisco's Homosexual Underground

By the late 1940s, SFPD Officer Thomas Cahill, raised on a farm in County Kilkenny, Ireland, had seen a lot. After arriving penniless in San Francisco in 1930, spending a decade performing manual labor there, and putting in four busy years on the force, Cahill was a seasoned veteran of San Francisco's seamy side. As a rookie officer, he had wrestled drunken sailors to the ground in Bayview–Hunters Point, tackled gun-toting bookies in the Tenderloin, and meted out his share of curbstone justice when the circumstances required. So he was a perfect fit for his new assignment on the "S-Squad," also known as the Night Investigations beat, downtown in 1946. Working from seven o'clock at night to three o'clock in the morning, Cahill and his fellow officers took "anything that was hot." Despite his extensive experience, Cahill was always mystified by the shadowy figure of the homosexual. Whenever his superiors issued one of their periodic orders to raid the Black Cat, most of the suspects fled before Cahill could reach them. "If there was a homosexual on the street, he'd see the car at the end of the block," Cahill later remembered, "and I don't know where the hell they used to go. I thought they went down into the sidewalk. By god, they could just disappear anywhere."[73]

Cahill's recollection of homosexual men vanishing into the sidewalk, and into the corners of the night, precisely captures the shrouded nature of homosexuality in San Francisco before the sexual revolution. Ostracized by friends and families, harassed by law enforcement agencies, and scared into silence by employers, most homosexuals in San Francisco and the rest of the United States simply repressed their desires, entering into unfulfilling heterosexual relationships or suffering in lifelong isolation. The small proportion with the self-awareness to recognize their homosexuality and the audacity to express it almost always found the large city a more comfortable habitat than the countryside or the suburbs. Because San Francisco was a cosmopolitan port city, it was better suited than most of the nation's cities to provide the dynamism, anonymity, and erotic possibilities that homosexuals desired. At the same time, the campaigns to forcibly suppress homosexuality were as intense in San Francisco as they were anywhere else in the United States prior to the sexual revolution.[74]

Prior to the 1930s, the openly homosexual population of San Francisco was small and discreet, and there were very few public places where homosexuals could safely meet to forge partnerships. The most publicly visible homosexuals were male, cross-dressing "queens" for whom Market Street was an essential promenade. Described in an early twentieth-century tour book as a "long bazaar and highroad of this port of all flags," Market Street served the commercial and transportation needs of the city's downtown workers and shoppers during the day.[75] But after dark, it served more illicit purposes, particularly in the Tenderloin, where it was given over to bookies, pickpockets, hustlers, actors, and queens. "Looking back," gay writer Lou Rand Hogan wrote of the 1920 and 1930s, "it must be repeated that 'Market Street' was the focal point of all the action...you 'met' on the street."[76] And at the end of Market Street, the Embarcadero waterfront was the site of countless furtive liaisons, particularly inside the YMCA Embarcadero Branch.

The repeal of prohibition and America's entry into World War II multiplied the opportunities for homosexual sociability among lesbians and homosexual men, stimulating the opening of bohemian bars like Mona's, Finocchios's, and the Black Cat. And World War II significantly expanded the numbers and the visibility of homosexuals nationally, but particularly in San Francisco, which served as a major port of embarkation for military personnel heading to the Pacific theater, and debarkation for men dishonorably discharged for homosexual behavior. The burgeoning population of homosexuals in San Francisco expanded the geography of homosexual congregation in the 1940s and 1950s. The most vibrant and publicly visible sites of homosexuality continued to be bars. Joining Mona's in North Beach were bars where some lesbians congregated, for example the Artist's Club, Tommy's Club, the Anxious Asp, Miss Smith's Tea Room, 12 Adler Place, downstairs from Tommy's Place, and the Copper Lantern. By contrast, the bars of the Tenderloin and the Embarcadero generally catered to homosexual men. Clubs such as 356 Taylor, 57 Powell Club, and Club Inferno catered to a variety of tastes from the "cuff link set" to the "rough" crowd. One, the Gaslight, opened in one of Sally Stanford's former brothels at 1144 Pine. The working-class bars of the Embarcadero generally served as rendezvous points for gay men seeking liaisons with sailors. There, the Sea Cow Café—according to a cheeky 1954 Mattachine Society convention bar guide—was known for "Beer, Wine and Seamen."[77]

Bars provided a sense of community for isolated homosexuals before the sexual revolution. Yet the comfort of the homosexual bar could be cold and fleeting. Writing in 1972 of the old lesbian bars that served as "reminders of an underground life," Sidney Abbott and Barbara Love described the world of the lesbian bars as "affirming" and "comforting" atmosphere but, they argued, a kind of "puritanical terror hangs over the client of a gay bar, the clandestine, guarded nature of the bars heightens the fear of consequences.... The beneficial effects wear off quickly, leaving the hard facts of the Lesbian's isolation unchanged."[78]

Furthermore, bars where homosexuals congregated were subjected to ceaseless harassment. As bar owners quickly discovered, moralists were adept at exploiting the national and local mood in order to eradicate sinful spectacles. During World War II, the army and navy easily enlisted the support of the Rossi-Dullea regime to close down known "deviate" hangouts, ostensibly to protect servicemen from disease and dishonor. Raiding bars, roughing up patrons, citing bar owners for violating state laws forbidding the maintenance of establishments that were "injurious to the public morals," and drawing up a list of establishments "off limits" to military personnel, the SFPD and naval shore patrols sought to drive homosexuals out of public view and back into the shadows. In the late 1940s, California moralists exploited the gruesome sex murders of two little girls—committed by heterosexual pedophiles—to legitimize campaigns against homosexuals whose alleged illness made them susceptible to similar sexual psychopathy. And by the 1950s, homophobes were given an additional ideological bulwark in anti-communism, whose suppression of political deviancy could easily be redirected to sexual deviants.[79]

The case of the Black Cat—one of the only definitively homosexual bars in San Francisco prior to the sexual revolution—illustrates homosexual bars' vulnerability to these shifting homophobic priorities. The Black Cat had long been a home for intellectuals and writers such as John Steinbeck and William Saroyan, as well as workers from the nearby Embarcadero. After a new owner, Sol Stoumen, bought the bar in the 1940s, its patronage became decisively more homosexual. "When the place changed hands," one former patron dissatisfied with the change later wrote, "the new owner encouraged the fruit and the place went to hell." In 1949, the California State Board of Equalization—then the alcohol-regulating agency for state—evidently shared this view and suspended the bar's liquor license on the grounds that it was a "hangout for persons with homosexual tendencies." Stoumen, however, was defiant and quickly hired a lawyer, who appealed the Board of Equalization's decision, finally taking the case to the California State Supreme Court. In 1951, the Court ruled in *Stoumen v. Reilly* that the mere congregation of homosexuals was not criminal unless there was actual illegal conduct on the premises.[80]

The *Stoumen* decision was a landmark victory because it validated the right of gays to public assembly. But, its greatest legacy, in fact, may have been that it stimulated innovative new forms of homosexual surveillance and repression in California. Four years after the *Stoumen* decision came the landslide election of Christopher with his promise to "clean up" San Francisco and the state legislature's creation of the ABC, installing as its director Russell Munro, a native Mississippian and former jail warden. Under Munro, the vigorous new agency made the revocation of homosexual bar liquor licenses a high priority. The records of the ABC reveal the extensive resources it devoted to training officers to expose "resorts for sexual perverts," a category that was added to the state's liquor law when the ABC was created. The ABC regularly assigned its youngest, "greenest" agents to the growing gay bar circuit in San Francisco and Los Angeles, teaching them to affect "homosexual mannerisms," "come on" to bar patrons, and engage in casual sexual contact in order to have documented proof of the establishment's status as a bastion of perversion.[81]

Though Stoumen had won the battle in 1951, he ultimately lost the war. Unable to afford the mounting legal costs associated with defending his business from Munro's hounding, Stoumen closed the Black Cat in 1963. Meanwhile, SFPD harassment continued virtually unabated. One gauge of its extent is the SFPD's annual number of arrests for vagrancy—a catchall charge frequently used against social undesirables generally and homosexuals in particular. The number peaked in 1947 and 1948 under Dullea and Riordan, dipped dramatically between 1949 and 1952, and then climbed again to a lower peak in 1954 under chief Michael Gaffey. After the sudden death of Chief Ahern in 1958, the SFPD Commission installed Cahill, whose early experiences on the S-Squad had prepared him well for the challenges of mounting "sex deviancy." Although vagrancy arrests declined under Cahill's tenure as chief, the patrolling of homosexual bars increased, earning him an unfavorable reputation among many homosexuals. In the largest and most dramatic raid of a homosexual bar in San Francisco's history, Cahill's SFPD—along with ABC officers—raided and arrested more than one hundred homosexuals gathered at the Tay-Bush Inn in 1961.[82]

Because the sites for "legitimate" encounters between homosexual partners were a rarity, homosexuals often put themselves in risky, if not dangerous, circumstances to have sex. This was particularly the case for gay men, who were more likely than lesbians to seek out public sex, and whose gender usually allowed them greater access to public spaces. Warner Jepson, an Oberlin-trained pianist who moved to San Francisco after college in 1953, has recalled that he searched for public sex sites when he arrived because, as a teetotaler, he did not feel comfortable in the bars. A working musician in local theaters where "everybody was gay," Jepson was "out with those people" but "in with everybody else." Afraid of the "suffering" that coming out in a homophobic society would induce, Jepson searched for discreet public sex in parks, where he discovered a brisk public sex scene in the 1950s. He used the restroom at Lafayette Park for sex many times and did "a lot of things with a lot of guys"; but he was arrested when he was simply walking through the park one evening— for being in a place homosexuals were known to hang out—and was sent to jail for the night. The next morning in court, "the judge basically says well we know what you do in there." "Don't let us catch you again," the judge admonished Jepson, "or we're really going to give it to you." But Jepson and others like him continued to search for sex in public sites, finding it in museum bathrooms, bus and train stations, and Golden Gate Park.[83]

At the beginning of the 1950s, a group of politically active homosexuals, jaded by the bars and shadowy parks, tired of isolation, and angered by their second-class citizenship and perpetual harassment, created what became known as the homophile movement. The Mattachine Foundation, a wobbly initial effort to organize against homophobia, was founded in 1950 in Los Angeles. In 1953, homosexual Harold "Hal" Call played a key role in resurrecting this organization in San Francisco. An experienced copywriter, Call started a newsletter and drafted a document that explained that the purpose of the renamed, reinvigorated Mattachine Society was to correct "bigotries and prejudices resulting from lack of accurate information regarding sex variants." By 1955, Call and other volunteers were publishing the *Mattachine Review,* and by 1958, in combination with several other homophile periodicals, this magazine had become part of a larger communication network emanating from the West Coast across the nation. That communication network, historian Martin Meeker has explained, was one of the most important new elements influencing the emergence of gay and lesbian communities.[84]

In 1955, a lesbian couple—Del Martin and Phyllis Lyon—and several other lesbians started their own homophile organization in San Francisco known as the Daughters of Bilitis (DOB). Initially envisioned as a social alternative to the bars, DOB quickly became explicitly political like the Mattachine Society, seeking to give lesbians visibility and self-esteem at a time when either could be an intense personal and professional liability. "The organization," its founders later remembered, "was to encourage and support the Lesbian in her search for her personal, interpersonal, social, economic and vocational identity."[85] Daughters of Bilitis communicated with lesbians through its monthly newsletter the *Ladder* and reached out to lawyers and legislators to eradicate restrictions against lesbians. Both DOB and the Mattachine Society also laid the foundation for the emergence of more specialized homophile organizations in the early 1960s, including the League for Civil Education (1961), the Tavern Guild (1961), the Society for Individual Rights (SIR) (1964), and the Council on Religion and the Homosexual (1964).[86] Cofounded by James Foster, Bill Beardemphl, and several others, SIR would strike a decidedly more assertive tone than its predecessors in the homophile movement: "SIR is dedicated to belief in the worth of the homosexual and adheres to the principle that the individual has the right to his own sexual orientation so long as the practice of the belief does not interfere with the rights of others."[87] This message would resonate with young homosexuals, and SIR would quickly eclipse earlier homophile organizations in both its membership rolls and its public visibility.

Before the founding of SIR, though, both the Mattachine Society and DOB created a communication network among homosexuals, while simultaneously raising their profile among heterosexuals. The central role of the Mattachine Society in a major political flap before the 1959 mayoral election is a case in point. In October 1959, the neighborhood newspaper *San Francisco Progress* blared: "Sex Deviates Make S.F. Headquarters." Seeing an opening, Russell Wolden, a challenger for Mayor Christopher's seat, accused Christopher and Chief Cahill of allowing San Francisco to become "the national headquarters of the organized homosexuals in the United States," specifically citing the Mattachine Society for its purported perversions. In the following two months, more than a hundred articles and a considerable amount of radio air time were devoted to discussions about the Mattachine Society.[88] But Wolden's plan backfired: once it was revealed that one of his operatives had infiltrated the society in order to foment a crisis, the major newspapers discredited him, and San Franciscans thoroughly rejected his brand of demagoguery at the voting booth. More significant, the flap did what several years of homophile activism had failed to do: it introduced thousands of Bay Area readers and radio listeners to the Mattachine Society and to homosexuality more broadly. The following year, the city was again introduced to homosexual activity and SFPD corruption when the full extent of "gayola"—police payoffs for nonharassment of gay establishments—became known. Of course, the rising visibility of homosexuals was not the same phenomenon as the later gay liberation, but it was a necessary step toward greater tolerance of homosexuals in the public eye.[89]

Even as homosexuals became more visible in the mainstream media, they were still largely invisible in public by virtue of their geographic isolation in, and immediately around, the Tenderloin. Most of the bars homosexuals frequented were in the Tenderloin, and so were the headquarters of homophile activism. The first office of the Mattachine Society was South of Market at Third and Mission, about half a mile from the Tenderloin; the first office of DOB was on O'Farrell, about one block from the Tenderloin, and a subsequent office was on Market Street in the heart of the Tenderloin; Guy Strait, the provocative gay magazine publisher and cofounder of the League for Civil Education, published out of an office South of Market between Sixth and Seventh streets, about two blocks from the Tenderloin. Ultimately, both homosexual people and homophile politics were still well contained.

From the Hearst campaign to shut down the Barbary Coast in 1913 to the early 1960s, San Francisco moralists expended enormous energy to restrain the cultural tide toward greater public sexual expression, and they were remarkably successful. Virtually all of the city's brothels were closed down, and an alarming number of street prostitutes filled the county jail as they waited out their quarantines. Exotic dancers were ever vulnerable to the wildly different definitions of obscenity held by patrons, club owners, the SFPD, and local judges. Advocates of birth control faced tremendous challenges in Catholic San Francisco, and untold numbers of women subjected themselves to unreasonable risks at Inez Burns's abortion mill. And homosexuals, though more visible than ever before, often lived in fear of reprisals for that visibility. For the time being, it seemed, the push for greater public expressions of sexuality among a healthy proportion of the population had been contained. But how long could it hold?

2

SEX RADICALS AND CAPTIVE PEDESTRIANS

When she was a blonde, doe-eyed teenager, Carol Doda's future was not bright. A high-school dropout from Napa County, she landed in the Tenderloin in the early 1960s, where she quickly found a roommate and friend in a male hairstylist who shared his makeup tips with her. Doda fell in love with her roommate and became inconsolably jealous about his mysterious preference for male company. Her love unrequited, Doda took a job as a dancing cocktail waitress at the Condor go-go bar in North Beach and moved into the district. "Big" Davey Rosenberg, a corpulent, hard-nosed club promoter, saw great profit potential in Doda and encouraged her to perform her dance in one of designer Rudi Gernreich's new "topless" bathing suits. On June 22, 1964, the twenty-year-old Doda metamorphosed from ingénue to internationally renowned sexual spectacle when she took to the stage at the Condor and revolutionized the local burlesque show circuit by baring her breasts in their entirety during her performance of the "swim" dance. She brazenly tossed aside the pasties that striptease dancers had worn for most of the century. Shortly thereafter—also at Rosenberg's urging—Doda received one of the first silicone breast augmentations, increasing her modest bust size to a double D. Doda's likeness, depicted on a forty-foot sign complete with red, illuminated nipples, towered over the intersection of Columbus Avenue and Broadway Street and became a landmark, drawing throngs of locals and tourists alike.[1]

Surely no one actually believed Rosenberg's claim to have "invented toplessness," but Doda was indeed something new. Playwright Ettore

Rella, who had worried in 1941 about the diminishing theatrical standards of burlesque, would have been aghast that by 1964, there were absolutely none. Doda's halfhearted "swim" and "twist" dances served only the purpose of revealing her breasts for the sake of male sexual excitement. But Doda's performance is best understood as the opening shot of the sexual revolution. During the next decade, spectacles of sexuality would dramatically transform the nature of urban life in San Francisco, particularly in North Beach, the Tenderloin, the Haight-Ashbury, and the Fillmore.

Barbary Coast Redux

Doda's daring feat was contingent on local changes to the neighborhood surrounding the Condor. In the late 1950s, San Francisco's literary renaissance changed the character of North Beach, bringing artists and writers to its cheap apartments and numerous cafes and bars, and infusing its nightlife with an air of intellectual urgency and sensual curiosity. Yet despite the long-term literary, artistic, and cultural influence of the "Beats," their impact on the landscape of North Beach was actually quite brief. Many of the leading lights of the literary movement—including Allen Ginsberg, William Burroughs, and Jack Kerouac—had left San Francisco by 1956, and many of the prominent Beat haunts closed shortly thereafter.[2]

But if the Beats' influence on the real landscape was brief, their impact on the imagined landscape was profound. After the 1957 publication of Kerouac's novel *On the Road,* mainstream media—including CBS, MGM, *Life,* and *Time*—popularized a parodic and highly marketable version of "the Beat" as a wine-gulping, marijuana-smoking dropout, vehemently opposed to employment of any kind. This media-made incarnation of the Beat, and particularly its aura of subdued bacchanalianism, fit well with the long-standing "tourist narrative" about North Beach's racy history and contributed significantly to the city's tourist industry. By the early 1960s, tour buses regularly introduced passengers to "North Beach—home of the Italian colony and the beatniks of San Francisco."[3]

Thus, by the time Carol Doda hit the stage topless, a North Beach nightlife revival was under way, but her act accelerated this revival dramatically. Doda's topless swim dance, and the dozens of similar acts that followed hers, drew thousands of tourists, servicemen, conventioneers, and locals to the streets of North Beach in unprecedented numbers, comparable only to the crowds of the original Barbary Coast in the days before 1913. Particularly appealing to revelers was the quite public nature of commercial sexual entertainment in

FIGURE 2.1. The Condor nightclub at Broadway and Columbus in North Beach, 1978. The Condor was the epicenter of a nightlife revival in North Beach following Carol Doda's first topless performances in 1964. Courtesy: San Francisco History Center, San Francisco Public Library.

the "new" North Beach: through picture windows, topless dancers advertised their talents, creating a sexual spectacle on the streets of North Beach that was distinct from what was happening inside nightclubs. By the 1970s, the explosion of storefront pornography would arrest more chaste citizenry. "I am sensitive," one Tenderloin property owner complained to the San Francisco Board of Supervisors, "to the pornography that must be viewed as a 'captive pedestrian' in the Tenderloin."[4]

Within a year of Doda's performance, there were an estimated thirty-five to forty topless clubs in the city, and nine stores downtown that openly sold pornography.[5] Within five years, the number of "adult bookstores" increased to almost fifty, and by the late 1970s there were thirty-nine adult movie theaters, fourteen "encounter studios"—where, officially, patrons paid to converse with nude women, but often had sex when they ran out of things to say—and dozens of peep shows and strip clubs.[6] Not only was there a proliferation of sex-related businesses but also they had become more publicly visible than ever before, displaying "hard-core" pornography in storefront windows, hiring "barkers" to describe, in lurid detail, the entertainment housed inside, and installing neon signs that vividly described sexual acts. The success of the barkers, as they frankly admitted, depended on their ability to surprise passersby with shocking and bizarre descriptions, of women "making love to a hubcap," for example.[7] Finally, as "topless" gave way to "bottomless" in the late 1960s, many ostensibly "legitimate" sex-related businesses, like strip clubs and massage parlors, encouraged actual sexual contact between entertainers and the predominantly male clientele, blurring the line between commercial sexual entertainment and outright prostitution.

The revival of commercial sexual entertainment in North Beach drew immediate fire from local religious leaders, including the Italian Catholic Federation and Lawrence Byrne, a priest who condemned the obscenity of toplessness. Alfred Lynch, a suburbanite and vice president of the Northern California chapter of Citizens for Decent Literature, said of the topless show he witnessed: "the thing sickens you, saddens you and could only delight a pervert." Meanwhile, "legitimate" nightclub owners feared the competition generated by the new topless clubs, and members of the North Beach Merchants and Boosters association argued that the severe pedestrian and traffic congestion on Friday and Saturday nights harmed local businesses.[8] Protesting to the San Francisco Board of Supervisors, the Merchants and Booster Association found sympathetic allies in supervisors William C. Blake, the influential Peter Tamaras—who served two terms as president of the board in the 1960s—and the board's Governmental Services Committee, who, undoubtedly aware of the potential political liability of prudishness in San Francisco, conjured up the specter of

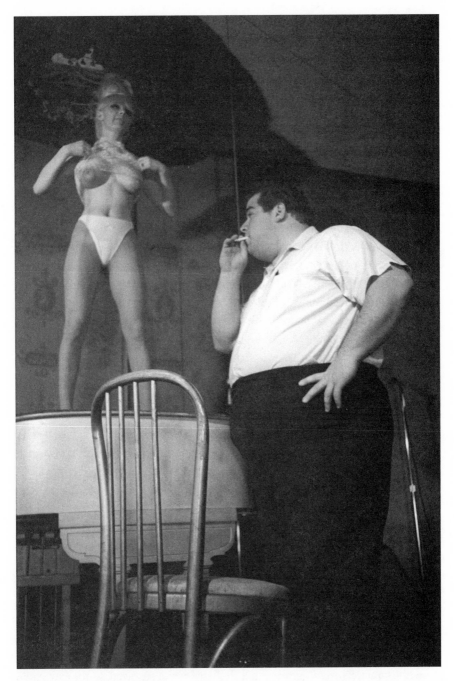

FIGURE 2.2. Topless pioneer Carol Doda stands atop a piano at the Condor as
club promoter "Big" Davey Rosenberg looks on, circa 1965. Courtesy: Bill Graham
Archives, LLC/ www.wolfgangsvault.com.

urban violence, rather than the nudity per se, to support their argument for the closure of the topless circuit. Flatly contradicting SFPD Central Station captain Charles Barca's assertion that the new North Beach was still an area of low crime incidence, the committee reported: "North Beach has drawn the most undesirable elements of the community in the persons of punks, muggers, cutthroats, molesters, and the rest of the street criminals who give life in any metropolis a taint of terror." "I know," Tamaras added, "fear is stalking the streets of North Beach and the entire city."[9]

Pressure mounted on the new mayor, John F. "Jack" Shelley—not even six months into his term. A native San Franciscan, longtime labor leader, and the first Democratic mayor in fifty years, Shelley was quickly dubbed the "crisis mayor." Three months into his term, civil rights demonstrators occupied the Sheraton Palace hotel, demanding an end to the hotel's discriminatory hiring practices and drawing national attention to the limits of racial tolerance in San Francisco. Later, Shelley would be instrumental in negotiating a citywide public nurses' strike and in responding to the 1966 race riots in Bayview–Hunters Point. Shelley reassured the Merchants and Booster Association, and other North Beach complainants, that under his administration, "this town is not to be an open town," but he also remained committed to the letter of the law. "The public just doesn't understand," Shelley told a crowd at City Hall in March 1965: "They direct their fire at me and the police when the real problem is the law and the courts."[10] No one in his administration or legal staff could definitively answer the question: was topless dancing obscene, and therefore illegal? With the support of Governor Brown—who told reporters "I think a woman looks better when she has a little clothing on"—Shelley sought to resolve this legal issue by ordering the SFPD to arrest topless dancers and waitresses and the owners of topless nightclubs in North Beach, the Tenderloin, and the Mission. And so, on a busy Thursday night in late April 1965, police arrested dancers and club managers at the Condor, Off Broadway, Big Al's, the Domino Club, Club Chi Chi, Tipsy's, Mr. Wonderful, the Moulin Rouge, Club Hangover, the Cellar, Chez Paree, and Relax With Evonne. "I don't think the Swim is obscene," Doda told reporters the next morning. "I wouldn't be ashamed to have my parents watch my act."[11]

Shelley took a drubbing in the *San Francisco Chronicle*, which heartily endorsed North Beach's bawdy rebirth and decried Shelley's "inquisition." But he was a practical man, and wanted the legal issue resolved so the city could move forward.[12] The raids and subsequent "topless trials" in early May served Shelley's goal of establishing a legal benchmark for the issue of nudity in San Francsico, but it was not the one the Board of Supervisors or the North Beach complainants had sought. Two San Francisco Municipal Court judges acquitted the dancers and club owners on the grounds that they had not violated "community standards," the test of obscenity for city and state statutes since their revision by the *Roth* ruling.

Meanwhile, across the Bay in the blue-collar suburb of San Pablo, Kelley Iser copied Doda's topless act but added a new twist: "wiggling around"—as arresting officers described it—on her hands and knees "with her breasts exposed" for about thirty seconds. Both she and the club's manager, Albert Giannini, were arrested late in 1965, and Iser was found guilty in municipal court of violating section 314 (formerly section 311) of the penal code by "willfully and lewdly" exposing herself—the same charge Rand had faced almost twenty years earlier.[13] One of the first topless dancers to be convicted, Iser appealed the verdict, but her appeal was quickly rejected, on the grounds that, the appeals court ruled, the jury that had convicted her in the municipal trial had, in fact, constituted the "community" whose standards were the benchmark of obscenity. This was a curious argument that antiobscenity groups like Citizens for Decent Literature had advanced since the *Roth* decision in 1957 and that seemed to willfully misinterpret the meaning of "community." Consequently, Iser and Giannini took their case to the California Supreme Court, arguing that they had been unfairly punished because the prosecution in the municipal case had failed to prove that the jury could be, in fact, a proxy for the community.

In November 1968, the California State Supreme Court agreed with Iser and Giannini, ruling that Iser's dance, no matter how "vulgar and tawdry in content," enjoyed First Amendment protections unless it could be proven obscene, and that the relevant "community" in question was not a jury but the state of California. Because toplessness was generally accepted in other California cities, the court concluded, it was not regarded as obscene by the community. Justice Louis H. Burke dissented, arguing that by making the "entire State of California" the community, "the new rules will impose a difficult or impossible burden on local communities combating obscenity." It was a prescient observation.[14]

The 1965 topless acquittals in San Francisco—and the subsequent 1968 ruling in favor of Iser and Giannini—paved the way for the spread of topless and bottomless entertainment, "nude encounter parlors," and massage parlors, many of which were actually fronts for prostitution. So ubiquitous was the massage parlor—there were approximately three thousand statewide in 1965—that the California Massage Therapy Association lobbied unsuccessfully for the passage of a bill requiring massage parlors to be licensed by the state in order to protect "legitimate" purveyors of massage therapy.[15]

In a failed effort to hold the line against pornography and to "clean smut out of California," E. Richard Barnes, a former Methodist pastor from New York

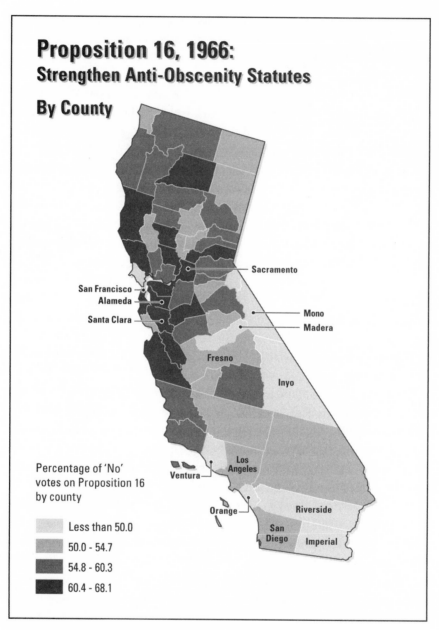

Proposition 16, 1966:
Strengthen Anti-Obscenity Statutes

By County

Sacramento

San Francisco
Alameda

Santa Clara

Mono

Madera

Fresno

Inyo

Los
Angeles

Ventura

Percentage of 'No'
votes on Proposition 16
by county

Orange

Riverside

San
Diego

Imperial

Less than 50.0

50.0 - 54.7

54.8 - 60.3

60.4 - 68.1

MAP 3. Although the majority of California voters rejected Proposition 16 in 1966, the county level returns revealed the growing geo-cultural divide in California, in which the residents of southern and suburban counties voted more conservatively on "social issues." Map by David Deis, Dreamline Cartography.

and current state assemblyman from San Diego, launched in 1966 a campaign called California League Enlisting Action Now (CLEAN). It introduced an initiative, Proposition 16, to greatly strengthen the state's obscenity statutes. The proliferation of obscene paperbacks, nudist magazines, live shows, and movies, Barnes believed, was conspiring to "attack" the California family. Though Barnes found an influential campaign director in William K. Shearer—credited with engineering the passage of Proposition 14 in 1964, which had overturned an antiracist housing act—Proposition 16 lost badly. But the county-level election returns were telling: they showed that a cultural and political divide was emerging in 1960s California. The initiative passed in the San Francisco suburb of Marin County and the Los Angeles suburbs of Orange, Riverside, and Ventura counties. Indeed, Proposition 16 heralded the emergence in California of a "family values" agenda among suburban conservatives that would gain great strength in the nation's West and Sunbelt in the coming decades.[16]

While Proposition 16 failed, several U.S. Supreme Court rulings checked the liberal assault on the legal parameters of obscenity. However, even they offered few concrete rewards to opponents of sexual entertainment. Shortly after Ronald Reagan won the 1966 gubernatorial election—partially with a promise to "clean up the mess at Berkeley"—he appointed a new director for the ABC, former FBI agent Edward J. Kirby. Concerned about debauched conditions at topless bars in which oral sex was occurring between patrons and entertainers, Kirby resurrected the moralist crusade of the Russell Monroe era. Kirby authored changes in the liquor control law that empowered the ABC to revoke liquor licenses for bars where there was conduct "contrary to public welfare or morals." A group of California topless bar owners filed suit against Kirby in the U.S. District Court in Los Angeles, and the court sided with bar owners, determining that for the ABC to revoke their licenses was a violation of First Amendment rights to free expression. But in December 1972, the U.S. Supreme Court upheld Kirby's restrictions in *California v. LaRue*. Setting aside First Amendment privileges and the issue of obscenity, the Court ruled that the Twenty-first Amendment, which repealed Prohibition, granted states broad discretion to repeal liquor permits. Vindicated, Kirby reinstated the 1970 policies, which created the very particular specifications under which California strip clubs operate to this day: permits can only be issued to topless bars where performers wear panties or G-strings, no "lewd" acts are performed, and performers are on stages at least eighteen inches high and six feet away from patrons.[17]

The *LaRue* decision, the front page of the *Los Angeles Times* blared, was the "Death Blow for Topless Bars." Predictably, it was not. First, the ABC had never been well staffed. With several hundred officers regulating thousands of licenses in the state, the ABC was largely a bureaucratic agency with little presence on the streets and in the bars of California's cities. Local law enforcement agencies were expected to carry out the duties of the ABC, but there was very little incentive for them to do so, particularly since the Tay-Bush Inn raid in 1961 and the subsequent "gayola" revelations. Second, while compliant, alcohol-serving topless bars continued to flourish, massage parlor prostitution became much more prevalent. The massage parlors would become the most dynamic component of the burgeoning commercial sex industry in California by the 1980s.

Perhaps the most enduring local legacy of the post-*LaRue* reorganization of commercial sexuality in San Francisco, however, was the ascendancy of the internationally renowned Mitchell Brothers O'Farrell Theater, one of the nation's first all-nude, alcohol-free, "lap-dance" theaters. The first thing Jim and Artie Mitchell did when they opened their theater in July 1969 was to revolutionize the commercial sex industry by screening their own films. Weeding out the prostitutes from the talent pool, the Mitchell brothers preferred what their biographer has described as "enthusiastic young hippies." In fact, pornographers of the era generally agreed that the talent was becoming better looking

FIGURE 2.3. Pornography and strip club impresarios Jim (*left*) and Artie Mitchell, 1977. Courtesy: AP/Wide World Photos.

and generally of a "better stock." "Most of the girls come from well-off, middle-class families," one of the Mitchell brothers' competitors-in-porn remarked in 1970. "They have gone to college, if not graduated. Their appearance in sex films is a way to show off their new found sexual freedom."[18] One of those actresses was nineteen-year-old Marilyn Chambers, who, shortly after wrapping the early Mitchell brothers film *Behind the Green Door* (1972)—reportedly the most expensive pornographic film ever made to that point—revealed that she had recently modeled for Procter & Gamble as the face of Ivory Snow laundry soap. The publicity made the movie an instant international hit—ultimately grossing more than $35 million—and brought pornography into the mainstream.

Capitalizing on the notoriety generated by the Chambers adventure, and unimpeded by the ABC, the Mitchell brothers quickly introduced live shows. By the late 1970s, they had opened the Ultra Room, which featured performances of lesbian bondage; the Kopenhagen, featuring nude dancing by pairs of women offering "lap dances" for male patrons; and New York Live, a cabaret-style show culminating in nude lap dances. These "customer-contact" live shows were among the first in the nation, real crowd pleasers for legions of American tourists as well as a number of international tourists, particularly Japanese businessmen.[19]

Although the brothers emphatically denied that any actual sex took place on the premises of the O'Farrell Theater, dozens of reports from undercover SFPD officers demonstrated the extent to which the line between erotic entertainment and outright prostitution was blurred. "Every seat was equipped with a flashlight," one detailed report from 1981 revealed. During the dance, the purpose of the flashlights became clear:

> She started to disrobe, while she continued to go around the room;
> eventually she was completely nude. While she danced nude
> she would fondle her breast, posterior and vagina: inserting her
> finger into the vagina. During the dances patrons would shine
> their flashlights illuminating the dancer. While nude she then
> got on her knees before [a patron] and simulated an act of oral
> copulation placing her head between his knees and her hands on his
> lap.... While in his lap, nude, [the patron] started to kiss, fondle her
> body and place his finger into her vagina.

An officer in another room of the club the same night observed "four different males with their penis's [*sic*] exposed in which the females who accepted tips from these patrons were actually masturbating these individuals with their hands."[20] Little wonder that journalist Hunter Thompson, who briefly managed the theater in the mid-1980s, described the O'Farrell Theater as "the Carnegie Hall of public sex in America."[21]

FIGURE 2.4. Pornographic actress and Ivory Snow Soap model Marilyn Chambers, 1973. Courtesy: AP/Wide World Photos.

Critics of the proliferation of sex shows and toplessness were quick to blame the scale of debauchery in San Francisco on "hippie culture," and the bearded, shaggy-haired, drug-addicted Mitchell brothers certainly fit the bill. But in fact, most patrons of pornography were well-educated, affluent, and "neat" looking whites. A careful study conducted by a research team led by California State University professor Harold Nawy, and commissioned by the Commission on Obscenity and Pornography, produced a finely grained portrait of the city's pornography industry and its many customers. In April and May 1970, Nawy and his associates observed more than 950 patrons of adult bookstores, 367 patrons of pornographic video arcades, and more than 3,100 patrons of adult movie theaters in San Francisco. Across all genres, the most common patron was not, in fact, the wild-eyed, long-haired, hippie but rather the purportedly upstanding white businessman. Among adult bookstore patrons, for example, about 35% wore a suit and tie, and another 29% were described as "casual (neat)" in dress; those wearing "hip" clothes only made up about 4%. The results of an in-depth questionnaire of adult movie theater patrons were similarly revealing: white-collar workers outnumbered all other types of workers; college and graduate school graduates greatly outnumbered non–college graduates, and high- and middle-income earners greatly outnumbered the poor.

Japanese tourists played an essential role as patrons in San Francisco's booming sex businesses. Before the early 1970s, Japanese tourism to the mainland United States was very limited; after 1964, when the Japanese government lifted travel restrictions, Japanese tourists and investors began to head west to Hawaii, but most did not travel to the American mainland until the mid-1970s. Beginning in 1976, a declining dollar and extensive American promotion in Japan of the Montreal Olympics made mainland United States travel much cheaper and more appealing. From the beginning of Japanese tourism, sex tourism was an essential component of it. The first Japanese-language magazines for Japanese tourists in America were produced in Los Angeles in the early 1970s and were funded almost exclusively by massage parlor advertisement revenue. San Francisco's Japanese-language tourist magazines also featured prominent advertisements for massage parlors and pornographic theaters. Sutter Cinema near Union Square, for example, advertised "the best of the pornographic movies" and the most "comfortable seats."[22] The advertisement for the Sutter Cinema was well placed because, as Nawy's team discovered, Japanese men disproportionately patronized relatively discreet adult theaters and were underrepresented in porno arcades and bookstores.[23]

As Fred Methner knew all too well, the handmaiden of toplessness and sex shows was storefront pornography; its explosion represented an even more spectacular assault than the topless and sex show craze on traditional ideas about the proper place of sexuality. And the sale of the merchandise got a healthy boost from the U.S. Supreme Court's 1966 decision in the so-called Fanny Hill case, in which the Court further expanded the criteria for obscenity, significantly diminishing prosecutors' ability to prove obscenity. After the 1966 decision, legal scholar Donald A. Downs has explained, "the Court began to overturn virtually every obscenity prosecution it encountered unless

Prostitution and Sex Businesses, 1976-1978

Marina

North Beach

San Francisco Bay

Russian Hill

Columbus Ave.

Broadway & Grant

Broadway

Grant St.

Pacific Heights

Nob Hill

Chinatown

Financial District

Polk St.

Post & Hyde

Post St.

Union Square

Hyde St.

Civic Center/ Tenderloin

Tenderloin

Western Addition

Hayes St.

Fillmore St.

Market St.

Hayes & Fillmore

South of Market

Castro/ Upper Market

Mission St.

18th St.

Mission & 18th

Mission

0   .5 km
0   .5 mi

• Sex Businesses
■ Areas of Protitution

Potrero Hill

MAP 4. By the mid-1970s, pornography businesses and prostitution had moved
well-beyond their historic concentration in the Barbary Coast and the Tenderloin.
Map by David Deis, Dreamline Cartography.

the material was sold to minors or advertised salaciously." The only mitigating ruling offered by the Court came with *Miller v. California* in 1973, in which the Court lowered the bar for determining obscenity slightly; but it was still extraordinarily difficult to prosecute obscenity charges. One only need look at the legal history of the Mitchell brothers to recognize this fact: charged more than two hundred times with lewdness and obscenity in their career, they only lost once, and that verdict was later overturned.[24]

The proliferation of pornography in the 1970s, essentially the product of changing values among young Americans and increasingly liberal Supreme Court decisions, was also the product of technological changes—in particular, the rising popularity of 16-millimeter film. As the newer, cheaper 8-millimeter film replaced 16-millimeter in the home-movie market, the once amateur 16-millimeter achieved a semiprofessional status and became the standard gauge for film school projects. Not only did 16-millimeter film change the styles of film being made but also the venues where they were screened. The limited brightness of 16-millimeter was not suitable for large theaters, thus encouraging the proliferation of storefront theaters, also known as "pocket theaters" or minicinemas. Low operating costs and small audiences allowed operators to regularly avoid zoning regulations and fire codes because they had too few seats to even qualify as theaters.[25] One of the first screenings of a 16-millimeter porno film was in the Mission District in 1967, but by the early 1970s, the 16-millimeter porno film was a national phenomenon. By 1970, all of San Francisco's pocket theaters used 16-millimeter film, and in 1971, the *Independent Film Journal* reported: "16 mm Skinflick Brush Fires Pock Nation."[26]

That "brush fire" blew obscenity onto the streets of other American cities. In New York's Times Square, Detroit's Eight Mile Road, Boston's "Combat Zone," Baltimore's "Block," Los Angeles' Hollywood and North Hollywood, and dozens of other American metropolises, urbanites could plainly see the sexual revolution writ large on the urban landscape. By 1969, the phenomenon of toplessness was so well known that the Gallup poll asked Americans about their views on "topless nightclub waitresses": 73% of respondents found them objectionable. More than 70% of respondents said that they found nude pictures in magazines objectionable, and 73% wanted stricter state and local laws restricting the sale of obscene materials on newsstands.[27]

By the early 1970s, San Francisco was increasingly identified as a national haven for vice and smut. In January 1971, journalist William Murray recognized this in an article in the *New York Times Magazine* entitled "The Porn Capital of America." "Prostitution is flourishing," he wrote, with open solicitation taking place on street corners in the heart of town and even outside such fancy hotels as the St. Francis, where a ring of teen-age boys and girls was doing a brisk business a few weeks ago at $50 to $100 a body. There are about 30 movie houses scattered all over that screen only hard-core films.

"Just walking around the city," Murray concluded, "can give the casual visitor the impression that porn, not tourism, is San Francisco's leading industry." That same year, the San Francisco Committee on Crime, a nonpartisan analysis group, declared that the "range of prostitution in this city is fantastic":

> Practitioners may be male or female; black, white, or oriental. They may be 14-year-olds hustling as part of a junior high school "syndicate" operation; they may be hippies supporting the habits of their "old man" (or their own habits); they may be moonlighting secretaries who sell their favors on a selective basis through legitimate dating services. Places of assignation range from run-down hotels to luxurious hilltop apartments.[28]

But even this "fantastic" range would pale in comparison to what it became by the mid- to late 1970s.

Street prostitution increased dramatically under the mayoral administration of native San Franciscan George Moscone. After narrowly beating John Barbagelata, a conservative supervisor and local real estate mogul, in a run-off election in 1975, Moscone sought the informal decriminalization of prostitution in the city. It was an open secret that Moscone himself had narrowly avoided arrest shortly after being elected to the Board of Supervisors in 1963 when police caught him with an African American prostitute in the Fillmore. When he became mayor in 1976, he quickly appointed Charles Gain, most recently head of the Oakland Police Department, to the position of chief of police. Gain soon broadcast his tolerance of prostitution by befriending the city's best known prostitution rights advocate, Margo St. James. In an effort to reduce police corruption and kickbacks from prostitution, Gain regularly consulted St. James about incidents of police payoff among street prostitutes. Gain then rotated officers suspected of taking payoffs, infuriating no small number of them, who felt that the force was taking orders from prostitutes. And Gain's well-publicized attendance at St. James's annual Hookers' Ball in 1977 appeared to confirm their suspicions.

The election of Joseph Freitas as district attorney further diminished the strictures against open prostitution. In striking contrast to his predecessor, who prosecuted nearly six hundred local landlords under the Red Light Abatement

Act, Freitas announced in January 1976 that the district attorney's office would no longer actively pursue prostitution convictions. This was less a reflection of tolerance than of prioritizing: the violent crime rate in San Francisco, and in cities nationwide, skyrocketed in the 1970s. Convinced that prostitution was a victimless crime, Freitas, Gain, and Moscone believed they should direct their resources elsewhere.[29]

The results of this new tolerance were palpable. By 1976, an average of 250 female prostitutes walking the streets each night. Beat cops in the Tenderloin were outraged. Sergeant Michael Dower of the Tenderloin's night-time vice squad said, "It's a hell of a situation out there. Outrageous. The girls are getting more brazen." Even Gain, whose popularity suffered as a result of the new policy, admitted that clearly there had been "an influx. I have had complaints from hotel owners that the increase in the number of prostitutes is substantial." Evidently, prostitutes had an informal network, and word traveled quickly that there was, as the San Francisco Chronicle described it, a new "Gold Rush" in the Tenderloin.[30]

But it was not only the old Tenderloin that experienced a surge in prostitution. Under the newly tolerant administration, a climate of sexual openness prevailed, and prostitutes fanned out across the city. While North Beach and the Tenderloin continued to be the most popular prostitution zones, new zones emerged at Eighteenth and Mission in the Mission District and in Hayes Valley on the periphery of the Western Addition. But perhaps the most conspicuous increase occurred in the heart of the African American Western Addition, on Fillmore Street.

Race and Prostitution in the Fillmore and Beyond

Like many black girls in the Fillmore, Monique grew up fast and hard. One of seven children with an alcoholic mother and a petty criminal for a father, childhood was—as she later remembered it—"pretty shitty." With absentee parents, too many siblings, and a "lousy school," she started hanging around with older kids on the street who quickly exploited her youth and naiveté. After she was forced into having sex at age eleven to complete her initiation into a local gang, she started "popping pills" to cope with her depression, and before long a local boy started to "pimp me off in part of the Fillmore around Webster Street." By 1967, she was a career prostitute in the Tenderloin, and she saw few better alternatives in San Francisco. "I never got a job because if you are black you can't get much of a job beyond cleaning a shit house and I can make a lot more pushing my ass."[31]

Monique was part of the vast expansion of prostitution in the Fillmore during the 1960s and 1970s. "Their dresses make them as obvious as peacocks in a flock of chickens," wrote the author of a 1965 exposé in the *San Francisco Chronicle*. "Their skirts are tight, tight, tight, and the hemline is halfway between the knee and hip. No man," he concluded, "can complain he is offered unseen merchandise." The streets had become so crowded that the officers at the SFPD's Northern Station received regular traffic complaints because it was virtually impossible "for a man to drive from one place to another these evenings without being subjected to all sorts of esoteric signals from girls standing on street corners." The San Francisco Committee on Crime reported that prostitutes in the Fillmore and the Tenderloin had even been known to "grab at the coattails of pedestrians."[32] Even the city's premier black newspaper, the *Sun-Reporter*, ran a story on a local prostitute who regaled the editor with stories of white convention "johns" and aggressive Fillmore pimps.[33]

The explosion of prostitution in the Western Addition in the 1960s and 1970s was part of the citywide relaxation of both social and legal codes against casual and even commercial sex. But in the Western Addition, this explosion was also the product of the deepening economic deprivation of many African

FIGURE 2.5. Western Addition prostitutes congregate on a street corner, 1965. Courtesy: *San Francisco Chronicle.*

Americans in the 1960s. Despite the real economic advances of the war and immediate postwar years, and the Bay Area's reputation for racial tolerance, most San Francisco employers were generally in step with the discriminatory hiring policies of the nation at large. Further displaced by the reconversion of wartime industries, the city's black population was often relegated to the burgeoning service and tourist sector, and even there they encountered discrimination in hiring, as the 1964 strike against the Sheraton Palace made clear. "It's the same old loaded dice for a Negro in San Francisco," one Fillmore resident complained. "They just sugar 'em up a little."[34] More concretely, black men were twice as likely as whites to be unemployed, and where blacks were employed, they tended to work in the lowest paying jobs, largely because of the rampant discrimination in labor unions.[35] Given these limited economic opportunities, it is not surprising that a disproportionate number of black women in the Fillmore turned to prostitution.

Deeply complicating the nature of prostitution in the Western Addition was the provincial culture that flourished in the SFPD. Comprised predominantly of San Francisco–born Irishmen, much of the SFPD rank and file was emotionally invested in preserving their vision of racial order of the city of their youth. They watched nervously in the postwar years as blacks came to occupy

FIGURE 2.6. A Western Addition prostitute approaches a "john," 1965. Courtesy: *San Francisco Chronicle*.

a greater share of both the population and the public space of the city. Less than 6% of the citywide population in 1950, blacks comprised more than 13% of it by 1970; more significant, blacks had moved beyond the Western Addition to occupy the once largely Italian Bayview–Hunters Point area and, even more problematically, had begun to move into the once solidly Irish Visitacion Valley, a district that Warren Hinkle, a fourth-generation San Franciscan and *Chronicle* columnist, described as "the last reservoir of the blue-collar ethic in a romantic city lately tilting towards narcissism."[36] The nearby Sunnydale housing complex, originally built for returning World War II veterans, was converted into public housing in the early 1970s and became predominantly black. The rising tension between the SFPD and the city's blacks was best exemplified by the 1966 SFPD shooting of an unarmed black teenager in Bayview–Hunters Point and by the SFPD's fierce resistance to hiring blacks. As late as 1979, when a consent decree went into effect to desegregate the SFPD, it was 85% white and 95% male. In short, racism became a more acute component of the provincial culture of the SFPD as longtime officers watched "their" town disappearing before their eyes.[37]

By inserting themselves into the public realm conspicuously, black prostitutes and pimps of the 1960s and 1970s violated not only actual laws against prostitution and solicitation but also the expectations of white officers who wanted to keep blacks "in their place." Not surprisingly, race-based selective enforcement of prostitution laws became the norm. For example, 48% of the 125 women who served time in the San Francisco County Jail in 1975 were black, despite the fact that black women represented a minority of all San Francisco prostitutes.[38] Sentencing was a problem: while about 60% of the women arrested for prostitution in 1976 were white, 62% of the women sentenced to jail for prostitution were nonwhite.[39]

Profiting from the black prostitutes was a cadre of black male pimps who became highly visible on the streets of San Francisco and other American cities. Of course, just as there had always been white pimps, there had always been black pimps. But during the Civil Rights revolution of the 1960s and 1970s, as public space in San Francisco and elsewhere became more democratic, black pimps moved into the public—white—eye. Part of the much-documented explosion of African American "pimping" in the era reflected a real increase in the practice, but much of the attention it got was simply a reflection of the increased *visibility* of pimps throughout the city. In the 1972 study *Black Players*, coauthor Christina Milner recounted her ethnographic research among the pimps of San Francisco. Working as an exotic dancer in North Beach, Milner got to know the pimps closely—so closely, in fact, that many attempted to lure her into their "stables." But she thwarted their advances by conspicuously handing over her earnings to her husband, Richard Milner, also a Berkeley graduate student and part-time writer for the *Berkeley Barb*, and certainly not, in the pimps' parlance, "a player." (The pimps took pity on his frumpiness and referred him to their tailor.)[40] In *Black Players*, the couple dispassionately dissected the pimps' paranoia, recklessness, misogyny, and shallow materialism. But they also showed sensitivity to the important economic role prostitution played in sustaining legitimate enterprises. Particularly noteworthy was that behind the fronts, "the psychological warfare," and "the deep defensiveness" was a desire to do "righteous business" in the black community, especially in the Fillmore. To her surprise, Milner discovered a great number of businesses that were owned by pimps—or supported by loans from pimps—including a gas station, a talent agency, a liquor store, a record store, a massage parlor, a photographic supply shop, several apartment buildings, a movie theater, a beer bar, a fried chicken store, and a black advertising agency. There is "clear evidence," she concluded, "that pimping is frequently used as a springboard for individual Black capitalism in the ghetto."[41]

From the perspective of many influential whites, the migration of both black prostitutes and pimps out of the Fillmore and into North Beach magnified the scope of the prostitution problem, generally. Both the *San Francisco Chronicle* and Mayor Shelley articulated the notion that black civil rights progress was to blame for the SFPD's unwillingness to rein in the migration of black prostitutes from the Fillmore to North Beach. And as historian Christopher Agee has shown, the SFPD in fact used this rationale to justify its relaxed prostitution enforcement in North Beach. The *Sun Reporter* snapped that this was "one of the most candid lies ever uttered by a law enforcement official in defense of dereliction of his duties." By contrast, the *Sun Reporter* blasted, white "johns" were allowed to freely patronize the black community with impunity, as "similar situations along Fillmore St" went unchallenged.[42]

Some African Americans decided to tackle the problem of streetwalking prostitutes in the Fillmore themselves. In 1971, a group of African American teenagers from the Western Addition organized themselves under the banner The Ghetto Youth Movement with the specific intention of curbing prostitution in their neighborhood. Their opposition was not a moralistic campaign against prostitutes. Instead, the problem, as one member described it, was that prostitution degraded black women who were not prostitutes, because "johns" "can't tell the difference between a black lady and a black prostitute. A day does not go by without a black mother or daughter or sister being molested by ignorant white tricks." Their response was direct and confrontational: "We're going to mess up the man's mind by taking down license plate numbers, taking pictures of all the tricks cruising the ghetto and put up big signs warning them that the war is on."[43]

Sex Radicals Storm the Haight-Ashbury

The last time anybody saw Bernard Mashioff, he was racing out of town in a new convertible with two fabulous cross-dressers in the back seat. Having jumped bail, written a string of bad checks, and filed a false police report, he probably drove fast. It was an appropriately theatrical end to Mashioff's tumultuous month in the Haight-Ashbury in 1964. In July, Mashioff resurrected the defunct movie house the Haight-Ashbury Theater as a veritable gay circus, screening Ed Wood's 1953 transsexual drama *Glen or Glenda,* hosting a *Mr. San Francisco* physique show, and featuring nightly drag contests. By inserting these brazen spectacles of homosexuality into what residents described as a "family neighborhood," Mashioff touched off a firestorm of protest during his month in the Haight-Ashbury.

In the *Haight-Ashbury Independent,* editorialist Richard Doyle, a longtime resident, demanded to know how Mashioff could continue to pollute a neighborhood "with many children. I do not believe children should be subjected to the realities of a harsh world at too early an age. I do not believe that any mother wants her child exposed to an environment of sexual deviation." Housewife Adria Garabadian, also a longtime Haight-Ashbury resident, complained that she and her neighbors were "afraid for our children." "Homosexuality is a disease," she said; "a contagious one." Evidently unafraid of immediate contagion, those young children—under close parental supervision—protested by carrying signs reading "Haight-Ashbury Is a Straight Neighborhood." John Klung, president of the Haight-Ashbury Neighborhood Association, saw Mashioff's introduction of his brand of obscenity to the district as tantamount to recent attempts to build a freeway through it. "Any form of deviation, sexual or freeway, is not good for this neighborhood."[44]

Ultimately, Mashioff's mendacity and unscrupulous finances drove him out of the theater business, and he drove himself out of town shortly thereafter, to the great delight of Haight-Ashbury residents. Given the vitriol of their rhetoric, it would be tempting to see them as conservative foot soldiers of the emerging, if not yet named, Moral Majority. But to do so would be to miss the nuance of the story and to ignore the profound discomfort that changes in sexual attitudes generated in people who otherwise proudly thought of themselves as democratic and highly tolerant.

To understand the Haight-Ashbury residents' attitudes on the eve of the sexual revolution, one must understand the Haight-Ashbury Neighborhood Council. Officially founded in March 1960, the council actually originated at least a year earlier, when residents met at the local Dudley Stone Elementary School to mobilize against a proposal to bisect the district, and the Panhandle area of Golden Gate Park, with a six-lane freeway. The Panhandle Freeway proposal dated back to a 1945 City Planning Commission Master Plan, formalized at the time in the commission's 1951 "Trafficways Plan," which provided for nine new freeways crisscrossing the city. Once formalized, the plan was vigorously opposed by the Recreation and Park Commission and dozens of neighborhood groups throughout San Francisco, including the Haight-Ashbury Neighborhood Council. Facing mounting opposition, the Board of Supervisors abandoned six of the nine proposed routes—including the Panhandle Freeway—in January 1959. But the California State Division of Highways and the City Planning Commission mounted a new offensive, changing the name of the Panhandle Freeway to the Western Freeway. On May 14, the Board of Supervisors unanimously recommended that the renamed and reinvigorated plan be rejected, and on the following day, more than ten thousand San Franciscans, many of them residents of the Haight-Ashbury, attended a "Save the Park Rally" to protest the route. In 1966, the Board recommended that all proposed projects be discontinued.[45]

While residents resisted changes to the physical characteristics of the neighborhood, they did not resist racial changes as one might expect. Many blacks displaced by the redevelopment of the Western Addition during the 1950s migrated just west of Fillmore to the Haight-Ashbury. Between 1950 and 1960, when the black proportion of the citywide population increased from about 6% to 10%, the black proportion of the Haight-Ashbury's population rose from 4% to almost 30%, and by 1970, blacks would represent more than half of the Haight-Ashbury's residents. This new black population was not confined to the lower portion of the district adjacent to the Fillmore but was widely distributed across the district's four census tracts.[46]

Remarkably, black migration caused less of a stir there than it did generally in other metropolitan neighborhoods nationwide and even in San Francisco. For one thing, the Haight-Ashbury was already ethnically diverse, and even as the proportion of the San Francisco population that was foreign-born declined between 1940 and 1960, the proportion of foreign-born in the Haight-Ashbury had increased. Furthermore, the district's abundant apartment stock, which became more affordable during this period because of its declining value, was appealing to successive waves of Irish, Germans, Poles, and Italians. The transitory nature of the rental district mitigated the emergence of deeply entrenched homeowner interests. On the eve of the hippie in-migration, the neighborhood, according to one close observer, considered itself "a liberal, sometimes radical, successfully integrated, bohemian, working class, residential area."[47]

Whatever their rationale, residents were successful in integrating the neighborhood, and the Haight-Ashbury Neighborhood Council took the lead. On the same day the *Haight-Ashbury Independent* celebrated the return of "family pictures" to the Haight Theater, its editor lauded Mayor Shelley's appointment of an African American, Terry Francois, to fill a vacancy on the Board of Supervisors: "It is most timely in a moral, political social sense that the city's 75,000 negroes have a voice in San Francisco's legislative body." The *Independent* demanded an expanded war on poverty, citing the poor chances faced by the "Negro youngster" and others in "the Fillmore, Polk, South of Market, Mission, Hunter's Point and even now the Haight Ashbury." And the paper asked, on the eve of the Western Addition redevelopment project, what accommodations would be made for those families displaced by the renewal. Finally, and more significant, both the *Independent* and the Neighborhood Council strongly opposed Proposition 14, the 1964 initiative to repeal the Rumford Fair Housing Act. Proposition 14 sailed through in the city and the state; the residents of the Haight-Ashbury rejected the measure 64% to 36%.[48]

Beyond racial issues, residents of the Haight-Ashbury were more staunchly democratic than other San Franciscans. In the presidential election of 1964, for example, almost 80% of Haight-Ashbury residents voted for Lyndon Johnson over Arizona Republican Barry Goldwater. Johnson won citywide as well, but by a smaller margin than in the Haight-Ashbury. Goldwater's opposition to civil rights and Medicare legislation earned him scorn in the pages of the *Haight-Ashbury Independent,* which called him a candidate running headlong "back to the nineteenth century."[49]

But the New Deal liberalism and racial tolerance of Haight-Ashbury residents did not predispose them to tolerance of sexual "deviance." This would become apparent in 1967, once the trickle of hippies into the neighborhood became a flood. There were lots of things that longtime residents disliked about the hippies: their languorous lifestyles, their confrontational attitudes, and their overwhelming numbers. But it was the hippies' sexual views and practices that made confrontation inevitable between them and the long-standing residents. By 1968, antihippie hostility was driven much more by the threat of violence from hardened criminals who had come to exploit the naiveté of hippies; but before then, it was free love that was most problematic.

The cultural transformation of the Haight-Ashbury began inauspiciously, and it began across town in North Beach. Two historic developments propelled the remnants of the Beat community out of North Beach and gradually toward the Haight-Ashbury. The first was a well-coordinated campaign by local media and law enforcement during and after 1958 to drive the Beats out of North Beach in order to rid the district of their purported depravity and sexual libertinism.[50] The second and final nail in the coffin of the Beat scene was the

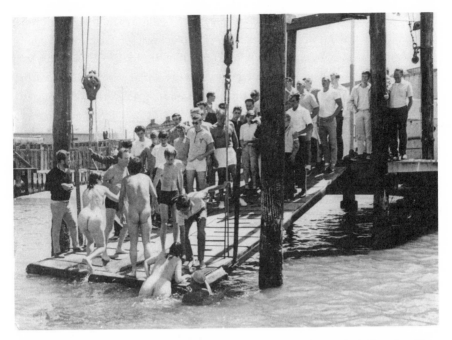

FIGURE 2.7. Jefferson Poland and fellow sex radicals Ina Saslow and Shirley Einseidel at a "wade-in" in Aquatic Park, 1965. Courtesy: *San Francisco Chronicle*.

topless craze that had turned North Beach into a sex tourism zone. As a result of this transformation, and a generalized backlash against the Beats, many of them migrated to the Haight-Ashbury—bringing with them new ideas about sexuality.

In 1958, sociologists Francis Rigney and L. Douglas Smith studied the Beats of North Beach intensely, publishing their results in their 1961 book *The Real Bohemia*. Devoting considerable attention to the sexual practices of the Beats, Rigney and Smith concluded that media portrayals of Beat promiscuity and sex radicalism were greatly overstated. Though many they interviewed said they had had homosexual experiences (just as had the American men surveyed in Kinsey's famous 1948 study) and others had "rather mixed-up sexual lives, involving premarital, marital, and extramarital intercourse and homosexual activity as well," exclusive homosexuality was quite rare. The explicit homosexuality of Ginsburg's 1957 *Howl,* and the Beats' identification with homosexual love more generally, was an important part of their legacy, but Rigney and Smith's study suggests that the Beats of North Beach tended to pair off in heterosexual couples, though marriage was less common and premarital sex more common than in the American population in general.[51] Nonetheless, though the sexual practices and beliefs of the Beats were not radical by the standards of the 1960s, their forays into sexual libertinism certainly laid the groundwork for the Haight-Ashbury scene.[52]

Most influential in creating a sexual revolution in the Haight-Ashbury was a young political radical named Jefferson Poland. After being expelled from Florida State University in 1960 for his integrationist work with the Congress of Racial Equality (CORE), Poland moved to California and quickly took up work as an agricultural labor organizer, renting a room in the Stockton home of labor leader Dolores Huerta. After working with CORE to register black voters in Louisiana in the summer of 1963, Poland traveled to New York, where he reconnected with a friend, Leo Koch, a University of Illinois biology professor who had been fired for advocating premarital sex. Mutually inspired by sex radicals in New York—including Allen Ginsberg, Tuli Kupferberg, and Randy Wicker—Poland and Koch founded the New York City League for Sexual Freedom in 1964. Drawing members from the Lower East Side bohemian community and the Columbia University student body, Poland led animated public discussions about sex, pickets against the imprisonment of prostitutes, and weekly "talkouts" on the streets of Greenwich Village in which passersby would sign up to stand on a wooden box and talk about sex.[53]

By 1965, Poland was back in San Francisco lending his support to the creation of the Sexual Freedom League (SFL), a West Coast analogue of the New York group. He found a sympathetic crowd at a little café just north of the Panhandle called the Blue Unicorn, where an anarchist had already begun a series of lectures.[54] Poland began hosting weekly lectures and discussions on topics such as "Sex in the Mental Hospital," "How to Be Queer and Like It," and "Sex and Civil Rights." He advocated, among other things, complete sexual freedom, legalized abortion, legalization of prostitution, the repeal of penalties for having sexual relations with persons under eighteen (he thought the age should be changed to sixteen), the introduction of sex education in primary education, and the elimination of laws requiring the wearing of clothing. The *Berkeley Barb* also published Poland's stinging critiques of beatnik sexuality: "Whatever the general public may think, most beatniks still practice conventional sexual possessiveness and jealousy." Part of his goal was to "free bohemia from monogamy, possessiveness, jealousy, and sexual 'faithfulness.' "[55] A self-described "all-around non-violent activist," Poland had long viewed sexual freedom as an essential component of human liberation. But in San Francisco, he was able to practice that freedom when a hippie commune of San Francisco State College students invited him to move in with them in 1965. Mostly women, they had a "clothing was optional and so was monogamy" policy.

Poland raised the public profile of the SFL on a chilly Sunday in August of 1965 when he and fellow sex radicals Ina Saslow and Shirley Einseidel conducted a nude "wade-in" in Aquatic Park, drawing national press attention. He and SFL members continued to advocate for public nudity, particularly on Ocean Beach near Fort Funston. From his jail cell, where he was placed for violating a local ordinance on proper swimming attire, Poland promised that he would hand out free copies of "so-called" obscene literature as an act of civil disobedience. In the pages of his newsletters *Lovescene* and *Sexual Freedom,* Poland reported on orgies and nudist romps, and directed readers to local pornographic movie theaters.[56]

Organized sex radicalism reached its zenith in the Psychedelic Venus Church (Psyven), founded by Poland in November 1969. Made up of former SFL members, art students, and new followers, the church fused group sex and marijuana consumption with Eastern mysticism and paganism to create what its leaders described as a "hedonist sexual-psychedelic-political-mysterious cult."[57] The president of the church was a man named Mother Boats, a native Californian, Vietnam veteran, and sailor who first learned of the SFL from reading the *Berkeley Barb* while stationed on a naval submarine in San Diego.[58] A closet gay-bisexual, Boats was inspired by the writings of Poland, as well as those of a gay liberation activist named Leo Laurence. Once back in Berkeley, Boats joined the SFL, participated in the emerging gay liberation movement, and then took the helm of Poland's new church. The church gave Boats the outlet he had been seeking, and he became one of the most active organizers in the history of organized sex radicalism. "We believed," Boats later recalled, "in breaking the chains of restriction, to liberate the body and turn it on and enjoy hedonistic comforts." Under Boats's guidance, Psyven became the epicenter of some of the most radical and performative sexual experimentation of the era. Boats hosted several nude rock 'n' roll dances—some with over four hundred attendees—that culminated in massive orgies for both gays and straights. In one Psyven "ceremony," more than one hundred people had sex in an old, two-story mansion. In another Psyven event, sex radicals gathered in a warehouse in which a woman wearing nothing but a winged helmet was hoisted by crane into the air and then landed safely to have sex with multiple onlookers. When Boats permanently left the United States in 1973, he did so in a way his fellow Psyven members would certainly have appreciated: he sailed off into the sunset with the mostly nude crew of the three-masted cargo schooner *S.V. Sofia.*

As many women soon discovered, sexual "freedom" did not mean gender freedom. While the most disciplined male sex radicals believed fundamentally in women's equality, many more hippies who behaved like sex radicals were gender conservatives. As historian Alice Echols has explained, "instead of undoing the deeply rooted sexual double standard, free love only masked it in countercultural pieties."[59] But for the sexually experimental women who were determined to challenge both gender and sexual limitations, the era gave unprecedented freedom. One of them was Margo Rila, who moved to San Francisco in 1965 after graduating from the University of New Mexico. "I was just not ready to settle into a long-term monogamous relationship," Rila later recalled. "I was ready for some sexual adventures with guys." She found those adventures in San Francisco. She and a female friend went to an SFL open house in Berkeley in 1966 and were soon invited to the parties.[60] In the course of her sexual adventures, Rila moved in with a man and began running the San Francisco chapter of the SFL. "We were trying…to live our lives and have fun by going to the nude beaches on weekends and to sex parties every Friday night." But her experience in the SFL not only expanded her experiences with men. Having seen naked women at the beaches and parties, Rila began to have "erotic feelings" about women but had no notion of bisexuality until she consulted a sympathetic psychologist. Affirmed in her preference, she began erotic relationships with women and came to the conclusion that bisexuality was "groovier than being strictly homosexual or strictly heterosexual."[61]

Even where rough equality prevailed, however, the ways men and women defined and practiced sexual freedom often varied. For example, Susan Elisabeth of the Psychedelic Venus Church argued that "true hedonism" required moderation. "The man whose primary interest in life is sex," she wrote, "really doesn't come to know his partners, but uses them as jackoff stations." Instead of raucous orgies and nightclubs, Elisabeth recommended an "intimate wine-tasting at home" as a more appropriate venue for achieving true hedonism. Another woman active in the Berkeley Sexual Freedom Forum—an East Bay sister organization to the SFL—between 1965 and 1967 characterized the nude parties as "a lot of people who did not know each other sitting around trying not to act self-conscious about having no clothes on." "Sexual freedom" meant something different for her, and likely for other women involved in the SFL, than for many of the men involved. For her, sexual freedom was not the freedom to participate in an orgy but the freedom to make her own choices about her body without government interference. Having dedicated her energies to making birth control information available at the University of California, Berkeley—still a radical act at that time—she found like-minded activists on the campus. "For me, the SFL [Sexual Freedom Forum] was a lot of work: schlepping to UC every day and sitting at a table on the street, engaging in conversation with anyone who came by, trying to listen thoughtfully and not react, often in the face of hostility." Her outspokenness against government intervention in the personal lives of American citizens drew the support of a surprising ally, the Young Americans for Freedom. In a show of support for the Sexual Freedom Forum's defense of individual liberties, the famously conservative student group defied its national leadership (and ultimately lost its funding) by allowing her to store her table at their nearby apartment. Ultimately, she remembers the SFL experience as one of "opening up a dialogue on subjects that had been taboo, and I hope it led the way to some of the breakthrough thinking about women's oppression that was part of seventies feminism."[62]

Had the sex radicalism of the SFL and later the Psychedelic Venus Church remained the exclusive territory of those fringe groups, the fabled tolerance of the longtime Haight-Ashbury residents might have extended to the hippies. In fact, there is abundant anecdotal evidence that residents initially tolerated hippies. Even before the Summer of Love, students from San Francisco State University had discovered the neighborhood and were drawn to its affordable, historic, Victorian apartments. Inspired by experimental psychology and drugs, these young residents became the customers of the first psychedelic shops, health food stores, craft boutiques, and coffee shops that began popping up in 1965. When San Francisco State College professor Sherri Cavan visited the Haight-Ashbury that year, she reported that the Neighborhood Council viewed the development with pleasure, telling her that "it was nice to see young faces in the area" and, perhaps more important, that their presence would "revitalize the neighborhood, bring a sense of life to it." In September 1965, Michael Fallon of the *San Francisco Examiner* shared their view: "Haight-Ashbury," he wrote "seems to be experiencing a renaissance that will make it a richer, better neighborhood in which to live." By the end of 1966, the neighborhood had about thirty "hippie" businesses.[63]

A small collection of gay and lesbian bars already existed in and around the Haight-Ashbury before Poland and other outspoken sex radicals descended on the area. These establishments generally avoided censure because they were discreet. Among them was D'Oak Room at 350 Divisadero, Romeo's at 1605 Haight, the Golden Cask at 1725 Haight, My Place #4 at 1784 Haight, and Maud's, the well-known lesbian bar in neighboring Cole Valley. They survived by following Park Station police captain Daniel Kiely's advice: "be discreet and don't dance."[64]

But the flamboyant sex radicalism of Poland and the SFL was shared by many other self-defined hippies, and this generated no small amount of friction in the historically tolerant neighborhood. To be sure, much of the neighborhood's shock in response to the hippies' invasion was a reaction to their generalized "lifestyle," of which sexual liberation was just one part. A psychiatrist at neighboring Mt. Zion Hospital observed the hostility of longtime residents who resented the "slovenly dress, and uncleanliness of the hippies, with

their sexual behavior, and with problems of drug abuse."⁶⁵ Beyond that, the
great hippie invasion created transportation problems, as many buses had to be
rerouted around the crowded streets. Beginning in March 1968, the city closed
the Haight-Ashbury to traffic on Sundays, an act that encouraged the revelry.
Waste management proved challenging, and piles of garbage lined the streets.
In this respect, sexuality was just one aspect of an overall hippie persona that
many longtime residents found objectionable.

A closer reading of the Haight-Ashbury residents' response to the hippie in-
migration of the mid- to late 1960s suggests that the overt sexuality of the hippies was longtime residents' chief concern. Early in 1966, a local church tried
to bring together members of the old and new communities; one exchange,
recorded by sociologist Sherri Cavan, captured the nature of the rising tension about sexuality: "Do you know what happened in the flat right across the
street from me? That I can see from my window?" a longtime resident asked
the crowd. "There were two Hippies, making love. On the porch. Outside. You
could see it from my window." At a meeting in which "straights" declared a
"war on hippies" in March 1968, longtime resident Raymond Hagan expressed
his outrage at the sight of a couple having sex in their backyard and "going
through everything imaginable." When residents of the Haight-Ashbury took
their list of grievances to Mayor Joseph L. Alioto two weeks later, they complained to him about the "prostitution" and the "lewd dances by drug addicts
on our streets." One woman complained of "couples loving themselves up"
on Haight Street. "Should we expose our children of tender ages to that?" she
indignantly asked the mayor. These local views squared with a national perception that hippies were rabidly promiscuous. *Newsweek* reported in February
1967: "There are no hippies who believe in chastity, or look askance at marital
infidelity or see even marriage itself as a virtue. Physical love is a delight—to be
chewed upon as often and as freely as a handful of sesame seeds."⁶⁶

Less publicly visible but no less public were the medical consequences
of free love. David E. Smith, the doctor who founded the Haight Ashbury
Free Medical Clinic and chronicled his experiences in a book he coauthored in
1969, *Love Needs Care*, marveled at the explosion of venereal diseases among
the youth of the Haight-Ashbury. "The problems they experienced," he wrote
of hippie youth, "became convenient symbols of the unbridled experimentation which characterized their life-style." Hemorrhoids among young men
and women who experimented with anal intercourse was probably the least
glamorous of these "symbols," and there were many others. "Some of the
younger adolescents seemed to view hemorrhoids as a necessary price to be
paid in exchange for food and rent. Others stated that they were willing to try
any and all sexual practices, the further out the better." Estimates from the

SFDPH concluded that there was at least a 100% increase in venereal diseases in San Francisco in 1966 and that it had increased another 35% by 1967. Clinic doctors maintained that at *least* half of the young women living in the Haight-Ashbury were infected with some venereal disease, though many were unaware of it.[67]

Most of the members of the Haight-Ashbury non-hippie community were probably equally unaware of that fact, but they were not unaware of the general significance of the building at 558 Clayton Street that became the home of Smith's clinic in 1967. The building had a long and storied history of sexual significance. In the mid-1960s, it was home to four leaders of the gay rights group SIR—numerous SIR meetings were held here, and SIR members lent their support to Smith's new clinic. Often associated with its drug treatment, the Free Clinic, as it was generally called, also stood as a symbol of the consequences of sexual liberation. It was precisely this synonymy that made establishing the clinic difficult at first, because merchants and homeowners opposed the project, but Smith finally was able to move into an abandoned dentist's office above the former SIR headquarters.[68]

By the fall of 1968, there was more need for the clinic than ever before. Little was left of the euphoric hippie community of the Haight-Ashbury. Hippies, most accounts suggest, were replaced by "hoodies." "There were no paisley-painted buses on Haight Street," Smith remembered, "no flower children parading on sidewalks, no tribal gatherings." Left in their wake, according to Smith, were AWOL soldiers and draft evaders, white and black winos, black and white thugs. What they generally had in common was their rejection of LSD and marijuana in favor of opiates, barbiturates, and amphetamines, and their predisposition to criminal—often violent—activity.

A spike in reported rapes in San Francisco was one horrible and profoundly misunderstood effect of the sexual revolution in the city. Reported rapes doubled abruptly in the early 1970s and doubled again in 1973. In California as a whole, the number of reported forcible rapes tripled between 1960 and 1972 and continued to climb through the 1970s.[69] These rates may be less sensational than they first appear, because they reflect—at least in part—new awareness about the crime of rape, an increase in the reporting of rapes, and a rise in law enforcement personnel's sensitivity in responding to rape victims—all the result of the impact of the women's movement. Nonetheless, there did appear to be a real increase, which was most striking in and around the Haight-Ashbury, served by the SFPD's Park Station.

Historically, incidents of rape had always been highest in the Northern District, which contained the Western Addition and the Tenderloin; the Southeast District (later renamed Potrero District), which contained Potrero

Hill, Sunnydale, Visitacion Valley, and Bayview–Hunters Point; and the Mission Station, which included the Mission District, Eureka Valley, Noe Valley, and Twin Peaks. But by the late 1960s, officers in the once sleepy Park Station found themselves inundated with rape cases. A close examination of the records of reported rapes between 1958 and 1978 reveals that the number of citywide cases increased gradually each year until spiking in 1969, maintained an alarmingly high rate through the 1970s, and then spiked again in 1978. During the same period, the Park Station's share of citywide reported rapes increased from its average of about 12% in the late 1950s and early 1960s to a remarkable 24% in 1967.[70] Patrolman Colin Barker, who joined the Park station in 1967, watched the Haight-Ashbury's rapid decline and observed in 1968 that rapes were so common that they were "hardly ever reported." And the Diggers, a countercultural agitprop troupe that distributed free food, complained: "rape is as common as bullshit on Haight Street."[71]

In the Haight-Ashbury, police officers and other "straights" initially blamed the sex radicals for this trend. In 1968, a lieutenant at the Park Station described the "runaway girls" he heard "all the time about" who "get picked up by Negroes or bike riders on the street, locked in closets and raped for days at a time. Gang bangs and turnouts occur all the time." When L. H. Whittemore visited the Haight-Ashbury to conduct research for his bestselling non-fiction book *Cop! A Closeup of Violence and Tragedy,* he participated in a "ride along" with an officer who was investigating a charge of rape by a young hippie woman. Whittemore reports, with misplaced irony, that the words "free" and "love" were posted in the victim's house and that she exhibited what he saw as utter indifference, apparently blurring the lines between voluntary sex and rape very easily: "I grooved on the whole thing," she told the officer. "I let it take me where he was going. He had a knife, but I told him to put it away. I figured as long as it was going to happen, we *both* might as well enjoy it. Chalk it up to civil rights."[72] Yet, the fact that the young woman, raped at knifepoint, courageously reported the rape belied Whittemore's portrayal of her alleged indifference. Furthermore, that Whittemore took the young woman at her word revealed his unwillingness to ask tougher questions about her emotional maturity and, perhaps, her bravado in the wake of a traumatic event.

Whittemore, who went on to write for the popular TV series *Baretta,* undoubtedly had a flair for the dramatic. But there was something more problematic in his account: it both understated the violence of rape and casually linked rape with sexual liberation. Rape was never part of the ideology of the sex radicals. When Poland and his fellow wade-in participants chanted "no rape, no regulation" before diving nude into the icy waters of Aquatic Park, they were not just posturing. Rape ran completely against the grain of what most sex radicals and free-loving hippies sought. But sexual predators exploited that openness as a cover and an outlet for their pathological sexual aggression. Whittemore recognized this much. He saw in the Haight-Ashbury only a "nightmare of frustration, anger, disillusionment, despair, racial conflict, and disease."[73]

Perpetrating the most infamous manipulation and exploitation of the free love ethos was Charles Manson. Shortly after the Summer of Love, Manson—freshly paroled from a seven-year stint in prison for forgery, theft, and pimping—arrived in the Haight-Ashbury, where he quickly lured young hippie women and fewer hippie men into a group that he would soon call the "Family." Combining the hippie-inspired affinity for communal living, drug use, and unfettered sexual expression with the megalomania and paranoia of a hardened sociopath, Manson created a band of wolves in sheep's clothing. The sensational 1969 killing of twelve victims, including actress Sharon Tate, by associates of Manson's commune appeared to a shocked nation as the natural by-product of the free love and hippie phenomenon. The *Los Angeles Times*, for example, regarded Manson's Family as an "occult band of hippies" that reveled in "mass murder sadistic sexual gratification."[74] It was a popular characterization, but it was based entirely on the aesthetic similarity between the members of the Family and the multitude of sexually adventurous and entirely non-violent hippies congregating in the Haight-Ashbury. For many readers, the two radically distinct groups simply became one and the same. Neither the nation's fascination with Manson nor Manson's easy exploitation of the communal and free-love ethos to cause unspeakable harm would be lost on writers and filmmakers in the subsequent decade.

Unfit Mothers, Illegitimacy, and Birth Control

One of the more subtle, but no less potent, symbols of sexual liberation in the Haight-Ashbury, San Francisco at large, and throughout the nation was the single mother. Childbirth out of wedlock, of course, was not a new phenomenon, and it was certainly on the rise before the sexual revolution, a product of wartime and immediate postwar relocation and massive migrations of Americans. Between 1950 and 1960, the proportion of births among unmarried women rose from 3.9% to 5.3%, and between 1970 and 1980, it rose again from 10.7% to 18.4%.[75] In California, the increase was even more spectacular: between 1970 and 1980 the proportion of births among unmarried women increased from 12.6% to 20.7%. Among black women, who had always had higher rates of out-of-wedlock births than white women, the increase was staggering. Mirroring a national trend, the proportion California's black mothers who had children out of wedlock rose from 31.6% in 1966 to 58.2% in 1985.[76] Locally, the cultures of distinct neighborhoods reflected these shifts. For example, while 18.7% of the children in San Francisco belonged to female-headed families in 1970, 32% of the kids in the Haight-Ashbury did.[77]

Throughout most of American history unwed mothers had been treated as social deviants or, at the very least, subjected to contempt. In the immediate postwar years, as historian Rickie Solinger has demonstrated, policymakers, health providers, and the media had begun to portray the experiences of unwed mothers in new ways. The rising rates of births to black unwed mothers after World War II, in particular, had forced policymakers to try to explain the differences between blacks and whites, so they distinguished between the two, Solinger asserts, by viewing unwed white mothers as treatable neurotics versus black ones as either pathological, "unrestrained, wanton breeders, on one hand, or as calculating breeders for profit on the other."[78] This rhetorical distinction became politically potent by the late 1950s and 1960s as welfare costs rose. Though the Aid to Dependent Children program, founded in 1935, benefited both black and white mothers, social perception deemed it a black institution, further raising the specter of the profiteering black mother.

Now the rising rate of out-of-wedlock births among white women challenged this historic distinction. Although the rate of unmarried births among black women in California was very high, it did not increase markedly between 1973 and 1985; the rate of increase among white women was much faster.[79] As a result, with an increasing number of unmarried white women not only conceiving but also keeping their babies, it became more difficult to hold up black illegitimacy as the counterpoint to virtuous white motherhood. The San Francisco Unified School District opened four special schools in 1967 to accommodate pregnant students, in response to what the *San Francisco Chronicle* deemed a "rash of S.F. schoolgirl pregnancies."[80]

Planned Parenthood responded most decisively to the explosion of out-of-wedlock births. Long an advocate of birth control, but silenced in the pre–sexual revolution era, Planned Parenthood saw the tide turn in 1963, when Elgin Orcutt was appointed as chief of obstetrics and gynecology at San Francisco General Hospital. A member of San Francisco Planned Parenthood's Medical Advisory Committee, Orcutt was surprised to find that there was no birth control program at the hospital and that it did not offer therapeutic abortions or tubal ligations. "When I first met the superintendent of the hospital," Orcutt later recalled, "he warned me that he didn't want 'any funny stuff' in the operating room. 'I know that some of you gynecologists have been getting away with doing sterilizations. I've got my nurses in the operating room watching for that.'" Shortly after Orcutt came in, however, the superintendent fell ill and took a six-month leave; in his absence, Orcutt consulted the city attorney, ascertained that there was no law against providing tubal ligations, and implemented a policy of offering them. He also began offering birth control advice in the outpatient department. To fund this, he added a line item to the hospital's budget, requesting that $10,840 be designated for the purchase of birth control supplies. It cleared the hospital budget office, but was contested when it reached Mayor Shelley's desk.

Not yet humiliated by the infamous topless trials, Shelley responded to the budget item reflexively as a Catholic. Before he even saw the item, his chief administrative officer, Sherman Duckel, cut it from the budget, claiming that the services would be redundant because Planned Parenthood was going to be opening an office near the hospital. When Planned Parenthood contacted Duckel to inform him that such a clinic would only be a "last-ditch" attempt to provide services, he then admitted that he had cut the item because, he said, the hospital superintendent was not very "hot" for birth control. Planned Parenthood's legal counsel, Alvin Pelavin, responded with a scathing editorial in the *San Francisco Chronicle*:

> I was not aware that it was necessary for the hospital
> superintendent to be "hot" for a recognized medical service before
> it was made available to patients.... Birth control services are a
> fundamental part of any adequate health service according to
> statements of the California Medical Association, the American
> Public Health Association, and the California Conference of Local
> Health Officers, with the concurrence of our own Public Health
> Director, Dr. Ellis Sox.

Cowed, Duckel returned the item to the budget; but when the budget went to Shelley, he removed the item himself. Like Duckel, Shelley offered a rather feeble excuse that was generally recognized as a cover for a decision made on the basis of his Catholic faith. In the ensuing weeks, during which all of the local newspapers ran front-page coverage of Shelley's decision and the fallout, high-profile Californians weighed in to support the birth control funding at the hospital, including the Episcopal bishop of California, James Pike, and Dr. John Schaupp, president of the San Francisco Medical Society. But Shelley refused to budge. And then in April, a wealthy, thrice-married poet and philanthropist from suburban Saratoga named Henriette de Saussure Goodrich Durham Lehman wrote a personal check to the Board of Supervisors for the exact amount requested. They approved it, Shelley agreed not to veto the budget, and birth control became part of the program at San Francisco General Hospital, bringing it in line with the city's other secular hospitals. Following suit, the SFDPH opened the first of a slated five birth control clinics in November 1966, the first on Pacific Avenue near Chinatown, offering free birth control advice and supplies.[81]

Far more daring was the opening of a teen clinic in 1967, the brainchild of Sadja (Goldsmith) Greenwood, a doctor who had moved from New York to San Francisco in 1958 for a one-year internship at San Francisco General Hospital. She had been a volunteer at Planned Parenthood on the East Coast since she was sixteen, and her mother, as she recalled, "began teaching me about birth control at the age of two." Undeterred by San Francisco General's official policy of silence on the issue of birth control, Greenwood discreetly distributed Planned Parenthood referral cards to young women in the hospital. She worked for two more years as a psychiatric resident at Langley Porter but was still uncertain about the direction of her career. Later, while living in Singapore in 1963–1965, she met the indefatigable Alan Guttmacher, then president of Planned Parenthood and chairman of the Medical Committee of the International Planned Parenthood Federation. Guttmacher, then in his sixties, had been a leader in the family planning movement since he had watched a botched abortion kill a young woman as an intern in the 1920s. Greenwood found Guttmacher inspirational, and followed his advice to become active in the family planning movement.[82]

Greenwood returned to San Francisco in 1965, earned a public health degree at the University of California, Berkeley, and completed a year of residency in obstetrics at the UCSF Medical Center. There she saw hundreds of pregnant, naïve young women who were utterly unprepared for the responsibilities of childbirth. "Haight Street at that time was beautiful and exciting," Greenwood later recalled, "but there was so much ignorance about sex." Recognizing that few hippie women would seek out comprehensive family planning education in the traditional setting of a hospital, Greenwood pushed Planned Parenthood to open a teen clinic. Catering specifically to the hippie lifestyle, she insisted that no appointments be necessary. The first clinic opened at 2340 Clay Street, opposite Presbyterian Hospital, followed by outpost clinics at Bayview–Hunters Point, Columbus Avenue, and the Haight-Ashbury. Greenwood welcomed not only teenaged girls but their boyfriends as well. To help the offices blend in with the scene, Greenwood hung Indian bedspreads on the ceiling and displayed patients' works of photography throughout the clinic.[83]

Greenwood and other family planning advocates in California benefited from the legislature's passage of the Therapeutic Abortion Act of 1967, which permitted doctors to provide abortions in cases where childbirth could endanger the life of the mother and only after extensive consultation with a medical review board. According to a poll by the California Medical Association, an overwhelming number of California obstetricians were deeply dissatisfied with these restrictions and wanted to make it easier for a woman to have an abortion.[84] After the passage of the Therapeutic Abortion Act, many obstetricians performed abortions, while their colleagues simply rubber-stamped the procedures. More to the point, according to Greenwood, this softening of the law effectively led to "abortion on demand" in San Francisco, a good six years before *Roe v. Wade*. Greenwood, her medical colleagues, and social workers routinely were able to secure abortions for women twenty-one and older, as well as for "emancipated minors" fifteen or older. Many pregnant girls made compelling cases for needing abortions, though perhaps none as effectively as one who marched into Greenwood's clinic, pearl-handled revolver in hand, and threatened to commit suicide unless granted an abortion.

On its face, nothing about single motherhood doomed a child, but when that arrangement was coupled with drugs and the free-love ethos of the sexual revolution, the results could be disastrous. At the Free Clinic, Smith observed that few expectant mothers heeded his advice to forgo LSD and marijuana for at least the first trimester of pregnancy, and most took LSD during labor with the hopes of "merging their consciousness with the fetus." In addition, the new trend of giving birth outside the hospital meant that both puerperal sepsis and gonococcal conjunctivitis were a constant threat. Equally problematic was the trend among these young women of forgoing vaccinations or attempting to immunize their children themselves. Finally, Smith was troubled by hippie parents' behavioral patterns. He complained that hippies tended to treat their children like "miniature adults or cuddly toys" and denied them an adult "reference point":

Children were rarely cleaned or disciplined, even when a father or father figure was present in the home. Toilet training was performed on an impromptu basis, sometimes not beginning until the infants were three or four years old and after they had been introduced to marijuana. As the children grew they became community property and were often shared. They were allowed to romp on Haight Street, were always present at such tribal gatherings as the Summer Solstice Festival and the be-in, played in places like the Psychedelic Shop and the Print Mint, and were exposed to the supposedly educational environment of their free school.[85]

The long-term psychological effects of hippie child-rearing practices were not ascertainable, but the physiological ones were. The doctors at the Free Clinic noticed alarming rates of malnourishment and bacterial infections due to extremely poor hygiene. And the malaise, tics, and behavioral problems they observed in these children did not bode well. Norman Sissman, a clinic doctor, observed that while little was known about the future, "one thing is certain: in spite of their desire to create superior children, the hippie parents are raising their offspring to be exactly like themselves."[86]

Joan Didion, perhaps the most trenchant of California chroniclers, immortalized the failures of hippie child-rearing in her now classic 1968 essay "Slouching towards Bethlehem." Didion arrived in San Francisco in the spring of 1967 because she believed it to be the center of a national "social hemorrhaging" that she sought to document. "All that seemed clear," she wrote, "was that at some point we had aborted ourselves and butchered the job." For Didion, the Haight-Ashbury embodied not only the general ennui of the nation but Americans' more troublesome failure to raise children properly. Compounding this tragedy was the fact that these languorous and often stoned youth were now having their *own* children, and not faring well at it, from any sober perspective.

Touring the devastation of the Haight-Ashbury like a war correspondent, Didion befriended a number of young people in their late teens and early twenties. Born into affluence, these youth had chosen to live close to the bone, often forgoing meals for a drug score. With journalistic dispassion, Didion laid bare the delusional fantasies of the drug-intoxicated kids. But at the end of the essay, when she met a five-year-old girl named Susan, Didion's detachment was shaken. Susan, Didion realized, was high on acid. Susan's mother, who lived with an assortment of "other people" but not with Susan's father, had been giving Susan both acid and peyote for a year. Another child, a three-year-old boy named Michael, had accidentally started a fire in his communal living quarters. Later the same day, he was nearly electrocuted while chewing on an electrical cord. When his mother screamed, no one inside the house came to help, because they "were in the kitchen trying to retrieve some very good Moroccan hash which had dropped down through a floorboard damaged in the fire."[87]

The sexual revolution that began in the early 1960s was not simply a revolution in private sexual behavior; it was revolutionary in dramatically increasing the public visibility of sexuality and sex. From North Beach to the Western Addition to the Haight-Ashbury, acts of heterosexual sexuality became not only more numerous but much more public, with profound consequences for the politics, economies, and reputations of the places where it took place. Yet one might argue that the heterosexual sexual revolution was merely an intensification of processes already in place. The gay revolution, by contrast, brought activity that had been largely underground into full view. And it would further expose the limits of longtime San Franciscans' fabled tolerance.

3

WHEN THE
STREETS
WENT GAY

Paul Kantus, a good friend of Fred Methner in Noe Valley, vividly remembered the day San Francisco went gay: he could tell by the look on his father's face. An Estonian immigrant, Kantus's father joined other immigrants at least one afternoon each week at the steam baths. He patronized Finnila's Finnish Baths on Market Street, right on the edge of what would soon be known as "the Castro" but then was still called Eureka Valley. It had been a quiet neighborhood of immigrant families—the neighborhood chamber of commerce called it "The Sunny Heart of San Francisco"; Chief Dullea raised his family there, and so did his friend George Healy, future chief of the SFPD. But in the early 1960s, Eureka Valley began to change, and for Kantus's father, the change was personal. He began to notice that the new, younger crowd of men at Finnila's took an unnatural interest in each other's bodies. So the senior Kantus and his friends marched to the front desk, handed in their membership cards, never went back, and never talked about it again.[1]

To the chagrin of Kantus's father and his friends, beginning in the early 1960s, San Francisco moved from being one of many sites of homosexual activity in metropolitan America to being the nation's gay capital. As historian Martin Meeker has demonstrated, this was largely the product of the expanded communication networks created by San Francisco's homophile movement, which in turn drew increased media attention to homosexuals generally and to San Francisco ones in particular. In 1961, Jess Stearn, a former *Newsweek* editor, wrote a best-selling book on homosexual men, *The Sixth Man,* and followed up in 1964 with his account of lesbianism, *The Grapevine.* Both books highlighted homophile activism in San Francisco, and in *The Grapevine* Stearns described the DOB headquarters as the "the Singapore of the lesbian world. It is the crossroads of lesbian news and views, the distillery of virtually all thought and activity in the lesbian grapevine."[2]

But it was *Life* magazine's two-part series on homosexuality in the United States in June 1964 that drew unprecedented attention to the nascent homosexual community of San Francisco. "Large cities," the article explained, "offer established homosexuals societies to join, plenty of opportunities to meet other homosexuals on the streets, in bars or at parties in private homes, and, for those who seek it, complete anonymity." "Homosexuals can find some or all of these advantages in many parts of the U.S.," the article concluded, "but because of its reputation for easy hospitality, California has a special appeal for them." This issue of *Life,* which sold more than 7.3 million copies, was a watershed in gay history: it permanently shattered the conspiracy of silence that had prevailed in mainstream news media. And for homosexuals, as Meeker has explained, San Francisco became "a symbolic homeland of an identity and a city that was a haven for institutional support unknown in most American cities." Most significant, the article started a gay stampede. Solly Blue, a character in Jack Fritscher's rollicking 1990 memoir-novel *Some Dance to Remember,* says of the article: "an engraved invitation to every faggot in America wouldn't have caused more of a sensation. Reading Life's expose in Iowa was like discovering a travel agent's dream brochure."[3]

The gay stampede utterly transformed the culture, politics, and social geography of San Francisco. While the domain of homophile politics had generally been the newsletter or the magazine, the domain of gay liberation was the street. While there had been gay bars and other more discreet sites of homosexual sociability, something unprecedented in the world history of cities now existed: the gay neighborhood. More remarkably, gay San Franciscans created several different gay districts, where varied sexual customs and personal histories intersected with distinctive geographies to produce subcommunities among gay San Franciscans. And because many San Franciscans believed that public spaces could only serve mutually exclusive social purposes, the gay revolution provoked heated, even violent, exchanges over the destiny of urban space.

In the process of claiming a place for themselves on the streets, in the chambers of San Francisco's City Hall, and in the broader American culture, gays and lesbians sometimes faltered as they tried to balance the demands of political agitation for full equality with an enjoyment of their new opportunities for abundant and unfettered sex. Freedom was new, and the transition from life in the closet to life in the public sphere was not always smooth or easy. While many gay and lesbian activists continued to lobby for cultural and legislative change while enjoying deeply satisfying sex lives through the 1970s, many more of them took away only part of the message of gay liberation. As the sites of gay sociability expanded in San Francisco, most gay men in the 1970s abandoned the political agitation of their forebears in the homophile and gay liberation movements and sought simply to enjoy active and free sexual lives. By contrast, as lesbians built a separate world for themselves in the Mission District—a world informed largely by the ideology of cultural feminism—lesbian sex became highly politicized, generally to the detriment of erotic freedom. Ultimately, however, if the immediate political legacy of gay and lesbian liberation was sometimes uncertain and unsettled, the geographic impact was profound and enduring.

From Homophilia to Gay Liberation

On New Year's Day, 1965, Chief Cahill made an old decision in a new era, and the results were disastrous. Under his command, several investigators from the sex crime detail, with the support of more than twenty uniformed SFPD officers and police photographers with still and motion-picture cameras, descended on California Hall, a historic building on lower Polk Street where a gay New Year's Ball was scheduled for the evening. Although the sponsoring organization, the Council on Religion and the Homosexual (CRH)—a new homophile group dedicated to promoting the integration of homosexuals into mainstream society—had secured all necessary permits and even met with the sex crime detail a week in advance and received the SFPD's assurances that there would be no harassment, the police made a gratuitous display of force. Blocking off the intersection, photographing and harassing the guests, and arresting several guests who challenged the SFPD's right to enter the establishment, the assault was an exaggerated instance of the SFPD's time-worn policy—in effect since World War II—of literally trying to force homosexuals off the street and back into the closet. But this time, as Cahill discovered on the following morning, it backfired.

It backfired largely because of the guest list. Among the lesbians, gays, and drag queens were the ostensibly straight members of the CRH, their wives, their lawyers, and their friends. Embroiled in the melee, they witnessed firsthand the kind of harassment that homosexuals had so long endured, and issued a clarion call for change. As the Presbyterian Theological Seminary newsletter explained: "It is the type of police activity that homosexuals know well, but here-tofore the police had never played their hand before Mr. Average Citizen.... It was always the testimony of the police officer versus the homosexual, and the homosexual, fearing publicity and knowing the odds against him, succumbed. But in this instance the police overplayed their part."[4] On January 2, organizers from the CRH held a press conference at the Glide Church in the Tenderloin and blasted the police for "intimidation, broken promises and obvious hostility." Speaking out were CRH organizers Ted McIlvenna, a young minister who was the adult director of the Methodist Glide Foundation; McIlvenna's recent hire Cecil Williams, a dynamic young African American minister at the Glide Church; Robert Cromey, special assistant to Episcopal bishop James A. Pike; Charles Lewis, a minister at the Lutheran North Beach Mission; and Clarence Colwell, a minister at of the United Church of Christ. Given the credentials of these protestors, the *San Francisco Chronicle* evinced sympathy for the guests and ran a story under the banner "angry ministers rip police."[5]

"This is the beginning," the ministers thundered in a statement, "and not the end of this determination to achieve full citizenship for homosexuals and all minorities, without discrimination and intimidation."[6] As public opinion quickly turned against the SFPD, it seemed they were right. Shelley took Cahill to task for the raid, signaling a new era in San Francisco policing. Cahill later remembered, somewhat grudgingly, that this was the era when relations between the SFPD and homosexuals permanently changed:

> In the old days, they locked them up. And when they went in, the cop on the beat and the captain would just say this is what they [were] doing on Market Street and they were causing trouble and here they are. Well, the word came out, you can't lock them up en masse. You have to have proof on each one as to what he was doing wrong and why you arrested him.

In essence, Cahill concluded, the SFPD stopped arresting gay men for doing "what was wrong" and only arrested them for a "violation of the law." Del Martin and Phyllis Lyon later recalled January 1, 1965, as a historic date marking a "contract of accommodation" between gays and the SFPD.[7] Ultimately, the fallout from the incident made San Francisco judges less tolerant of SFPD abuses and more sympathetic toward homosexuals—a local variation on the theme of diminished police power that was characteristic of the Warren Court era.[8]

The 1965 New Year's Eve raid both raised the profile of homosexuals in San Francisco and spurred the revision of the decades-old policy of harassment against homosexuals; the "Armed Forces Day protest" of May 1966 brought

FIGURE 3.1. Del Martin delivers an address in front of the Federal Building in San Francisco during the Armed Forces Day protest of 1966. Courtesy: GLBTHS.

together the largest group of homosexual protestors to date. Scheduled for May 21, 1966—Armed Forces Day—the protest was conceived at the National Planning Conference of Homosexual Organizations, which had been held in Kansas City the previous February. At the meeting, more than forty homosexual rights activists—including representatives from CRH and the San Francisco chapters of the Mattachine Society and DOB—discussed strategies for combating the "second-class" citizenship of homosexuals in the United States. What emerged was the Committee to Fight Exclusion of Homosexuals from the Military—a loose confederation of homophile groups across the country—and a plan to launch the largest coordinated gay demonstration the nation, and the world, had ever known.

Targeting discrimination in the military laid bare the larger hypocrisy and intolerance of American society. The Selective Service medical exam form included a box labeled "homosexual tendencies" that, if checked by the medical examiner, subjected the patient to medical discharge. Once inducted into the military, the revelation of homosexual tendencies could, and often was, grounds for less-than-honorable discharge. On the other hand, gays who admitted their homosexuality were subject to ridicule and discrimination that could follow well beyond the ranks. In the private sector, open discrimination against homosexuals often mitigated against "openness" and visibility. As Del Martin put it in a letter to a sympathetic professor at the Church Divinity School of the Pacific in Berkeley: "This is quite a daring adventure for us. It is not like any other civil rights demonstration—having no popular support and being somewhat hazardous, if not disastrous, to the individual who reveals himself."[9]

Planning for the event was meticulous; homophile leaders in San Francisco notified the SFPD Public Relations Bureau of the impending protest, and now in the post–New Years' Ball era, received little resistance. Volunteers printed more than twenty thousand leaflets and distributed them throughout the city. Del Martin was indefatigable, coordinating with both local and national groups to assure the success of the event. She tried—in vain, ultimately—to recruit well-known speakers to the event, including swashbuckling civil liberties attorney Jake Ehrlich, writer and Beat icon Kenneth Rexroth, and liberal California congressman Phillip Burton. Ehrlich never responded; Burton declined, citing congressional duties outside of San Francisco; Rexroth, a pacifist, was not comfortable supporting a plan that would effectively *increase* military enlistment, and he was busy that day anyway.[10] But the lack of star power proved to be no impediment.

At two o'clock on Saturday, May 21, more than forty protestors and four to five hundred supporters met on the steps of San Francisco's Federal Building. Posting a large sign reading "The Draft Dodges Homosexuals—Homosexuals

Don't Dodge the Draft" on a truck, protestors demanded that the military change its discriminatory policies. Cecil Williams, among others, spoke from the truck. "There is a homosexual revolution here and across the land," Williams shouted through a megaphone. "We protest against the Armed Forces' policy of discharging 'discovered' homophiles under less than honorable conditions."

From the perspective of the early twenty-first century, it is hard to recognize the Armed Forces Day protest of 1966 for the success that it was. After all, it was held on a Saturday, when protesting would not intrude unnecessarily on the operations of government, and when the crowds of onlookers would be much smaller; it was done with the courteous permission of the police; and it failed to change the policy of the Selective Service. Yet according to *Vector*, the organ of SIR, the event was a "resounding success." "Such," *Vector* celebrated, "is the consensus of the sponsoring organizations in the Bay Area." Guy Strait's *Citizen News* was more restrained, calling the event a "qualified success." Bob Ross, secretary of the Tavern Guild, wrote that the reaction of the general public was "favorable" and that it was just the beginning. "This was the communitys [*sic*] first try at demonstrating nationwide, and we understand that reaction was quite favorable across the country.... We must move forward now, and there can be no turning back."[11]

The success of the protest lay not in its measurable effect on Selective Service policy—and surely organizers must have expected very little in that regard—but in significantly raising the profile of gay people in the nation. The story was picked up in the local press, although the title of the *San Francisco Chronicle* article—"Deviates Demand the Right to Serve"—scarcely challenged conventional portrayals of homosexuals. More influential was the Channel 7 local news devoting approximately five minutes of airtime to the event, including an interview with Robert Cromey of CRH. Nationally, the *New York Times, Los Angeles Times,* and *Newsweek,* as well as dozens of smaller media outlets covered some phase of the protest. What readers and television viewers learned was that homosexuals existed and believed themselves worthy of first-class citizenship. In this regard, the editor of *Vector* described the event as a "pilot project."

> So long as members of the homophile community act as second
> class citizens, then so long will they be subjected to second
> class citizenship in various facets of life. When the members of
> the homophile community demand first class citizenship, and
> demand the opportunity to assume the responsibilities of first class
> citizenship, then we are on the road to achieving those rights which
> are ours and to shouldering those responsibilities which are rightly
> ours also.[12]

Only three months later came jarring new evidence that homosexuals were making that step.

In August 1966, while homophile leaders were still assessing the impact of the Armed Forces Day protest and developing new political strategies, an anonymous drag queen at Compton's Cafeteria in the Tenderloin fired one of the opening shots in the battle for transgender liberation in the United States. Compton's had been a hangout for Tenderloin youth and cross-dressing "street queens" particularly for several months, and by August the management had tired of allowing bands of social misfits to linger over a single cup of coffee for hours. Because the spectacle of street queens represented one of the most visible assaults on the moralists' geography, and because cross-dressing was not decriminalized in California until 1962, street queens had always endured unchecked harassment from police. When Compton's management finally called the SFPD to rout a group of street queens, it probably expected little resistance. Instead, one of the street queens splashed hot coffee in an officer's face, touching off a melee. Susan Stryker, an historian and documentarian who has almost single-handedly resurrected the story of the Compton's riot through extensive oral history interviews, describes the event:

> Plates, trays, cups, and silverware flew through the air at the
> startled police officers, who ran outside and called for backup.
> Compton's customers turned over the table and smashed the plate-
> glass windows and then poured out of the restaurant and into the
> streets. The paddy wagons arrived, and street fighting broke out in
> Compton's vicinity, all around the corner of Turk and Taylor. Drag
> queens beat the police with their heavy purses and kicked them with
> their high-heeled shoes.[13]

The riot forced the SFPD to recognize both the humanity, and the new militancy, of street queens. But it was only a sign of things to come. In April 1969 the Committee for Homosexual Freedom (CHF) became the first gay liberation organization in the United States.

The story of the CHF is ultimately the story of Leo Laurence and Gale Whittington. A native of Denver, Colorado, Whittington knew that he was gay by the time he graduated from high school in 1966. But he had difficulty accepting it, and so did his lovers. In 1968, a lover who did not accept his own homosexuality broke off relations with Whittington and "went straight," a crushing blow for Whittington that sent him into a suicidal depression. After recovering, Whittington vowed to move to San Francisco. "Even back then in 1967 and 1968," he remembered, "I had heard that you could hold hands on the street and nobody would think anything of it." In one of those rare examples of

reality matching—and perhaps exceeding—expectations, Whittington found a
lover only minutes after arriving at the bus terminal, an unforgettable man in
a white Monte Carlo convertible.[14]

Whittington quickly set about finding work, and took a job at the States
Steamship Lines Company in the heart of the Financial District. First hired as
a mail clerk and then as an accounting clerk, Whittington soon recognized that
virtually "the entire freight department was gay." This was not atypical of cleri-
cal staffs in downtown businesses by the early 1960s. Even the city's venerable
capitalist landmarks employed, as one homosexual remembered it, a "horde of
effeminate men" who quietly joked that the "SP" atop the Southern Pacific building stood for "Swish Palace."[15] But Whittington soon realized that homosexual
employment was still contingent on silence. "Everyone thought they had it pretty
good. As long as they keep quiet, it was OK." "That's the way it was, even in San
Francisco," Whittington recalled. "It was understood that people were gay, but
nobody talked about it." Meanwhile, Whittington pursued a more "out" existence
by responding to an advertisement for an unpaid position as a staff writer at
SIR's *Vector* magazine, where he met the new *Vector* editor, Leo Laurence.[16]

Laurence brought a wealth of journalistic experience to the magazine.
After graduating from Westminster College in Missouri in 1960, he became
a reporter for an Indianapolis radio station and then a lobbyist for the Indiana
Retail Council. At thirty-one, he was a well-paid, politically conservative lobbyist who knew the governor on a first-name basis, drove a Ford Mustang given
to him by the Retail Council, and even carried a card certifying him as a deputy
attorney general—a novelty title customarily bestowed on lobbyists of the Retail
Council by the governor. Yet, in an incident that is telling of the tenuousness of
life "in the closet" at that time and place, Laurence lost all of this just because
he forgot his lunch one day.

Unlike Whittington, Laurence had not been tormented by the awareness
of his own homosexuality. Even in Indiana, he remembered "as long as you
were in the closet, nobody much cared." But this changed when he asked his
younger lover, Johnny Willoughby, to bring him his lunch at work. Willoughby
was young, "pretty," and effeminate, and when he arrived, a loquacious recep-
tionist shared the news with her boss that Laurence must be gay. Laurence was
fired that day, shortly before Christmas 1966.

Crestfallen, Laurence traveled to Fort Wayne, Indiana, to plot his next
move. There his homosexuality again proved to be a liability, and nearly a
fatal one. After meeting several "good looking guys" at a café, he was savagely
beaten by the men. "The only reason they didn't kill me right there," Laurence
recalled, "was that they found my Deputy Attorney General card and figured
I was law enforcement." Bleeding profusely, Laurence dragged himself to the

Fort Wayne Police Department. But once the attending officers understood that Laurence was gay, they sent him—still bleeding—back out the door. The next night, Christmas Eve, Laurence drove to San Francisco and quickly settled in the Haight-Ashbury.

In San Francisco, Laurence easily found work as a reporter for KGO Radio and a writer for the *Berkeley Barb,* where he reported on the antiwar and sexual freedom movements. While he was covering the activities of the SFL, he began to think seriously about coming out. Until then, his pieces on sexual freedom and homosexuality had been published under the pseudonym Gary Patterson. But in the summer of 1968, Laurence became "radicalized." On his way back to California from a quick trip to Indiana, he stopped in Chicago for the Democratic National Convention. "It was a war zone," he recalled of that infamous convention, "and it is what turned me from a conservative Republican to a Leftist democrat. I was never the same."

Back in San Francisco, Laurence was increasingly influenced by Cecil Williams, as well as the Black Panther Party. These radical leanings appealed to SIR president Larry Littlejohn but were not apparent enough, evidently, to initially concern SIR's more conservative board of directors, which hired Laurence as editor in January 1969. He met Whittington when Whittington came down to the SIR office with a plan to write a piece on men's fashion. After a photo shoot in which the lithe Whittington posed seductively in cropped jean shorts, Laurence made the fateful request that the photographer snap a "few shots" of the two of them. Laurence wrapped his arms around the shirtless Whittington's waist, and the picture was taken. What harm could a picture do, especially in San Francisco?

Shortly afterward, Laurence found himself listening to a radio broadcast of a Martin Luther King speech and thought "If I replaced the word 'black' with the word 'gay,' we would have a gay revolution." Frustrated by what he perceived as the glacial pace of change espoused by SIR, the Tavern Guild, and other homophile organizations, Laurence lashed out in the April 1969 issue of *Vector* against the leadership of SIR, which had quickly unseated the Mattachine Society as the vanguard of gay radicalism when it was founded in 1964. But for men like Laurence, it was not radical enough:

> Homosexual organizations on the west coast are doing very little
> to spark the Homosexual revolution of '69. Timid leaders with
> enormous ego-trips, middle class bigotry and racism, and too
> many middle-aged up-tight conservatives are hurting almost every
> major homosexual organization on the West Coast and probably
> throughout the nation.[17]

Laurence later recognized that his claims of racism, based on the Tavern Guild's failure to support Cecil Williams's Citizen's Alert—a group organized to monitor complaints of police abuse—was overblown. But he stood by the core of his criticism, and it struck a nerve. The board of directors of SIR immediately called for his resignation, and he was immediately fired from his other job at KGO Radio.

On the same day the *Vector* mailed the issue containing his diatribe to its three thousand subscribers, Laurence sharpened his attack in an interview in the *Berkeley Barb*. "Society has made us perverts for too goddamn long. It's time for a change—right now." Laurence described the leadership of gay organizations as "timid, uptight, conservative, and afraid to act for the good of the whole homosexual community."

> Tell your boss, family—everybody, that you're gay.... After we can admit "gay is good" the revolution will come.... All our lives we've been made butts of jokes, laughed at, made to feel guilty. Human beings shouldn't have to live like that.... If the uptightness of the present leaders breaks the revolution, then they must go.

While his inflammatory editorial appeared in *Vector*, the *Barb* interview with Laurence contained something that the *Vector* article did not: the picture of the shirtless Laurence embracing the shirtless Whittington. Without considering the consequences for Whittington, Laurence had handed the picture to the *Barb* interviewer, saying: "I want this picture to become reality."[18]

The impact of the two articles was immediate. The strong reaction from within the homophile community, and the generally favorable reaction Laurence heard among young gays, encouraged him to push forward his radical vision of gay pride and acceptance. But for Whittington, the consequences of the *Berkeley Barb* article were utterly terrifying.

Unlike *Vector*, the *Berkeley Barb* was available in newsstands throughout downtown San Francisco. It was very popular, particularly in the otherwise buttoned-down Financial District, because it generated most of its revenue from vividly illustrated advertisements for nude female masseuses. Consequently, it did not take long for the issue containing Whittington's picture to circulate throughout the States Steamship Lines Company office. "Immediately I was fired. I was told my services were no longer needed. I cried on the way home on the bus," Whittington recalls. "The first thing I did was panic. Your reputation is shot. You'll never be hired again," he told himself.

That night, Whittington called Laurence in tears. Laurence recalls it as the "phone call that started the gay revolution." When Laurence learned of

Whittington's firing, he responded: "Gale, we can do something big here. I mean huge." The next morning, they met with Max Sheer, the editor of the *Berkeley Barb,* and together they devised a plan to challenge the firing of Whittington and raise the profile of gays in San Francisco, the nation, and, they hoped, the world. For Whittington, it was the beginning of a life completely reconceived: "I was a very shy kind of guy, so it was hard for me to do that stuff. But I managed to get out there and fight. I was not an activist, not a militant, none of that. It was an overnight change." That overnight change created the modern gay liberation movement, almost three months *before* the Stonewall Rebellion, the historic gay riot in New York which is widely credited as beginning the gay liberation movement. The action these men planned in response to Whittington's firing moved on two fronts, one legal and one public. The San Francisco Neighborhood Legal Assistance Foundation, a law service specializing in low-income clients, demanded from the States Steamship Lines Company Whittington's reinstatement with back pay, and a fair employment pledge not to discriminate against homosexuals and to urge other firms in the shipping industry to follow suit. Meanwhile, what the *Berkeley Barb* was calling "the militant Committee for Homosexual Freedom" run by "gay revolutionaries" made its presence known in the heart of San Francisco's Financial District.[19]

Unlike the Armed Forces Day protestors, who had picketed on a weekend, the CHF began daily picketing at lunchtime for maximum visibility at the offices of the States Steamship Lines Company at 320 California, in the heart of the Financial District and just outside the comfort zone of previous homophile activism. They also held meetings at Cabaret, a club located at 260 Valencia in the Mission, even further from the traditional locale of homophile politics in San Francisco.

The picket captain, a young Texan named Pat Brown, had been politicized in the streets of San Antonio after being kicked out of the house by his drill-sergeant, "Jesus Freak" father at the age of fifteen in 1960. Though San Antonio had a surprisingly vibrant gay scene in the early 1960s, the level of homophobic violence was staggering: by the time he was eighteen, six of Brown's "queenie bopper" friends in San Antonio had been murdered. After being kicked out of local beauty schools for his flamboyance, Brown left San Antonio in 1963, worked in Reno as a hair stylist for *The Golden Girl* showgirls, and then settled in San Francisco in June 1966. He immersed himself in the antiwar movement and the nascent gay rights movement. Nominally involved with SIR in the 1966 and 1967, Brown threw himself into the CHF. "I knew this was it," he later recalled; "I knew this was do or die, and it was exhilarating." Brown picketed every day for almost three months, maintaining order on the picket line, distributing leaflets to passersby and civil disobedience manuals to marchers, produced by the American Friends Service Committee.[20]

Brown and his colleagues were unabashedly radical. Fellow picketer Charles P. Thorpe, for example, did not shy away from violent rhetoric:

> It's a matter of survival and pride in my people. Homosexuals are
> stepping out of their ghetto-bars and double lives and into the power
> struggle. We must be freed from the chains of fear and death that
> have now repressed all but our sexual organs. We will take our
> freedom. We will burn our faces with tears and cover our hands with
> blood, but will get our freedom as homosexuals.[21]

Elsewhere, Thorpe excoriated "middle class society." "If need be we will burn down their cities to build beautiful ones."[22] The appearance and behavior of the protestors themselves challenged traditional homophile protests, which usually sought to project the image of respectability and professionalism. The CHF eschewed this tradition. Whittington remembered that because SIR was "afraid of us being stereotyped," its leadership discouraged participation by "drag queens," "anybody who looked effeminate," and particularly "gender fuckers." "But we just accepted anybody who came. And that was why we were successful."

Though the protest was initially about getting Whittington's job back, for most of those involved it quickly came to be about simply coming out of the closet and standing up for one's rights. The protest was the opening shot in the revolution Leo Laurence had demanded in his incendiary *Vector* editorial. The restoration of Whittington's job, CHF organizers quickly realized, would not be effectively accomplished by a consumer boycott, because the vast majority of the States Steamship Lines Company contracts were with the federal government. Less fortunate, however, was Tower Records, the Sacramento-based record store whose flagship store in North Beach had opened a year earlier. In May 1969, at the height of the States Steamship protest, a clerk at Tower Records, Frank Denaro, was fired—he claimed because of his homosexuality. Denaro became the vehicle for a more aggressive protest as marchers from CHF picketed Tower Records for two weeks. The vice president of the company flew down from Sacramento and agreed to rehire Denaro, offered back pay, and agreed to institute a nondiscrimination policy in hiring that would also be posted in the store. The gay rights revolution had scored perhaps its first victory.[23]

The States Line Steamship Company protests by Whittington, Laurence, and the CHF inaugurated an era of gay radicalism, which became a well-known phenomenon after the evenings in late June 1969 when the Stonewall Inn exploded in rebellion. Laurence was eager to create an umbrella organization for CHF and other emerging gay rights groups in the black and Latino communities. And he was determined to pick a name that broke from the homophile tradition of using the word "homosexual." Inspired, as many on the Left were, by the National Liberation Front in North Vietnam, he chose the name Gay Liberation Front, which quickly became known simply as GLF. The revolution in the streets had begun in earnest.

Late in October 1969, CHF held a demonstration in front of the *San Francisco Examiner* building South of Market to protest the portrayal of gays in a piece written by journalist Robert Patterson. Patterson described gay bars as sites of "sick, sad revels" replete with "semi-males." The protest led to a violent confrontation with police, which attorney Terence Hallinan, who later became district attorney, argued was instigated by an undisciplined Tactical Squad. Fifteen CHF protestors were arrested, and Pat Brown was cited for contempt of court for shouting "Power to the People" in the courtroom.[24]

Late in June 1970, a small but determined band of gays marched down Polk Street from Aquatic Park—the site of Jefferson Poland's nude wade-ins five years earlier—to City Hall in San Francisco's first gay rights march. This was followed quickly in July by a march and picketing in front of Macy's at Union Square in response to Macy's "pervert" sting operation. Responding to complaints from customers about homosexual sex encounters in the men's

FIGURE 3.2. Protestors at the States Line Steamship Company headquarters in April 1969. Holding the "California Cops" sign are gay rights activists Pat Brown (*left*) and Charles P. Thorpe. Courtesy: GLBTHS.

restroom, the store had hired young, handsome security guards and entrapped forty cruisers. Without defending sex in public places, opponents decried the entrapment, the felony charges, "unreasonable searches," and the store's failure to consult the city's gay leaders first.[25] There was no parade in 1971, but in June 1972 organizers launched the First Annual Christopher Street West parade, and a new tradition was born.

The sex radicalism of San Francisco homophile and gay liberation activists reached a national audience for the first time one month after the First Annual Christopher Street West parade, when San Francisco activist and SIR cofounder James Foster became the first openly gay delegate to address a national convention, the Democratic National Convention in Miami. Having recently cofounded the influential Alice B. Toklas Democratic Club, in San Francisco, Foster also benefited from a new delegate selection process coengineered by the Democratic candidate, George McGovern.[26] Foster took full advantage of his newly exalted position to inform convention attendees, and the television viewing public, about gay rights:

> We do not come to you pleading your understanding or begging
> your tolerance. We come to you affirming our pride in our life-style,
> affirming the validity to seek and maintain meaningful emotional
> relationships and affirming our right to participate in the life of this
> country on an equal basis with every citizen.[27]

Foster electrified gay rights advocates, raised his own political profile, and again fixed the nation's attention on San Francisco's sexual "deviation."

The public gay protests of the late 1960s, as radical as they were from the perspective of most city dwellers, simply blended in with their sense of San Francisco in the sixties. As one editorial put it, describing the Macy's protest, "shoppers in downtown San Francisco have probably noticed another 'only in San Francisco' sight this past week to add to the parade of sidewalk preachers and chanting Krishna worshippers." Of course, protests of this sort were not at all "only in San Francisco" but part of the national urban landscape—a very unappealing part from the perspective of most city dwellers. Why, one concerned citizen asked, were the gays "perpetually blazoning their sex life in public"? The simple answer was that they finally felt free to.

Gay Youth, Prostitution, and Transgenderism in the Tenderloin

Sally Stanford must have been disheartened by what she saw in the Tenderloin of the 1970s. Even by the standards of her brand of burnished bawdiness, the district had deteriorated dramatically in the 1950s and 1960s. *New York Times* writer Herbert Gold's 1977 description of the district as a "desolate Pigalle," a haven for "freaks, welfare cripples, runaways and drug hustlers," was certainly sensationalized, but not by much. The landscape of the Tenderloin—flophouses, cheap eateries, tenement hotels, and a soup-kitchen known as the St. Anthony Dining Room—confirmed the overwhelming poverty and growing hopelessness of the district. As it always had, the Tenderloin was the location of a dispropor-tionate number of the city's rapes, beatings, and thefts. In 1976, 40% of the city's overdoses and one quarter of its homicides occurred in the Tenderloin. All of these developments represented mere extensions of earlier problems. "The San Francisco Tenderloin," Robert Patterson wrote in the *San Francisco Chronicle* in 1970, "just as potent an underworld clearing house and night life center as ever, has lost its one-time piquant color and picaresque conviviality."[28]

By the 1960s, a much more significant, visible, and essentially novel phenomenon was afoot in the district: the increased presence and visibility of homosexuals in the streets there. *The Tenderloin Ghetto,* a 1966 study con-ducted by the CRH, was the first published report to explore the taxonomy of the Tenderloin. Among young men, the report revealed, "homosexual behav-ior is the most predominant," particularly among the hustlers. Not only were many of the women of the Tenderloin prostitutes, but many were also lesbi-ans. "A training ground for new prostitutes," the Tenderloin offered dead-end employment to marginal people. In short, during the 1960s, the alienation of the homosexuals of the Tenderloin exacerbated the historic poverty and misery of the district.

National audiences were briefly exposed to the Tenderloin in John Rechy's 1963 best-selling novel *City of Night.* Rechy's protagonist, youngman—an auto-biographical character based on Rechy's years as a male hustler—wends his way from New York to Los Angeles to San Francisco, living in the nation's "dark cities," "from 42nd Street to Market Street," from "Times Square to Hol-lywood Boulevard," forming "one vast City of Night." But even the jaded young-man is stunned by one of the bathhouses he visits near his Market Street hotel. "I'm struck," he wrote "by the atmosphere of overwhelming debauchery here." Even the seedy streets of Los Angeles, to which Rechy devotes considerable attention, are no match for San Francisco's Tenderloin. "San Francisco," his new hustling friend Buzz warns him, "isn't like L.A. The street scene here can get pretty mean after a while."[29]

Typical of Tenderloin denizens was an anonymous young woman inter-viewed in 1967. She had suffered bouts of depression because of her guilt over her lesbian yearnings, and her affluent but emotionally distant parents had shuttled her from one hospital to the next, eventually placing her in an institution where she underwent four months of heavy sedation. In the course of her treatment she became addicted to barbiturates. After leaving the facility, she suffered an overdose and ended up in a juvenile facility for another two years. After that, it was hard to account for the two-year gap in her life, and employers were naturally unenthusiastic about hiring her, but she finally found a job as a hotel waitress. However, her lecherous boss immediately "tagged" her as being gay. "He blackmailed me into going to bed with him." After having sex with him several times to keep her job, she became pregnant, and to help support her child entered into a brief, unsuccessful marriage with a gay man. "Hopefully when I meet my future wife," she concluded, "I'll quit the [drug] habit because then I'll have a good reason."[30]

While the Tenderloin's burgeoning gay population suffered the same debilitating poverty that had haunted the district's residents for so long, they had an unusual group of advocates. Perhaps the most unusual and effective was "the Night Minister," Ted McIlvenna. Born in 1932 and raised on an Indian reservation and in other "tough little towns" in rural Oregon, where his father was a social gospel minister, McIlvenna took a winding path to San Francisco. After briefly pursuing careers in acting and professional athletics, McIlvenna ultimately decided to follow his father's example; he studied theology at the University of Edinburgh, Scotland, and became a minister at a church in suburban Hayward, California, in 1962. Inspired by McIlvenna's crowded Sunday services, representatives from San Francisco's Glide Church recruited him to revive their flagging ministry through the new Glide Urban Center. Founded in 1931, Glide Church had watched its parish thin during the 1950s, and by the early 1960s, attendance was so low that the well-endowed Glide Foundation was worried about losing its tax-exempt status. Charged with the task of evangelizing the youth of the Tenderloin through innovative programming, McIlvenna reached out to them by opening an interdenominational "coffeehouse ministry" called Intersection for the Arts in the heart of the Tenderloin in 1965. A master fundraiser, McIlvenna sponsored a rock concert in Golden Gate Park and raised funds to support the Diggers' "free" food giveaways in the Haight-Ashbury.[31]

Meanwhile, McIlvenna and fellow Glide Urban Center director Louie Durham sought an African American pastor to revive Glide Church. They looked no further once they met Cecil Williams, a Texas native who had most recently practiced in Kansas City. Williams quickly offended the lingering conservative membership by enthusiastically embracing McIlvenna's campaigns for justice for homosexual youth. Joining McIlvenna and others in the CRH, Williams made Glide a sanctuary for the dispossessed, famously removing the cross from the building in 1967 because he believed it symbolized death.

Both heterosexual, Williams and McIlvenna were at the core of an emerging group of liberal ministers who collectively rejected the discourse of pathology and immorality with which most religious groups had addressed homosexuality for so long. In 1964, shortly after cofounding CRH, McIlvenna hosted a conference of ministers in San Francisco in which the "sex identity" of the young adult was regarded as an essential part of understanding and reaching metropolitan youth.[32] The CRH was one of the first organizations *anywhere* to argue that homosexuals represented not simply a socially marginalized but also an *economically* depressed group. The CRH was unusually sensitive, for example, to the problems of the male hustler. "As the hustler gets older (past his early twenties)," a CRH publication read, "it becomes increasingly difficult for him to make money by selling his body."

> His well established pattern of hustling, his lack of trade, of work experience, of education, and his psychological problems make it very difficult for him to obtain and then sustain himself in satisfying employment. The difficulties are so overwhelming that their only recourse seems to be further criminal activity such as pimping, pill pushing, shoplifting, robbing and rolling.[33]

The Tenderloin Committee, an umbrella organization for the CRH and other organizations, expanded on the point. "As profound and profane as the problems of the Tenderloin are," a 1966 report read, "none of them outrank in seriousness the confusion of identity and purpose of the sexuality of its young adults." This confusion, the report concluded, made the Tenderloin's homosexual youth prey to exploitative adults, a fact that virtually guaranteed debilitating self-esteem and chronic poverty.[34]

As a direct result of the work of McIlvenna, Williams, and other activists, as well as the rising tide of homosexual and transgender militancy in the Tenderloin, an activist doctor named Joel Fort convinced the SFDPH to open the Center for Special Problems. Though its name smacked of the same old pathological approach to homosexuality, the center was a progressive force for transgender integration into mainstream society. Offering hormone prescriptions and psychological counseling, the center also provided transgender patients with ID cards, signed by a public health doctor, that matched the patient's social—rather than biological—gender. These ID cards allowed transgenders greater access to official forms of documentation such as bank accounts and job applications. Later, the Center created the Sexual Minority Youth Service, a drop-in employment center to help Tenderloin youth find jobs outside the sex industry.[35]

There were other reasons to be hopeful about the rising profile of homosexual and transgender Tenderloin residents. In 1962, Elliot Blackstone, a veteran SFPD officer who had recently transferred from the Potrero to the Central Station, approached Chief Cahill about creating a community relations post in the Tenderloin. Still reeling from the gayola scandal, Chief Cahill approved the plan and gave Blackstone the post. A heterosexual, Montana native, and SFPD officer since 1949, Blackstone had very little in his personal or professional history to suggest that he would become one of the chief allies of gays, lesbians, and transgenders. But unlike his captain—who believed that the best way for homosexuals to gain acceptance was to "stop committing homosexual acts"—Blackstone insisted that understanding and tolerance were the best tools of public relations.[36] Blackstone worked persistently to reform the homophobia of the SFPD and to gain respectful treatment for the Tenderloin's exotic denizens, even organizing peer support groups for male-to-female transgender prostitutes. "I just want people to understand that these people are individuals in their own right," Blackstone said of transsexuals long after his retirement.[37]

Even as these individuals and institutions worked to expand opportunities for Tenderloin residents, the Summer of Love and its aftermath took a terrible toll on the district. In *The Final Report of the Tenderloin Ethnographic Research Project* (1978), researchers noted the dire turn after 1967:

> The "Spirit of the Haight" spread across the country—then turned
> to ashes in the wake of the hard drugs and a hardened economy.
> Harder times have heightened San Francisco's appeal to young
> people in search of a city in which they can live as they wish and
> survive. But many, particularly adolescent males without educational
> and economic assets, end up on Powell and Market streets—where
> they survive by selling themselves to older men for sex along the
> borders of the Tenderloin.

In 1967 a survey found that not only was there a very high youth population in the Tenderloin—about twenty-seven hundred males and females between the ages of twelve and twenty-eight living in the fourteen-block area bounded by Leavenworth, Market, Powell, and Ellis—but that at least 14% of them were hustling.[38] If the Tenderloin had once functioned as a neighborhood for those in transit, it was now an end place for those whose poverty drove them to sexual limits that would become lethal by the early 1980s.

Polk Street: Forerunner of the First Gay Neighborhood

As San Francisco's gay men acquired new rights, as gay liberation activists lobbied for continuing legal reform, as local courts checked long-standing patterns of police harassment, and as the SFPD became more tolerant of gay people in public places, gays began to move out of the Tenderloin. No longer forced to seek the sheltered camaraderie and anonymity of the densely packed district, gay men began aggressively claiming sections of historic residential and business districts, often creating vibrant nighttime street scenes that would have been suppressed even a few years earlier. They followed Polk Street north of the Tenderloin into the Polk District; they followed Third, Fourth, Sixth, Seventh, and Eighth streets south of Market Street to Eighteenth, Folsom, Bryant, and Harrison streets; and they moved west on Market Street to Castro Street in Eureka Valley. By the mid-1970s, San Francisco had four geographically distinct gay male neighborhoods, which were beginning to reflect the diversities in class, style, and sexual behavior among gays. At no time in the history of the world had as many openly gay men claimed as much urban terrain as they did in San Francisco during the 1960s and 1970s.[39]

FIGURE 3.3. Gay men overlooking the Castro Street Fair in August 1979. Photograph by Don Eckert.

Before the 1960s, most homosexual activity on Polk had been limited to the Civic Center area of Lower Polk, near California Hall, the site of the 1965 New Year's Ball. But during the 1960s, gay men began opening businesses and nightspots as far north as the area around Union Street. Beginning in the mid-1950s, the Mattachine Society had advertised several Polk establishments in its convention bar guides, most conspicuously the 1228 Club at 1228 Sutter. A later retrospective in the *Bay Area Reporter* described Polk Street as the "mid-'50s jewel of San Francisco's gay café society."[40] Indeed, in that account and others the gay Polk of the early 1960s is often remembered as a meeting spot for downtown's white-collar gay workforce. "Gay men would come home from work...toss off their Brooks Brothers suits and polished cotton shirts, slip out of their wing tips...and go for an evening stroll."[41] If the gay Polk's habitués were relatively affluent, they were also generally older than gays in other neighborhoods. When Peter Groubert came out and moved to San Francisco in the late 1960s, for example, he remembered Polk as full of "quieter restaurants for older men."[42] If, as local leather columnist "Mr. Marcus" put it, South of Market was the "Valley of the Kings," Polk Street was the "Valley of the Queens."[43]

Older, more affluent, and perhaps more effeminate gay men were not the only ones there. Unlike the Castro, the Polk never became a predominantly gay residential or commercial district, and it retains a high degree of heterogeneity today. "Along the street," one offbeat travel guide to the city stated in 1966, "you'll find every classification of human represented: there are sprinklings of homosexuals, lesbians, real and fake artists, real models, model prostitutes. You name it and it can be had on Polk."[44] A sizeable "traditional" population was there as well. For example, the 1970 census tracts surrounding the area of greatest gay business concentration reveal that the solitary male resident was only slightly overrepresented and the male-female household was still by far the most typical of the area.[45]

Yet the gay imprint on Polk Street was unmistakable. When the editors of the gay magazine *California Scene* set out to identify all the gay spots on Polk Street in 1971, they described it as the "gayest street in San Francisco" and listed more than thirty sites. The diversity of the sites demonstrated the extent to which Polk also became a district of wider gay entrepreneurialism during the 1960s, and not just a district of gay rendezvous. In addition to nightclubs and bars, *California Scene* identified as gay-owned a hotel, a florist, several clothing and gift boutiques, a record shop, a bookstore, and an art framing business.[46]

As Polk developed as a district of gay commerce, rendezvous, and residence during the 1960s, it also became the informal seat of gay politics several years before the Castro took on that function. On June 27, 1970, gay liberationists staged a march on Polk Street from Aquatic Park to City Hall, where they held a rally in honor of the first anniversary of Stonewall. Subsequently regarded as the first event in what has become the San Francisco Pride Parade, the march galvanized existing gay liberation forces.

By the mid-1970s, Polk was beginning to lose some of its luster as a site of upscale gay living. The legions of young men who hustled in the Tenderloin increasingly set their sights on Polk Street, particularly on the four-block corridor of lower Polk between Ellis and Sutter. Male-to-female transgender Regina McQueen, who moved to San Francisco in 1975, recalled the vitality of Polk Street:

> You could walk down Polk Street and the whole street would be full
> of prostitutes. One side would be men standing out there posing,
> luscious little creatures—oh! And on the other side of the street
> would be women dressed in evening gowns with feather boas and big
> hair and lots of make-up. And the next night, some of the boys would
> be over there on the other side of the street, in femme drag, and vice
> versa.[47]

Similarly, Kevin Bentley, in his autobiographical novel *Wild Animals I Have Known* (2002), recalled Polk Street at night in the late 1970s as a street "teeming with hustlers and cruisers and crazies." When he spots young men loitering, he reminds readers: "This is Polk Street, and anyone of youthful mien loitering may be taken for a hustler."[48]

Sex without Politics South of Market

Whereas Polk Street reflected a diversity of interests, enterprises, and some political activism, this was not the case for the gay world of South of Market. There nightclubs and bathhouses emerged in the 1960s and 1970s to serve the singular purpose of providing a place for gay men to have unlimited sex: sex with friends, sex with strangers, sex in groups, sex in showers, sex in leather harnesses, and sex with inanimate objects. "Public sex is revolution," hustler and novelist John Rechy wrote in 1977; "courageous, righteous, defiant, revolution."[49]

The culture of radical sex that emerged South of Market beginning in the 1960s may have been revolutionary, but it was not political. Homophile activists and gay liberationists viewed free sexual expression as one among many elements of the complete social and legal equality they sought. By contrast, the culture of radical sex South of Market sought no legal or social reforms. Instead, practitioners sought to enjoy what freedoms had already been won and to explore the sexual limits of their imaginations in what they regarded as one of the most ecstatic, liberating, and glorious—if ultimately brief—moments of their lives.

According to anthropologist Gayle Rubin—the foremost authority on San Francisco's South of Market leather culture—a hypermasculine gay leather subculture emerged in large American cities in the mid-1950s. In San Francisco, gay "leathermen" patronized hardscrabble waterfront bars on the Embarcadero until 1962, when the Tool Box, one of the city's first leather bars, opened South of Market on Fourth and Harrison. The Tool Box quickly became iconic because it was the backdrop to the famous 1964 *Life* magazine piece on homosexuality in America. Febe's and the Slot followed, and by 1970 there were almost twenty gay bars and bathhouses South of Market; by 1980, the introduction of discos and the expansion of gay bars and bathhouses brought the total number close to forty.[50]

Even at the height of the gay revolution, South of Market was generally only gay by night. Historically, the area was home to San Francisco's light manufacturing businesses and machine shops. After the blue-collar workers finished their shifts and went home to other districts, the streets were transformed. Journalist Mark Thompson observed in 1982: "A few hours later, men in black leather...will step out on these same streets to fill the...gay bars, restaurants and sex clubs in the immediate vicinity."[51]

The Folsom Street Barracks was one of the biggest and best known clubs South of Market. "In its prime," *California Hotline* reported in 1977, "the Folsom Barracks created a world standard as to what baths could be in terms of hotness, honesty, outstanding music and general outrageousness." In his memoir-novel, Jack Fritscher described the Barracks as a "four-story maze of fantasy sex." "In its long corridors, men stripped down to combat boots and jockstraps. Most carried a white towel over one shoulder and a bottle of poppers tucked in their gray wool socks."[52] After a fire that destroyed the building in 1981, Chief Casper of the SFPD truthfully—if artlessly—announced: "It was reported to me that there was an S & M slave quarters at the back of the alley. We can't write this off as a lifeless fire. There may have been people chained to a bed."[53]

The Brig, according to *Drummer Magazine,* was "as heavy as you could get." The Ramrod, opened in 1967, still packed a punch nine years later: "This is one of Folsom's true-blue, hardcore leather bars and it is still a top favorite for many," *QQ Magazine* reported in October 1976. The sex clubs were remarkably active as well, the Corn Holes, Hot House, Glory Holes Ballroom, and South of the Slot being the most prominent. The *Spartacus Gay Guide* called South of the Slot "Heavy S & M and fetish scenes." "Only San Francisco could have baths further out than the Barracks," the *California Hotline* reported in 1977. The Caldron at 953 Natoma was known for "watersports" and resembled a "large one-level playground that seemed to corner the market on sleaze," according to Robert Payne of the *Manifest Reader*.[54]

One gauge of the enormous popularity of these clubs was their profitability. Gay journalist Randy Shilts estimated that by the late 1970s, the gay bathhouse and sex club industry in the United States and Canada was grossing $100 million a year. Locally, two *San Francisco Chronicle* reporters found that one bathhouse brought in an estimated twelve hundred customers per week, and another reported grossing $500,000 annually.[55]

The culture of extreme promiscuity that was characteristic of the South of Market scene ushered in fundamental changes in the nature of gay male relationships. Shilts, writing shortly after the demise of the South of Market scene in the wake of the AIDS crisis, was ambivalent about the change:

> At first you'd sleep with a person, hug all night, talk and have
> omelettes in the morning. Then, you skipped the breakfast because
> just how many omelettes can you make before it gets boring? Then
> you wouldn't spend the night. With the bathhouses, you wouldn't even
> have to talk. The Glory Hole and Cornhole clubs came into vogue next.
> There, you wouldn't even have to see who you had sex with.

The increased anonymity of gay sexual encounters was also the target of Larry Kramer's graphic and wildly controversial 1978 book *Faggots*, which satirized the outlandish hedonism of New York's gay men, which he viewed as a symptom of self-loathing rather than a sign of liberation.[56]

However, the continuing demand for the clubs is evidence that most gay men were untroubled by the kind of doubts Shilts and Kramer shared. The depersonalization of sex and the hypermasculine narcissism that were characteristic of gay sexuality South of Market in the 1970s were voluntary arrangements that were of no detriment to anyone who chose not to engage. On the other hand, much of the energy that might have been devoted to advancing the cause of complete social equality for gays and lesbians was drained off by the indefatigable partying of the era. The rampant narcissism of this culture was embodied in the so-called Castro clone look, the popular and hypermasculine aesthetic achieved by wearing leather boots, strategically tight Levi's jeans, flannel shirts, and leather jackets. The clone look demanded scrupulous physical fitness; by one account, it was difficult to find a clothing boutique on Polk Street that carried pants with waistlines larger than twenty-four inches.[57]

More problematically, gay men broke sharply with lesbian women, with whom they had shared social space before the sexual revolution. Given their freedom, many gay men simply replicated the same sort of misogynistic "boys only" policies and attitudes that had once impeded them. "Leave your fag hag girlfriend behind," *Drummer* advised its readers in a piece about Folsom Street. "Many of the bars do not have a ladies room at all; and most of the private clubs bar admission to women altogether. For the most part, Folsom is a men-only environment," the article concluded, adding the disingenuous suggestion that these policies were established because the action "gets too raunchy for female company."[58] Of course, there were very, very few women who might have sought admission to these goings-on, but this exclusion of women spoke volumes about a deeper misogyny among gay men that was typical of the era.

In addition, as many gay men in the midst of their revolution too easily adopted the sexism of American society, they often adopted its racial mores as well. As interviews conducted by historian Horacio Roque Ramírez have revealed, Latino gays were sometime subjected to strict ID requirements for admission to gay bars or clubs, while their white peers were not. And as Ramírez has demonstrated, Latino anger over white racism fueled creative new political strategies among gay Latinos in the Mission.[59] Blackberri, a gay African American folk singer from the East Bay, excoriated both the racial arrogance and the apolitical nature of gay white men in the pages of the *Advocate* in 1981: "The majority of gay white men are real self-serving and don't get any further than their needs." "There doesn't seem to be a commitment to anything other than getting the right to screw whomever you want. After that," Blackberri concluded, "it's fuck everybody else."[60] It was a harsh indictment that bore a great deal of truth.

The Castro: America's First Gay Neighborhood

While gay men developed social, commercial, and sexual communities on Polk Street and South of Market in the early 1960s, a few of them ventured into the unexceptional Eureka Valley district. Part of a continuum of residential and shopping neighborhoods that included the Mission District and Noe Valley, the community of Eureka Valley was almost indistinguishable from its neighborhood church, Most Holy Redeemer, dedicated in 1902. Heavily Catholic, Eureka Valley was a neighborhood of second- and third-generation immigrants. Into the 1940s, Norwegians were the most numerous immigrant group, followed by Germans, Irish, and Swedes; by 1960, the Irish were more significant, ranking third behind Germans and Italians. Ethnically diverse but mostly blue collar, and spiritually unified, Eureka Valley was one of the last provincial pockets in an increasingly cosmopolitan metropolis.[61]

The integrity of Eureka Valley was threatened by postwar suburbanization. Longtime residents and their counterparts in Noe Valley and the Mission

FIGURE 3.4. A longtime Eureka Valley resident observes the 1976 Castro Street Fair from her window. Photograph by Don Eckert.

watched as their children moved out to suburbs in Marin County, eastward into Alameda County, and southward into Daly City and the more distant peninsula communities. As they did so, the value of the properties in Eureka Valley began to decline, remaining well below the citywide median value until the mid-1970s. Increasingly, Eureka Valley's once proud homeowners became absentee landlords of low-rent properties, an arrangement that worked wonderfully for the long-haired, hippie gays just over the hill in the Haight-Ashbury.

In 1963, the first gay bar in the Castro opened its doors on Market Street. It was called the Missouri Mule, and it was only a few doors down from Finilla's Baths, where Paul Kantus's father had first sensed the change in the neighborhood. Shortly thereafter, a small men's clothing store on Castro Street called Valet Men's Wear began advertising its clothes in local gay periodicals, drawing a handful of gay male shoppers to the neighborhood before it was identified as a gay neighborhood. By 1965, the trickle of gay men had turned into a stream, sparking the opening of several more gay bars and restaurants, such as I-Do-No (1967), Burke's Corner House (1968), and Mistake (1968). By 1970, there were still fewer gay businesses in the Castro than there were either South of Market or on Polk, but the change was coming, and longtime Eureka Valley residents took note. For them, particularly after the Summer of Love, the specter of another Haight-Ashbury loomed large. One resident later remembered the day her husband, an SFPD officer, came home and announced their imminent departure. "He was totally afraid that our neighborhood was going down the tubes. So he says, 'our house is for sale!' We're selling the house. I don't want the kids raised here any more. All that stuff in the Haight, it's coming over the hill at us."[62]

For a gay hippie like Peter Groubert, the Castro was a great fit. When he finally admitted his homosexuality to himself in 1972, he moved out of his Berkeley commune and moved to San Francisco. He was turned off by most of the gay bars in the city, which seemed to cater to drag queens, "go-go boys," and collegiate preppies, but a friend soon told him about a bar for "long hairs" called the Midnight Sun, just off Castro Street. Indeed, a number of gay hippies had migrated from the Lower Haight-Ashbury over to the Midnight Sun, the Missouri Mule, and Toad Hall, which had opened the year before and quickly become the most popular bar in the Castro, and was described later in a gay newspaper as the "nerve center of the Castro."

When Cleve Jones, a future aide of supervisor Harvey Milk, arrived in the spring of 1973 from Phoenix, he was immediately captivated by the district. "There was just this electricity," Jones later remembered, "this knowledge that we were all refugees from other places and we'd come here to build something that was new." Acknowledging that he probably romanticized it in retrospect, he still remembered it "as a very happy, remarkable time." And Groubert delighted in watching "the neighborhood grow, wave after wave of people from different parts of the country, huge influxes. They found a place to be themselves after hearing all their lives that homosexuals were sick and the best thing for them to do was commit suicide."[63]

Neighborhood kids resisted the changing culture of Eureka Valley as long as they could. Back in 1961, when there were very few openly gay men in Eureka Valley, three boys from the Holy Redeemer School confessed to having killed a gay man by beating him savagely and then rolling him onto the tracks of the oncoming light rail train that passed through the neighborhood. Later, the school's students were caught yelling "fags" into new gay bars in the neighborhood and beating up gay men cruising in neighboring Collingwood Park. But

FIGURE 3.5. Supervisor Harvey Milk and Mayor George Moscone signing the city's gay rights bill in March 1978. Courtesy: AP/Wide World Photos.

by the mid-1970s, there were too few children left in the neighborhood to keep the school open, and it was closed in 1979.[64]

By the mid-1970s, the tipping point had passed: the streets were thick with throngs of young men cruising for sex partners. Most of the old family-oriented businesses of the Castro were replaced by gay-oriented businesses. The iconic Twin Peaks bar at the corner of Castro and Market, opened by a lesbian couple in 1972, is thought to have been one of the first gay bars in the country to have picture windows, in striking contrast to the painted windows or heavy walls that had historically shrouded gay meeting places. Particularly vital to the sex lives of the Castro's new residents was the Jaguar Bookstore, opened in 1971 near the intersection of Castro and Eighteenth Street. Ostensibly an erotic bookseller, the Jaguar was legendary as the "Quick-Stop of casual sex." A small fee granted patrons access to the rest of the house, furnished with bunk beds, a maze for sexual pursuit, and disco floor rarely used for dancing. "It was specifically designed for 'grab and go,'" one patron later remembered, "making a trip to the store for a quart of milk less than a chore."[65]

The transformation of the built environment in the Castro has become the stuff of legends. Gay residents' meticulous renovation of the neighborhood's dilapidated Victorians gave the neighborhood a fresh new look. The Castro Victorians, essayist Richard Rodriguez playfully recalled in his essay "Late Victorians," were "dollhouses for libertines."[66] That passion for renovation also reached to frumpy Castro Theater, which was restored to its 1920s glory in the mid-1970s. More significant, gay renovation of the Castro also contributed to a rapid ascent in property values. The 1970s saw a phenomenal rise in property values citywide, as downtown redevelopment spurred commercial growth and the in-migration of white-collar workers from all over the country. In that decade alone, the median price of a home in San Francisco increased by a whopping 270%. The increase in the Castro was more remarkable, exceeding the citywide number. At the end of the decade, the median value of a Castro home was 37% higher than the citywide average.[67]

The creation of a gay district in the Castro brought gay men the community they had sought for so long, but it also gave them something else they could scarcely have dreamed of even a decade earlier: political power. Since 1972, neighborhood associations throughout the city had advocated the introduction of district elections. Shortly after entering office in January 1976, George Moscone voiced his support for district elections, and a Castro neighborhood activist and camera salesman named Harvey Milk prominently supported a growing coalition of labor unions and neighborhood associations across the city in calling for a referendum on the issue in November 1976. In that referendum, voters chose to have district elections, and the Board of Supervisors was then slated to have its first district election in November 1977. Having quickly established himself as the default "mayor of Castro street" in his campaign for district elections, Milk—who had already made two unsuccessful bids for the Board of Supervisors—knew that victory was within easy reach, even though a far more qualified candidate existed in Rick Stokes.

A longtime homophile activist and early supporter of SIR, Stokes had developed deep connections with San Francisco's liberal elite. By contrast, Milk had arrived in San Francisco in 1972 with no political experience, except that he had enthusiastically distributed Barry Goldwater leaflets in 1964.[68] In fact, Milk had never lifted a finger for the cause of homophilia or gay liberation until it suited his political ambitions. That said, Milk resonated with the younger generation of gays flooding the Castro. As his chief biographer, Randy Shilts, wrote, "to Milk supporters, Rick Stokes was just another part of the wealthy elite, salving his wounds by kissing ass to liberal friends." Milk found his support among "the teeming thousands of angry street gays who had come during the 1970s."[69] It was their time, and they chose their man overwhelmingly. Gays would never again be ignored in San Francisco politics.

Dramatic proof of this came in March 1978, when Milk initiated an ordinance barring discrimination against homosexuals in employment, housing, or public accommodations. The bill won by a ten-to-one margin, with Dan White casting the only dissenting vote, ostensibly because it violated the beliefs of his Catholic constituents, but really to spite Milk for not supporting him on a key vote months earlier. Moscone signed the bill into law in April, and San Francisco belatedly joined the growing list of American cities where homophobia had lost much of its historic functionality.

The Incomplete Lesbian Revolution of the 1970s

Less than a mile from the heart of America's gay male revolution, lesbians in the Mission District inaugurated a revolution of their own. Like gay men, lesbians now made themselves more visible on the streets than they had ever been, showing the legions of closeted women throughout the nation that women could love whom they wished, when they wished. By writing and performing poetry and folk music in bohemian coffee shops, lesbians moved past the limited bar scene of an earlier era, articulated their long-forbidden desires, and encouraged their sisters to do the same. By learning business basics and manual skills, they proved that they did not need men to open bars and bookstores, or lay tiles and build bookshelves. By publishing countless magazines and newsletters, they created a nationwide network of lesbian communication and support and simultaneously laid claim to a burgeoning women's literary world. And beginning with the 1972 Christopher Street West Festival—the second event of what is today known as the annual Pride Celebration—lesbians marched alongside gay men and served notice to San Franciscans and to the world that they were out and proud and never going back. "Our goal," lesbian authors Sidney Abbott and Barbara Love wrote in 1972, "is to be able to go about our lives—as human beings, as women, as Lesbians—unselfconsciously, and to be able to spend all of our time on work or fun, and none on the arts of concealment or on self-hatred."[70]

Yet the lesbian revolution of the 1970s was not all that it could have been—largely because of the ascent of cultural feminism among many lesbians. Emerging in the early 1970s, and quickly eclipsing both liberal and radical feminism, cultural feminism emphasized the physical and moral superiority of women over men and sought the creation of a completely separate women's counterculture.[71] To a certain extent, lesbians in the Mission accomplished this; the do-it-yourself ethos of cultural feminism led to the creation of a vibrant, thriving lesbian presence where there had been virtually none. At the same time, by conflating personal choices with feminist politics, cultural feminism was highly doctrinaire and prescriptive. Even as the lesbian revolution advanced, cultural feminists stifled erotic opportunities for lesbians, marginalized bisexuals, and completely ostracized transgenders. But the lesbian revolution did not start this way.

FIGURE 3.6. Lesbian couple repairing a car in front of their Mission District apartment, 1971. Photograph by Cathy Cade.

In the early 1960s, before the rise of cultural feminism, the lesbian sexual revolution in San Francisco had overlapped conspicuously with the simultaneous gay and straight sexual revolutions. Many San Francisco lesbians continued to socialize with or near gay men and other sexual revolutionaries and bohemians in the mid-1960s. Because many of the historic lesbians bars of North Beach had closed by the early 1960s, a rising number of lesbians abandoned the North Beach and downtown areas and followed gay men, hippies, and other sex radicals westward across the city. In 1966, one of the first gay bars, Ebbtide, opened in the Mission on Valencia Street, and it was decidedly mixed gender. "This bar," Guy Strait wrote shortly after its opening, "specializes in peaceful coexistence and serves all three sexes (are there four now?) with equal ease and enjoyment."[72] Many other lesbians found their way to the Haight-Ashbury. In 1961, Romeo's opened on Haight Street near Clayton, and in 1966, Maud's—which would become one of San Francisco's most enduring lesbian bars—opened in neighboring Cole Valley. When writer Sue-Ellen Case pulled up a stool at Maud's for the first time in the late 1960s, there was both tension and erotic opportunity in the "an old butch-femme scene" as well as a collection of "hippie dykes."[73] And one block away from Romeo's was a "hip" boutique called Mnasidika, opened in 1964 by Peggy Caserta, a woman who derived local celebrity from having lots of sex with Janis Joplin from 1966 until her death in 1970.[74] When coupled with the exploits of the women in the SFL and, later, the Pyschedelic Venus Church, Joplin's sensational and well-documented sex life is just another example of the broader culture of the Haight-Ashbury, in which female sexual experimentation was not always political and often simply playful.

But for many lesbians—particularly ones who had been involved in left-wing politics and student movements in the 1960s—the cavalier, ambiguous, and largely apolitical lesbianism and bisexuality of the 1960s was either unattainable or undesirable. In their search for comfort, meaning, and legitimacy in a largely hostile society, many lesbians turned toward feminism. To be sure, in the mid- to late 1960s, feminists had not generally allied themselves with lesbians; locally, San Francisco's small consciousness-raising women's groups had been entirely silent on the issue of lesbianism, and nationally prominent feminist pioneer Betty Friedan had infamously described lesbians as the "lavender menace" in 1969.[75] But in the early 1970s, the tide quickly turned, particularly after May 1970, when lesbians at the second Conference to Unite Women in New York declared their independence from mainstream feminism. The National Organization of Women (NOW)—the most influential feminist group in the country—followed suit in 1973, rebuking Friedan's earlier homophobia and welcoming lesbians into the ranks. By the early 1970s, lesbianism and feminism were not only compatible but often indistinguishable.

Meanwhile, in San Francisco, lesbian-feminists were also breaking away from the gay liberation movement. Members of DOB had been complaining of tokenism in the male-dominated homophile movement since the mid-1960s, and for all the fiery rhetoric of the GLF in 1969, gay liberation had not offered lesbians much more than the homophile movement had. By 1970, DOB cofounder Del Martin had simply had enough. Inspired by the January 1970 publication of Robin Morgan's essay *Goodbye to All That*—a manifesto of feminist separation from the New Left—emboldened by the lesbian breakaway from the second Conference to Unite Women in May, and particularly infuriated by the condescension male homophile leaders had shown her at a recent dinner for Assembly speaker Willie Brown, Martin penned a new lesbian manifesto entitled "If That's All There Is" in October 1970.[76] Like Leo Laurence's 1969 article "Gay Revolution" in *Vector,* published one year earlier, Martin's piece hit the gay and lesbian press like a bombshell. "I've been forced to the realization that I have no brothers in the homophile movement." "Fifteen years of masochism," Martin wrote of her time working with men in that movement, "is enough."[77]

Though few lesbians were as outspoken as Martin, many shared her separatist sensibility. As lesbians increasingly learned the building trades and business management skills, they could literally afford to write that separatism into the urban landscape. Having lived in proximity to gay men and other sexual radicals in the Haight-Ashbury and the Castro during the 1960s, many lesbians began to push south and eastward into the Mission District in the early 1970s. One of the first lesbian businesses of this era—the Full Moon Café—was actually in the Castro, but the members of the lesbian-feminist collective that gathered around it soon brought their energies eastward to the Mission. Opened in 1974, the café reached out to women by posting advertisements in the women's restrooms at the Main Branch of the San Francisco Public Library. One of those drawn to the Full Moon was a lesbian book-hound named Carol Seajay.

Fleeing Michigan for San Francisco in 1973, Seajay arrived "with a ray of hope about living life as a lesbian woman" and quickly joined up with the collective.[78] The collective laid cement floors and installed new plumbing in the building. "It was a dyke thing to do everything ourselves," she recalled in a 1999 interview with Elizabeth Sullivan. "So if you open a dyke coffeehouse, and it needs a new cement floor, you learn how to lay cement floors."[79] The Full Moon—which boldly maintained a female-only admission policy in the heart of the male-dominated Castro—soon closed its doors because of permit violations. But Seajay's commitment to the literary scene only deepened, particularly as a growing number of lesbians began coming out through poetry readings at local coffeehouses in the mid-1970s. In 1976, Seajay and her partner, Paula Wallace, took out a loan from the Bay Area Feminist Federal Credit Union and opened what would be the longest running lesbian-feminist bookstore in the city, Old Wives' Tales on Valencia near Sixteenth Street, in the heart of the Mission District. Old Wives' Tales was quickly followed by Amelia's, a bar that opened on Valencia near Seventeenth Street, and Osento, an all-women's bathhouse on Valencia between Twentieth and Twenty-first streets. Most significant was the opening of the Women's Building at Eighteenth and Valencia by what one founder described as "feminists with a lesbian priority." Located in a former Sons of Norway meeting hall, the woman-owned and -operated building became the meeting place for lesbian and feminist groups from around the city. Surrounding these establishments was a quickly growing community of lesbians, many of whom moved from outside California into the district in the late 1970s, particularly into the area between Dolores and Valencia and Seventeenth and Army Streets—renamed Cesar Chavez Street in 1995.

Historically an immigrant neighborhood of European ethnic immigrants—with the Irish predominating—the Mission had become home to Mexicans and a smaller number of Central Americans after World War II. In 1962, David Braaten of the *San Francisco Chronicle* still described the Mission as a diverse, "international" neighborhood, but in truth it was well on its way to having a Latino majority. Though an occasional "Murphy's pharmacy or Shamrock Cleaners" could still be found, Braaten recognized that they existed only as "reminders of the past." Indeed, the once solidly Irish parish of St. Peter's Catholic Church on Twenty-fourth Street was at least one-third Latino by 1965.[80] As more ethnic whites moved out to the westerly Richmond and Sunset districts and eastward across the Bay to more distant suburbs, the Mission became heavily Latino, and the 1970 census revealed that Latinos represented nearly half of the population there.

Complementing their numerical strength in the Mission was the rising political consciousness of the second-generation Latinos of the district in the 1970s. During the 1960s, thousands of predominantly Latino Mission denizens repelled redevelopment efforts, fearing the fate that had overtaken the Western Addition. In the 1970s, Latino artists in the Mission pioneered *la raza* arts movement, in which they creatively articulated both ethnic and neighborhood identities. Initiated by the Pocho-Che Collective, Latino artists in the Mission connected local issues to a larger Latin American consciousness. In 1977, the Centro Cultural de la Misión (now the Mission Cultural Center for Latino Arts) opened, housing artist studios and Mission newspapers like *El Tecolote*.[81] Finally, Latino-identified gangs proliferated in the 1970s, claiming their part of the city, sometimes violently.

Given the politically charged context of the Mission in the 1970s, still firmly attached to Catholicism regardless of the radical politics, the arrival of predominantly white lesbians seemed destined to create conflict. But this never happened. In striking contrast to the gay men of the Castro, the lesbians of the Mission left a relatively light footprint on the Mission District. In addition to creating a vibrant social world for themselves, the lesbians of the Mission became vital contributors to the preexisting cultural and ethnic diversity of the district without ever colonizing it. This was partly a simple function of numbers: though no certain figures exist, lesbians probably represented no more than approximately one-third of San Francisco's gay population.[82] But it was also a function of the smaller earning potential of women versus men in the 1970s and the existing housing stock of the district. With many more apartments available than houses—in comparison to the Castro—lesbians were generally renting apartments rather than buying buildings. And they were renting apartments in a very soft rental market: the population of the Mission was declining at an even faster rate than the population of the city during the 1970s. Finally, many were cohabitating in cooperative housing arrangements. The effect of all of these developments was that lesbians in the Mission were generally not gentrifiers.[83]

The opposite was true for gay men, as assassin Dan White wrote in his prison notebooks in 1979. "The people in my neighborhood," he said of his neighbors in Visitacion Valley, "felt that gays have made things even harder for big families because they don't have any children to worry about and several of them can put their salaries together and pay more rent than a single family, and this has the effect of driving up prices."[84] At the opposite end of the political spectrum, the editors of *Foghorn*—the student newspaper of the University of San Francisco—pilloried the "urban genocide" perpetrated by gay men against "Third World people" who had been forced out of the city into "shanty towns" like Daly City.[85] Here, as everywhere, the charges of gentrification missed the target: it was landlords who raised rents, not tenants. But since at least the late 1960s, it was an open secret among landlords and real estate professionals that to have your property "queenized" was a great financial boon.[86]

Further mitigating hostility to lesbian newcomers in the Mission was the fact that many envisioned and described themselves as part of a larger struggle of ethnic and racial minorities and "Third World people," while white gay men generally did not. Consequently, racism among white lesbians was probably much less common than it was among white gay men. Moreover, if the extensive written correspondence between the staff and customers at Old Wives' Tales was an indicator of lesbian attitudes generally, lesbians were extraordinarily sensitive to differences in race, class, physical ability, and even weight among women.[87] This had concrete implications that likely ingratiated them with the Mission's Latino population. From the beginning, the Women's Centers emphasized multicultural programming, a fact that became visible on the muraled façade of the building in the mid-1990s but was at play much earlier. Finally, the taboo against antifemale violence in the machismo culture of the Mexican gangs of the 1970s and early 1980s probably gave white Mission women an ounce of protection relative to men during an era of otherwise rising crime rates. During the 1970s, the Mission Station reported the highest number of auto thefts in the SFPD's nine stations, and the third highest number of aggravated assaults and burglaries. But the Mission Station ranked a distant fourth in reported rapes, with just over half the average number for the Northern Station, which covered the Western Addition and Polk Gulch areas.[88]

If, by the late 1970s, lesbians had reshaped the sexual landscape of San Francisco and carved out a space for themselves, cultural feminism still hindered the ability of many lesbians to imagine queerness more broadly. Sadomasochists, bisexuals, and transsexuals, in particular, were marginalized not only from the mainstream but also from the emerging lesbian community. Because many lesbians viewed "coming out" as a political act, the personal choices of lesbians were often subjected to close scrutiny by their peers. A 1972 article in the lesbian periodical the *Furies* argued that lesbianism was "more than a sexual preference, it is a political choice."[89] This pressure from the self-appointed spokeswomen of lesbian feminism—the "queen bees," as some critics described them—sharply delimited the terrain of acceptable lesbianism. Deborah Sundahl, a lesbian-feminist who later went on to spectacularly reject the central tenets of 1970s lesbian feminism, recalled that "lesbians were hiding by appealing to political feminism for legitimacy." Part of that "hiding" involved the repression of sexual practices that the lesbian-feminist leadership deemed politically incorrect. In an unfortunate and ironic twist that was ultimately stultifying to unfettered lesbianism, the lesbian-feminist leaders of the 1970s demanded allegiance to their sexual strictures at least as adamantly as did the patriarchal society against which they were ostensibly revolting.

The dutiful lesbian of the 1970s and early 1980s was expected to resist patriarchy on the streets and phallocentrism in the sheets. In a fabulously self-serving and melodramatic keynote address to the 1973 West Coast Lesbian Feminist Conference in Los Angeles—which drew about twelve hundred women from around the country—feminist Robin Morgan warned the lesbian crowd from adopting the "male style."

> Every woman here knows in her gut the vast differences between
> her sexuality and that of any patriarchally trained male's—gay or
> straight. That has, in fact, always been a source of *pride* to the lesbian
> community, even its greatest suffering. That the emphasis on genital
> sexuality, objectification, promiscuity, emotional noninvolvement, and
> coarse vulnerability was the *male style,* and that we, as women, placed
> greater trust in love, sensuality, humor, tenderness, commitment.[90]

In her address, Morgan also savaged transvestitism as "an ingenious new male approach for trying to seduce women"; the Rolling Stones, whose lead singer, Mick Jagger, she regarded as the "high priest of sadistic cock-rock"; and the campaign of "attempted gynocide" presumably sweeping the nation.[91]

In a similar vein, lesbian feminist Sue Katz argued that healthy lesbian sexuality should only involve "touching and rubbing and cuddling and fondness." "It's only goal is closeness and pleasure. It does not exist for the Big Orgasm. It exists for feeling nice."[92] And even lesbian pioneers Del Martin and Phyllis Lyon—whose pathbreaking 1972 book, *Lesbian/Woman,* generally avoided polemics in its affirmation of lesbian love, relationships, and sexuality—could not resist the anti-phallocentric line of cultural feminism. After describing the "three most popular" methods of lesbian sex—mutual masturbation, cunnilingus, and tribadism—they described "two other methods by which women may achieve sexual gratification" but which seemed to be "relatively rare in practice." One of those was through the use of a dildo, but "its most prevalent use is by heterosexual women," they wrote, citing absolutely no proof of this assertion. Not only had most lesbians never even seen a dildo, they wrote, but the lesbian use of the dildo was merely "the fancy of most men who cannot feature women enjoying or being satisfied without a penis."[93]

If many lesbian-feminists were hostile to any hint of the "male style" in their sisters' lovemaking, they were utterly contemptuous of sadomasochism, which they regarded as an eroticized metaphor for patriarchal power relations. That contempt was deeply alienating to those lesbians who openly admitted to having S/M fantasies. One of these was Pat Califia, who came out in 1971—from behind the "Zion curtain," as she referred to the boundary between her home state of Utah and the "rest of the world"—and migrated to San Francisco in 1973. Working at the San Francisco Sex Information (SFSI) switchboard and as a volunteer for DOB, Califia was deeply committed to feminism, and particularly to lesbian separatism. "We got to be heroes who were going to change the world and rescue women from male evil," she later recalled, "instead of a bunch of twisted, mentally-ill drunks hovered and hiding from the world in dirty, dark, tiny, bars."[94]

But Califia—who would become Patrick Califia thirty years later when she transitioned to a male identity—soon found that there were limitations to the new world she and her lesbian sisters were creating. Still reeling from her rejection from her Mormon family, she had dutifully suppressed her budding S/M fantasies and entered into a monogamous relationship in which she felt stifled. But a trip to a Los Angeles feminist conference in 1976 changed her perspective. Despite being harassed by anti-S/M feminists outside the S/M workshops, Califia attended a workshop entitled "Healthy Questions about S/M." Dazzled by the female presenters, Califia was transformed. "When I got back to San Francisco, I began to tell everyone I knew that I was into S/M and looking for partners and support." Through the *Berkeley Barb,* Califia learned of an S/M support group for women. That group, which become known as Cardea, was a part of the Society of Janus, an S/M club started in 1973 by a bisexual woman named Cynthia Slater and her male partner, Larry Olsen. Despite her earlier separatist stance, Califia found some temporary camaraderie at Janus-hosted parties at the Catacombs and other predominantly male venues because the only bar to welcome leather-clad lesbians at the time was Scott's Pit, a mixed-gender gay bar at Duboce and Sanchez, on the edge of the Castro.[95]

In 1978, Califia met a like-minded lesbian named Gayle Rubin, a University of Michigan graduate student in anthropology who had come to San Francisco to study gay leather sexuality. Rubin, Califia, and sixteen other women met that June and decided that they wanted to create what Rubin later described as "a social and political space" where "where kinky lesbians could find friends and partners" and "carve out protected space in otherwise increasingly antagonistic lesbian communities." That desire led to the creation of Samois, the first lesbian S/M educational and political organization, in 1978. "As feminists," the members of Samois declared in their first publication, "we oppose all forms of social hierarchy based on gender. As radical perverts, we oppose all social hierarchies based on sexual preference."[96]

But many lesbians were simply not willing to accept "radical perverts." Grudgingly allowed admission into the Pride parade, Califia and the others were physically harassed by the lesbian security staff. Califia did not dare attend the Michigan Womyn's Music Festival because she received death threats. And leading feminists felt that the threat of sadomasochism among lesbians was so severe that an anthologized polemic was necessary.[97] Despite this pressure, Califia, Rubin, and other S/M lesbians continued to pursue their interests, and by 1981 they were finding greater acceptance among local lesbians. In September 1981, Samois hosted its first annual leather dance and Ms. Leather contest at a lesbian bar in Oakland, with more than three hundred women in attendance.

Bisexual women represented another source of discomfort for many lesbians because of the prevailing belief that bisexuals simply had not "made up their mind" or, worse, were attempting to access the privileges of heteronormativity while indulging exotic lesbian fantasies. Furthermore, the gay press—a touchstone of identification for gays, bisexuals, and lesbians—was virtually silent about the existence of bisexuals. One of the first to challenge the obvious "bi-phobia" was Maggi Rubenstein, who had come out as a bisexual while working as a nurse for the Center for Special Problems in 1969. In 1972, she began working with the National Sex Forum at McIlvenna's Glide Urban Center, giving lectures on bisexuality throughout the city. She also cofounded the SFSI switchboard service, along with bisexual Margo Rila and several others. Describing the "rage of being discounted, invalidated," Rubenstein, Rila, Hariett Leve, a bisexual man named David Lourea, and several others founded the Bisexual Center in 1976.[98] Located first downtown and later in the Haight-Ashbury, the Center was the only place in the country—besides a small discussion group in New York—where bisexuals were encouraged and educated. Unlike lesbian-feminist organizations, the Center also accepted transsexuals and talked openly and nonjudgmentally about S/M. It was a radically inclusive group, as Lourea later recalled, whose members believed that "anybody who identified as a woman had the right to be there."[99] Capitalizing on the demand for their services and growing expertise, Rubenstein and other bisexual activists soon joined Ted McIlvenna in founding the Institute for the Advanced Study of Human Sexuality in 1976, the first institution to grant advanced degrees in sexology.[100]

Few lesbians felt the sting of lesbian antitransgender sentiment as acutely as Beth Elliott. A Bay Area native, Elliott was born a male but recognized that she was really "a girl and a lesbian" at the age of nineteen in 1970. Finding support and hormone supplements through the Center for Special Problems, Elliott had begun to establish herself as a woman and a lesbian by early 1971, soon joined DOB, and was elected vice president of the San Francisco chapter that summer. All the while, she was developing a following in the Bay Area and in Los Angeles as a "hippie-chick" lesbian singer-songwriter. She came to be so well regarded by lesbians and other folk music fans in California by 1973 that she was a shoo-in as a main act for the West Coast Lesbian Feminist Conference in Los Angeles.

But when Elliott took the stage on the first evening of the event, an old friend of hers "outed" her to the crowd and accused her of sexual harassment, touching off a firestorm of protest that culminated with Robin Morgan's hostile address. Insulted by Morgan and members of the audience, and ostracized by lesbian-separatists, Elliott became fodder for the lesbian-separatist press. Sharing Morgan's disdain for transgenders, an East Bay group called the Gutter Dykes described Elliott's attendance at the conference as "the most bizarre and dangerous cooptation of lesbian energy and emotion [we] can imagine." In the *Lesbian Tide*, Ann Forfreedom refused to use Elliott's name, describing her instead as a "being-with-a-penis," bent on disrupting the conference.[101] The transphobia of lesbian feminism reached its zenith in 1979 with the publication of Janice Raymond's vicious manifesto, *Transsexual Empire*, in which she infamously asserted that "all transsexuals rape women's bodies by reducing the real female form to an artifact, appropriating this body for themselves."[102]

Elliott was personally devastated by the attack, but it did not stop her from working. While many lesbian-feminists spent their time policing the borders of femininity and lesbianism—to no one's benefit, as it turned out—Elliott went on to champion gay rights as a board member of the California Committee for Sexual Law Reform, a group that organized in support of Willie Brown's "consenting adults" bill, which repealed prohibitions against "unnatural sex acts"—a euphemism for oral copulation or sodomy—between consenting adults. And she found comfort in the Haight-Ashbury as a lesbian musician because, as she remembered later, "I wasn't one of those angry dykes giving them attitude." Her performances in Haight-Ashbury coffeehouses and in rural Mendocino County brought her the respect of her musical peers. Life in the Bay Area music scene of the mid-1970s also brought her into contact with other hippies, many of whom were bisexual, and she took on their cause as fellow outcasts from mainstream lesbian feminism, publishing extensively on bisexuality as a feminist issue. "Bisexuality could be the best thing that has ever happened to lesbian feminism," Elliott would later write. "It delivers the benefits of loving women—and the freedom to do so—to more women."[103] Victimized by the intolerance of

1970s cultural feminism, Elliott championed bisexuality, transgenderism, and sex positivity almost two decades before it was fashionable to do so.

Just as Elliott was celebrating the 1975 victory of the consenting adults bill, Joani Blank, an East Coast transplant with a master's degree in public health education, was also testing the limits of femininity. Blank arrived in San Francisco in 1971 and quickly befriended Maggi Rubenstein, joined the first group of volunteers with SFSI, and then became a counselor for preorgasmic women at UCSF. By 1975, Blank had amassed enough experience teaching women about their bodies to write *My Playbook for Women about Sex*, a "sexual self-awareness book for every woman" published by her own press, Down There Press.[104] Because sex stores were the exclusive domain of gay and straight men—and generally not inviting for women—Blank decided to start her own store. In 1977, she opened Good Vibrations—the first women-oriented sex toy store in the world—at Twenty-second and Guerrero, on the edge of the Mission and adjacent to Noe Valley.

Early on, a few lesbian-feminists dismissed her because she was not a lesbian, and in one instance a lesbian couple, when asked if they needed assistance, pointed to an already-sheepish male customer and said "not with him in here!" And some men—conditioned to the separatist ethos of the 1970s—told Blank that they felt like they were invading a "women's space." But what Good Vibrations ultimately proved was that there was a wide spectrum of the population who wanted Blank's wares. By advertising Good Vibrations as a store "especially—but not exclusively—for women," Blank served notice to both female separatist and potentially disrespectful male customers that the store would have something for everyone. It did, and it worked.

About two years after arriving in San Francisco, Gayle Rubin reflected on the state of lesbian feminism. A rigorous thinker, Rubin challenged the "confusion between sexual orientation and political belief" that had become a widely accepted component of lesbian feminism: "it has prevented the lesbian movement from asserting that our lust for women is justified whether or not it derives from feminist political ideology. It has generated a lesbian politic that seems ashamed of lesbian desire. It has made feminism into a closet in which lesbian sexuality is unacknowledged." Finally, Rubin concluded, "the idea that there is an automatic correspondence between sexual preference and political belief is long overdue to be jettisoned."[105] Rubin had rejected that dangerous idea herself, and she was not alone. The true female sex revolutionaries of the 1960s and 1970s were those women—lesbian, straight, or bisexual—who engaged in the precise sexual practices that they desired, with whom they desired, and where they desired. They were women who cared about other women, and about feminism, but withheld public judgment about their sisters' private lives and private practices. They were the lesbian sex revolutionaries but it was not yet their day.

4

THE UNSPOKEN
SEXUALITY OF
GOLDEN GATE PARK

To wander among the dense, winding cypress groves of Golden Gate Park during the sexual revolution was to enter a world of virtually limitless sexual possibility. So dense in places as to be almost impassible, the thicket easily shrouded anonymous gay and straight trysts. At the "wasteland"—as locals described the western end of the park at Ocean Beach—the decrepit Beach Chalet building and defunct windmills were given over to sex-hunters, squatters, vandals, and raccoons. For those San Franciscans who had seen the park in better times, its demise was a shocking symbol of a city run amok. Indeed, no public space in the city was as thoroughly transformed by the sexual revolution as was Golden Gate Park in the 1960s and 1970s.

Delight and Deviancy in the Most Public Space

Beginning with its construction in the 1870s, Golden Gate Park occupied a central place in both the geography and imagination of San Francisco. The city's largest park—and slightly larger than New York's Central Park—it encompassed over a thousand acres of once sandy and generally unruly land in the western half of the city formerly known as the "outside lands." Its groves, lakes, and gardens lured millions of tourists throughout the twentieth century, and tourist guides described the park as a "must see" site, "one of the most picturesque parks in the world," full of "outstanding attractions for young and old"; "Golden Gate Park is the aureole of San Francisco's recreational haunts."[1]

Unlike the streets of San Francisco—whose public nature was always mediated by the intrusion of the private concerns of both businesses and residents—Golden Gate Park was more purely public. From the park's inception, the most prevalent discourse about it celebrated its palliative properties for the human body and the body politic. "Those who are weary and worn from head work, or hand labor," a 1916 park tour guide read, "may refresh themselves by breathing the pure breezes from the Pacific Ocean, and delight in the fragrance of tree and flower."[2] The park's beauty and its purportedly curative properties were the product of careful planning on the part of William Hammond Hall, its designer. Appointed park superintendent in 1871, Hall envisioned a place that would convey "warmth, repose, and enlivenment" and soothe the urban denizen. Roads were deliberately winding to discourage the park's horse and buggy traffic from speeding, walkways were at a distance from roads to protect pedestrians, and shrubbery was planted in abundance to attract birds and wildlife to low-lying and isolated dells. In 1887, Hall hired John McLaren, a Scottish landscape gardener, who not only improved the park by vastly expanding its plant life with plants from across the globe but also decided to maximize public access, vowing that there would be no "Keep off the grass" signs under his stewardship.[3]

Both Hall and McLaren's vision of the park quickly made it a great site of recreation and repose in nature for countless San Franciscans. By the mid-1880s, three different streetcar lines connected to the park, bringing thousands of visitors daily. A conservatory was built in 1877 on North Drive, an adjacent music stand built in 1882, and the Children's Playground was dedicated in 1888. In 1894 at the Midwinter's Fair, more than two million people passed through the park's gates in only six months, and the event added new attractions to the park, including the Japanese Tea Garden, the Fine Arts Building, and the Grand Concourse, which later became the Music Concourse. McLaren's addition of a chain of lakes also enhanced the bucolic setting of the park.

Yet despite the genteel discourse of the park, it also served unsavory purposes from the beginning. The very design of the park—its winding roads, high shrubs, and isolated dells—allowed people to act out their human penchant for violence and sex with anonymity and, usually, impunity. From its inception, the park was the site of numerous acts of horrific violence. In April 1886, the body of a young man who had been murdered, his skull "frightfully crushed," was discovered in the park. The body of a "beautiful" young female telephone operator who had been shot in the head was found there in February 1900. In October 1921, a young woman who had been sitting alone in the park was strangled to death by a teamster. A young woman was sexually assaulted, beaten, and strangled to death in a park tunnel in May 1934.[4] These incidents of murder, as well as countless suicides, belied the prevailing discourse about Golden Gate Park.

The most conspicuous locus of this tension between the discourse of the park and its actual use was sex. Ideas about sexuality clearly informed ideas about the park, but these were distinct from ideas about sexual relations taking place in the park. From the perspective of Gilded Age park advocates, the romantic properties of the park were an extension of its health-inducing properties. The intended serenity of the park was a natural lure for those who could, by law and custom, express some degree of affection in public—in this era, heterosexual couples. A 1936 *San Francisco Chronicle* editorial on the many uses of the park concluded: "And, of course, there are the couples. 'The trees get ya,' a seventeen-year old Romeo tells his yellow-haired beauty."[5] *Golden Gate: The Park of a Thousand Vistas*, a 1950 paean to the beauties of the park, described the irresistible romanticism of the "portals of the past," a group of smoke-stained marble columns from pre-1906 mansions that were installed on the shores of Lloyd Lake: "romantically picturesque in sunlight or moonlight, the 'Portals' are a favorite haunt of lovers and all others who delight in sentimental associations and the beauty of reflections in still water."[6]

Yet even within the context of heterosexual romantic relations, the park incited stronger passions than some could bear to watch. The more chaste found the open expressions of affection among heterosexual couples in the park quite scandalous. In the late 1870s, the Park Commission purchased a hundred iron benches and distributed them throughout the park, where they became popular with young couples eager to escape their Victorian chaperones. Editorials criticized the excessive "hugging in the park." A letter to the editor of the *San Francisco Examiner* complained that the park had been given over to "certain hoodlums, who are in the habit of driving through Golden Gate Park almost daily with fast horses, and who are supported by a class of 'fast women.' They do not work but live on the proceeds of the ill-gotten gains of those women." From this perspective, the park was a pleasure-ground for pimps.[7] One film critic for the *Los Angeles Times* denounced the trend toward "maulish" and aggressive "love making" in the cinema of the late 1920s. Actors today, she argued, "act like soldiers and nursemaids in Hyde Park or Central Park or Golden Gate Park and wrap themselves all around each other, no matter what lack of privacy is evident."[8] And at least through the 1940s—and probably much later—horse-mounted police officers regularly rousted "spooning" couples parked in shadowy lanes of the park.[9]

The Beach Chalet posed particular difficulties for moralists. Designed by the architect Willis T. Polk, this Spanish-inspired building opened in 1925 as the crown jewel of the park and its furthest western outpost. The Chalet housed a restaurant and various concessions that served beachgoers. Owned by the city and controlled the Park Commission, the building also had many other tenants, including local Boy Scouts troops and the Veterans of Foreign Wars. The prestige of the building was further enhanced by Federal Works Project–funded frescoes by French painter Lucien Labaudt.[10]

But the wide public access to the building, its geographic remoteness, and the unwillingness of the Richmond Station of the SFPD to patrol the area allowed the building to be used in alternate ways that neither the San Francisco Recreation and Park Department nor the general public endorsed. In 1932, a party at the Chalet featured exotic dancers who offered, according to the SFPD report, "rotten performances and nauseating spectacles." But it was a large 1952 party that drew fire from the San Francisco Recreation and Park Department. Called a "smoker," this event was part of a traveling show arranged by Sunset District promoter Salvatore "Tarbaby" Terrano. In addition to providing "stag" films, Tarbaby brought two exotic dancers from Oakland to the party and planted them in the crowd. On his cue, the women would walk to the stage, take off their clothes, and conduct what the police described as "abnormal acts." The winner of the door prize got to have sex with the woman of his choice. In short, it was what guests likely regarded as a really good party.[11]

Even more frequent, though scarcely discussed, was the use of Golden Gate Park for clandestine homosexual encounters. The most compelling source of information on homosexual relations in the park before the sexual revolution is a study conducted by the Sexual Deviation Research project at Langley Porter Psychiatric Institute in the early 1950s. This project was the product of a $100,000 appropriation in 1949 that grew out of the "sex crimes" panic of 1949. In their report "Sex Crimes in San Francisco," the doctors and researchers at the Langley Porter Clinic made effective use of citywide juvenile sex offender records and one of the first large vacuum-tube IBM machines at the Sacramento State Department of Mental Hygiene to create statistical profiles of juvenile sex offenders.

Most female "juvenile sex delinquents"—as the study described them—had been detained for voluntarily having sex with older men, while male sex delinquents either had heterosexual relations with much younger girls or homosexual relations with males of any age, though usually older. One of the most revealing aspects of the investigation into juvenile sex delinquents was the data concerning locations of offenses. Although about 43% of all sex offenses committed by juvenile sex delinquents occurred in the delinquent youth's home, a companion's home, or a hotel or motel room, gender-specific tabulations revealed a sharp discrepancy: while only 3% of female sex delinquents committed their sexual offenses in public parks or beaches, 16% of the male ones did. According to the study, the park was a site not just of sex but of a definitively *male* underground sexual culture. In most cases, boys detained for homosexual offenses in the park were likely "tricking" for money with older gay men. Because most were from poor sections of town—the Mission, the Tenderloin, and Bayview–Hunters Point, they found a market in the hidden pathways of Golden Gate Park long before the closet doors opened.[12]

The homosexual sex trade in the park was apparently well enough known to provide easy fodder for homophobes' sensationalizing. For example, the neighborhood newspaper *Truth* excoriated the degradation of the park in 1949.

> The parks of San Francisco are a sexual cess-pool. Old men who have been practicing homesexuality [*sic*] for decades, journey to the parks of the city for the sole purpose of making contacts and they prey largely not on their own kind, but on the very young and very innocent. Was the original intention of the designers and builders of these parks that they were to be used for illicit homosexual purposes? Or was it their intention that they were to be the playgrounds of the children and young people of the city?[13]

Russell Wolden, whose homophobic 1959 campaign for mayor had backfired, mailed postcards to supporters that featured a map of "authenticated homosexual hangouts." Above a detail of Children's Playground in Golden Gate Park, Wolden drew a large and ominous question mark.

Gay trysts in California parks were both common enough and sufficiently well known for the state legislature to mount a response to them. By 1950, the long-standing vagrancy code had been amended to include anyone who "loiters in or about public toilets in public parks." In 1955, the statute was again amended to solidify the connection between loitering and deviancy: "every lewd or dissolute person, or every person who loiters in or about public toilets in public parks."[14] The law had the effect of bolstering the legal apparatus of the SFPD's vice officers, with sometimes comical results. One SFPD vice duo consisting of officers Murphy and Gallagher took advantage of their mismatched heights—Murphy was unusually tall and Gallagher unusually short—to simultaneously peer over and under public bathroom stalls in the park.[15] Of course, the misdemeanor charges that resulted from such arrests were no laughing matter for those who sought sex in Golden Gate Park. Although the repeal of California's vagrancy law in 1961 was regarded as a victory for homophile activists, the legislature retained an antiloitering subsection that continued to prohibit loitering around toilets for the purpose of "engaging in or soliciting any lewd or lascivious or any unlawful act."[16]

Despite the aggressive sex surveillance and "crackdowns" of the 1950s, there is no evidence that the use of the park for homosexual encounters diminished.

In fact, given the fierceness with which the bar scene had been corralled, the use of the park for sex may have actually increased during this closeted decade. By 1958, the year in which the SFPD began to report on sex offenses by district, the Richmond District Police Station, which covered most of Golden Gate Park and the district north of the park, had an unusually high number of sex offense arrests, particularly given its quasi-suburban status. Of the nine police districts in San Francisco, Richmond was probably the quietest. Much of the Richmond district was residential and built up during and after World War II. Unlike North Beach or Market Street, it had no history of a street prostitution scene. Yet in 1958, the quiet Richmond station had the third highest number of sex arrests after the Taravel Station, which covered the Sunset and particularly Ocean Beach, where people had sex, and the Mission District. Richmond continued to rank within the top five districts through the 1960s.

The Golden Gate Park Torture Rapist

Melvin Bakkerud, a twenty-one-year old, unemployed body-building drug addict from the Sunset District, changed the course of park history in the summer of 1957. Bakkerud attacked a young couple in the park, raped a young nursing student, and sexually assaulted a nine-year-old girl in a park bathroom. Bakkerud's vicious sex crimes—and the sensational media coverage of the "Golden Gate Park Torture Rapist"—contributed to the transformation of the historic discourse about Golden Gate Park.

Bakkerud had been in trouble with the law frequently as a child, earning juvenile charges for traffic violations, auto theft, and possession of a firearm by the time he was fourteen. His mother sent him off to work on a farm with his brother in New Mexico, where he finished high school; he returned to San Francisco in 1954. Standing at a mere five feet, Bakkerud had compensated by lifting weights and come in second place in a 1955 physique contest, an accomplishment of which he was quite proud, according to his testimony several years later.

In 1956, Bakkerud was in an automobile crash that resulted in a serious head injury. After his operation, he was laid off from his job as a warehouseman and lived with his parents in the Inner Sunset, less than two blocks from Golden Gate Park. While in the hospital, he had developed a drug addiction that made him increasingly irascible. He attacked his father with a small knife, ground out a cigarette butt on his mother's forearm, and wrote notes to himself about his desire to attack girls. His imagination was stimulated by pulp detective novels, which he read compulsively, delighting in passages about binding

FIGURE 4.1. Melvin Bakkerud—"the Golden Gate Park Torture Rapist"—displays his torture kit for reporters, 1957. Courtesy: *San Francisco Chronicle*.

women. One morning in July 1957, after waking up to a fix of heroin and morphine, he read another detective story, this one about a rapist who handcuffed
his victims. He went to the garage and pulled out items from a "torture kit"
he had been assembling, which contained scissors, a safety razor and shaving
cream, two pillowcases, a nylon stocking, a knife, rolls of cord, steel manacles,
and rolls of adhesive tape. Then he headed to Lincoln Boulevard, adjacent to
the park, and found a young couple parked in their car.

Bakkerud yanked open the door of the car and forced the couple to drive
to one of the park's many isolated paths. He beat the man and bound him, and
then turned to the nineteen-year old nursing student, stripped her, beat her
with a belt, cut off her hair, and raped her. "I wanted her hair to look like mine,"
Bakkerud later confessed. The case drew immediate sensational coverage and
so much pressure for a conviction that police first arrested the wrong suspect,
a San Quentin parolee with a record of sex offenses. Bakkerud was arrested
eleven days later on unrelated charges. He was captured South of Market in
possession of drugs he had stolen at a pharmacy, including morphine, codeine,
opium, and Demerol. After his capture, he happily confessed to the crime, as
well as an additional sexual assault on a nine-year-old in a park bathroom.[17]

The exceptionally brutal and well-publicized Bakkerud assaults fueled a
shift in discourse about Golden Gate Park to one that emphasized its potential
for the incubation of pathological behavior—a sharp break from the health pro-
motional discourse that had prevailed since the nineteenth century. During the
1950s and 1960s, local political and business leaders worried about the decline
of the city, fearing that it might follow other more spectacular declines in cities
like Detroit and Pittsburgh. This perception was most evident among several
of the commissioners of the San Francisco Recreation and Park Department
who attempted essentially to reverse McLaren's historic policy of complete,
unfettered access to the park. For example, in response to a perceived increase
in vandalism in the park in 1953, David E. Lewis, the general manager of the
San Francisco Recreation and Park Department, recommended that pedestrian
traffic in Golden Gate Park be dramatically curtailed and that any pedestrian
who "looked suspicious" or loitered could be arrested.[18]

Through the early 1960s, San Franciscans increasingly complained about
the "declining" state of the park, and it was frequently asserted to be a mirror
to—or metaphor for—the purportedly simultaneous process of urban decline.
But it was the Summer of Love that contributed most significantly to changing
ideas about the park. Certainly, some of that sense of the park's decline had
to do with increased foot traffic, garbage, and vagrancy. But one of the most
conspicuous and talked-about changes was in the moral character of the park.
It had, according to many, been taken over by "sex maniacs."

The Summer of Love and the Hedonistic Jungle

The Summer of Love brought new spectacles of sexuality to the streets of the Haight-Ashbury. But the hippie glorification of nature—and the district's proximity to the Panhandle and eastern end of Golden Gate Park—combined to bring the public sexuality of Haight-Ashbury Street to the park. Hippies began gathering in large groups in the Panhandle in 1966. On January 14, 1967, the park's Polo Fields was the site of a gathering of twenty thousand people known as the "Human Be-In," or "A Gathering of the Tribes," billed by the Haight-Ashbury's *Oracle* newspaper as a "joyful Pow-Wow and Peace Dance" and a "union of love and activism."[19] Those who attended took acid, danced, and reveled in the spectacle they had created, as well as the entertainment, which included Allen Ginsberg, Gary Snyder, Timothy Leary, and the musical groups Big Brother and the Holding Company, Jefferson Airplane, and members of Country Joe and the Fish, among others. As first-hand observer Charles Perry wrote: "The speakers from the platform were curiously irrelevant, a slightly absurd center to things—if a center was even necessary." To be sure, previous events had brought hippies together en masse before, including the Trips Festival, the Love Pageant Rally, and the New Year's Wail, but these were much smaller than the Be-In.[20]

Although the SFL brought a small contingent of nude dancers to the Be-In, the event was not—in the main—about sex. It was about taking drugs and experiencing other people. But the event was nonetheless critical in intensifying the eroticism of Golden Gate Park. People began experiencing freedom and the beauty of anonymity in the public space, a lesson that influenced future explicitly erotic uses of the park. More directly, the Human Be-In was a foray into a very different experience from what Hammond Hall had envisioned. For the Be-In crowd, the value of the park was not the appreciation of the beauty of nature— plants, wildlife, trees, flowers—but of other people. "Twenty thousand young people," sixties radical turned sociologist Todd Gitlin has written, "reveled, dropped acid, burned incense, tootled flutes, jingled tambourines, passed out flowers, admired one another, felt the immensity of their collective spectacle."[21] Helen Swick Perry, a student and Be-In participant, recalled that it was not the entertainment, wine, or pot that defined the event but the encounter with strangers. "It was the people that turned me on—the spectacle of people from so many walks of life, some come in curiosity, some in search of something, some in worship of the idea, some to be initiated into a new rite: It was the people being together, unprogrammed, uncommitted, except to life itself and celebration."[22]

It did not take long for that enthusiasm for mutual experience to transmute into sexual freedom. Though the public sexuality of the hippies reached

FIGURE 4.2. Mother holding her child at a Be-In in Speedway Meadows, Golden Gate Park, 1969. Photograph by Robert Altman.

all corners of the park, it was mostly concentrated on and around Hippie Hill, a gentle slope on the eastern end of the Park near the Haight-Ashbury, and in the Panhandle. There nudism and open sexual relations took place with regularity. As Chief Cahill later remembered, "it wasn't uncommon for a gal to come out of the bushes there in the Panhandle without a damn stitch and stand right in front of you with her hands up." "I was out in the Park and two started going to it on the lawn beside me." Contemplating arrest, Cahill remembered, "well, you may as well be looking for a needle in a haystack." Hippies were emboldened by both the spirit of the moment and the inability of the police to catch them "in the act" and became increasingly brazen in their escapades— even in front of the chief of police. The SFPD generally could not stop it. "If you arrested one, you had to arrest a dozen," Cahill remembered. "As long as it was contained and there was no problem and the people in business didn't complain, we just about let them alone."[23]

But people did complain. "The Hippie Problem," as newspapers, older residents, and the Recreation and Park Department described it, consisted of several elements. One was the tendency of hippies to sleep in the park; another was trash; but the biggest problem was the open display of sexuality. Opponents of the hippie migration to the park voiced their concerns at the Recreation and Park Department meeting in May 1968. More than fifty citizens, "most of

FIGURE 4.3. A couple dances on Hippie Hill in Golden Gate Park, 1969. Photograph by Robert Altman.

them middle-aged and older and very angry," according to the *San Francisco Chronicle,* complained that "open acts of sexual relations—both between heterosexuals and homosexuals—are commonplace." Edward Heavey, an attorney and frequent park user, claimed that "a lewd, lascivious, depraved sex maniac" had exposed himself to a fourth-grade teacher and her class. "Women and children may not safely venture into this jungle at any hour of the day or night." According to the meeting minutes, citizens complained about "the 'open bedroom' area of Golden Gate Park; the indecent exposure and nudity; and the pursesnatchers and homosexuals."[24]

Frank Foehr, the exasperated superintendent of parks, demanded that at the very least the hippies should "stay on Hippie Hill," and he allegedly pursued the judicious use of fertilizer on the hill to corral hippies.[25] "They are panhandling and smoking pot all over the place. They strip off and dance."[26] Naturally, they did not stay on Hippie Hill. After the summer solstice of June 1967— which some have marked as the beginning of the Summer of Love—entertainment brought hippies further west to Speedway Meadows, where regular rock concerts were held by a promoter named Teddy Bear and his organization, the Thirteenth Tribe.[27] By 1969, the *Berkeley Barb* declared that in Speedway Meadows "Hedonism" was in "full bloom," long after the Haight-Ashbury Street scene had ended and many hippies had moved on, leaving abandoned storefronts in their wake. But, the *Berkeley Barb* reported, "the Mayor got wind of the free souls who found clothes to be a drag last week and showed the rest of us how beautiful bodies are in the sun. The Mayor (who could be hiding some horrible physical deformity) came down real hard on the Tribe about it."[28] But this was pure hippie badgering, as Mayor Joseph Alioto had been no enemy of free lovers.

In fact, Alioto—an Italian businessman and moderate Democrat, whose term had only just begun in January 1968—proved immune to the shrill complaints of "sin" and "evil" in Golden Gate Park issuing from the city's "square" community. Unjustly vilified then and later by hippies for the SFPD sweep of Haight Street in 1969, Alioto was generally quite affable. Savvier and far less impulsive than his predecessor, Jack Shelley, Alioto rejected park superintendent Foehr's plea to keep hippies contained solely on Hippie Hill. "We will see that everyone has access to the park, as we have seen that the streets will also be kept open." Not satisfied with newspaper accounts of sin, Alioto decided to find out for himself what was going on by taking Sunday afternoon walks in the park. "Saturday and Sunday afternoons," he announced at a May 1968 press conference, "I plan to go down to North Beach, buy a sandwich, and take it into the park to eat while I walk around." The son of a Sicilian immigrant and fish wholesaler, the sandwich-touring mayor made at least five trips to the park that

May in search of what the *San Francisco Chronicle* had described as "lewdness, muggings, pursesnatching, and just plain sin," but he only complained about a lack of trash cans. The "park-prowling Mayor" found that charges of nudity and crime in the park were "greatly exaggerated."[29]

While there was clearly an increase in crime in the park, it was not generally related to either hippies or to sex. As had happened in the Haight-Ashbury, there were those who exploited the free-love ethos and general tolerance of hippies. Rhetorically, the connection between free love and crime was an easy association to make, as opponents of free love frequently did. But it was merely rhetoric. About 60% of the strong-arm robberies, purse snatchings, assaults, and vandalism in the park were committed by juveniles under the age of eighteen, widely believed to be toughs from the Lower Haight-Ashbury and the Western Addition.[30] Experiments in law enforcement abounded, most quietly with the creation of a "silent scooter" patrol in 1970, which featured twelve officers on quiet motorbikes who could sneak up on criminals quickly. Almost seventy felony arrests were made in the first month of the silent scooter patrol.

Ultimately, however, neither strategic fertilizer applications nor stealth motorcycles could contain what the Summer of Love had unleashed. Through the 1970s and into the late 1980s, public sex in Golden Gate Park would only intensify.

Gay Cruising in Golden Gate Park and Beyond

As the spectacle of nude men and women frolicking on Hippie Hill developed, gay men began to openly "cruise" the western end of the park. The day after the first gay march on Polk Street in June 1970, gay liberationists met at Speedway Meadows for the first "Gay In," an event that brought young gays to a part of the city that most of them had never visited. They quickly took advantage of the erotic possibilities of the park's many secluded dells, woods, and restrooms. Open and extensive gay cruising in the park was mostly a product of the culture of radical gay sex, but that culture flourished in part because of changes in the law and its enforcement. As they had on the streets and bars after reaching the contract of accommodation in 1965, gays asserted their radical sexuality in the park, confident that they would not endure the same harassment their predecessors had. But they also benefited enormously from the eleventh-hour passage of the so-called consenting adults bill in 1975.

Authored by then state assemblyman Willie Brown, Jr., and dubbed the "homosexual bill of rights," Assembly Bill 489 decriminalized "adulterous

FIGURE 4.4. Couple at a Be-In at Speedway Meadows, Golden Gate Park, 1969.
Photograph by Robert Altman.

cohabitation," sodomy, and oral copulation. The bill, which Brown had been pushing for at least five years, finally cleared the Assembly in 1975 and then went to an uncertain fate in the Senate. With a twenty-twenty split in the Senate, majority leader George Moscone summoned lieutenant governor Mervyn Dymally back from a trip to Denver just to cast the tie-breaking vote in favor of the bill.[31] The bill was hailed as a long overdue victory by gay rights activists and burnished the already favorable image of Moscone and Brown in the city's growing gay community. But it left the Recreation and Park Department with one less legal tool for preventing the use of public restrooms for public sex.

These legal changes, coupled with the sexual radicalism of gay liberation, transformed the park into a public sex paradise, though it was rarely visible to the public. As Laud Humphreys argued in his now classic 1970 book *Tearoom Trade*, public sex had rarely been fully public, as people relied on sometimes cryptic signals to avoid "coming on" to potentially hostile straights. Indeed, SFPD incident reports from September 1976 suggest that arresting officers were not confronted by the spectacle of gay sex in public restrooms, but rather sought out visual confirmation of its existence. For example, when a Richmond Station officer was ordered to patrol the public restroom at Forty-first and JFK Drive on the western end of the park—a well-known cruising spot—the only immediately visible cue of illegal activity was the unlikely concentration of parked cars in front of the bathroom. After tying his horse to a tree, the officer walked along a path to the rear of the bathroom, where he peered through a window that was four feet above the ground. There he could clearly observe the "obscenities" taking place, which he did for "approximately 30 seconds."[32]

To be sure, there was no unanimity within the gay community on the appropriateness of public sex. For example, in response to the highly publicized indecency arrest of Mississippi congressman John Hinson in a House of Representatives restroom in 1981, Eric Jay of the gay newspaper the *Washington Blade,* excoriated the gay record on public sex. Jay wrote that if gays did not "come to terms" with the issue of public sex, "we are doomed to frustration in attempting to overcome the public's perception of us, to say nothing about adding to the burdens of our supportive friends and families and to the tension between us and our Gay sisters." "The fact of the matter," Jay continued, "is that we are not living any longer in the 1950s." Public sex was simply "indefensible."[33]

The AIDS epidemic and the closure of the bathhouses would temporarily transform the nature of the sexual uses of the park. While AIDS increased the risks involved in the encounters, the closure of the bathhouses likely made them more common, particularly in the early years before people realized the extent of the epidemic. In neighboring Buena Vista Park in the Haight-Ashbury, for

FIGURE 4.5. This public restroom at 41st Avenue and JFK Drive in Golden Gate Park became an active site for gay sex in the early 1970s. Photograph by author.

example, 1984 bathhouse closures led to a trebling of gay trysts the following year, according to Park Station officer Bob Del Torre. The extent to which San Francisco's gay men had come to recognize "quasi-public" sex as a right was evident in the responses of challenges to curb the Buena Vista Park scene. "I don't think we are infringing on people's rights," said one thirty-two-year old park cruiser. "We are pretty discreet and don't cruise where the kids and public are." He compared the park to a neighborhood bar or a Playboy Club. "It's a ridiculous issue. These are modern times, an age of sexual freedom."[34]

In fact, in the heyday of gay cruising in the park, homosexuals were more likely to be the victims of violence than the perpetrators of it. At the "waste-land" at Ocean Beach on the western end of the park, antigay violence became an increasingly common phenomenon in the 1970s. In June 1974, a popu-lar transgender entertainer named Jae Stevens was stabbed to death at Thirty-fourth Avenue in the park, about ten blocks east of the wasteland; and two gay men were found stabbed to death in the heart of the wasteland at Ocean Beach that year.[35]

But neither gays nor lesbians reduced their public sexual excursions to Golden Gate Park. As gay men in particular continued to find sexual rendezvous in Collingwood Park and Buena Vista Park, in the Castro and the Haight-Ashbury, respectively, both gay men and lesbians began to explore the varied physical and cultural geography of neighboring regions of northern California. During the 1970s, gay men created a quasi-private sexual landscape near San Gregorio State Beach, about one hour's drive south of San Francisco. After making their way down several treacherous trails, gay couples and single cruisers built cabanas or "condos" out of piles of driftwood, or sheltered under a collapsing railroad trestle. Providing privacy and a windbreak, the structures also allowed for "gay creativity," as one patron remembered. Regarded as little more than a public sex venue for telescoping homeowners nearby, San Gregorio was much more to its patrons; it was a place to explore sexual freedom, but also to forge lifelong relationships. "It was as if Beach Blanket Bingo," a patron remembered, referencing the 1965 film, "had finally been released in Living Gay."

About an hour north of San Francisco, gays and lesbians also created a new nudist colony at Hacienda Beach on the Russian River and a seasonal gay resort in the river town of Guerneville in western Sonoma County. A nineteenth-century resort area for San Francisco's Irish and Italian communities that had become rather rough-and-tumble by the early 1970s, the Russian River and the town of Guerneville first attracted gays and lesbians after a man named Peter Pender opened Fife's, the area's first gay resort, in 1978. One early patron later recalled: "At night at Fife's, men would leave the doors of their cabins open, just in case a passing stranger wanted to drop by.... I'd have sex with someone and I'd never learn their name."[36] Gays and lesbians found sexual gratification among the ancient redwoods of the Russian River, laid claim to yet another public space, and simultaneously reinvigorated the tourist economy of the once flagging region.[37]

5

TAKING BACK
THE STREETS OF
SAN FRANCISCO

"I am not going to be forced out of San Francisco by splinter groups of radicals, social deviates and incorrigibles," Dan White wrote in his campaign literature in 1977. The supervisorial candidate tapped into longtime residents' festering resentment. "You must realize that there are thousands upon thousands of frustrated angry people such as yourselves waiting to unleash a fury that can and will eradicate the malignancies which blight our beautiful city."[1] White was exceptionally incendiary, but his message was pedestrian: more San Franciscans shared his views than is commonly believed, and they organized with increasing effectiveness through the late 1970s.

San Franciscans invested in rolling back the perceived excesses of the sexual revolution were certainly not all of one stripe. Christian moralists made little ground statewide after the defeat of the 1966 CLEAN initiative, and by the 1970s, they maintained a very low profile in San Francisco. A handful of sandwich-boarding preachers continued to excoriate sinners, whoremongers, and sodomites on Market Street, but even the most hardened moralists recognized them for the crackpots they were. Far more effective were municipal leaders' campaigns to legislate limitations on public spectacles of sex. They approached purported obscenities as symptoms of urban decline, the process of urban divestment that plagued many cities during the 1960s and 1970s. An economically diverse city whose fate was never as closely tied to the manufacturing sector as that of many other American cities, San Francisco nonetheless shared the escalating rates of crime typical of

American cities during the era. As a result, supervisors, city planners, the SFPD, and, most prominently, Dianne Feinstein sought new ways to reduce the spectacles of decay, of which prostitution and pornography were often the most visible symbols. Meanwhile, in the provincial world of San Francisco's ethnic neighborhoods, violence prevailed. Unable or unwilling to recognize the complicated nature of the city's transformation during the 1970s, young men from these neighborhoods physically assaulted and sometimes killed gays, lesbians, and hippies because of their nontraditional behaviors, lifestyles, or appearances.

Meanwhile, Hollywood began to reflect and reinforce the story of San Francisco's unique depravity to national audiences. Beginning in the late 1960s, film directors increasingly chose San Francisco as the locale in which to tell a dark story of America's sexual revolution. The city welcomed the enormous cash influx that accompanied blockbuster film production, and Mayor Joseph Alioto created the Film Production Office to streamline the city's historically cumbersome permitting process. But here was the rub: not only did most films depict San Francisco as a city overrun by sex radicals but they also portrayed most sex radicals as violent deviants. Like local critics of the sexual revolution in San Francisco—though much more self-consciously—film directors like Don Siegel, Paul Schrader, and Stuart Rosenberg conflated sex radicalism with predatory violence. In their case, however, this portrayal purely served the purpose of entertainment: it created a context in which the unchecked violence of the smut-busting vigilante was glorified. But the box office success of these films had the unintended and remarkable effect of legitimizing not only the tough talk of the sexual counterrevolutionary but also the deployment of physical violence to restore the moral balance of society. Popular culture, in short, turned on San Francisco, and the political consequences of this turn would become fully evident by the 1980s.

The Anti-smut Ascendancy at City Hall

Although Jack Shelley had been mercilessly ridiculed for dragging Carol Doda and her scantily clad cohort to jail in 1965, he continued to quietly pursue strategies to prevent San Francisco from being "wide open," even as he dealt with the much more pressing problems of a public nurses' strike and a race riot in Bayview–Hunters Point. After the topless trial acquittals, Shelley sent his public service director, Bill Roddy, on a nighttime walking tour of downtown pornography stores to assess the volume of "objectionable" material. Roddy found a whole lot of it. But Cahill was already on the case, pursuing obscenity charges against one of the larger local distributors, ultimately dislodging him from his tenancy of a Market Street storefront.[2] Indeed, in the final years of his career, Cahill increasingly operated independently of the mayor's office and with surprisingly little oversight. Late in 1968, fewer than two years before his retirement, Cahill took the unprecedented step of arresting male prostitutes in San Francisco.[3]

As Joseph Alioto's 1968 sandwich tours of Golden Gate Park proved, he and Shelley were men cut from different cloths. Both were Catholics, Democrats, and native San Franciscans; Alioto had far greater executive and political experience than Shelley. Having chaired the Redevelopment Agency in 1955, directed the Rice Growers' Association of California, and cofounded the First San Francisco Bank, Alioto quickly rose to prominence in the California Democratic Party.[4] When Shelley bowed out of the mayoral race in 1967, citing "health concerns," it was generally understood that Democrats in Sacramento had leaned heavily on him to withdraw. Once elected, Alioto invested a great deal of his time and energy in the redevelopment and expansion of the downtown area, including the massive Embarcadero project and the construction of the Transamerica pyramid building, the city's tallest building, opened in 1972.[5] Unlike Shelley, Alioto was tolerant of diverse tastes and made no effort to rein in pornography in the city, despite steady badgering by the president of the Board of Supervisors, Dianne Feinstein.[6]

Born in San Francisco in 1933 to a former model and a prominent UCSF surgeon, Feinstein quickly ascended California's political ladder, earning a post at the California Woman's Parole Board shortly after graduating from Stanford University. She ran for the Board of Supervisors in 1969 at the age of thirty-six and received the most votes in the city-wide election, catapulting her automatically to the position of president of the board, a position she would occupy again in 1974–1975 and yet again in 1978. In 1970, Feinstein met with city attorney Thomas M. O'Connor to discuss drafting an ordinance forbidding the purchase or display of pornographic films in San Francisco, but the ordinance was rejected by fellow supervisors who knew that it would not stand up to a court test of constitutionality. But Feinstein would not be so easily deterred; she began marshalling influential allies and mounted her first mayoral campaign against Alioto in 1971.

Crime continued to rise and smut continued to spread, and Feinstein exploited the coincidence in a January 1971 *New York Times* interview. In a seven page Sunday magazine exclusive, Feinstein—described as an "attractive brunette"—complained that San Francisco had "become a kind of smut capital of the United States."[7] In addition, she led a walking tour of San Francisco porno shops, hosting a press conference to call attention to the extent of smut.

She quickly drew the support of John Barbagelata, a real estate magnate and Republican supervisor; the head of the SFPD vice detail, Lieutenant Gerald Shaughnessy; and the chief of the SFPD, Alfred J. Nelder. Nelder had already raided the Mitchell Brothers on numerous occasions but had never secured a conviction. Meanwhile, Feinstein talked tough with her gay supporters: "Porno movie houses and bookstores and smut papers," she warned gay voters at an SIR meeting in May 1971, "are making it harder for the gay community to become part of the accepted mainstream of America." In an interview in *Ladies' Home Journal* seven years later, she said: "The right of an individual to live as he or she chooses can become offensive—the gay community is going to have to face this. It's fine for us to live here respecting each other's lifestyles, but that doesn't mean imposing them on others."[8]

As a direct result of Feinstein's rising influence, Alioto adopted an uncharacteristically authoritarian tone in the months leading up to the mayoral election. Claiming the law-and-order high ground for himself, he decried Feinstein's proposal to create an independent police commission. He warned an audience at a Chamber of Commerce luncheon not to "let anybody interfere with your police department." "There's a volcanic undercurrent in San Francisco, beautiful as it is. It's better to have somebody with toughness of mind and toughness of spirit to keep that from erupting." Feinstein, he argued, was "pressured and influenced by the lunatic fringe of the left." His campaign advertisements also claimed that "children and mothers are safer in Golden Gate Park" than when he took office. Feinstein staked her own ground, "This is not a safe city." "If I'm elected mayor, we are going to serve notice on the pusher, the mugger and the thief and we're going to break the back of crime in this city once and for all."[9] Although Alioto easily won reelection in 1971, Feinstein not only dramatically raised her political profile but also forged a new political identity as a socially conservative Democrat.

Alioto's record of tolerance was vindicated by the findings of the San Francisco Committee on Crime, a nonpartisan analysis group that released a report on "non-victim crimes" in 1971. The report criticized the shortsighted devotion of scarce SFPD resources to victimless crimes like prostitution. The committee found that while only 13% of the killings, rapes, robberies, and assaults were solved in 1969, 50% of all arrests, and 54% of the jail occupancy, were for nonvictim crimes, including indecency and prostitution.[10] Similarly, the committee argued, the targeting of gay men for indecency arrests was a waste of resources. Although the committee struck a balance, arguing that "few respectable citizens care to look upon the exposed view of vice, and they should not have to," it unabashedly recommended a relaxed enforcement policy for "discreet" off-street prostitution.[11]

Moreover, the committee explained, law enforcement should follow public sentiment. While there was a consensus among the city's disparate populations about the evil of "crimes of violence," there was much less of one about "drinking, gambling, prostitution, homosexuality, adultery, abortion, pornography and the use of drugs." Because "all the world loves San Francisco" because it was not "straight-laced," it was essential to protect the city's reputation as "tolerant, free, with room for every taste."[12] Unless a citizen impinged on or injured others, the committee concluded, he should be "left free to conduct his life in his own way, to 'go to hell in handbasket' or to heaven in his chariot, to act the fool as others see it."[13]

Chief Nelder was "flabbergasted" by the committee's findings and rejected them wholesale. "There is no such thing as discreet prostitution." Nelder also rejected the committee's recommendation to erase remaining statutes against homosexuality because it would make it more difficult to prosecute male prostitution. To the committee's recommendation that the continued sale of pornography to adults be permitted, Nelder responded: "You have to regard this as a nefarious business which portrays degrading and illegal sex acts and which uses juveniles, drug addicts and mentally disturbed persons in its portrayals." Feinstein shared Nelder's chagrin, arguing that the findings had "no connection to what is really taking place in San Francisco."[14] And so Feinstein went back to the business of trying to prosecute smut. With Barbagelata's strong support, Feinstein lobbied successfully in 1973 for an ordinance forbidding the display of signs or pictures that showed nude bodies, an achievement that significantly diminished the public nature of sexual spectacle that had prevailed in North Beach for most of the previous decade.[15] For his part, Alioto remained unperturbed by the city's alleged transgressions: "If you like the city," he said toward the end of his administration, "you have to take what the city has. It involves dirt, it involves some measure of pollution, prostitution and crime.... You don't expect Walden Pond; if you like that better, you better go to Walden Pond."[16] Truer words were never spoken, but they were not the words Feinstein and her supporters wanted to hear.

The election of 1975 marked a decisive turning point in the history of sexual politics in the city. When the well-qualified and famously charming George Moscone announced his candidacy, most regarded him as a shoo-in. Having served on the Board of Supervisors between 1963 and 1966, he rose through the ranks of the California Democratic Party as a state senator, closely allied with the "Burton Machine," which included liberal legislators John and Phillip Burton and Assembly speaker Willie Brown, with whom Moscone had authored the "consenting adults bill." But it was Moscone's battle for the lesser political role of mayor that proved to be his most bruising. Polls conducted one month before the election showed Moscone and Feinstein neck and neck, with Barbagelata at a distant fourth after state senator Milton Marks. Moscone's campaign literature, which compared his record only to Feinstein's, misjudged not only his competition but the issues as well. It primarily emphasized his strengths in the realm of personal liberties, extolling his participation in the consulting adults bill and liberalizing marijuana laws. By contrast, the literature read, Feinstein had only "led battles against 'dirty movie' advertisements in San Francisco newspapers."[17]

But Barbagelata, a former airline executive and local real estate mogul, sensed the mood, particularly among older San Franciscans, and zeroed in on several issues. His political career was triggered by his revulsion toward "the mess in the Haight," and he claimed to live by two "commandments": "Love God and secondly, Love Your Neighborhood."[18] A consummate businessman, he deplored the financial mismanagement of the city, raising the specter of the recently bankrupted city of New York; he rode the rising wave of antilabor sentiment that had swelled in the wake of a police and firemen's strike during Alioto's administration; and he deplored crime and particularly "public displays" of sexuality. He went on record as opposing the Polk Street fair, saying he didn't like "public displays" of any sort. When asked at a preelection brunch hosted by prominent gays whether he applied the same standard to the Chinese New Year festival, he responded: "No, that's a traditional thing. A bunch of people running around with dragons....I don't like sex displays on streets." He had worked closely with Feinstein on the passage of antibarking and antinewsstand ordinances. "I went out and cleaned up Broadway. Little kids could walk on Broadway on the way to school and to the shops in that area."[19]

To the shock and chagrin of both Moscone and Feinstein, Barbagelata's message resonated with a great many San Franciscans. When the results were in, Moscone had won a plurality with 66,672 votes, with Barbagelata taking 40,842 votes to Feinstein's 39,610. Because 1975 was the first year in which pluralities triggered automatic runoffs, Moscone would have to go toe-to-toe with Barbagelata in December. Moscone beat Barbagelata, but the margin was telling of the changing mood in San Francisco: with 200,804 of the 302,344 registered voters turning out, Moscone's margin of victory was only about forty-three hundred votes.[20] "He didn't win by a mandate when he should have won decisively," John Burton later recalled of Moscone. "There were old San Franciscans being vituperative toward him because of his position on issues like gays and race— guys he went to high school with. These people saw the world changing and didn't understand it....What you don't understand, you don't like."[21] Nonetheless, Moscone quickly set out to advance the social liberalism in San Francisco that had earned him accolades among his peers in the state Senate.

In November, thirty-six-year-old liberal Joseph Freitas handily beat the incumbent and became district attorney. Born in 1939 to a Catholic Portuguese family in the rural town of Merced in San Joaquin Valley, Freitas moved into politics quickly after graduating from college, becoming staff director of the Bay Area Urban League in neighboring Oakland—an unlikely position for a white man.[22] Within two months of becoming district attorney, Freitas effectively decriminalized prostitution in the city, declaring that his office would no longer actively pursue prostitution convictions. The staggering result of this policy shift was that a flood of prostitutes poured into the city.

Rounding out Moscone's liberal administration was the reelection of Richard Hongisto as sheriff and the appointment of Charles Gain as chief of police. Hongisto grew up in the Richmond and Fillmore districts, and his parents were shopkeepers in Visitacion Valley, a neighborhood undergoing a massive racial transformation that horrified locals like Dan White but inspired a different reaction in Hongisto. After he joined the SFPD in 1961, Hongisto was one of a few lone white SFPD officers who supported the Officers for Justice Campaign as it pursued the racial integration of the police force. When first elected to the sheriff's post in 1971, he had appointed the first openly gay deputy and actively recruited racial minorities.[23] When Moscone appointed Gain, who quickly supported Freitas's nonprosecution stance toward prostitution and would infamously appear at the Hooker's Ball in 1977, Moscone sent an unmistakable signal that the gains of both race and sex liberals would not be rolled back by counterrevolutionaries.

The great prostitute in-migration of 1976 galvanized antismut forces in San Francisco as nothing yet had. Most influential was the Hotel Employers Association, a professional association representing more than forty area hotels and wielding enormous clout; many of the executives on the board of this organization also sat on the board of the San Francisco Convention and Visitors Bureau. During the deluge of 1976, the Hotel Employers Association, the Chamber of Commerce, the Market Street Merchants, and other powerful downtown interests co-opted the language of the era's social movements and organized under a faux-grassroots umbrella group that called itself the Tenderloin Citizens Committee. In a remarkable statement that fused constitutional rhetoric about citizens' "unalienable [sic] rights" to life, liberty, and the pursuit of happiness with Rooseveltian rhetoric about "freedom from" unsightly spectacles, this organization asserted its constituents' "right" to "streets free of prostitution," "streets free of narcotics," and "streets free of garbage."[24] Demanding that City Hall and the SFPD reverse the tolerance of prostitution, hoteliers in the Tenderloin began their own crusade by photographing suspected prostitutes in their lobbies and on the sidewalks and distributing the photographs among other hoteliers to create a united front.[25]

Certainly, on the face of it, there was nothing unreasonable about hoteliers' desire to keep prostitutes away from their hotels. But their moral outrage was the most flagrant hypocrisy. While the Hotel Employers Association insisted that sex businesses "degrade and cheapen San Francisco," it was an open secret that hotel patrons and conventioneers regularly patronized prostitutes and sex businesses.[26] As prostitutes' rights advocate Priscilla Alexander observed, "a significant number" of traveling conventioneers "feel that a visit to a strange city is not complete without a visit to a prostitute." Hoteliers not only were aware of the practice but frequently encouraged bellboys to provide references to "high-class" call girls to inquiring male guests.[27] According to Margo St. James, another prostitute rights activist, who arguably knew more about San Francisco prostitution than anyone, some SFPD officers moonlighted as security guards in hotels, doubling as "pimps or procurers" for guests.[28] Ultimately, hoteliers were not opposed to prostitution per se; they were opposed merely to the spectacle of "low-class" and African American prostitutes who walked the street, potentially undercutting their vested interest in the prostitution business. "If she is Black, or if she is garishly dressed," Alexander observed, "or if she is seen as being too noisy, or drunk, she is more likely to be stopped than if she is elegantly dressed."[29]

As they always had, opponents of prostitution exploited general crime trends to make their case about the dangers of tolerating prostitution. But it had never been so easy. At the end of Moscone's first year in office, aggravated assaults had increased by 22% from the previous year, auto thefts by 16%, and burglaries by 25%.[30] The fact that there was absolutely no evidence—nor was it at all likely—that this increase was related to the lenient prostitution policy did not stop foes of prostitution from exploiting the figures. Supervisor Quentin Kopp quickly seized on the issues, blaming the rise in crime on the "confusing dialogue about victimless crimes....That confusion," Kopp asserted, "was a signal to people engaged in prostitution to come to San Francisco. Now prostitution brings other crime."[31]

As political pressure mounted for a crackdown on prostitution, San Francisco prostitutes gained something they had never had: an advocate, in an eccentric woman named Margo St. James who founded the first prostitutes' rights group, COYOTE—Call Off Your Old Tired Ethics—on Mother's Day, 1973. Born in Bellingham, Washington, in 1937, St. James had migrated to San Francisco with her infant son after a divorce in 1959, held an eclectic array of occupations, started her own company—Margo's Miracle Maids—and acquired a California private investigator's license. A teetotaler, she also claimed to have jogged down every street in San Francisco, and she had set several records for mountain running. But her politicization came after she was accused and convicted on charges of prostitution, though she adamantly denied the charges. Hostile to both male treatment of prostitutes and feminists' contempt for them, St. James became an activist for the decriminalization of prostitution and ultimately provided legal, educational, medical, and financial services for prostitutes through COYOTE.

St. James's most lasting achievement was her single-handed defeat of the prostitute quarantine policy, which had been in effect since Dullea implemented it in 1944. Having complained to the SFDPH in 1974 to no avail, St. James hired Nancy Roscoe, an attorney at the offices of Michael Stepanian, an attorney Margo knew from his days as a doorman at a North Beach night club, who would go on to be a high-profile advocate for medical marijuana patients.[32] In 1975, Roscoe convinced a local judge to issue an injunction forbidding the SFPD's historic, odious practice. The repeal of the preliminary quarantine policy not only represented a radical assertion of prostitutes' rights but also vastly increased their visibility and mobility, now that their legal situation had become far less capricious.

Though St. James enjoyed very close relationships with both Moscone and Gain, she could not dissuade them from responding to the mounting antiprostitution pressure exerted by Kopp, Feinstein, the Hotel Employers Association, and the Tenderloin Citizens Committee. In December 1976, just eleven months after the new laissez-faire prostitution policy had gone into effect, Freitas and Gain terminated it, announcing that they would now vigorously prosecute prostitutes and pimps. Immediately, the SFPD conducted raids in North Beach, the Tenderloin, the Western Addition, and particularly Union Square, which had been most transformed by the policy. "Protecting" Union Square remained a high priority, as it had been in the case of Sally Rand.[33]

Meanwhile, Feinstein began to make headway in her plan to reduce the quantity, availability, and visibility of pornography in San Francisco. She was particularly smitten with the "Anti–Skid Row Ordinance" the Detroit City Council had implemented in 1972. In an attempt to check an expanding cluster of sex shops on Detroit's West Eight Mile Road, the authors of the ordinance had entirely sidestepped the problematic legal issues surrounding obscenity and morality, citing instead the deleterious "secondary effects" of such business congregations. In a novel approach, they argued that the increased traffic and crime that verifiably accompanied the expanding cluster of businesses warranted zoning restrictions of the type that already existed for industrial and other special uses, and established the following restrictions: no new sex businesses could be established within one thousand feet of an existing sex business, and every new sex business required owners to obtain the approval of 51% of the residents within a five-hundred-foot radius of the prospective site in residential areas. It was a simple solution that was utterly effective: by 1977, the number of topless bars on West Eight Mile Road was halved, and the number of bookstores and theaters was significantly reduced.[34]

The success of the Detroit "dispersal" approach stood in glaring contrast to Boston's strategy of containment in its Combat Zone. In the early 1960s, the Boston Redevelopment Agency had embarked on an extensive renewal project in Scollay Square that had dislodged the area's long-standing commercial sex establishments, most of which then moved to the lower Washington Street area, which was quickly dubbed the "Combat Zone." Concerned that the spread of sex businesses beyond the Combat Zone would derail redevelopment and threaten downtown real estate development, but unable to implement a Detroit-style plan because of Boston's relatively small size and preponderance of residential areas, the Redevelopment Agency proposed containing all sex-related businesses in the Combat Zone. Approved by the Boston Zoning Commission in 1974, the ordinance even included $2 million in redevelopment money to draw visitors to the city's officially sanctioned adult entertainment zone. Within months of implementation, however, it was clear that the Combat Zone ordinance was a complete failure. The apparent civic endorsement of illicit activities created a documented crime wave that culminated tragically in the 1976 slaying of Harvard football player Andrew Puopolo by a pickpocketing prostitute's "muscle men."[35] For sex district opponents nationwide, Boston's notorious Combat Zone became an example not only of the wickedness of sex districts in general but also of the folly of the containment strategy in particular.

In San Francisco, the city's legal counsel instructed Feinstein to wait until the Detroit ordinance passed the constitutionality test of the U.S. Supreme Court before introducing such a plan in San Francisco. In the meantime, Feinstein found ideological and logistical support among Bay Area feminists, although she did not publicly identify herself as a feminist and had even run afoul of feminists on a number of occasions.[36] The most prominent feminist organization to aid Feinstein's campaign was Women Against Violence in Pornography and Media (WAVPM), which had been founded simultaneously in several cities and whose immediate impetus was the release of the 1976 film *Snuff,* which purportedly showed the real murder and evisceration of a young woman. Although WAVPM initially limited its activism to eradicating pornography that depicted women being "bound, raped, tortured, or murdered for sexual stimulation," it quickly expanded its scope to include all pornography. This programmatic shift was consistent with the increasingly popular belief among cultural feminists—most closely associated with activist, writer, and

WAVPM member Andrea Dworkin—that pornography, by its very nature, inflicted violence on women by objectifying their bodies.[37] Beginning in 1976, WAVPM staged numerous picketing actions in North Beach, culminating in the Take Back the Night March on November 18, 1978, in which more than five thousand women marched down Broadway in protest of the district's objectification of women. "For thirty minutes," one reporter wrote of the 1978 march, "Broadway, between Columbus and Kearny, belonged to the women."[38]

Though undoubtedly meaningful to the marchers, who frequently described the emotional impact of momentarily claiming the space of the notorious district for themselves, WAVPM's Broadway marches had no appreciable effect on sex businesses. Yet behind the scenes, feminists did contribute concretely to the legal campaign against the spread of pornography in San Francisco. Most influential was Laura Lederer, director of WAVPM and the Berkeley Women's Center, whose father was the commissioner of buildings and safety in Detroit and had worked vigorously for the Detroit ordinance. Lederer and Feinstein met regularly to prepare a comparable ordinance in San Francisco. Lederer traveled to Detroit, conducting interviews with city officials and collecting data on the effectiveness of the ordinance, which she then passed along to Feinstein. Correspondence between the two women suggests that Lederer's research was influential in shaping Feinstein's final proposal for an antipornography zoning ordinance in San Francisco.[39]

Feinstein, Lederer, and others monitored the Detroit situation closely as challenges to the ordinance wound their way through the courts. Finally, in 1976, the U.S. Supreme Court upheld its constitutionality in their landmark decision in *Young v. American Mini Theaters*.[40] Shortly after the *Young* decision, Feinstein pushed through a four-month moratorium on the issuance of permits for sex businesses as she worked on a more permanent solution. That came in January 1977: the proposal of an ordinance—virtually identical to Detroit's—that prohibited new sex businesses from operating within a thousand feet of existing sex businesses and fewer than five hundred feet from residential areas. The plan received immediate and enthusiastic support from downtown hotel, tourism, and real estate interests, most conspicuously the Hotel Employers Association and the Travelers Aid Society. Marjorie Montelius, executive director of the latter, heartily endorsed Feinstein's plan, arguing that "anything less than total closure" of adult bookstores, theaters, and encounter studios in the Tenderloin, "is a compromise." The San Francisco Board of Realtors pleaded with the Board of Supervisors to adopt Feinstein's ordinance, so that they might repair the badly "damaged character of our city."[41]

But many San Franciscans strongly opposed Feinstein's plan. Most obviously opposed were sex business owners, who portrayed Feinstein and her backers as a small minority trying to impose their puritanical values on the cosmopolitan city. Harvey Milk derided the "hypocrisy" and "demagoguery" of the supervisors. "Bookstores," he scolded, "don't create crime."[42] And the San Francisco chapter of the American Civil Liberties Union (ACLU) opposed the ordinance on the grounds that it was really an attack on the First Amendment "wrapped in the cloth of a zoning regulation." "Whatever the merits of restricting the right to read and participate in private sexual activity may be in Detroit," Arthur Brunwasser of the San Francisco ACLU wrote, "this is San Francisco and we suggest that our policy be adopted with full respect for the Constitutional rights of free speech and privacy."[43] The most unexpected and formidable opponents of Feinstein's ordinance were the African American mothers of the Bayview–Hunters Point Neighborhood Association, who viewed the ordinance as a threat to their already beleaguered community.

As Feinstein and supporters of the proposed ordinance intended, the stipulation that sex businesses be located at least five hundred feet from residential areas greatly limited the number of places in the city where such businesses could relocate. In addition to parts of Potrero Hill and the South of Market area, the most likely location for relocating sex businesses was Bayview–Hunters Point, which had long stretches of industrial and warehouse buildings along and adjacent to its main thoroughfare, Third Street. Hunter's Point also had a sizeable residential population, particularly in the large public housing developments adjoining the naval shipyard, where many African Americans had worked during World War II. Already physically isolated from central San Francisco on a hilltop on the far southeastern edge of the city, Bayview–Hunters Point was also besieged by a wave of crime and poverty and had been the epicenter of the 1966 race riots. Thus, when the African American women of the Bayview–Hunters Point Neighborhood Association heard about the creation of what critics were calling a "porno zone" in their neighborhood, they appealed to Feinstein, supervisor Peter Tamaras, and their pro-ordinance allies to reconsider. Appearing before a meeting of the Supervisors' Planning, Housing, and Development Committee, Bayview–Hunters Point resident Enola Maxwell exclaimed, "We already have enough combat zones where we are." "We're out there fighting, and we don't want to start another war where we are."[44]

Bolstering the objections of the Bayview–Hunters Point residents were the members of the City Planning Commission, who concurred that the distance-from-residence stipulation would have the effect of simply relocating "porno zones" from one area of the city to another rather than breaking up the "degrading concentration" of sex businesses, Feinstein's expressed intention.[45] Ultimately, Feinstein decided to drop the distance-from-residence stipulation, retaining only the injunction that no new sex business be built within a thousand feet of another. In September 1978, the Board of Supervisors, citing the "adverse effects of [the] proliferation and concentration of adult entertainment establishments," unanimously approved resolution no. 8064, establishing a watered-down version of the Detroit ordinance in San Francisco. After a struggle that spanned almost eight years, Supervisor Feinstein and her supporters had finally scored a victory against smut.

Murdering Robert Hillsborough

In the early hours of Wednesday, June 22, 1977, Robert Hillsborough, a professional gardener who spent most mornings planting rainbows of hyacinths at one of San Francisco's finest children's playgrounds, was savagely murdered in the Mission, making him the nineteenth gay man killed in as many months because of his homosexuality.[46] His young Latino assailant stabbed him fifteen times, piercing his heart, lungs, and liver, and left him to bleed to death at Nineteenth and Lexington. Pensive and mild-mannered, Hillsborough seemed like the last person anyone would have expected to die so violently. It was partly the horrible incongruity between Hillsborough's serene life and ghastly death that made his name a rallying cry for gay activists both locally and nationally. Widespread outrage among gays and lesbians in San Francisco contributed to an unprecedented attendance of 250,000 at that weekend's Gay Freedom Day Parade, making it the largest demonstration for gay liberation that had ever taken place in the United States. A makeshift shrine on the steps of City Hall, adorned with many of the floral varieties Hillsborough loved so much, became the virtual wailing wall of the 1977 Gay Freedom Day Parade.[47]

After an evening out on the town with his lover, Jerry Taylor, the thirty-three-year-old Hillsborough had pulled his light blue Land Rover into a late-night hamburger stand known as the Whiz-Burger on Eighteenth Street and South Van Ness, just blocks from their apartment on Nineteenth and Lexington. After receiving their food, Hillsborough and Taylor sat in their car, ate, and hugged. A waitress at the Whizburger testified that the four assailants—John Cordova, nineteen, Thomas Spooner, twenty-one, Michael Chavez, twenty, and Richard Ojeda, sixteen—got out of their car, apparently to confront Hillsborough and Taylor for their public display of homosexuality. Shouting "faggot," Cordova punched Hillsborough repeatedly through the opened driver-side window. Hillsborough backed quickly out of the lot, shouted "Fuck you, you fucking punk," and swerved out onto Eighteenth to head home. Apparently unbeknownst to either Hillsborough and Taylor, the assailants gave chase, attacking them when they got out of their car at their apartment building. When Taylor

FIGURE 5.1. On the eve of the 1977 Gay Pride Parade, mourners gather at a makeshift shrine on the steps of City Hall for Robert Hillsborough while SFPD officers look on. Photograph by Don Eckert.

did not fight back, the teens turned their rage to Hillsborough, who struggled in vain to fight them off. In a final savage moment, Cordova pulled out a knife and began stabbing Hillsborough to death. "Oh my god," Hillsborough gasped in his last words, "what are you doing to me?"

What Cordova was doing to Robert Hillsborough—according to Hillsborough's friends and family, contemporary gay activists, pundits, thousands of Gay Freedom Day participants, Mayor George Moscone, and subsequent scholars—was the inevitable outcome of a national crusade against homosexuality that had been launched several months earlier in Dade County, Florida.[48] In February 1977, in response to the demands of Miami's small gay population in Coconut Grove, the Dade County Commission had passed an ordinance barring discrimination against homosexuals in housing, employment, and public accommodations. Anita Bryant, a thirty-seven-year old mother of four and a nationally known singer who had become a spokeswoman for Florida Orange Juice, had immediately challenged the ordinance. She quickly found a new role as founding leader of Save Our Children, Inc., an antigay group whose members shared her belief that laws protecting homosexuals would force schools to hire gay teachers who would use their positions to proselytize and molest schoolchildren. Required to collect only ten thousand petition signatures to force the law to a ballot for a referendum, Bryant's group collected more than six times that number. More important, during the four months between the passage of the ordinance and the referendum of June 7, Bryant's high profile forced the issue of homosexuality into the national spotlight, making it one of the top media stories of 1977. Bryant's crusade also politicized gays nationwide, and gay communities from New York to San Francisco joined "Miami Support Committees," donated hard-earned money for the campaign, and boycotted Florida orange juice.[49]

On the day before the Dade County referendum, California state senator John Briggs, from Fullerton in Orange County—one of the few California counties that had passed the 1966 CLEAN initiative—flew to Miami to lend his support to the Bryant campaign. Warning Miami voters about the danger of "the San Francisco influence," he vowed to carry Bryant's fight back to California.[50] Bob Green, Bryant's husband and manager, also warned that failure to reverse the ordinance would mean "Dade County will become like San Francisco where many 'gays' dominate daily life."[51] Voters in Dade County repealed the ordinance by a of two-to-one margin—a blow to advocates of gay rights in Florida and nationwide; on the following day, Briggs stood on the steps of City Hall in San Francisco and announced the "Briggs Initiative"—Proposition 6—to ban homosexuals from teaching in California schools. "San Francisco," Briggs told the crowd, "is the fountainhead of all homosexual activity in the country. It is in a captured-nation status, and the people want to be liberated."[52]

In the months leading up to the general election, Briggs skillfully wove together the strands of rhetorical populism and moral and fiscal conservatism that would become the hallmark of the Reagan revolution. Citing both the moral decline of California and the vindication of the recent property tax–cutting measure Proposition 13, Briggs warned that citizens' rights as parents and taxpayers were threatened by the employment of homosexuals in public schools:

We know that the undermining of traditional values which began in the sixties has left many Americans in a moral vacuum which they try to fill with drugs, alcohol, and "alternative life styles." . . . In June, we Californians gave the nation a new idea. The Jarvis Amendment has made fiscal responsibility respectable again and is serving as a model of inspiration for the rest of the nation. Now the nation is watching us again. We're going to put America back on the high road, not because the politicians want it, but because people demand it.[53]

For Briggs, California's role as vanguard in a national tax revolt augured well for its role as vanguard in the national restoration of traditional values.

The Briggs Initiative failed miserably, but the county-level returns, as they had in the case of Proposition 16 in 1966, bespoke a growing geocultural divide in California, with social conservatives congregated in rural and suburban regions of that state, particularly in Southern California. But the rhetoric of the Briggs campaign, coupled with the Dade County and similar subsequent victories against gay rights in St. Paul, Eugene, and Wichita, fanned the flames of a newly emerging form of national homophobia: a backlash against the American public's perception of gay excesses and depravity—a misperception that had accompanied the rising visibility of gays in the early 1970s.[54]

Exceptionally troubling to gay rights advocates was the rhetoric of this new wave of homophobia, which not only asserted the general depravity and criminality of homosexuality but often implicitly condoned violent attacks against homosexuals themselves. After her victory, Bryant thanked God for helping to rein in a lifestyle "both perverse and dangerous." Her book *The Anita Bryant Story: The Survival of Our Nation's Families and the Threat of Militant Homosexuality*, published a month after her victory, was viciously homophobic. With unshakable self-righteousness, a literal interpretation of the Bible, and a penchant for paranoia, Bryant warned readers of the "social epidemic" of homosexuality and conjured up the specter of "militant homosexuals" who sought human rights as a "camouflage" for "flaunting their devious ways," which included "sadistic sexual rituals, and abominable practices." More pointedly, while insincerely denying the charge that she encouraged antigay violence, she proudly quoted Leviticus 20:13: "If a man also lie with mankind, as he lieth with a woman, both of them have committed an abomination: they shall surely be put to death; their blood shall be upon them." Not to be outdone, Briggs's campaign pamphlets urged support for both Proposition 6 and Proposition 7, an initiative to stiffen California's death penalty law. The pamphlet, which featured a photograph of a bloodied

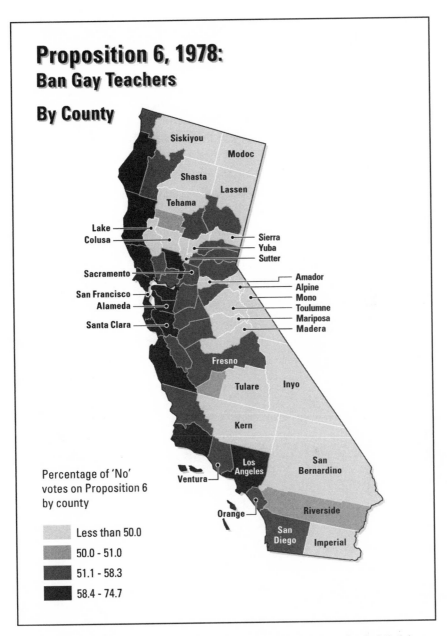

Proposition 6, 1978:
Ban Gay Teachers

By County

Siskiyou

Modoc

Shasta

Lassen

Tehama

Lake

Colusa

Sierra
Yuba
Sutter

Sacramento

Amador
Alpine
Mono
Toulumne
Mariposa
Madera

San Francisco

Alameda

Santa Clara

Fresno

Tulare

Inyo

Kern

Ventura

Los
Angeles

San
Bernardino

Orange

Riverside

San
Diego

Imperial

Percentage of 'No'
votes on Proposition 6
by county

Less than 50.0

50.0 - 51.0

51.1 - 58.3

58.4 - 74.7

MAP 5. The attempt to ban gay teachers from California's public schools failed, but the county level returns again revealed the geo-cultural divide first evident in the Proposition 16 returns in 1966. Map by David Deis, Dreamline Cartography.

teenager bludgeoned to death on its cover, effectively linked violent predators with openly homosexual teachers.[55]

Around the country, and particularly in San Francisco, homosexual men complained of increased incidents of "gay bashing" or "fag bashing," in which roving bands of teenagers attacked gay male couples. Struggling to explain this increase, even in a city believed to be uniquely tolerant of homosexuality, many homosexuals blamed Bryant and Briggs. The city's largest gay newspaper, the *San Francisco Sentinel,* implicitly blamed Bryant for the twenty-plus incidents of antigay violence that it documented in San Francisco in the weeks after the defeat of the Dade County ordinance. Mayor Moscone accused Briggs "and other demagogues" of contributing to a "climate of hate and bigotry" that had led to Hillsborough's murder. The Coalition for Human Rights, an ad hoc group organized in response to the increased level of antigay violence in San Francisco, explicitly named Briggs and Bryant, whose "campaigns of hatred and slander against gay people" created "a climate of violence" that, they said had "allowed this murder to occur." Up-and-coming gay leader Harvey Milk blamed "Dade County and Anita Bryant," and another gay coalition wrote Bryant personally, telling her Hillsborough's "blood is on your hands." Helen Hillsborough, the victim's mother, sued Briggs and Bryant in civil court, charging that they had created an "atmosphere" of hate leading directly to the murder of her son.[56]

Only a small handful of observers challenged the link between the "climate" and Hillsborough's death. One was pioneering gay scholar Martin Duberman, whose 1977 essay "The Anita Bryant Brigade" argued for a much longer historical view. "Simple equations between her inflammatory rhetoric and Hillsborough's murder should be avoided," Duberman wrote; "homosexuals, after all, had been beaten, tortured and burned to death for centuries before Anita Bryant began her crusade." More immediately, there were those who seized on a significant detail: that John Cordova himself had a history of homosexual activity. A district attorney investigator spoke with four men who claimed to have had sexual relations with Cordova, who went by the name Jose. Allegedly, Cordova regularly "cruised" the Mission, engaging in homosexual sex, while feigning disinterest. This revelation prompted the theory that Cordova's extreme violence was a product of self-loathing, a popular notion in the field of psychology. But neither the defense nor the prosecuting attorney, assistant district attorney Gene Sweeters, introduced this information, fearing that it would prove little and potentially backfire.[57]

What few contemporaries appreciated sufficiently was the very provincial nature of the crime. Ultimately, neither the "climate of hate" created by Bryant and Briggs—of which Hillsborough's assailants were probably unaware—nor

Cordova's alleged self-loathing sufficiently explained the tension between Hillsborough and his young assailants. Ultimately, Hillsborough's murder was a tragic example of the rising levels of homophobic violence in San Francisco as neighborhood toughs acted out their determination to keep "fags," "dykes," and hippies out of what they considered "their" neighborhoods. As Tim Speck, a gay man who left the Castro for the Mission, wrote, "one of the greatest joys of my life is to walk through my neighborhood and be in the middle of such stunningly beautiful latino people, and hear their marvelous language.... The only problem is that I have to be back in my room before dark, when the teenagers come out with lead pipes, knives and guns."[58]

Hillsborough and Taylor must have known about the dangers of the Mission as well; their new apartment was on the third floor of a brightly painted—and heavily gated—Victorian building. When they had moved in, four months before Hillsborough's death, they had weighed the benefits against the risks. Affordable and with good light for Hillsborough's plants, the apartment echoed with the sound of busy streets and children. He was determined to make it his home, repainting the interior, making the hardware shine, and expanding his indoor garden. He was finally "out" to his mother and was happily in love with Jerry—at a point of clarity of life and purpose that people of any sexual preference are lucky to find at thirty-three.[59]

But gay men's affection for the Mission was rarely reciprocated. In fact, during the mid-1970s, as Speck's comment indicates, explicitly antigay violence became a real and regular threat. One Mission teenager assaulted gays by throwing rocks and chasing them in the area of his home on Folsom Street. He said: "if they want to do something, they should do it at home, not in front of little kids. I have to walk my girlfriend home every night, and what we see makes me a little sick. I just hate them."[60] White gays in the Mission began to decry the "thuglettes" of the neighborhood. Significantly, Feinstein, who sought to downplay conflicts between gays and Latinos, implicitly recognized the tension after Hillsborough's death when she warned: "we can't blame his death on every single young person in the Mission." And after she became mayor, she ordered SFPD officers to go "under cover" in the Castro and Mission to deter homophobic attacks by Latino gangs.[61]

Many Mission youths resented gays for their effeminacy, their renunciation of mainstream Mexican and American notions of masculinity, and—for some Latino youth—their open embrace of practices deemed sinful by the Catholic Church, a major cultural force in the Mission. But many of the Mission's Latino youth also resented gay men for their public expressions of affection, which they likely interpreted as an assault on the aesthetic character of their neighborhoods. Simply put, they believed that they possessed an entitlement to be shielded from behavior they deemed offensive. According to newspaper reports of assaults on gays in the Mission, most were immediately triggered by gay men hugging, kissing, holding hands, and occasionally groping in public. Significantly, hostility to gay expressions of public affection was rarely a manifestation of the same strict moralism that white, middle-class opponents of public sexual activity espoused. For example, in the predominantly African American Western Addition—which was also a haven for streetwalking prostitution—the in-migration of gays prompted a vehement reaction on the part of black mothers. At a 1979 community meeting called to address the issue of gay in-migration to the Western Addition, Idaree Westbrook expressed her revulsion at openly gay couples walking the streets of her neighborhood. Complaining that her grandson had been "repulsed" by the sight of an openly gay couple, she worried openly about how "this permissiveness [will] affect future generations of black kids." But what about the prostitution that plagued her neighborhood? "I don't think seeing a prostitute is nearly as bad as seeing two males kissing," Westbrook told the crowd: "There's a normality to prostitution in the black community that kids learn to understand."[62]

Moreover, hostility to gay in-migration to the Mission—or to the Western Addition or dozens of other ethnic neighborhoods throughout metropolitan America, for that matter—was not, and has never been, just about homophobia. At least as important, though rarely cited, have been the racial and social class dimensions of these migrations. In the case of the Mission, this was demonstrated most conspicuously by Mission residents' relatively benign response to the rising visibility of gay Latinos, as well as lesbians of all races, in the Mission during the same historical moment that white gays were moving into the neighborhood. Not only were there very few reported antigay attacks against Latinos or lesbians in the Mission but district leaders also recognized the legitimacy of—and worked in cooperation with—an organization known as the Gay Latino Alliance (GALA). Operating in the Mission in 1975–1983, GALA's founders and members sought to mitigate both the sense of marginalization they felt in the predominantly white Castro District and in the heterosexually oriented public spaces, nightclubs, and bars of the Latino Mission. Historian Horacio N. Roque Ramírez has carefully sorted out the ways the politics and fissures of this organization revealed a complex negotiation of sexual, gender, and racial identities among members.[63] More remarkable, however, is the way GALA—despite its purported beliefs in human equality and freedom—actually reinforced and legitimized community hostility to the in-migration of white homosexual men to the Mission.

Masking their own racial hostility in the rhetoric of La Raza, leaders of GALA pushed the issue of gay white migration to the forefront of their political agenda in the November 1977 city election, the first district elections in San Francisco. Arguing that Mission Latinos who supported white candidate Carol Ruth Silver were "cocos"—"brown on the outside, white on the inside"—members of GALA threw their support behind Mission activist Gary Borvice. "GALA seeks," representatives of the organization wrote in the *Sentinel*, "to preserve the familial and cultural character of the Mission. We are Raza and we are familia! There is no need to convert the Mission or any other racial or cultural community into a Castro or Polk Street. There is room in the city for all of us."[64]

Race-based defense of neighborhoods, when deployed by whites, has rightly earned the condemnation of liberal contemporaries and like-minded historians. Indeed, it was one of the nastiest and most potent forces for segregation in urban America in the twentieth century. But it has been blithely tolerated—and in some cases, perversely celebrated—as an affirmative act of cultural pride when nonwhite groups do the same. The folly of this hypocrisy was plainly evident in the Mission, where non-Latino gays—themselves victims of a unique brand of homophobia—were discouraged from moving where they pleased, from exercising the same democratic rights that politically active Latinos demanded for themselves. Yet the difference in this case was that Latinos in the Mission lacked either the political clout or the real property to fully exploit their own prejudice. Consequently, defenders of the Mission's *latinidad*—its essentially Latin American character—could do little more than complain, intimidate, and threaten. These actions, however unpleasant and sometimes dangerous, were not sufficient barriers to keep white gay men out of the Mission.

So they came. And to John Cordova, Michael Chavez, Richard Ojeda, and Thomas Spooner, this was unacceptable. Though all four regularly prowled the Mission at night—and ringleaders Chavez and Cordova had been harassing gays in the Mission long before meeting Hillsborough—none actually lived there; three of them lived directly adjacent to Mission Street in San Francisco's oldest and closest suburb, Daly City. (Non-Latino tagalong Thomas Spooner lived in neighboring San Bruno.) They did not live in the "new" Daly City, west of Route 280, which boasted shopping malls and classic suburban homes, but in the suburb's east side, a joyless blue-collar neighborhood of dilapidated, aging homes, anchored by a flagging business district of auto and vacuum cleaner parts stores, used car dealerships, and used clothing shops. Described by *Mother Jones* writer Bill Sievert as a "treeless, gray, cloud-covered place where the fog rolls in early and stays late," east Daly City had an equally gloomy economic profile; between 1970 and 1980, the average income remained stagnant at a time when San Francisco's was increasing dramatically.[65]

The chief recreational activities of high-school dropout John Cordova and his neighborhood friend Mike Chavez were drinking lots of beer, smoking marijuana, and picking fights with friends and strangers. In the daytime hours, both tinkered with cars in their driveways, and John had even managed to secure an apprenticeship with a local mechanic with the help of his father. But mechanics really seemed to be a diversion from the principal aim of nighttime rowdiness. Cordova had already spent a night in jail for harassing gay men on a city bus in the Mission, and Chavez was a constant companion on their nighttime cruises into the district. Chavez's recent acquisition of a green 1974 Buick Opel had quickly expanded their options. The body needed work, but it got the teenagers around.

The evening began, as so many did for Chavez, Cordova, and the others, at Lincoln Park, two blocks off Mission Street in Daly City. That night, Chavez was hanging around with Thomas Spooner, drinking on the park grounds. At around half past ten, they went cruising, and on Mission they ran into Cordova and Ojeda. They drank more beer, smoked some joints, and cruised down Mission, ending the evening at the Whizburger. Hillsborough and Taylor were already there, eating their burgers. When Cordova and the boys began harassing them, Hillsborough pulled his Land Rover out abruptly. Cordova claimed that Hillsborough's vehicle had brushed Cordova on the way out of the parking lot, but no eyewitnesses corroborated this, and a city bus driver said he saw Cordova trip while kicking Hillsborough's car. The boys piled back into Chavez's Opel and followed Hillsborough and Taylor back to Nineteenth and Lexington. Chavez chased Taylor while Spooner, Ojeda, and Cordova pummeled Hillsborough. Spooner and Chavez fled to their car, but Cordova stayed on, climbing on top of Hillsborough, shouting "Faggot, faggot!" and stabbing him repeatedly. Cordova finally got into the car, and the boys sped off. "I fucked up," he said. "I don't know what made me do it."[66]

Nowhere in subsequent accounts of the trials was there any mention of Anita Bryant. In fact, only Cordova's defense attorney mentioned Bryant; he argued that the prosecution was overstating the antigay nature of the slaying and that it was (as reporter Randy Alfred put it in his courtroom notes) "a drunken tiff turned into an antigay slaying by a politically active gay community and a hysterical press in the days between the Dade County gay rights defeat and San Francisco's Gay Freedom Day."[67] The neighborhood context, on the other hand, was inescapable: the white, gay Hillsborough and Taylor in their shiny new Land Rover; the predominantly Latino, heterosexual youth piled into the rundown Opel. Hillsborough and Taylor must have seemed to the provincial boys like the most extreme type of outsiders.

When Wednesday morning broke, the four went their separate ways, so apparently untroubled by the murder that they simply fell into old patterns;

shortly before their arrest, Cordova, Spooner, and Ojeda were seen drinking beer and playing pinball at the Westlake Bowling Alley in Daly City. But extensive publicity about the murder thwarted their plans. This antigay murder would not go unpunished. On Thursday, Moscone offered a $5,000 reward from the city's general fund for information leading to the arrest of the killers and ordered that all flags at city offices be flown at half-mast. The Tavern Guild, an organization of gay bar and restaurant owners, also put up $5,000, Café Biarritz and N'Touch Disco Bar each offered $1,000, and the Council of Emperors—a gay charity group—added another $1,000. Supervisor Dianne Feinstein was filled with "shame and alarm [because of] the increasing incidence of violence against members of San Francisco's gay community."[68]

This aggressiveness—coupled with the work of the San Francisco and Daly City police departments—produced results; on Friday, Chavez—who had already shaved his beard, cut his hair, and was apparently making plans to go to Mexico—was arrested after taking his car to an auto body shop to paint it yellow, presumably a response to the well-publicized tip about the green getaway car. At two o'clock Saturday morning—just as all-night revelers in the Castro were making final preparations for that day's Gay Freedom Day parade—Daly City police officers arrested John Cordova at his home, where they found the still-bloody murder weapon. They picked up Spooner and Ojeda the next day. By the time of Hillsborough's funeral—over three thousand people packed the city's historic Grace Cathedral atop Nob Hill on Monday—all of the suspects were in custody.

The trials were under way by late November. Because he was a minor, Ojeda was sentenced only to spend time at the California Youth Authority facility in San Mateo. District attorney Freitas offered Chavez immunity in exchange for his testimony in the case. Spooner pled to aggravated assault and was briefly imprisoned at the California Men's Colony in San Luis Obispo. Cordova was convicted of second-degree murder and given a sentence of five years to life at the Correctional Training Facility in Soledad. The relatively light sentencing infuriated the gay community in San Francisco and nationwide. Freitas, who had made a preelection pledge in 1975 never to plea-bargain in violent felonies, outraged gays in the city by offering the plea bargain to Spooner and offering immunity to Chavez, who had turned eighteen several days after the murder and was tried as a juvenile, despite a new state law allowing for the prosecution of minors.[69] But Freitas's options were also limited because he could not pursue the punitive enhancements that soon would become standard in cases of gay bashing only a year later when California became the first state to pass "hate crime" legislation.

"The days are gone," Randy Alfred wrote in a pointed editorial in the *Sentinel*, "when we can be taken for granted. We are tired of shabby, liberal gestures."[70] After Hillsborough, this attitude of defiance became a hallmark of rhetoric in the city's gay community. "This is our city too," one gay activist reminded reporters from the *San Francisco Examiner*, "and we're going to take the streets back."[71] Gay men defended themselves in the Castro by organizing the Butterfly Brigade, a group that detained suspects in antigay attacks. But it was an uphill battle. Dolores Park—across the street from the historic Mission Dolores—had become "a hotspot of antigay harassment by Latinos," according to Dick Stingel, head of the gay organization Community United Against Violence. "If anybody who doesn't think there's antigay violence, I'd like to dress them up in a Castro clone outfit and walk them through Dolores Park on a Saturday night.[72] "Any gay person who goes into the Mission area can be attacked," said Wayne Friday, the president of Tavern Guild. "The Latinos have carved out that area as their turf, and it's a political statement. A number of gays are buying homes in the Outer Mission area, and the line has been drawn at Church Street. Anybody who comes across Church Street is considered fair game."[73]

Both the horrific violence and the light sentencing of the Hillsborough incident prefigured the assassination of Mayor George Moscone and supervisor Harvey Milk less than one and a half years later. Supervisor Dan White had grown increasingly frustrated by his diminishing influence on the liberal Board of Supervisors, and particularly resented the rising influence of Milk, who had recently "betrayed" White on a key vote. Further strained by the financial pressures of his failing baked-potato concession at the Pier 39 tourist site, White resigned his supervisor seat in a huff, only to ask for a reappointment shortly thereafter. Moscone gave it serious consideration but was swayed by liberal allies, including Milk, to deny White the reappointment. On November 27, 1978, White met with Moscone to make one final appeal. When Moscone denied White the reappointment, White shot and killed Moscone. He proceeded down the hall and shot and killed Harvey Milk.

When Dan White assassinated Moscone and Milk, he followed through on a festering vendetta that was only partially about homosexuality.[74] But given the mounting homophobic violence in San Francisco before the assassinations, it was very difficult for gays, lesbians, and their supporters to interpret the assassinations as anything other than homophobia carried to its gruesome extreme. "The more I observed what went on at the jail," an undersheriff at the city jail said, "the more I began to stop seeing what Dan White did as the act of an individual and began to see it as a political act in a political movement." "To a lot of these cops," he concluded, "Dan White was a hero."[75] Further proof of this assertion was the brisk sale of "Free Dan White" T-shirts, the proceeds of which contributed to the $100,000 defense fund that policemen, firemen, and the other sympathizers raised for White.[76] But it was the trial, in which the mostly white and Catholic jury found White guilty of voluntary manslaughter rather than first-degree murder, that smacked most of homophobia. White's light sentence triggered the "White Night Riots," in which thousands of gays caused more than one million dollars in damage to City Hall.

Rather than abating in the wake of the tragedy, antigay violence only continued. Historically insulated—to a greater extent than gay men—from physical violence by ostensibly "straight" men, lesbians came under increasing attack in the 1970s. Their visibility, their assertiveness, and their claiming of urban spaces—both public and private—angered men who were already predisposed to beating up gays and women and unleashed a campaign of violence. In one of the more egregious moments, Peg's Place, a Richmond District lesbian bar, was the site of unchecked male aggression in 1979. A group of intoxicated men, including off-duty SFPD officers, were out celebrating a bachelor party for their friend, Bernard Shaw, who was about to marry Patty Hearst, the infamous heiress to the Hearst fortune who had participated in a bank robbery led by the Symbionese Liberation Army and had only recently been released from prison. When the doorwoman denied the rowdy crowd admission because of their drunkenness, they pushed their way in, reportedly yelling "Let's get the dykes!" They put the doorwoman in a choke hold and beat bartender Alene Levine with a pool cue. Levine spent ten days in the hospital as a result of injuries to her skull.[77]

In January 1979, two lesbians leaving Amelia's, a lesbian bar in the Mission, were harassed by SFPD officers and dragged to jail without being informed of the charges against them. At the Hall of Justice, they were allegedly strip-searched by male sheriff's deputies. This incident prompted the founding of a new organization in Oakland, Lesbians Against Police Violence.[78] In February 1980, arsonists set fire to the Women's Building in the Mission, causing close to $50,000 in damage. In September 1980, it had to be evacuated because of a bomb threat, and in October of that year, someone detonated a pipe bomb in front of the Women's Building, shattering the front windows and blowing off the marquee signs.[79]

Suburban moralists came to San Francisco to fan the flames of antigay violence. Richard Zone of the suburban group "In God We Trust, Inc.," announced a $1 million "media blitz" to repeal the 1978 gay rights ordinance, and Dean Wykoff of the Santa Clara County Moral Majority campaign advocated imprisonment for homosexual behavior and later ominously warned that there would be a "bloody battle" to restore morality in society. He subsequently refined his position, arguing that homosexuals should be executed because they were committing a capital offense. And while these groups drew little public support in San Francisco, antigay violence showed no signs of abating through the 1980s.

In 1990, the National Gay and Lesbian Task Force reported that, for the third year in a row, San Francisco had more antigay and antilesbian physical assaults than in any other city in the country.[80]

Hollywood and the Smut-busting Vigilante

"Considering the movies recently announced for production," *Los Angeles Times* film critic Joyce Haber wrote in 1968, "there's a fair chance that every actor and actress at next year's Academy Awards will have been nominated for portraying a sexual deviate."[81] Haber's prediction turned out to be slightly premature: only one of the screenplays she cited—*Midnight Cowboy*—made it to film the next year. But she was only off by a few years. Beginning in the late 1960s, the figure of the sexual deviate became an increasingly pivotal one in Hollywood's action and thriller genres. As a proxy for sexual and political radicalism run amok, the sexual deviate became the perfect foil for a new kind of hero: the smut-busting vigilante, whose extralegal crusade to restore moral order and safety on the streets resonated with millions of American moviegoers. To further intensify the dramatic effects of the vigilante's crusade, directors easily exploited San Francisco's national renown as a capital of filth, creating a moneymaking formula that likely reinforced public perceptions of the city as a moral cesspool.

Of course, San Francisco had made its screen debut long before the sexual revolution. Howard Hawks's 1935 *Barbary Coast* relived the raucous days after the Gold Rush. "Killers! Courtesans! Croupiers!" the trailer said, fulfilled "their wildest desires" in the "sinful, bawdy, Barbary Coast." But generally, it was not the city's moral reputation but its variegated topography that drew directors and production crews north from Los Angeles. As writer Nathaniel Rich has observed, San Francisco's dark alleys, notorious fog, and abundant public spaces made it an irresistible locale for shooting film noir, including such classics as *The Maltese Falcon* (1941), *Born to Kill* (1947), *The Lady from Shanghai* (1948), *I Married a Communist* (1949), *D.O.A* (1950), *The Sniper* (1952), *City on a Hunt* (1953), and *Vertigo* (1958).[82] As many film scholars have observed, film noir's focus on the "rotten underbelly" of American cities reflected a great deal of anxiety and ambivalence about postwar changes in urban life.[83] In this context, San Francisco was only one of a constellation of cities in which this theme was developed. In short, and with the exception of Hawks's 1935 *Barbary Coast*, Hollywood at first exploited San Francisco merely as a set.

The reimagination of San Francisco as a moral tableau that came later took place in a sexually and politically charged context, but it was cold financial calculation—as always with Hollywood—that drove the shift. The financially savvy Alioto was the first mayor in San Francisco's history to aggressively court Hollywood directors. Prior to his election, he had watched from a distance as a spate of directors chose San Francisco over Los Angeles as the setting of their films; in 1967, eight major films were being produced in San Francisco, including *Petulia*, *Guess Who's Coming to Dinner?* and *Point Blank*. Citing the city's natural beauty and vibrant culture, and their own displeasure with the "overwhelming" nature of Los Angeles, enough directors moved production to San Francisco to alarm Los Angeles mayor Sam Yorty. By 1971, the *New York Times* described San Francisco as Hollywood's "home away from home."[84] One of the first films to locate sexual deviancy in San Francisco was Richard Rush's 1968 film *Psych-Out*, featuring Susan Strasberg, Dean Stockwell, Bruce Dern, and Jack Nicholson. The film opens with a montage of threatening iconography: the atom bomb, the Ku Klux Klan, race riots, and pollution, immediately followed by actual footage of the Haight-Ashbury, whose warmth is a conspicuous counterpoint to the madness of American society. When Strasberg's deaf ingénue, Jenny Davis, arrives at the "scene" by bus in search of her long-lost brother, she is immediately bedecked with flowers and beads by her new neighbors. But with the help of Nicholson's Stoney, Jenny soon discovers that evil lurks beneath the city's façade. Her lost brother, played by Bruce Dern, has become a cultish guru known to followers as "the Seeker" and travels with dubious allies. In their pursuit of him, Jenny, Stoney, and Stoney's rock band–mates are confronted by a group of thugs—also seeking the Seeker—who attempt to gang-rape Jenny. Narrowly escaping, they decide to attend a mock funeral in Golden Gate Park, at the end of which a naked woman mounts the "corpse" while being showered with flowers. After the Seeker is killed in a fire, Jenny drops acid and wanders out into the crowded streets of the Haight-Ashbury, where she is harassed, manhandled, and solicited while seeking the solace of a private walk. In essence, the acid allows Jenny to see the Haight-Ashbury for what it really is: a sinister place where the free-love ethos masks pathological violence.

A tepidly reviewed, low-budget film destined only for cult status, *Psych-Out* was influential nonetheless. The first film to challenge the hippies' free-love mythology, it also depicted the imagined relationship between sexuality and violence that was essential for the emergence of the smut-busting vigilante in *Dirty Harry* (1971). Director Don Siegel specifically chose to make the film in San Francisco because he thought that permissiveness—both real and perceived—would create dramatic tension in the film's story of the unabashedly misogynistic, xenophobic, and misanthropic "Dirty" Harry Callahan.[85] Harry is a plain-dealing, pistol-wielding, suffer-no-fools vigilante for "old" San Francisco before it was ruined by what he calls the "loonies." "If a political inference is to be drawn from the picture," a sympathetic biographer of Don Siegel and Clint Eastwood wrote, "it is certainly not a liberal one, but a highly conservative one in which the audience is pulled into siding with a policeman who knows that he must take the law into his own hands."[86]

Dirty Harry's enemies are many, but sexual psychopaths, pimps, and pornographers are his prime targets. Already on thin ice for shooting down an attempted rapist in the Fillmore, Harry is assigned to catch the serial killer Scorpio, a character modeled on the real Zodiac killer, who terrorized northern Californians in 1968 and 1969 and taunted the press with cryptic letters. Having lost many partners in the line of duty, Harry is assigned a new partner, the rookie Chico, played by Reni Santoni, whom we assume has been elevated to his position through race liberals' hiring policies. As the two drive through North Beach, Harry wags his head at the "loonies" on the street: "They should throw a net over the whole lot of 'em," he growls. Meanwhile, Scorpio taunts Harry, revealing that he has buried alive a fourteen-year-old girl with "nice tits." When Harry finally captures Scorpio after a shootout, the police captain berates Harry for violating the suspect's rights, and Scorpio goes free, never revealing the location of the girl, who soon dies as a result. Against direct orders, Harry pursues Scorpio, finally kills him, and in a final act of defiance tosses his SFPD badge into a reservoir. There is no room in the modern police force, the film suggests, for Harry's brand of heroic vigilantism.

Both the message and the popularity of *Dirty Harry* proved worrisome to liberal intelligentsia, most famously film critic Pauline Kael. "Dirty Harry," she wrote in the *New Yorker,* "is not about the actual San Francisco police force; it's about a right-wing fantasy of that police force as a group helplessly emasculated by unrealistic liberals." For Kael and others, the "fascist medievalism" of the film was downright ominous.[87] But Kael appeared to be swimming against the cultural current: box office receipts for *Dirty Harry* topped $18 million in the United States and more than $50 million worldwide.[88]

Some in San Francisco did not share Alioto's enthusiasm for filming in San Francisco. Herb Caen and the Downtown Association shared the view that "if moviemakers persist in giving the impression that San Francisco is a crime-ridden city where police chases are an every day occurrence, let them make their movies elsewhere."[89] And the SFPD was particularly sensitive, given their rather grim portrayal. Chief Donald Scott weighed on the Mayor's Film Production Office to force Richard Rush, the director of *Freebie and the Bean* to "tone down" ethnic references made by the police officers in the original script. Subsequently the words "spic" and "spade" were dropped from the dialogue. More significantly, Scott insisted that the proposed scene at a "topless massage parlor" be changed so that the girls were costumed, so as not to give the impression that there were actually topless massage parlors in San Francisco.[90]

The unremarkable Dirty Harry sequel *Magnum Force* (1973), in which Harry turns his vigilantism against corrupt and homicidal cops, undermined Kael's assertion that Harry was a right-wing fantasy, while still highlighting the city's many sexual "loonies." (Its production also brought an infusion of more than $1 million to local coffers.)[91] A more pointed portrayal of sexual loonies came in *The Laughing Policeman,* released within months of *Magnum Force* and described in the *New York Times* as the latest contribution in "the continuing love affair between movie makers and the violent and photogenic San Francisco."[92] Director Stuart Rosenberg dug much deeper into San Francisco's sexual landscape than any mainstream film director had and exaggerated the violent threat that sex "deviants" posed to the city's residents. Featuring Walter Matthau and Bruce Dern as SFPD detectives Jake Martin and Leo Larsen, *The Laughing Policeman* begins violently, with a machine-gun massacre on a San Francisco bus in which Martin's former partner is killed. The hunt for the killer brings Martin and Larsen into the world of sex radicals: to North Beach strip clubs where underage girls dance; to a furtive discussion among transvestites at a North Beach café; to a street where a black pimp beats his white prostitute; to the Ramrod and Frolic Room, where go-go boys dance for gay patrons. Their investigations lead them to a suspect named Camerero, a "fruiter," as Dern's hostile Larsen describes him. "Couple of years ago," Larsen says nostalgically while observing the obviously gay Camerero, "it was enough to ruin you." Fortunately, Larsen and Martin kill the gay psychopath just before he launches another bus massacre. The third Dirty Harry installment, *The Enforcer* (1976), directed by James Fargo, tackled sexual politics in San Francisco more directly than the other sequels. A liberal campaign to "winnow the Neanderthals in the department" and thrust unprepared women into the homicide squad brings Harry a new partner in Inspector Kate Moore, played by Tyne Daly. The two are out to stop the People's Revolutionary Strike Force—based loosely on the Symbionese Liberation Army, famous for its kidnapping and alleged brainwashing of Patty Hearst—who ultimately take the mayor hostage. The tomboyish Moore infuses sexual tension into the relationship by relentlessly psychoanalyzing Harry, insisting that his use of the more powerful .44 rather than the standard issue .357 has phallic implications. In a dramatic foot-chase scene, the suspect falls through a glass ceiling directly into a pornographic film shoot; and the key tip in the investigation comes from a racketeer at Tiffany's sex parlor in North Beach, where Harry is offered a sex lesson in the thirty-two positions of lovemaking with a rubber doll. Despite Harry's contempt for his inexperienced female partner, she saves his life twice before being killed, and the film ultimately celebrates the bravery and heroism of women in the SFPD.

Reinforcing the demand for drama about vigilance against sexual psychopaths was the 1979 release *Hardcore,* directed by Paul Schrader and featuring George C. Scott in the role of the smoldering Jake Van Dorn, a tightly wound religious conservative from Grand Rapids, Michigan—precisely the sort of fellow disinclined to wax poetic about the city by the Bay. After his daughter, Kristen, runs away and he discovers that she has become a porno film actress, he travels to California and embeds himself in the pornographic underworld of Los Angeles, San Diego, and ultimately San Francisco's North Beach. Taking a nod from *Dirty Harry* and more directly from Martin Scorcese's *Taxi Driver* (1976), *Hardcore* revels in retributive violence against the urban porn industry. Van Dorn's sleazy sidekick Andy Mast avenges the pornographer who has exploited Kristen Van Dorn by shooting him to death, and Van Dorn personally assaults an amateur pornographer on the streets of North Beach. In a pathos-inducing subplot, Van Dorn befriends a hapless prostitute, Niki, who helps him track down his daughter. At the end of the film, Van Dorn wants badly to "save" Niki from the life she has chosen, but the zoom out on Broadway and Columbus suggests that she is marked for this territory, bound to its tawdry fate.

The ascendancy of the smut-busting vigilante films collided head-on with the rising gay liberation movement, whose activists decried inflammatory portrayals of homosexuals in film. This was first evident in Los Angeles, where gay activists protested the screening of *The Laughing Policeman,* much to Bruce Dern's chagrin. The film, well-reviewed in the *New York Times,* elevated Dern from the status of reliable television actor to a movie star, but gay pickets at theaters apparently robbed him of some of the joy associated with such a career break. "Finally, I am a fucking movie star," he said in response to protests, "and I got pickets in front of my theater. For Christ's sake!"[93]

The small Los Angeles protests over *The Laughing Policeman* in 1974 paled in comparison to the nationwide protests over director William Friedkin's *Cruising* (1980), which features Al Pacino as an undercover officer who infiltrates New York's gay leather and S/M scene in search of a murderer. Filmed in gay S/M clubs in New York's meat-packing district, the sex-club scenes were filled with sixteen hundred regular patrons because the Screen Actors Guild was unable to find enough extras who fit the "leather bar look" or would agree to simulating explicit sexual acts. *Cruising* offered Americans an unprecedented glimpse—a remarkably candid and even graphic glimpse—of that scene. Pacino's young, straight detective, Steve Burns, poses as a leatherman at the behest of his captain, and as Burns immerses himself in the culture of the

FIGURE 5.2. George C. Scott's Jake Van Dorn assaulting a pornographer on the streets of North Beach in Paul Schrader's 1979 film *Hardcore*. © 1979 Columbia Pictures Industries, Inc. Courtesy of Columbia Pictures.

clubs, his own emotions become tangled, and his sexual life with his estranged girlfriend takes on aggressive elements of the hardcore scene. Sniffing poppers, dancing wildly, and participating voyeuristically in the outlandish sex practices of the S/M club, Burns also becomes embroiled in a gay lovers' quarrel that ends with the brutal murder of his new gay friend.

The protests started before filming in New York and spread west. The National Gay Task Force, which had gained access to an advance copy of the

FIGURE 5.3. Gays protest Transamerica Corporation, whose subsidiary released the 1980 film, *Cruising*, directed by William Friedkin. Courtesy: *San Francisco Chronicle*.

screenplay, asked New York mayor Ed Koch to withdraw the shooting permit, arguing that it would trigger a "potentially inflammatory and explosive" reaction among homosexuals because the film presented a "gross distortion of the lives of gay men by portraying them as violent or sex-obsessed." David Rothenberg, a New York City human rights commissioner, called the film "odious and inflammatory" and laid down the gauntlet: "We will no longer tolerate Hollywood interpreting and reflecting on gay men and lesbians at our expense." More sensationally, a spokesman for an ad hoc group of gay activists argued that to make the movie in Greenwich Village was tantamount to "the Ku Klux Klan making a movie about the black community on 125th Street in Harlem." The mayor refused to revoke the permit, and producer Jerry Weintraub—who was hit with a bottle during one protest—responded in characteristically smug Hollywood bravado: "All this publicity will turn into big box office!"[94]

In San Francisco, gay activists gathered beneath the iconic Transamerica Pyramid building, demanding that the Transamerica Corporation prevent one of its many subsidiaries, United Artists, from distributing the film. One protestor described *Cruising*, hyperbolically, as "the most massive attack on lesbian and gay men since Hitler." The day before the opening of the film in San Francisco, mayor Dianne Feinstein arranged for an unprecedented private screening at the Transamerica building with her new police chief, Cornelius P. Murphy, to assess the potential impact of the film and anticipate the nature of the scheduled protest at the St. Francis Theater the next day. Feinstein attempted unsuccessfully to persuade United Artists executives to cancel San Francisco screenings. Failing in that, she and her top aides excoriated the film publicly. Feinstein called it "trash," Deputy Police Chief James Ryan called it "a zero," and the mayor's press secretary Mel Wax called it a "lousy movie" not worth the "four bucks" it would cost viewers.[95]

When *Cruising* opened the next day, hundreds of picketers gathered at the St. Francis Theater on Market Street, under the watchful eye of Mayor Feinstein, who viewed the spectacle through binoculars from a window across the street. A large crowd passed out leaflets and shouted, but the theater was full. There was none of the predicted violence, due in no small part to the large SFPD presence. In retrospect, many of the responses to *Cruising* seem shrill. Yet not three years earlier, Anita Bryant had successfully whipped Floridians into a frenzy about the specter of homosexuality; teenagers had savagely murdered Robert Hillsborough; fag- and dyke-bashing still occurred with alarming frequency; and two years earlier, Dan White had acted out his own revenge fantasy and killed Mayor Moscone and Harvey Milk. There were, in short, many good reasons to worry about how the public would react to *Cruising*.

6

THE MANY
LEGACIES
OF AIDS

Selma Dritz was the last person you would expect to be an expert on the outlandish gay sex scene South of Market. Born in Chicago to Russian parents in 1917, Dritz finished medical school in 1941 and became the chief resident of the Cook County Contagious Disease Hospital before retiring in 1947 to raise her three children. She and her family moved to San Francisco in 1949, where they bought a house in the sleepy southwestern edge of the outer Sunset District, and Dritz became a stay-at-home mom for almost two decades. Once her kids were grown, she got a master's degree in public health at Berkeley in 1967 and quickly accepted a post as assistant director of disease control for the SFDPH. As a doctor and a mother, she already knew the terrain well. "At first," she later recalled, the work "was the usual standard chasing down of measles, mumps, whooping cough, making sure that children in school had their proper immunizations."[1]

Very little in Dritz's daily work routine changed during her first decade at the SFDPH. To be sure, rates of syphilis and gonorrhea increased, "but that didn't bother anybody; one shot of penicillin and you were cured." But by 1977, Dritz remembered, there was a "complete change": the number of enteric diseases, typically associated with the fecal contamination of food, escalated dramatically. Because virtually all of the patients were men, she knew that "these cases weren't coming from eating establishments."[2] Instead, she came to learn, they had been transmitted through the exotic sex taking place in South of Market bathhouses and sex clubs. When she followed up her observations with close research, the findings were alarming: between 1974 and 1979, the annual number of amebiasis cases in San Francisco had risen from 10 to 250; annual cases of giardiasis had risen from fewer than 2 to 85; annual shigellosis and hepatitis A cases had doubled, and hepatitis B cases had trebled. By 1980, she estimated that 70–80% of the patients at the SFDPH Venereal Disease Clinic were homosexual men.[3] Dritz's findings paled in comparison to those of Edward Markell, a doctor who conducted research among a sample of Castro District residents in 1982. Almost 60% of the subjects in Markell's study tested positive for intestinal parasites.[4]

"Too much is being transmitted," Dritz warned a group of San Francisco physicians in 1980. "We've got all of these diseases going unchecked. There are so many opportunities for transmission that, if something new gets loose here, we're going to have hell to pay."[5] Dritz was no scold; she was a consummate professional, and she never indulged in moralistic hand-wringing. Instead, she immediately reached out to the city's prominent gay political clubs, gay business associations, and gay physicians to warn them about the threat. Her professionalism immediately earned her the trust of the gay community, and that of gay physicians in particular. In her early sixties and nearing retirement, Dritz had unwittingly become—as her children joked—"sex queen of San Francisco" and "den mother of the gays."[6]

In June 1981, an article in *Morbidity and Mortality Weekly Report* reported on an unusual pneumonia appearing in gay men in Los Angeles.[7] This was the first official announcement of the new condition that would become known as AIDS. Within one month of its publication, Dritz began seeing the first cases of Kaposi's sarcoma and *Pneumocystis carinii* pneumonia, opportunistic diseases that accompanied the AIDS infection. Dritz recognized before others did that the sexual revolution, as it had been understood, was over.

That the AIDS epidemic was devastating to San Francisco is very well known. Yet the full complexity of the epidemic's impact on the city's disparate communities and neighborhoods remains elusive and largely unexplored. The gay male community of the Castro—indisputably the hardest hit in the epidemic's first twenty-five years—has collectively, and justly, claimed responsibility for telling the story of the epidemic.[8] Yet despite the legitimate authority of the gay Castro to tell the story of AIDS, their influence has obscured other dimensions of the story. Peoples' social and economic class status, race, and location within the city all shaped responses to AIDS in ways that elude quick calculation. And the changing epidemiology of the disease after the early 1980s also changed the meaning of the disease for San Franciscans. In short, the historic devastation to the Castro must be seen in its proper context—as the most affected district of a city in which other affected districts and numerous people were also deeply transformed by the debilitating virus.

The Politics of AIDS South of Market and in the Castro

Largely because of Dritz's outreach prior to the arrival of AIDS, the SFDPH responded to the disease with remarkable alacrity. Within a month of the publication of the *Morbidity and Mortality* article, the department implemented a reporting system and registry for AIDS cases, allowing doctors to quickly look up existing cases and improve treatment. In coordination with doctors at UCSF Medical Center, community groups, individual sex educators, and sex radicals, the SFDPH created an extensive network that became known in health-care circles nationally as "the San Francisco model."

At the center of this network was Dritz's boss, Mervyn Silverman, the city's public health director. Fresh from a stint as public health director of Wichita and medical director of Kansas Planned Parenthood, Silverman arrived in San Francisco in 1977, extraordinarily qualified and unusually experienced for his new post.[9] His quick coordination of doctors and public health providers after the AIDS outbreak was remarkably effective, and by early 1983, health educators from his department were conducting regular education and outreach through Silverman's new AIDS Activity Office. Meanwhile, the AIDS ward at San Francisco General, Ward 86, became a model of superb patient care that would be replicated elsewhere in the country. Simultaneously, the UCSF Medical Center opened a clinic for the treatment of Kaposi's sarcoma, one of the more cruel manifestations of the AIDS complex. Late in 1982, Dr. Marcus Conant and Cleve Jones, Harvey Milk's former assistant, founded the Kaposi's Sarcoma Research and Education Foundation, which was soon renamed the San Francisco AIDS Foundation.

Because of aggressive education efforts by these organizations, gay San Franciscans were well informed about the behaviors most likely to transmit the virus. But having lived in the shadows for so long before finding their sexual paradise, many gay men were loathe to abandon the freewheeling promiscuity that had become such a central feature of gay culture. A 1984 study commissioned by the San Francisco AIDS Foundation concluded that most gay and bisexual men were knowledgeable about the risk factors for the disease. The challenge, the study's authors frankly admitted, was "motivating people to act on the information they already have." Although the study found that significant "attitudinal and behavioral changes" were taking place among gay men in

San Francisco, it also concluded that "much of the safe behavior is perceived to be sexually unsatisfying."[10] An earlier study conducted in November 1983 had yielded the same findings. Researchers had been puzzled: "knowledge of health guidelines was quite high," they had written, "but this knowledge had no relation to sexual behavior." Gays who had regularly sought sex at the bathhouses continued to do so with alarming frequency. By the late 1980s, the rate of unprotected sexual encounters among gay men would decline precipitously, but meanwhile, the disease ravaged the city.[11]

Probably the most successful education campaigns came from within the gay community. Despite their historic marginalization from both gay and lesbian communities, bisexuals were very active sex educators. David Lourea, a cofounder in the 1970s of the Bisexual Center, became one of the most important sex educators among gay and bisexual men. Lourea was probably the first sex educator to actually bring his workshops to the bathhouses and sex clubs South of Market. One of his workshops, entitled "Safer Sex South of Market," not only introduced gay men to safe but erotic sex techniques but also engaged their feelings about the demise of a culture of radical sex: "What do you miss," he asked his pupils, "about the 'good old days'?"[12] Lourea was so well regarded as a sex educator that Mayor Feinstein invited him to join the newly formed Mayor's AIDS Educational Advisory Committee in 1983.

The sad reality was that the educational campaigns simply were not working fast enough. In San Francisco, 24 AIDS cases were reported in 1981, 94 in 1982, 248 in 1983, and more than 500 by 1984. Almost half of all these patients were dead by 1985.[13] Though Feinstein was loathe to publicly say it, for fear of alienating gay voters, the bathhouses needed to be closed, and she pressured Silverman to implement a closure policy.

An appointed public official, Silverman was not significantly swayed by political ambitions, but he approached the idea of closure very reluctantly. "My feeling was," he later remembered, "it's not the role of the health department to 'clean up' the city; it's to make sure that there are not any unhealthy situations in the city. It's like inspecting restaurants: the food may taste lousy, but if it's not unsafe, it's not my role to interfere."[14] This metaphor did not quite work; within the medical community, there had long been general agreement that the bathhouses were a vector of the disease.[15] Silverman did develop an additional public health rationale that was sounder: if he closed the bathhouses, gays would simply find sex in other venues where the department would have no educational reach at all. Better, he reasoned, to face the enemy he knew.

Silverman was in an unenviable position, buffeted from all sides. A poll by the *San Francisco Examiner* revealed that 80% of San Franciscans wanted to ban sex in bathhouses or close them all together.[16] Feinstein continued to press him for closure, while the city's legal counsel warned him that closure might violate the bathhouse owners' civil rights. In the pages of the *San Francisco Policeman,* the monthly newspaper of the Peace Officers Association, SFPD officer Jim Higgins wrote: "this 'bathhouse' situation amounts to an excess quantity of garbage being thrown in San Francisco's face. They are an embarrassment to our City and to God-fearing people. Why must they always take away from San Francisco what is good, while pursuing their lifestyle?"[17] Gay supervisor Harry Britt, whom Feinstein had appointed to fill Milk's seat, supported bathhouse closure, as did SIR cofounder Larry Littlejohn, but the gay press was vehemently, even hysterically, opposed. Randy Shilts's close reading of gay newspapers during the crisis reveals this deep hostility. Shortly after Silverman formally floated the idea in early 1984, the *Advocate* lashed out: "there is no proof that even one of the 3,775 cases of AIDS tallied by the Centers for Disease Control had involved sexual transmission." In the *Bay Area Reporter,* Paul Lorch wrote that supporters of the bathhouse closure were trying to "kill" gay liberation and sought the "annihilation of gay life." He published a list of "traitors" that included Harry Britt, Larry Littlejohn, and several former Milk aides.[18] The Association of Independent Gay Health Clubs pledged more than half a million dollars to fight the assault on "the freedom of sexual expression."[19] Few things were more dangerous to public health at that moment than willful ignorance wrapped in revolutionary rhetoric, but that was exactly what the gay press delivered.

The most outspoken gay critics of a closure policy were the bathhouse owners. A flier distributed by the owner of Animals, a leather den, proclaimed: "we do not intend to be singled out, subjected to an inquisition-like atmosphere.... We find no evidence either from the medical community or health department, which indicates that bathhouses are either the source of or a primary contributing factor to the AIDS threat." Less truculent owners, responding to reduced business in the wake of the mounting epidemic, published healthy sex guides, and a few posted warnings. But most simply ignored the crisis. The owner of the Jaguar Bookstore and sex club, for example, told the *Bay Area Reporter:* "I don't want that [passing out brochures] going on. People come here to forget what's going on." In fact, the most organized response opposing closure was the creation of the Northern California Bathhouse Owners Association, an organization whose sole purpose was to resist it.[20]

Eventually, Silverman—after sending health inspectors into the bathhouses in March 1984 to document high-risk behavior—moved aggressively to shut down all fourteen bathhouses the following October:

Today I have ordered the closure of 14 commercial establishments which promote and profit from the spread of AIDS—a sexually transmitted fatal disease. These businesses have been inspected on a number of occasions, and demonstrate a blatant disregard for the health of their patrons and of the community.... Make no mistake about it. These 14 establishments are not fostering gay liberation. They are fostering disease and death.[21]

Yet, Silverman's bathhouse closure came far too late to be highly effective: patronage at the bathhouses was so low that The Hothouse, Cornholes, Liberty Baths, Bulldog Baths, and the Cauldron had already closed their doors voluntarily. Their patrons were either dead, dying, or afraid of dying.

The following month, Superior Court judge Roy Wonder ruled that the bathhouses could reopen, but only if they hired monitors to survey the premises every ten minutes and expel men engaging in unsafe practices. They were also required to remove all booths and doors. The health inspectors' reports the following year suggested that these policies, coupled with the panic over AIDS in the gay community, had dramatically curtailed patronage. At Folsom Gulch Books, health inspector George Bush wrote, the booths "have been removed and movie viewing now occurs within a single more easily monitored area." Conditions there were no longer "conducive for inappropriate activities." At the beloved Boot Camp baths on Bryant, Bush observed: "the premises are totally vacant and gutted." At the Club Baths on Eighth Street, the "labyrinths and slings appear to have been removed," and "glory hole rooms have either been boarded up or dismantled." At both the Ritch Street and Jacks's Turkish Baths, the "premises are vacant." At the legendary Jaguar Bookstore, the sex facilities for the "grab and go" crowd were entirely dismantled, leaving only "the porno book store portion of the establishment" open for business. "Soon," Bush concluded, "even that will be closed." A more complete erasure of the urban landmarks of gay male liberation could not have been imagined.[22] "An era is ending in the South of Market district," *San Francisco Focus* reported in November 1985. "The man in black leather is going the way of the beatnik and the hippie.... AIDS, which has claimed so many San Francisco lives, has also killed a subculture."[23]

In the wake of the dying South of Market sex scene, a group of gay and bisexual safe-sex advocates gathered at 890 Folsom in October 1986 to create a new model of public sex. Organized by a man named Bernard "Buzz" Bense, the 890 Folsom building became a clubhouse where men and a few women who were determined to preserve their sexual lifestyles could do so, provided they obeyed the strict safe-sex rules Bense established. Hosting dozens of sex clubs—the SF Jacks, J.O. Buddies, the Premier Jacks, K'thar Sissies, Bondage Buddies, Blow Buddies, and many more—890 Folsom earned the approval of the San Francisco AIDS Foundation, which regarded the establishment as a "state-of-the-art model in terms of promoting a sex positive and a safe sex environment for consulting [sic] adults desiring sexual expression in the age of AIDS."[24] But 890 Folsom was the exception to the rule: everywhere else South of Market, a culture was dying.

In the Castro, the effects of AIDS were immediately palpable. Most transformed was its commercial core, which relied on active gay sociality for its survival. When Bobbi Campbell, a young man who was one of the first victims of AIDS, posted a picture of himself with Kaposi's sarcoma in the window of Star Pharmacy at Eighteen and Castro in December 1981, the neighborhood began to witness the ravages of the disease. One shopkeeper interviewed by Kevin Jackson remembered the years 1985 and 1986: "during this period I really noticed the bars becoming very, very empty. I began wondering how they were even going to exist, how they were going to keep going, because they seemed to be completely empty."[25] Other Castro businesses that catered to straights and gays also declined during the early days of the epidemic because of fear among both homosexuals and heterosexuals that AIDS might be communicable through patronizing these businesses. Dennis Mitchell, who owned Buck's, a large clothing store, lamented the loss late in 1984.

> We don't consider Castro Street an upward, gay area anymore.
> Business isn't what it used to be because of AIDS, even though only
> about half of my customers are gay. Straight people don't want to
> try on clothes that gays have put on, and many straights just aren't
> coming here anymore.[26]

Further intensifying downward pressure on Castro businesses were insurance companies, which allegedly charged higher rates to insure businesses in the Castro and Mission because of the risk of AIDS-induced deaths and business closures.[27]

Beyond these economic changes were changes in the spirit of the district, which, while not statistically measurable, were overwhelming. Historian Allan Berube, who was interviewed by the New York Times, had already lost thirty friends by 1987. "I'm learning how to incorporate grieving into my daily life," Berube said. "It's now as much a part of my life as eating and sleeping."[28] In Fritscher's memoir-novel, the protagonist, Ryan, "hated the changing Castro." "Old faces gone. New faces eager to find the party they did not know was over."[29] "Back then on a sunny day like this," a Castro boutique owner said in 1986 of the late 1970s, "that corner would have been packed with guys with their shirts off, taking in the sun. Now it's quiet."[30] Through the early 1990s, San Francisco's Castro District—that internationally famous conglomeration of gay life, residence, and community—was a mere shadow of its former self.

The Forgotten AIDS Crisis of the Tenderloin

Because AIDS quickly devastated so much of the Castro—and because gay residence, affluence, political power, and intellectual influence had been concentrated there since the mid-1970s—the impact of the disease on the Tenderloin was often overlooked. Yet most of earliest cases, as public health scholar Michelle Cochrane has concluded, were in fact among extremely impoverished, drug-addicted, gay or bisexual men living on the margins of society and, most likely, in the Tenderloin. Because the disease was so closely associated with homosexuality from its inception, epidemiologists, policymakers, and scholars were slow to recognize the impact of AIDS on intravenous drug users.[31] Furthermore, the social isolation of the Tenderloin's many transgender prostitutes from the larger gay community—a legacy of both the hypermasculine narcissism of many gay men and the rigid cultural feminism of many lesbians—further obfuscated their crisis.

The hidden toll of AIDS on the Tenderloin did not become generally clear to San Franciscans until 1984. Elizabeth Prophet, an African American prostitute and intravenous drug user, was found not only to have the disease herself but to have passed it on to her children, born AIDS-infected in 1978 and 1979—San Francisco's first known AIDS cases.[32] Early in 1985, further sensational media attention was drawn to the Tenderloin, and to heterosexuals' risk for AIDS infection, when a thirty-four-year old Tenderloin prostitute whose boyfriend-pimp had AIDS was believed by prostitutes of having it as well. Other prostitutes who feared that the publicity her case was bringing to the area was hurting their business literally chased her off of the street.[33]

The women of COYOTE resurfaced to play a critical role in AIDS prevention for prostitutes in the Tenderloin. Prostitutes' rights activist Priscilla Alexander founded the California Prostitutes Education Project (CAL-PEP) in 1985 in order to better educate prostitutes about AIDS prevention techniques. Funded by the Centers for Disease Control (CDC) and the California Department of Public Health, CAL-PEP led what surely must have been the most effective health promotion campaign in the history of prostitution since Julius Rosenstirn's clinic closed its doors in 1913. Beginning in 1985, CAL-PEP workers drove a maroon van into the Tenderloin every afternoon, identified prostitutes, and distributed condoms, spermicides, and bleach bottles (for decontaminating intravenous needles). Alexander and St. James recruited Gloria Lockett, a former prostitute in the Tenderloin who had long been impressed by St. James. "She was the only person I had ever heard talk positive about prostitution," Lockett later recalled.[34] Because of Lockett's connections with local prostitutes, she became a valuable outreach worker and later codirector for CAL-PEP. "What people don't realize," she said in 1988, "is prostitutes are receptive to helping themselves and other people. Their bodies are their tools and they know they have to take care of them."[35]

Primarily because of the nature of the disease—but surely bolstered by the efforts of CAL-PEP—incidents of HIV transmission by prostitutes to clients in San Francisco and nationwide remained very low. But once it was understood that prostitutes could pass AIDS to heterosexual clients, and the specter arose of the disease "jumping the fence" from the gay and poor communities into suburban white homes via philandering husbands, prostitutes figured much more prominently in the AIDS discourse than was warranted. In 1984, less than 1% of known cases of HIV were derived from heterosexual contact; a decade later, only 7% were.[36] A 1987 study by the SFDPH demonstrated that HIV was certainly prevalent among the Tenderloin's prostitutes. Of the 146 street prostitutes tested in and around the Tenderloin, 9—all of them intravenous drug users—tested positive for the HIV virus. But because of CAL-PEP's efforts, they were much more willing to wear condoms than they had been even a few years earlier. In short, the risk of HIV transmission to the male patrons of female prostitutes was extraordinarily low.[37]

Among the Tenderloin's prostitutes, intravenous drug users were most at risk of contracting the disease. In 1985–1986, the number of San Francisco AIDS cases traced to intravenous drug use more than doubled, and much of that concentration occurred in the Tenderloin.[38] By 1988, Tenderloin AIDS cases represented almost 7.7% of cases citywide.[39] Particularly hard hit were transgenders. Their risk was intensified by the high incidence of poverty-induced sex work among transgenders and the chronic low self-esteem that has historically made them more likely to engage in unsafe sexual practices. One survey of transgenders seeking hormone therapy at a San Francisco public health clinic found that 15% were infected with HIV. There was a cyclical pattern to their misery, as one male-to-female transgender observed: "I cannot go to school because I'm HIV-positive, and I'm going to end up being a prostitute again, get arrested, lose my apartment. If I sell my body or use drugs, I don't have my self esteem...this whole circle." Another confessed:

> All the girls that I know about, when they have HIV, they have
> nothin' goin' for themselves whatsoever. When they get out of jail,
> only thing they have to do is resort back to prostitution....When you

FIGURE 6.1. Gloria Lockett and fellow CAL-PEP workers distribute condoms and safe-sex information to Tenderloin prostitutes, 1988. Courtesy: *San Francisco Chronicle*.

have HIV, and you did nothin' for your entire life but prostitution,
what is there else to do?[40]

Other male-to-female transgender prostitutes fell back into sex work after their
HIV diagnoses because the experience of attracting male customers validated
their sense of femininity.

While the gay community of the Castro responded remarkably to the disease, opening hospices and hotlines, raising funds, and offering care, few such
services existed in the Tenderloin because of the profoundly impoverished and
highly transitory population there. The absence of permanent, adequate, and
affordable shelter had long been a problem for the district's marginalized residents, and the AIDS crisis only exacerbated this dynamic. Housing discrimination against AIDS victims cut across all San Francisco neighborhoods, but
was more acute in the Tenderloin. A survey the ACLU conducted reported
approximately thirteen thousand complaints of HIV-related discrimination
nationwide in 1983–1988; housing discrimination was the second most prevalent form after employment. Though the fear of casual transmission loomed
large for evicting landlords, the ACLU reported that "the perception of HIV/
AIDS as an impoverishing illness seems to compel landlords (who may or may
not also fear infection) to dump tenants perceived as likely to become less rent-
reliable in the future."[41]

The effects of AIDS discrimination in housing could be devastating.
Chuck Morris, former editor of the gay newspaper, the *Sentinel,* contracted
AIDS before the disease had a name, and by 1983 he had suffered more than
thirty symptoms, including three debilitating brain seizures. Because of his
condition, he was forced out of two apartments by a landlord and roommate,
respectively—the roommate threatened to kill him if he returned. In an interview with the *New York Times* in 1983, Morris recalled the combined effects of
his illness and his evictions:

> I was standing at Castro and Eighteenth Street with a little plastic
> bag with all my possessions that I could grab, and all of a sudden the
> enormous horror of all this hits me. At this point I had been working
> for 25 years, and I felt that the year before I was a reasonably wealthy
> man. I had my own newspaper, and now here I was, standing on the
> street, homeless and broke, and I had no idea where I was going to
> stay.[42]

Morris's experience was exceptionally cruel, but others suffered similar fates. The furor at the Civic Center Residence was another case in point.
A low-income building owned by the nonprofit Tenderloin Neighborhood

Development Association, Civic Center Residence voted overwhelmingly to reject the admission of homeless people with AIDS in 1988, citing fears of exposure to the AIDS virus, despite an educational presentation by a spokesperson from the San Francisco AIDS Foundation.[43] The rejection was authoritatively supported by Warren Kleinmaier, a doctor at the Tenderloin Detox Clinic who chose to live in Civic Center Residence, near and among his Tenderloin patients. Kleinmaier shocked AIDS educators but apparently rallied denizens of Civic Center Residence with a circular arguing that AIDS was proof of God's disdain for unnatural behavior:

> There *does* seem to be a magnificent, extremely subtle, yet powerful, connection between the abberant [*sic*] sexual and self-abusing *behavior*—a behavior which is anti-evolutionary, which reflects vividly a lack of faith in the overall guidance of the universe and a massive selfish self-centeredness and lack of moral and spiritual values in our society—and its *outcome,* in the form of the present plague of humankind.

Rather than agreeing to house AIDS victims in the same complex where he and his neighbors lived, Kleinmaier was content merely to hope that "the people who are bringing the plague among us, will see the Light... before it affects all of us."[44]

Despite resistance from Kleinmaier and others, and despite still falling short of the demand for AIDS housing, San Francisco became a model of AIDS care in the realm of housing. Emphasizing home care rather than institutional care, the San Francisco model was more affordable and was considered more humane. One portion of housing came from the Department of Social Services, which used its authority to provide emergency housing for homeless AIDS patients. The department contracted with twenty-three hotels for short stays in hotels with vouchers. The San Francisco AIDS Foundation also had its own program that provided limited hotel stays of up to two weeks. The largest residence was the Episcopal Sanctuary, which, appropriately enough, opened in an old bathhouse South of Market at Eighth and Howard in 1986, where it initially provided fifty beds for short-term emergency housing. In 1987, the Coming Home Hospice leased the defunct convent of Most Holy Redeemer Church in the Castro and established comfortable rooms for dying AIDS patients.[45]

For longer term care, the Shanti Project's Residence Program was the most successful. The foundation was established in 1974 by Dr. Charles Garfield to care for people with terminal illnesses, so its infrastructure was already established when AIDS hit. The program provided low-cost permanent housing in various buildings throughout the city, assisting approximately a hundred patients each year. "Virtually all of the residents would be homeless were it not for the Residence Program," program director Ellie Cousineau said. "Fear combined with the financial constraints of AIDS has forced many people with AIDS onto the streets."[46] These locations were kept quiet to protect occupants' privacy and diminish neighborhood resistance. Still, many people with AIDS chose to live at home, an option that improved as San Francisco developed innovative alternatives to institutional care and aggressive hospice programs. The passage of the AIDS Discrimination Ordinance of 1985 changed the landscape. The following year, the San Francisco Human Rights Commission—empowered to investigate charges of AIDS discrimination—reported the lowest number of AIDS-related discrimination complaints since it had first begun keeping track in 1982.[47] That said, in 1986, the Homeless Service Providers Coalition estimated that "taking into account an unknown number staying in Golden Gate park," as many as 150 AIDS victims were homeless. A decade later, when the cost of housing had reached astronomic levels, more than three thousand of the nearly eight thousand people living with AIDS in San Francisco signed on to the HIV/AIDS Housing Waitlist at the San Francisco AIDS Office to receive housing assistance.[48]

Profoundly complicating the issue of housing for AIDS victims was a simultaneous increase in San Francisco's homeless population. An exaggerated regional variation on a national theme, homelessness in San Francisco accelerated dramatically in the 1980s as a result of dwindling job opportunities, inflation, federal budget cuts in social welfare programs, and the arrival of new and highly addictive drugs like crack cocaine and methamphetamine. Homelessness was a more acute problem in California than in other states, and not just because the homeless were drawn to its relatively mild atmospheric and political climate: state spending on social welfare programs declined precipitously in the wake of Proposition 13.

In the case of Chuck Morris, AIDS brought homelessness; in many other cases, homelessness brought AIDS. In 1986, the Homeless Service Providers Coalition belatedly wrestled with the problem of AIDS, but not until the late 1980s and early 1990s did research demonstrate that the problem was more severe than anyone had expected. According to an unpublished study conducted by a UCSF researcher in collaboration with the Haight-Ashbury Free Clinic, approximately 15% of the homeless heterosexuals in San Francisco were infected with AIDS. A more careful examination found that the proportion of homeless among AIDS victims was approximatey 4%; but by 2002, it reached 18%.[49] Not surprisingly, these inconsistent but generally alarming figures intensified pressure to "solve" the homeless problem. The homeless were no longer simply a nuisance; they were also perceived as disease vectors.

Mayor Feinstein, after seeing a man eating out of a garbage can for the first time in her life in 1982, established a system of emergency winter shelters, providing cheap hotel rooms and directing homeless people into existing church shelters, most notably Glide. But without permanent affordable housing programs, these were stopgap measures. Inheriting the problem of homelessness from the Feinstein era, Mayor Art Agnos, a former social worker who served in 1988–1991, vowed to end the problem by converting two Tenderloin buildings into city-owned multiservice shelters. Meanwhile, the homeless began to congregate at the Civic Center in what residents began grimly to call "Camp Agnos." The shelters were completed in 1990, but his vision of a self-sustaining multiservice center was not realized because of immediate overcrowding.[50] Partially because of this debacle, police chief Frank Jordan easily won the mayoral election in 1991 with a mandate to clean up the Civic Center. Midway through his term, Jordan announced a new, ominously named program called Matrix: police, social workers, and health workers were to approach the homeless as a team and make recommendations for their care; but these police also issued about six thousand citations for misdemeanors—like sleeping in doorways—in the first six months of Matrix. Widely decried as heavy-handed and unsympathetic, Matrix was also very expensive: according to figures in the *Tenderloin Times*, it cost the SFPD more than $600,000 in its first four months, and a report by the budget analyst to the Board of Supervisors concluded that Matrix cost the Department of Social Services another $276,000 annually.[51] It was an often-quoted charge—not easily contested—that Jordan was criminalizing the poor. Though Jordan never cited AIDS, its legacy was hard to miss. The San Francisco chapter of the AIDS Coalition to Unleash Power (ACT-UP) asserted that "the Mayor's war on the poor is a war on people with AIDS."[52]

AIDS and the Pyrrhic Victories of the Sexual Counterrevolutionaries

One of the great tragedies of the early days of the AIDS epidemic, as has been well documented elsewhere, was the lethargic response of the Reagan administration to the disease, a response that contrasted strikingly with the San Francisco model of compassionate and comprehensive care.[53] Though sometimes handicapped by oversensitivity to gay "public opinion," San Francisco's AIDS health-care providers created the first dedicated AIDS ward in the country, experimented with new treatments, and innovated programs for long-term and hospice care. By contrast, Ronald Reagan did not deliver his first speech on the disease until 1987, after more than thirty-six thousand people had been diagnosed with AIDS and almost twenty-one thousand had died.[54] That silence amounted to more than a public relations gaffe: Reagan's failure of leadership undoubtedly worsened the mortality of the epidemic.

Even before President Reagan could have been reasonably expected to respond to the disease, he drastically cut the CDC's budget to half what it had been under his predecessor, Jimmy Carter. That was the beginning of a decade in which both the AIDS programs of both the CDC and the National Institutes for Health (NIH) would be chronically underfunded. Although Reagan increased HIV/AIDS discretionary funding for the Department of Health and Human Services (HHS) every year of his presidency, scientists with the CDC and NIH maintained that the increases were entirely inadequate. To make matters worse, Reagan explicitly forbade C. Everett Koop, whom he had appointed surgeon general, to make speeches about the disease or field any questions about it from the news media. "For an astonishing five and a half years," Koop later recalled, "I was completely cut off from AIDS."[55] Not until 1986, after the death of his close friend and fellow actor Rock Hudson, did Reagan break his silence and order Koop to prepare a special report on the disease to be mailed to American families. Reagan's next decisive action came in 1987, when he appointed a commission known as the President's Commission on the HIV Epidemic.

Neither overtly homophobic nor devoid of compassion, Reagan was utterly ineffective at leading the nation toward a clear-eyed understanding of the epidemic. Reagan biographer Lou Cannon has portrayed Reagan first as a man profoundly ignorant of the disease prior to Hudson's death, then uncomfortable with any frank discussions of condom use, and unduly influenced by evangelical Christian advisors.[56] This last point is particularly important, because it reveals the extent to which fundamentalists—both in the federal government and in the broader population—exploited the AIDS crisis to advance a family values agenda that had taken a drubbing in the high-water-mark years of the sexual revolution. As Koop sagely recognized later in his life, "within the politics of AIDS, lay one enduring, central conflict: AIDS pitted the politics of the gay revolution of the seventies against the politics of the Reagan revolution of the eighties."[57]

The counterrevolutionaries close to Reagan were also bitter enemies of Koop. Selected for the post of surgeon general because of his impressive medical career and his very active role in the anti–abortion rights movement, Koop alienated those fundamentalists who loathed his failure to describe AIDS in the moralistic terms they preferred. The particular influences on Reagan were William Bennett, secretary of education; Gary Bauer, a Bennett aide who became White House domestic policy advisor; Patrick Buchanan, White House director of communications; and Carl Anderson, an aide to North Carolina senator Jesse

Helms. Bauer and Bennett worked feverishly to guarantee that the president never advocated condom use, since it seemed to condone nonmarital intercourse. Before joining the White House staff, Buchannan wrote a column in which he sarcastically lamented "the poor homosexuals." "They have declared war upon nature," he wrote, "and now nature is exacting an awful retribution." "The sexual revolution," he continued, "has begun to devour its children. And among the revolutionary vanguard, the Gay Rights activists, the mortality rate is the highest and climbing."[58]

Reagan did not share Buchanan's smugness at the apparent vindication of "family values," or appear to believe, as so many did, that AIDS was a sign of "God's wrath," but this hardly mattered to fundamentalists of Buchanan's stripe: they saw in AIDS the opportunity for political gain. At a conference entitled "How to Win an Election," hosted by the American Coalition for Traditional Values, Georgia congressman Newt Gingrich said about AIDS: "It's something you ought to be looking at....AIDS will do more to direct America back to the cost of violating traditional values, and to make America aware of the danger of certain behavior than anything we've seen.... For us it is a great rallying cry."[59] Indeed, on the eve of the 1984 Democratic Convention in San Francisco, Buchanan argued that Democratic support for civil rights—which extended to gay teachers and gay waiters—would directly endanger American children by exposing them to the virus.[60] Televangelist Jerry Falwell preached his belief that "AIDS and syphilis and all the other sexually transmitted diseases are God's judgment upon the total society for embracing what God has condemned: sex outside of marriage."[61] Even after the facts of transmission were known, many religious fundamentalists called for the quarantine of AIDS patients.

Orange County congressman William Dannemeyer, who coauthored Proposition 102 with Proposition 13 coauthor Paul Gann, was one of the most aggressive of these fundamentalists in California. Proposition 102 was an attempt by Dannemeyer and Gann—who had contracted HIV through a blood transfusion in 1982—to establish a public directory of all AIDS patients in California to prevent further infections through blood transfusions. Dannemeyer once told Koop that if it were possible to identify all HIV-infected people, he would like to "wipe them off the face of this earth," but he evidently viewed the septuagenarian Gann as an innocent victim.[62] Proposition 102, placed on the California ballot in 1988, long after the modes of transmission were well known, would have required all people testing positive for the HIV virus to be reported to public health authorities—effectively gutting the elaborate confidentiality rules then in place—and mandated that public health officers pursue the known contacts of those infected. Republican governor George Deukmejian endorsed the proposition; virtually every health-care association in the state roundly criticized it as a pointless diversion of critical resources that would worsen the crisis by sending potential carriers into hiding. Many physicians in San Francisco were so incensed by the proposition that they vowed to destroy their medical records if it passed. Laurens P. White, a San Francisco internist and president of the thirty-four-thousand-member California Medical Association, said: "if Proposition 102 passes, I will tear the page out indicating the (AIDS virus) status of my patients and throw it away." Fortunately for White, that was not necessary; the proposition was crushed by the California electorate.[63]

AIDS Activism in the Streets of San Francisco

As the political exploitation of the disease reached its high-water mark around 1987, AIDS victims fumed at the fatal slowness of the Food and Drug Administration (FDA) in approving drugs for treatment. "There is no question on the part of anyone fighting AIDS," Larry Kramer wrote in a *New York Times* editorial in 1987, "that the FDA constitutes the single most incomprehensible bottleneck in American bureaucratic history."[64] It was not until 1985 that scientists at the National Cancer Institute, in collaboration with the pharmaceutical company Burroughs Wellcome, began experimenting with an old drug called AZT. Burroughs Wellcome filed for a patent on the drug and, after tests showed that it could extend the life of AIDS patients, the FDA approved the drug's use for AIDS treatment in March 1987. The drug was highly toxic, had a high side-effect profile, and would later become just one of many choices for AIDS sufferers, but at that time it was the last best chance for many infected with AIDS.

The release of AZT in March 1987 was highly problematic. First, it was one of only a half dozen drugs that had been tested by the FDA. Why, activists asked, was the FDA so slow to approve the other treatments, particularly when they were widely believed to be less toxic? Second, and most immediately, AIDS victims were stunned by the price: about $10,000 annually, making it one of the most expensive drugs ever produced.[65] Outraged by the apparent profiteering, New York activists, under the auspices of the weeks-old protest group ACT-UP (AIDS Coalition to Unleash Power), staged a demonstration at the intersection of Broadway and Wall Street on March 24.[66] At seven o'clock in the morning, more than 250 demonstrators gathered outside Trinity Church to protest the FDA's sluggish response to the epidemic and Burroughs Wellcome's exorbitant price for AZT. Shortly thereafter, a group called San Francisco AIDS Action Pledge reorganized under the name ACT-UP, and chapters formed quickly in other cities as well. Generally comprised of white, middle-class gays and lesbians, ACT-UP, combining aggressive street theatrics, disruptive protest, and clever graphics and chants, demanding immediate material goals from various agencies within the federal government.[67]

Before ACT-UP New York and ACT-UP San Francisco made national headlines, AIDS protest in San Francisco had started with a remarkable vigil that would last an entire decade and have a profound effect on the city's downtown. On October 27, 1985, several protestors with AIDS chained themselves to the doors of the Federal Building at the United Nations Plaza in the heart of the Tenderloin, home of the regional office of HHS. Nearly a hundred victims of the disease, many homeless, joined them in a vigil in the plaza, erecting a small tent city and pooling resources. They demanded a $500 million increase in federal funding for AIDS research, FDA approval of all AIDS drugs that were legal abroad, and an expanded definition of AIDS to include "AIDS-related complex" (a term not used today) so they could be eligible for Social Security benefits.

Although the vigil cannot be said to have had any significant impact on federal AIDS policy, it did accomplish at least two other goals. First, it provided an ad hoc community for AIDS victims who were homeless. "When I am out here, there is so much love," said a thirty-one-year-old AIDS victim who was disowned by his parents after his diagnosis. "When I'm at home alone, I get scared—I think of dying. Here, I feel I'm doing something."[68] Another vigil keeper with a similar experience said that "it was like getting my family back that I had lost."[69] Second, the vigil arguably had an even wider impact on people without AIDS, particularly those with little exposure to the disease. By claiming a public space as their own residential space, the AIDS vigil keepers educated the many passersby—particularly Federal Building employees—about the nature of the disease and its devastating toll. Employees began bringing coffee, doughnuts, casseroles, barbeque grills, and other immediate necessities. The vigil brought the disease out of the places where AIDS victims congregated—clinics, hospices, and house gatherings in the Castro—into the visible public space.

FIGURE 6.2. AIDS Vigil at UN Plaza, 1985. The makeshift vigil remained in the plaza for a decade, dramatically raising the profile of the AIDS epidemic to San Franciscans. Courtesy: *San Francisco Chronicle.*

The vigil—though a clear violation of ordinances against camping on public grounds—won quick support from the Board of Supervisors, and San Francisco congresswomen Sala Burton and Barbara Boxer. Supervisor Harry Britt pushed forward a resolution of support for the protestors in November 1985, and Terence Hallinan—who would go on to become district attorney— helped the vigil keepers get a license as "city contractors" to put a stop to the SFPD's sporadic raids on the camp. A year after the vigil began, George E. Miller, regional director of HHS, began pressuring Feinstein to tear down the camp, arguing—correctly—that tolerance of the vigil amounted to "selective law enforcement." "The mounting filth," he wrote Feinstein, "is becoming a serious health hazard to the health and safety of our community."[70] Despite his protests, the mayor did not challenge the board's policy of tolerance, and the vigil continued.[71]

Because AIDS care in San Francisco was generally superior to that available in New York, it took slightly longer for the same kind of radicalism that arose in New York to emerge in San Francisco.[72] When it did, it caught San Francisco officials, and the SFPD in particular, off guard. One of the most disruptive protests occurred in January 1989, when protestors—some affiliated with ACT-UP—linked arms and blocked traffic on the Golden Gate Bridge.

FIGURE 6.3. Jack Hanna, an AIDS victim, chains himself to the Federal Building to demand more research funding for AIDS in December 1985. Courtesy: *San Francisco Chronicle*.

FIGURE 6.4. AIDS activists block the Golden Gate Bridge protesting the lack of AIDS funding in January 1989. Photograph by Rick Gerharter.

Though few protests that year matched the drama of that blockade, the SFPD, having grown weary of ACT-UP's antics, lashed out in October 1989. When 280 ACT-UP protestors filled Castro Street for more than three hours, more than a hundred police officers rushed the crowd, allegedly calling protestors "faggots" and jabbing them with batons until they dispersed. Mayor Frank Jordan later acknowledged the overreaction of the SFPD and was forced to fire his own brother, deputy chief John Jordan, for his role in the blunder.[73]

The largest AIDS protests in the city occurred in June 1990, when protestors used the occasion of the Sixth International Conference on AIDS, hosted by San Francisco, to draw international attention to the crisis. On the eve of the convention, protestors blocked the doors of the Marriott Hotel for two hours, demanding faster production of AIDS drugs, a repeal of a 1987 law barring entry of immigrants with AIDS, and passes to the convention. Three days later, more than five hundred protestors blocked Market Street with their bodies, resulting in 140 arrests.[74]

By the mid-1990s, ACT-UP's influence was waning. The high-water mark for AIDS infections in San Francisco was 1992; in each subsequent year the number of new cases diminished, reducing some of the resentment that had built up about the slow pace of medical research and educational efforts. With the exception of a high-profile raid of Frank Jordan's office by sixty protestors

FIGURE 6.5. Five hundred protestors block traffic on Market Street to demand faster access to affordable AIDS medications on the occasion of the Sixth International Conference on AIDS, June 1990. Courtesy: *San Francisco Chronicle*.

in June 1993, AIDS activism in San Francisco diminished. The single most important cause of declining AIDS activism in San Francisco and elsewhere was the introduction of treatment using so-called drug cocktails—unique and potent combinations of preexisting drugs—in 1996. These treatments dramatically cut the rates of death from AIDS in the United States, and allowed many people infected with HIV to live relatively long and productive lives.

As AIDS activists worked toward and finally succeeded in forcing the hand of policymakers and pharmaceutical companies, they also became more internally unified. During AIDS protests, gay, lesbian, bisexual, and transgender activists began to describe themselves collectively as "queer," reclaiming a name they had been called in hatred for almost two centuries, and unifying the disparate and separatist strains among sex radicals into one critical mass. The term caught on in academia as well, spawning an entire generation of scholars of "queer studies," which found more commonalities throughout the queer communities than it found differences. Though many separatisms persisted, queers increasingly saw the political value of recognizing their shared experiences.

Race and the New Frontier of AIDS

While the almost exclusively white membership of ACT-UP challenged the sluggish federal response to AIDS, the disease was cutting a grotesque and often-overlooked swath through African American neighborhoods across the nation. As has been widely noted, the disease represented something of an "invisible crisis" as far as mainstream media outlets were concerned—both black and white—until basketball celebrity Magic Johnson's 1991 announcement of his HIV-positive status. The main causes of the initial outbreak of the epidemic in black communities were primarily institutional: the persistence of race-induced poverty, the inadequacy of schools, the paucity of health care and health education—just a few of the badges of second-class citizenship to which African Americans had long been subjected. But the worsening of epidemic among blacks after the early 1990s was also the uneasy product of a distinctive culture that had emerged in America's poorest communities—black, white, and Latino—in which casual, unprotected sex and extensive drug use was dangerously common.

In the first years of the AIDS outbreak in San Francisco, both the epidemiology and the politics of the disease clearly focused on white gay men—and for good reason. During the period 1980–1986, just under 130 cases of AIDS were diagnosed among African Americans in San Francisco, at a time when the city's total known cases were more than twenty two hundred.[75] This represented about 5 to 6% of the AIDS diagnoses in San Francisco, at a time when blacks represented about 10 to 11% of the population. Thus the disease was underrepresented among blacks, a fact that diminished the chances of an alarm being sounded. Second, because 87% of the cases of AIDS among nonwhites by 1986 were among homosexual or bisexual men, and another 6% were among intravenous drug users, AIDS was not generally perceived as a disease that affected "normal" African Americans.[76] In fact, the first case in San Francisco of an African American diagnosed with AIDS —other than that of Elizabeth Prophet and her babies, who were only diagnosed several years after their deaths—was that of a bisexual black man who lived near the Tenderloin, out of sight and, by virtue of his lifestyle, out of mind of the Bayview–Hunters Point area.[77]

Because the threat was clearly more pronounced for gay men, most of the educational efforts by the SFDPH and the AIDS Foundation focused, quite naturally, on the risk to gay men. Yet the fact that "normal" blacks were still largely unaffected by the disease need not have led to widespread community ignorance about the disease. The initial cause of that community ignorance was largely a legacy of school segregation, which had produced substandard educational opportunities for blacks who lived in predominantly black neighborhoods and attended predominantly black schools. Under California state law, school districts were allowed—but not required—to offer sexual education classes as long they contacted parents in advance and did not penalize students whose parents objected. This changed in 1992, when the state legislature mandated HIV/AIDS prevention programs at least once in middle school and once in high school; before the mandate, sex education in general and HIV/AIDS prevention education in particular was only implemented in the San Francisco public schools when individual teachers initiated it. There is evidence that such initiation was quite uneven. A survey conducted in May 1985 of adolescents in the San Francisco Unified School District about the cause, transmission, and treatment of AIDS revealed sharp disparities in knowledge by race. Only 59.9% of black and 58.3% of Latino students knew that using a condom would lower the risk of AIDS transmission, while 71.7% of white students knew this. There were more stunning misconceptions. Almost 20% of black students interviewed believed that all gay men had AIDS. The findings were disheartening for the public health researchers conducting the study. "The findings suggest," they concluded, "that adolescents, particularly Black and Latino adolescents, may be at greater risk of HIV infection as a consequence of engaging in unsafe sexual practices attributable to insufficient information."[78]

Given the minimal effect of the disease in the mainstream black community at this time, and the uneven record of schools in transmitting more sophisticated knowledge of the disease prior to 1992, it is not surprising that neither white nor black media outlets paid much attention to the disease.

When and where the black press did report on AIDS in these early days, they did so in a way that was profoundly unproductive. "Instead of engaging in battles to transform the consciousness of black people, offering an oppositional understanding of AIDS as a political issue fundamental to the survival of black people," political scientist Cathy J. Cohen has noted in her important study of black community response to AIDS, "the black press focused on elite declarations, conspiracy theories, celebrity fund-raisers, and the provision of basic information."[79]

Further interfering with the transmission of sophisticated knowledge about the disease to African Americans were the attitudes of many black church leaders. As he always had, Cecil Williams shared relevant knowledge to his Glide parishioners in the Tenderloin. But the predominantly Baptist ministers in Bayview–Hunters Point were reluctant to discuss a disease that was principally associated with behavior they deemed immoral. In this regard, black clergy were little different from white clergy in their response to the AIDS crisis in the 1980s, but the impact of their attitudes was quite different: black preachers had always enjoyed disproportionate influence as educators about secular matters because of the historic exclusion of blacks from white institutions. When one Baptist preacher decided to break the mold and allow an AIDS educator to talk to parishioners about the importance of condom use, the educator was shouted down by older African Americans, one of whom yelled "we don't teach sex here." A graduate student conducting research in Bayview-Hunters Point as late as 1990 attended a church workshop and found that most of the parishioners were "poorly informed about the disease."[80]

That knowledge gap became lethal after 1987, when the extent of AIDS in black communities first became acute. The number of African Americans diagnosed with AIDS in San Francisco nearly doubled that year, largely as a result of a new medical classification system that recognized as proof of AIDS a wider array of opportunistic infections accompanying the HIV virus. But even after that system was established, the proportion of AIDS diagnoses among African Americans continued to rise, finally reaching parity with their proportion of the population, and by the end of 1991, almost twelve hundred African Americans in San Francisco had been diagnosed with AIDS since 1980.[81] Most striking was the explosion of cases of AIDS among black women. In 1980–1987, only thirteen black women in San Francisco had been diagnosed with AIDS; in 1988–1991, ninety-two were.[82] The epidemic not only had reached crisis proportions but, clearly, had moved beyond the presumed demographic of gay men. That transition—which was mirrored among whites, though less acutely—spoke volumes about the very fragile state of black neighborhoods in the late 1980s and early 1990s.

Throughout the nation, black neighborhoods were transformed in the 1980s by economic shifts that took many able-bodied African Americans out of the workforce. The simultaneous diminution of semiskilled, unionized, industrial employment opportunities and the expansion of service sector and high-skill finance and technology industries left many blacks in the lurch. According to a 1988 survey of two 1980 census tracts where poverty was most acute, more than 26% of the residents were unemployed, and 40% of all families lived below the poverty line.[83] Despite an unusually high rate of black home-ownership in the area, poverty was rampant. At the very moment that traditional employment opportunities were disappearing, "crack"—a cheap and highly addictive form of cocaine—hit the streets; and sex trade for crack became very common. The cruel admixture of crack addiction and poverty led many people, women in particular, to offer the last thing they possessed in exchange for the drug: their bodies. Frequent sex-for-crack exchanges intensified this dynamic. William Cates Jr., the director of the CDC's Division of Sexually Transmitted Diseases Prevention, argued that "the crack house of today has become what the gay bathhouse was yesterday with regard to all sexually explicit diseases."[84] This was an exaggeration, because even in the context of sex-for-crack exchange HIV transmission was rarely as efficient as in the bathhouse, but the point was well taken, nonetheless.

Bayview–Hunters Point was never a monolith—the area encompassed a number of neighborhoods and communities. The public housing complex adjacent to the decommissioned naval yard was the most isolated and was particularly hard hit by the disease. "Groups of teenagers and young men wander the project grounds all day and night," a sociologist observed in 1988, "and clearly dominate and control the public space. There are literally no recreational services or facilities in the projects. The children's areas have not been used by children in years."[85] Battling the disease in this context was extraordinarily challenging, but several individuals and organizations worked toward the goal of eradicating the disease among blacks in the mid- to late 1980s.

The most visible, from the perspective of African Americans in the area, was the Bayview–Hunters Point Foundation, founded in 1971. It emerged as an important social force in the community, providing legal services for blacks and, later, drug and alcohol counseling. With the help of large grants from the U.S. Department of Housing and Urban Development, the foundation expanded to operate mental health clinics in Bayview-Hunters Point, as well as the Tenderloin and Mission districts. Central to the foundation's efforts was Shirley Gross, an outspoken African American woman who rose to prominence by haranguing the leadership of the National Urban League for not being aggressive enough in their educational efforts. "We can't afford to sit by and let this disease fester among us," she told the leadership at the League's annual convention in San Francisco in 1986.[86] Beginning 1985, before most blacks recognized the potential crisis of AIDS, Gross introduced the foundation prominently into the field by demanding equal partnership in an emerging research program sponsored by UCSF and the SFDPH. Under this partnership, the foundation launched its AIDS Research program, which supported pioneering research on AIDS transmission in the area, and its AIDS Education and Support Unit, which had a visible presence in Bayview-Hunters Point. Volunteers walked the streets, handing out fliers in bars and black businesses and leading safe sex workshops. Black business owners posted signs reading "Black People Get AIDS Too," and educators even handed out condoms on Bayview-bound city buses. The foundation used its methadone program to enforce AIDS education. As one health worker at the foundation explained, "I'll hold their dose until they come in for AIDS education 'cause they don't forget about their dose."[87] Most innovatively, the foundation hosted a rap competition in 1987 called "Rapn' Down Drugs, STDs and AIDS," in which approximately fifty teenagers rapped about AIDS. One teen's rap concluded: "So you better watch out if you know what I mean / don't date a floozy, be choosy and you'll stay clean."[88]

Another great exception to the silence in the black community was Reggie Williams, a black gay man, who founded the AIDS Task Force in 1985, as a committee of a group that dated back to 1980: Black and White Men Together. An X-ray technician in Los Angeles in the late 1970s and early 1980s, and an active homosexual, Williams became immediately aware of the danger of AIDS and particularly frustrated by the fact that African American gays were somehow not getting the message about transmission methods. He moved to San Francisco in the early 1980s and discovered his own HIV-positive status in 1986. Working from an office in the Western Addition, he sounded the alarm about the threat of the disease not only to gays but to blacks and Latinos more generally.

In a 1986 letter to David Werdegar, Director of the SFDPH, Williams pushed Werdegar to change the focus of efforts in Ward 86. Citing the disproportionate minority population there, Williams explained that black women, children, and heterosexual male drug users were not being adequately informed by medical literature being distributed at the Ward. "Cultural circumstances often dispose these groups to be hostile toward gay men. Intravenous drug users, for example, are not typically gay, and may have trouble receiving information about AIDS that is primarily directed at a gay audience."[89] He asked for more special outreach to these populations, for more minority staff at Ward 86, and for interpreters for the Spanish-language patients. Werdegar took the issue seriously enough to contact Dr. Paul Volberding, chief of

AIDS activities at San Francisco General Hospital. Having already met with Williams, Volberding assured Werdegar that as new positions in the Ward were becoming available, "we are attempting to fill the positions with persons of color and/or persons who speak Spanish fluently." Volberding ordered two sensitivity training seminars for his entire staff and collaborated with the SFDPH's application to the NIH for the "further study of issues of IV drug abuse and AIDS, including a major emphasis at defining the most effective educational approaches to the communities involved in this part of the AIDS epidemic."[90]

Williams was successful in bringing resources to the problem. In addition to substantial funding from the San Francisco AIDS Office, Williams secured a grant of $200,000 in 1988 from the CDC.[91] He also recognized that even when the message was transmitted, blacks were slow to acknowledge the disease. "Prevention messages," he wrote in 1989, "have generally not penetrated the veil of denial."[92] One of the chief problems, he argued, was that "there was no critical mass of educated men within the social circles in which minority gay and bisexual men move." Put another way, homophobia among blacks was so strong that it hampered outreach efforts. Williams's strategy to get past this problem was to go after gay men with "Hot, Horny, and Healthy" workshops that were sex positive. He also brought his leadership to the Black Coalition on AIDS, founded in 1986. His concern for others in the black community was remarkable, given what he perceived to be their reaction to him. "My personal struggle with AIDS has forced me to demand respect and dignity from my people." "Black, gay men," he once said, "need to be able to come home."[93]

By the late 1980s, the state of AIDS education among African Americans had improved markedly. In San Francisco, part of this could be directly credited to Reggie Williams, Shirley Gross, and a handful of other black AIDS volunteers. But it was also the product of a new—if tragically belated—federal intervention. In May 1988, the CDC mailed an AIDS brochure called "Understanding AIDS" to every household in the United States, the largest mass mailing in the country's history; one of the five photographs on the cover featured a young black woman and her child. Complementing these efforts was the CDC's public service radio announcements entitled "America Responds to AIDS." Several months after the mailings and radio spots began, the National Center for Health Statistics conducted an extensive national telephone survey, and the results were encouraging: "patterns of knowledge and attitudes about AIDS and HIV are essentially the same within the black population as for the U.S. population as a whole," the survey revealed, "with the greatest levels of knowledge in both groups occurring among the young and well educated." In fact, the only striking difference between black and white knowledge, according to the survey, was that blacks were less knowledgeable about the very low risk of casual transmission, tending to overestimate the risk of transmission through, for example, "working near someone with the AIDS virus."[94]

In a very disturbing development, however, this apparent parity in the AIDS knowledge of blacks and whites did not translate to parity in proportional cases. The rate of AIDS diagnoses among San Francisco's blacks skyrocketed in the 1990s. Mirroring trends in the general population, the number of blacks infected climbed steadily until reaching a peak in 1992, and then declined in subsequent years.[95] The *percentage* of blacks who were diagnosed followed a different path: it increased steadily, reaching more than 20% by the millennium, even as the black proportion of the city's population fell below 10%. Staggering rates of infection of blacks with other types of sexually transmitted diseases also suggested that messages about safer sex—even when understood—were not always heeded. In 1999, the Sexually Transmitted Disease Prevention and Control Services division of the SFDPH surveyed data since 1994 and concluded that rates of gonorrhea, early syphilis, and chlamydia were highest among African Americans, "four to ten times the rates for whites." The rate for chlamydia among African Americans was nearly twelve times that among whites.[96]

That transmission of HIV and sexually transmitted diseases continued at such alarming rates among blacks even as education programs succeeded in transmitting knowledge points to clear—and widely acknowledged, in some black circles—cultural resistance to active prevention. This resistance resulted not from ignorance about the disease but from people's stubborn preservation of traditional notions of black male sexual privilege. The best evidence of these cultural beliefs in the 1990s came from a series of interviews that a research team, led by Mindy Fullilove at UCSF Medical Center, conducted with low-income black teenage girls and women in Bayview–Hunters Point. Fullilove's team found that "teenage girls maintained their own respectability by being faithful to a teenage boy in spite of his unfaithfulness to her. In that situation, her respectability was not threatened by his infidelity: the behavior of each was sanctioned by the double standard." In effect, the study concluded, "men have been empowered to have greater sexual freedom" while "women have lost gound in their ability to insist on protection from infection."[97] The implications of the research were clear: in order to reduce heterosexual transmission among blacks, women would have to have the self-confidence and courage to resist the double standard and insist on condom use. Summoning such confidence and courage in the context of poverty, single-parent households, and epidemic drug addiction would be no mean feat.

At the millennium's end, the legacy of the sexual revolution in San Francisco looked quite bleak: having lost many of its best and brightest, and many of its young, the Castro was a mere shadow of its former self; the SFDPH now regularly described Bayview–Hunters Point as the "hot spot" for new HIV and AIDS cases; the once dowdy charm of Sally Stanford's Tenderloin had long ago been replaced by drug-induced desperation; and AIDS made that wound even deeper. Even in the Haight-Ashbury, whose free lovers had left in the 1970s, the effect of AIDS was palpable; mingled with the increasingly high-end boutiques were the faces of young and sick panhandlers—so many latecomers to a party that had ended long ago.

7

NEWCOMERS, NEW REVOLUTIONARIES, AND NEW SPACES

Back to the wasteland, that abandoned patch of Golden Gate Park at the foot of John F. Kennedy Drive, where the park meets the Pacific Ocean: preservationists had tried to revive it, bless their hearts. They quixotically restored one of the park's oldest windmills in 1980, but the propeller proved too heavy to spin, so it never did. A few paces to the south, a dark tunnel opened to a small clearing behind the Beach Chalet where the foliage was dense enough to provide shelter for the homeless and the public sex hunters. In 1981, the last of the Beach Chalet's long list of disreputable tenants—in this case a rough-and-tumble motorcycle bar—closed its doors, and the building was abandoned for almost two decades. The subsequent isolation of the area further enhanced its appeal as a public sex venue, even at the height of the AIDS epidemic in the early 1990s.

After allowing the historic Beach Chalet building to languish, the city began investing in its structural rehabilitation in the late 1980s, and in 1997 the building opened once again.[1] The storied structure now hosts the upscale Beach Chalet restaurant and microbrewery, and the grounds behind the building—once the site of countless sexual trysts—host the genteel Park Chalet beer garden. The parking lot in front—long invisible under piles of windswept sand—is filled with shining BMWs, Infinitis, and Lexuses, appropriate conveyances for the patrons who come to the Chalet for the fried wedges of French brie, served with balsamic vinegar that has been aged for exactly twenty-five years. Among the dozen or so variations of beer served on the bright back patio is the Saison du Chalet de Plage, advertised as a "farmhouse-style Belgian Ale with earthy, peppery, and spicy notes." This tony resurrection of the historically shabby Beach Chalet and its environs is a window onto the shifting passions, priorities, and sexual politics of San Franciscans in the 1980s and 1990s. It is one example among many of the pronounced repurposing of public space that accompanied massive economic growth in the region.

Developers, planners, and businesses both small and large repurposed much of the urban landscape of San Francisco during these decades, and though the intent was rarely to diminish public spectacles of sexuality, it often had that effect. Many of the public spaces that were once an essential part of the erotic life of San Franciscans went the way of the Chalet. From one long-time Richmond District resident's perspective, this was great news. Finally, he wrote, the city would be in a position to "weed out and uproot those who use the area next to the Beach Chalet for public sex acts." "This area and all areas of the park," he concluded, "are for everyone's enjoyment and shouldn't be spoiled by the deviant few."[2]

As one group of historic sex sites was being erased from the landscape, new ones were being created, a testament to the strong countercultural current that continued to run through the transforming city. Where new sites of public sexuality were being created, they were being created by lesbians. In 1995, in Yerba Buena Gardens—which opened in 1993 as the crown jewel in the

FIGURE 7.1. A "kiss-in" among lesbians in Dolores Park, prior to the 1999 Dyke March. Photograph by Phyllis Christopher.

city's South of Market redevelopment plan—two lesbians decided to kiss each other. A private security guard approached them and told them to stop kissing because "it is a family park." It was a mistake he would soon regret, because the lesbian couple went home, called all of their friends, and staged a kiss-in at the park: during a busy Monday lunch hour, fifty lesbians showed up and made out freely. It was perhaps the most sensational moment in a decade in which lesbians occupied more public space, opened more businesses, published more magazines, and resided in more neighborhoods than they ever had before. They were living proof that neither AIDS nor the massive economic shifts of the 1980s and 1990s could stop the sexual revolution in San Francisco.[3]

The New San Franciscans and the Repurposing
of Public Spaces

During the 1980s, as AIDS attacked the culture the sexual revolutionaries had wrought, San Francisco capitalized on its historic strengths in the banking and finance sector by vastly expanding its business services, which grew in conjunction with the computer industry in neighboring Santa Clara Valley. The staggering success of Apple Computer's 1980 initial public offering attracted the largest global venture capital pool to the region. By 1986, the Bay Area's gross regional product was $141 billion, and if the Bay Area were a nation unto itself—as both its greatest boosters and harshest detractors believed that it was—it would have ranked fifteenth among national economies.[4]

This vast economic shift had immediate geographic implications. It greatly intensified the demand for downtown office space. Almost nine million square feet of office space were added to San Francisco in 1985–1988.[5] Much of that growth came in the form of new construction downtown. Finance firms ventured South of Market in the late 1980s, at the very moment much of the hardcore gay leather scene was disappearing in the wake of the unfolding epidemic. In 1987, *San Francisco Business* described the southeastern portion of the city as "San Francisco's last frontier" and gushed about the prospect of creating a "city within a city" with new zoning favorable to business uses. In 1983, more than three million square feet of office space were added south of Market at First Street, and significant rezoning on Mission Street and Rincon Hill—in 1984 and 1985, respectively—promised even greater business expansion.[6]

No less dramatic than the changing geography of the downtown business district was a pronounced shift in many San Franciscans cultural values of in the 1980s. Liberalism, particularly in social and sexual matters, continued to be a dominant political ideology among San Franciscans in the 1980s, but many liberals—particularly those in the booming professional and business service sectors—replaced the bohemianism and antimaterialism of the sexual revolutionaries with a robust, even insatiable, appetite for material acquisition. And no individual represented this shift more acutely than the fabled "yuppie," the young urban professional of the 1980s.

A media-made symbol, the yuppie was the subject of ad nauseam reportage during the early to mid-1980s. The parodic *Yuppie Handbook* (1984) described a new urban class whose members thrived on "aspirations of glory, prestige, recognition, fame, social status, power, money," and the tireless quest for tasteful home decorations.[7] While there were undoubtedly those who bristled at this characterization of themselves, others who fit the "yuppie demographic" embraced the label ironically. Susanne Houfek, then a recent graduate of Stanford and the Business School of the University of California, Berkeley, conceived of and organized the First Annual Yuppie Cotillion, held at the California Academy of Sciences in Golden Gate Park in 1985. A tongue-in-cheek fundraiser for an unsuccessful bid to build a downtown baseball stadium, the event was saturated with the trappings of yuppiedom. Houfek arranged to have a floodlit BMW parked at the entrance, and the official logo of the event was the BMW icon surrounded by the words "Beauty, Money, Wealth." More than eight hundred guests attended, proof that there was, among San Franciscans, a receptive audience for Houfek's "call of the Yuppie." The event even drew protestors chanting "Let Them Eat Brie." The local alternative press was less playful; *Express*—an East Bay weekly—regarded yuppies as "mutant rats" who "multiply without even reproducing."[8]

The Yuppie Cotillion was certainly a parody; Houfek even remembers it as a piece of "performance art."[9] But the economic indicators of yuppiedom were very real. In 1986, for example, per capita spending on dining out in San Francisco significantly exceeded that of any other American city.[10] In 1988, San Francisco boasted the highest per capita retail sales of the ten largest metropolitan areas in the United States. And the shopping areas of Union Street and the downtown Financial District captured the second highest volume of retail business in the country, with $1.2 billion annually in sales. San Francisco ranked first in department store sales per household and was second only to New York in apparel and accessory store sales per household.[11]

In retrospect, the changes wrought by the yuppies of the 1980s were diminutive when compared to those wrought by the affluent migrants of the 1990s. By virtue of their numbers, their remarkable affluence, their ability and willingness to pay exorbitant prices for housing, and their affinity for urban life, they transformed the city in ways never imagined during the previous decade. The census gives us the most remarkable gauge of the implications of this shift. The

most important change was the large-scale in-migration of white-collar professional and independently wealthy young people during the 1990s. In 2000,
about 20% of the population of San Francisco (more than 145,000 people)
had moved to the city since 1995 from somewhere else in the United States.
This was more than double the number of newcomers who had come in 1985–
1990. More remarkable is that during the period 1990–2000, the population
of the city only grew by about twenty thousand people, which meant that the
vast majority of the 145,000 newcomers were *replacing* existing residents who
had left. Hence the New San Franciscans.[12]

Overwhelmingly white (66%) and, to a lesser extent, Asian (16%), the newcomers of the 1990s were very well educated, and most of them came from
California's suburbs. Quickly securing jobs in the booming dot-com industry,
these young technology workers earned the best salaries in the nation. Of the
282 "metropolitan regions" identified by the census of 2000, the San Francisco Bay Area ranked highest for median earnings among white workers.[13]

In San Francisco and surrounding areas, the arrival of these new migrants
fueled an exaggerated regional variation on the national housing price "bubble"
of the 1990s and early 2000s. The statistics were dizzying: between 1980 and
2003, the median home price increased by about 450%, along with almost
exactly the same increase in the cost of renting a two-bedroom apartment during the same period. By contrast, the consumer price index—a measurement
of the average cost of all goods—only rose by 178%. Thus, even in a market of
high salaries, for most San Franciscans, salaries were not keeping pace with
this swift increase in housing costs. As a result, the real cost of shelter for San
Francisco residents almost doubled between 1975 and 2000. Whereas median
rent had been about 10% of median income in 1970, it was about 46% in
2000.[14]

Generally speaking, these shifting economic circumstances were antitheti-
cal to bohemianism because they vastly increased the value of the spaces in
which bohemian pursuits had taken place.[15] The economic upsurge also shrank
the space in which the sexual revolution could continue. Yet the specific way
in which these circumstances affected sexual geography varied tremendously
from neighborhood to neighborhood, as a close look at the Tenderloin, Polk
Gulch, and North Beach reveals.

If one compares the uses of 105 sites known to have been sites of sexual activity and commerce in 1978 to their uses in 2008, a revealing picture
emerges.[16] Citywide in 2008, more than 70% of the 1978 sex sites had been
repurposed for different uses. While almost 30% of the 1978 sites continued
to be used for similar purposes, almost 20% of them had been repurposed for
retail uses, and another 18%—mostly in the Tenderloin—were boarded up and

empty by 2008, likely candidates for future retail uses. Twenty percent of the sites had been converted to restaurants and hotels; another 7% were being used by service businesses. The remaining sites were being used for housing, office spaces, and parking. All told, this repurposing pointed to an enormous shift in the urban landscape, economy, and culture of San Francisco over the previous three decades. Citywide, the once-visible sexual economy of the 1970s had been largely erased by 2008.

This transformation was starkest in the Tenderloin, whose 1978 sex sites had the lowest rate of continuity; only 14% of them were still operational in 2008. About 25% of the 1978 sites between lower Ellis and lower Eddy were wiped out in one fell swoop when the Ramada Renaissance hotel was built in the early 1980s. Completed in 1985, the hotel was renamed Parc 55 in 1989 and transformed into a luxury hotel catering to business travelers, particularly women. When it opened, many in the area regarded the Ramada as a harbinger of improvements. And the facility even hosted meetings of the newly formed Concerned Business Persons of the Tenderloin.[17]

Critics were quick to decry these block-by-block changes as part of a larger process of gentrification throughout the city, wiping out housing for people who then could no longer afford to live there. In fact, the story was considerably more complex in the Tenderloin. First, most of the 1978 sites were neither demolished for hotels nor repurposed for retail uses; rather, they simply went out of business, casualties of nearly universal internet access in San Francisco and pornography consumers' changing tastes. These consumers now generally chose to make their purchases using the anonymity of the Internet, and evidently not enough of those who craved the illicit companionship available at a porno theater still existed to sustain these businesses. Second, by 2008, many of the 1978 sites had been converted to spaces serving the needs of the large homeless population—a development not consistent with the general trend of gentrification in which private properties are upgraded for more affluent buyers and renters. Several sites in the Tenderloin proper, and just south on Sixth Street, were converted to housing service offices, often single-room-occupancy hotels above the former storefronts. The storied building at 101 Taylor—first the site of the Compton' Cafeteria riot, later the site of a pornography emporium—became the Oshun Center, a program of the Haight-Ashbury Free Clinic dedicated to helping women and their families struggling with drug addiction.

To a much greater extent than any other San Francisco neighborhood, the Tenderloin of the 1990s and 2000s was transformed by the nonprofit sector. Most influential was the Tenderloin Neighborhood Development Corporation (TNDC), the brainchild of housing activists in 1981 who rallied against the hotel boom in the area and convinced the Board of Supervisors to adopt a new zoning ordinance protecting SRO housing. Beginning in the 1980s, the TNDC's remarkable fundraising efforts allowed them to purchase twenty five buildings, and by 2008, they were offering housing units to more than twenty-five hundred people. A much newer organization, the North of Market Neighborhood Improvement Corporation (NOMNIC), founded in 1999, sought to stimulate the economic development of the neighborhood. Among other things, NOMNIC acted as a liaison between Tenderloin landlords and potential businesses. The corporation's executive director, Julian Davis, saw particular potential for the transformation of defunct pornographic storefronts and theaters, and in 2009 was negotiating to get tenants into both the former Doll House Theater on Turk and the Art Theater on Taylor. "Because of the protections on low income housing," Davis said, "the Tenderloin gives you the unique opportunity to revitalize the streetscape without creating the gentrification that affects other neighborhoods."[18]

One of the most dramatic shifts in the Tenderloin and neighboring Chinatown during the 1990s was the changing nature of prostitution. During the 1990s, the streetwalking female prostitute—that historic icon of urban sexuality—virtually disappeared. When sociologist Elizabeth Bernstein went undercover as a Tenderloin prostitute in the 1990s, she watched the number of prostitutes on the street dwindle from several hundred "to as few as ten or twenty a night."[19] Part of this shift, as Bernstein argues, was due to the introduction of the "First Offender" program by district attorney Terence Hallinan in 1994, under which citations of "johns" were vastly intensified and those cited were forced to attend a day-long "reeducation program." As potential "johns" recognized the risk, fewer ventured into the street trade, preferring the safer venue of the massage parlor.

The shift from the street to the massage parlor was also likely a function of changing demographics and tastes. Affluent and very well educated, the men among the New San Franciscans likely regarded the street trade as too "low-class" and dangerous. By contrast, the massage parlor offered relative privacy, a veil of therapeutic legitimacy, and the illusion of "cleanliness."[20] Usually owned and operated by Asians—Chinese and Vietnamese in particular—massage parlors became the modern brothel for the New San Franciscans. While massage parlor licensing records do not indicate which were "legitimate" and which were not, the proliferation of parlors in the 1990s and early 2000s is suggestive. According to figures from the SFDPH, the industry grew fairly steadily from 1995 (84 parlors) through 2008 (132 parlors). While certainly some of those were nonerotic massage establishments, the strong growth in Chinatown and the northern border of the Tenderloin suggests the expansion of erotic establishments. And while there is no data available on private escort services, there is abundant anecdotal evidence that this niche of the prostitution industry expanded significantly as well.[21]

On Polk Street, a very different story unfolded. Though the sex sites showed a significant degree of continuity, with about 30% of the 1978 sites still in use for similar purposes in 2008, almost 60% of them had been repurposed for retail storefronts, services like gyms and athletic clubs, and restaurants by 2008. Most significantly, the historic distinction between Lower Polk, sometimes known as Polk Gulch, and Upper Polk had largely disappeared by 2008. While Upper Polk had always been the site of more affluence, with retail stores and services, Lower Polk had been associated with male hustlers, prostitutes, pornography shops, and particularly transgender sociality.

Many of the well-known sites of transgender, homosexual, and hustler sociality closed their doors in the 1990s and early 2000s as more affluent and heterosexual professionals "discovered" the neighborhood. Famous queer hot spots like the Polk Gulch Saloon, Reflections, Rendezvous, and the Giraffe were replaced by tonier establishments. In 2005, restaurateur Myles O'Reilly opened his $6.5 million ornately designed restaurant O'Reilly's Holy Grail in the historic Maye's Oyster House building at Polk and Fern streets. According to one of his neighbors, "Myles O'Reilly is a man who cannot look at ugliness. He changed the neighborhood overnight."[22] A writer for the alternative weekly the *Bay Guardian* did not share this optimistic view of the change: "where scores of hustlers lined up against seedy sex shops and gay bars just a few years ago," he wrote with inexplicable nostalgia, "crowds of twentysomething Marina [District] look-alikes now clog the sidewalks in front of upscale clubs."[23]

As O'Reilly's heavy investment in Polk Street demonstrated, the transformation of Polk Gulch was often the result of individual initiative rather than simply larger economic forces. Most active were the couple Carolynn Abst and Ron Case, architects who moved to Polk Gulch in 1999 and opened Case+Abst Architecture on Polk Street between Post and Geary. Drawn by the relatively low property costs there—by San Francisco standards—they quickly became disillusioned by the drug dealing and street hooking that took place in plain view. They soon founded Lower Polk Neighbors, and Carolynn personally hired neighborhood youth to plant four hundred trees along Polk Street.[24] More significantly, they drew the attention of district attorney Kamala Harris, who sent representatives from her office and the SFPD to document crimes taking place on Polk. One of the immediate rewards of their labors was the inclusion of Polk Street in the new Neighborhood Marketplace Initiative introduced by Mayor Gavin Newsom. Ron Case captured the changing mood of the street: "the bars are changing

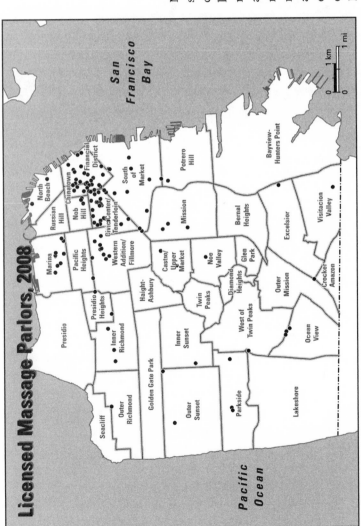

Licensed Massage Parlors, 2008

Pacific Ocean

San Francisco Bay

Seacliff

Outer Richmond

Presidio

Presidio Heights

Inner Richmond

Golden Gate Park

Outer Sunset

Inner Sunset

Parkside

Lakeshore

Marina

North Beach

Russian Hill

Pacific Heights

Nob Hill

Chinatown

Financial District

Civic Center/ Tenderloin

Western Addition/ Fillmore

South of Market

Potrero Hill

Haight-Ashbury

Castro/ Upper Market

Noe Valley

Mission

Bernal Heights

Twin Peaks

Diamond Heights

Glen Park

West of Twin Peaks

Outer Mission

Excelsior

Bayview-Hunters Point

Ocean View

Crocker Amazon

Visitacion Valley

0   1 km
0   1 mi

MAP 6. The diminishment of streetwalking prostitution and the changing preferences of affluent clientele led to a significant increase in the number of massage parlors in the 1990s and early 2000s. Although this map does not distinguish between "legitimate" massage parlors and those operating as sexual service providers, ample evidence suggests that most of the growth occurred in the latter. Map by David Deis, Dreamline Cartography.

FIGURE 7.2. Mayor Gavin Newsom kisses Del Martin as Phyllis Lyon looks on, shortly after the two became one of California's first legally married gay couples, June 2008. Courtesy: AP/Wide World Photos.

from down and outs to upscale, and people are realizing it can be nice and safe here, and they don't have to walk over passed out people and vomit."[25]

But from the perspective of many transgenders, sex workers, and other habitués of the long-standing sites of queer sociality on Polk Street, the transformation of Polk Gulch in the 1990s and early 2000s represented an attack on a lifestyle. "As for that so-called Lower Polk Neighbors Association," transgender Polk resident Rosalyne Montgomery wrote the *San Francisco Chronicle* in 2005, "it sure doesn't include any of the Lower Polk neighbors such as myself who have lived here for a long time and have no problem with human diversity." "We were here first," she concluded, "and we will stop this nonsense! The poor and non-trendy have just as much right to live in San Francisco."[26] Sharing Montgomery's perspective were the members of Gay Shame, a direct action group of radical queers, most of whom were sex workers. The loose affiliation of individuals who came to constitute Gay Shame got their start in the San Francisco LGBT Pride Celebration parade in 2001, in which they protested the materialism of the mainstream queer communities of San Francisco, particularly of Castro Street. By 2003, they were responding to the campaigns of Lower Polk Neighbors quite dramatically. Members of the group pasted "wanted" posters throughout Polk Gulch that featured pictures of Carolynn Abst and described her as the leader of a "progentrification attack squad."

A close look at census figures suggests that the claims of gentrification in Polk Gulch were both oversimplified and exaggerated. It is indisputable that the commercial streetscape of Polk Gulch was repurposed in the 1990s and early 2000s for new commercial uses that appealed to a more affluent and hetero-sexual crowd. But that crowd generally did not live in the neighborhood. If one compares median household incomes in Polk Gulch to those citywide between 1990 and 2000, the results are suggestive of the limits of gentrification. If it were as pervasive in Polk Gulch as its critics insisted, one would expect median household incomes there to approach citywide averages or, at the very least, to show an increase relative to citywide averages between 1990 and 2000. In fact, on many blocks in the Polk Gulch, the ratio of Polk Gulch median incomes to citywide incomes decreased during this period, sometimes dramatically. In the six-block area surrounding Polk and Pine, for example, median income actually decreased from 75% to 55% of the citywide average over this period, suggesting that those residents were not keeping up. Similarly, in the fourteen-block area surrounding Larkin and Sutter, median incomes slipped from above 50% to below 50% of the citywide median during this period. The only area that showed spectacular growth in its median income over this period and was the twelve-block area bound by Van Ness, Post, Ellis, and Larkin. Significantly, Case + Abst Architects sat within these boundaries. Beyond this area, gentrifi-cation was largely limited to commercial spaces.[27]

More broadly—and seen in the longer historical context—the cries of foul play in the Polk Gulch were not easily defensible. The transformation of Polk Gulch from a site of hustler and transgender sociality to a site of affluent, pre-dominantly heterosexual consumption might have been undesirable for some longtime Polk Gulch habitués. Their frustration about the decline of affordable housing in the area was surely warranted. But it is also an unpopular fact that the repurposing of Polk was no more or less radical or transformative than the repurposing of the late 1960s in which homosexuals and other sex radicals claimed what had been a "family" business district for their own purposes. The shift of the 1990s and early 2000s was simply another phase of urban trans-formation, where streetscapes reflected the shifting values and characteristics of the local population.

The story of North Beach in the 1990s and the early 2000s is a reminder that the arrival of the New San Franciscans could change the sexual geogra-phy of the city without eliminating it. During the 1980s, much of the raucous nightlife of the area had disappeared as strip clubs closed their doors; North

Beach restaurateurs and other "legitimate" business owners hailed the arrival of a new North Beach, free from the sleaze of earlier eras. But their hopes were short-lived. Although fewer than half of the 1978 sex sites remained in 2008, North Beach was the only community that added new sex sites during the 1990s and 2000s. These were not the same honky-tonks of the 1960s and 1970s. These new businesses targeted the New San Franciscans by billing themselves as luxury "gentlemen's clubs." The first was Centerfolds, which opened in 1993, before the dot-com boom was in full swing. Featuring a gourmet chef, the club boasted "fine dining and exciting, sophisticated entertainment under one roof."[28] They abandoned the food and went fully nude in 1996. In 2000, a former stockbroker opened the club Boys Toys, which offered limousine service, a business center, a chef, and imported wines.[29] When Hustler Club opened in March 2002, famed pornographer Larry Flynt said, "I want to get this business out of the gutter," and then concluded enigmatically: "There's a difference between style and class. We want this club to be about class."[30]

As such club openings had in the 1970s, the opening of the Hustler Club in 2002 drew protestors. Most vocal were women who were opposed to pornography and to Flynt in particular. Among them was Diana Russell, one of the original organizers of WAVPM who had rallied against similar businesses in North Beach in the famous Take Back the Night march of 1978. Russell, who had built an academic career by challenging rape and violence, told the *San Francisco Chronicle* that she wished Flynt's "would-be murderer had been a better shot! I hate and despise this man for all the harm he has done—and continues to do—to women and girls."[31] In many ways, the scene could have been lifted directly from 1978, except for one thing: among the crowds that gathered were women—self-identified feminists, in fact—who *supported* Flynt. Most conspicuous was Heather Findlay, a feminist, lesbian, and the editor of a sexually explicit lesbian magazine called *On Our Backs*. "Larry Flynt is a hero of mine. He's a hero to anyone interested in the First Amendment. Not all feminists are against porn," Findlay said, "some of us like it."[32] Proudly articulating a stance that would have drawn cries of treason from other feminists in the 1970s, Findlay was not alone. She represented the voice of a new generation of lesbians, indeed of a second sexual revolution among lesbians.

The Second Lesbian Revolution

During the 1990s, lesbians in San Francisco created a second sexual revolution. The lesbian revolutionaries were feminists, but they rejected the rigid ideological mandates of 1970s lesbian feminism. Unlike their predecessors, these new lesbian revolutionaries adopted an eclectic aesthetic, vastly more complicated than the traditional "butch" and "femme" categories of earlier years. They endorsed, embraced, and even produced explicit erotica and pornography. They sometimes sought group sex, and occasionally even anonymous sex. They sometimes engaged in S/M and used dildos, two practices reviled in most lesbian-feminist circles of earlier days. And they laid claim to a much wider area of urban space than their predecessors had. In these ways and others, San Francisco lesbians of the 1990s transformed the history of lesbian sexuality, the history of San Francisco, and the history of female sexuality in America. As San Francisco lesbian writer and pornographer Shar Rednour wrote of her experiences in the 1990s, "the straight people had their free-love years" and "the gay men had discoed into the bathhouses and beyond." "We were finally having," she concluded, "our slut coming of age."[33]

To fully understand the culture of the new lesbian revolutionaries, one must first look at its antithesis: the Castro Street of the 1990s. The predominantly white gay community of Castro Street became largely indistinguishable from the world created by the New San Franciscans. Once the site of a scrappy gay bohemianism, Castro Street came to represent the apogee of the gentrification trend of the 1990s and 2000s. By 1999, median income in the Castro was 126% of the citywide median; median asking rents were 168% of the citywide figure, and median home values were 150% of the citywide figure.[34] The commercial streetscape of Castro and Upper Market streets—battered by the AIDS epidemic in the 1980s—was again vibrant, saturated with high-end retail and restaurants catering to the affluent habitués of the area. For the older, newly affluent gay male population of the 1990s and 2000s, domesticity and materialism became vital—if only mildly mitigating—palliatives in an era of tremendous loss.[35]

By contrast—and undoubtedly with many exceptions—young lesbians created a dynamic, even revolutionary new world for themselves in San Francisco during the 1990s and early 2000s. There were at least two wellsprings for this second lesbian revolution. First was the ascent of sex-positive feminism in the mid-1980s. Shattering the taboos of mainstream feminism and mainstream cultural expectations of women, these women radically altered the course of feminism, of lesbians' sexual behavior, and, arguably, of women's sexual behavior generally. Though a number of women were associated with these new ideas, few were more influential than Nan Kinney, Deborah Sundahl, and Susie Bright.

Kinney grew up in the hardscrabble, meat-packing town of Austin, Minnesota. She knew she was gay from childhood; she came out as a lesbian when she attended the University of Minnesota. An antiwar protestor, Kinney also became passionate about challenging violence against women. She earned a master's degree in physical education and then began teaching martial arts for women. When she first heard about WAVPM, she was drawn to the cause. At the first WAVPM meeting in Minneapolis in 1979, she met a like-minded woman, fellow University of Minnesota graduate Deborah Sundahl, who was volunteering at a Minneapolis battered women's shelter. They became, as Kinney later recalled, "quick friends and quick lovers."

In the first month of their work with the Minneapolis WAVPM, Kinney and Sundahl shared their peers' hostility to pornography. But they quickly came to the conclusion that pornography was not the cause of the pervasive violence against women in American society. Furthermore, Kinney began to sense that the Minneapolis WAVPM's verbal harassment of sex workers smacked of elitism, pitting relatively privileged, well-educated feminists against lower class, minimally educated women who hustled for a living. Finally, the duo's sexual practices and values simply did not square with the "party line" of WAVPM. Both believed in the relevance of pornography for women's sexual education and sexual pleasure, and they also believed lesbians should be free to explore any aspect of their sexuality, including S/M. As so many gays and straights had before, they moved to San Francisco in 1982, as Kinney put it, "for the sex."[36]

And they found it. Having started a lesbian S/M club in Minneapolis, they soon joined Pat Califia, Gayle Rubin, and others in Samois to explore lesbian S/M. Sundahl edited the Samois newsletter and worked as a stripper at the Mitchell Brothers O'Farrell Theater, while Kinney broke a gender barrier at the Pacific Gas and Electric Company by becoming one of the first female jackhammer operators in San Francisco. But even in that city, the two were quickly frustrated with the pervasiveness of sexual repression among lesbians. To be sure, Samois was a haven, but it was very marginal among the lesbian mainstream, and it fell apart in 1983. Kinney and Sundahl determined to draw on all of their resources to create something radically new: erotica by lesbians, for lesbians.

Pooling money from their jobs and taking tips from publishers of gay magazines, Kinney, Sundahl, and Sundahl's business partner, Myrna Elana, began scouting out literary, photographic, and modeling talent among San Francisco lesbians. One evening, Elana heard a young woman named Susie Bright reading a love poem at Modern Times, and wrote her a fan letter. "I was delighted," Bright later recalled, "and asked to help out."[37] As a journalist for several New Left newspapers and a reporter for the *Long Beach Press Telegram*, the *Long Beach Union*, and the *L.A. Weekly*, Bright brought significant editorial experience to the table. Nor was she a stranger to controversial media; as a high school student, she had been hounded by Los Angeles news anchorman George Putnam for writing "birth control stories" in an underground newspaper. At *On Our*

Backs, Bright quickly signed on as a columnist and cofounder. A playful homage to *Off Our Backs,* the feminist magazine based in Washington, D.C., that the founders read voraciously, *On Our Backs* promised to be "entertainment for the adventurous lesbian."

First published in 1984, *On Our Backs* featured erotic fiction and erotic photographic centerfolds and boasted—probably without exaggeration—"the largest collection of sex-oriented business advertising for lesbians ever assembled under one cover."[38] Bright's first column in *On Our Backs* extolled the many virtues of the dildo, that masturbatory device long vilified in feminist circles. It was exhilarating to produce the new medium, even joyful, but it was also political work. Sundahl recalled that for too long lesbians had been downplaying "our sexuality." "Lesbians were hiding by appealing to political feminism for legitimacy." Publishing lesbian erotica became a way for Sundahl to say to the world: "we are lesbians because we love women" and not "because we hate men."[39] There was a growing urgency among prosex feminists, Sundahl recalled, "to set ourselves back on the road to sexual liberation."

Among lesbians, the initial reception to *On Our Backs* was chilly. *Off Our Backs* described the magazine's content as "pseudo-feminist" and "so-called 'feminist' pornography," and the editors of *Off Our Backs* warned Kinney and Sundahl not to use the acronym OOB in reference to their magazine because *Off Our Backs* was seeking a trademark. Kinney, Bright, and Sundahl received threatening letters, and women's bookstores refused to carry their magazine. And when Kinney and Sundahl decided to show selections of the first release of their new video company, Fatale Private Pleasures and Shadows—featuring makeup, leather, and penetration—at the 1985 Frameline film festival in San Francisco, the audience hissed, threw food at the screen, and came very close to physically assaulting Kinney. Wildly controversial, and deeply in debt, the magazine nonetheless quickly planted the seeds of a new attitude among lesbians. Subscriptions and sales accelerated in the late 1980s, and Fatale Media became the world's largest producer of lesbian pornography. When *On Our Backs* sponsored a night of female erotica with Susie Bright at the Castro Theater in 1989, the reaction was quite different from that in 1985. The lesbian crowd spilled onto the streets; there were complaints again—this time the chief complaint that there was not *sufficient* lesbian erotica to satisfy demand.[40]

As Kinney, Sundahl, and Bright worked to reverse the sex-negative strain in lesbianism, others worked on a parallel track to challenge lesbian hostility toward bisexual women. The bisexual movement of the late 1980s and 1990s was the second wellspring of the second lesbian sexual revolution. The bisexual movement had the effect of dislodging some of the bi-phobia that had been inherent in the lesbian feminism of the 1970s. This was no small task, since the bi-phobic sentiment redoubled during the 1980s, when many lesbians worried that bisexuals would be the vectors of HIV transmission into the relatively unscathed lesbian community. Challenging bi-phobia engendered sexual freedom by allowing queer women to openly engage in more varied sexual experiences without incurring the chastisement and prohibitions of fellow queers. In addition, the bisexual movement engendered political empowerment among queer women. "Never before," bisexual scholar Dawn Atkins has written, had there been a movement "composed of and for the benefit of both men and women that was predominantly and publicly led by women."[41]

In the late 1980s, bisexuals in San Francisco remade the flagging bisexual movement of the 1970s. Galvanized in part by the negative media attention bisexuals were receiving in the context of the AIDS crisis, bisexuals generally sought greater public visibility and stronger representation in mainstream gay organizations. Toward that end, they began to organize the first national bisexual conference, slated to take place in San Francisco in 1990. One of the dynamic leaders of the bisexual movement, a woman whose work would be foundational for the lesbian revolutionaries of the 1990s, was Carol Queen. Born and raised in rural Oregon, Queen recognized her "queerness" at an early age and discovered feminism shortly thereafter. But she soon found that the lesbian feminism of the 1970s was greatly at odds with one peculiar aspect of her sexuality: though "mostly" a lesbian, she also liked to have sex with men. Further alienating her from the mainstream of lesbian feminism was her enthusiasm for S/M. Refusing to accept that she was just a "bad dyke," Queen lit out on her own path.[42]

As Califia and Rubin had been a decade earlier, Queen was drawn to the predominantly gay male world of S/M and leather. But Queen's foray after the arrival of AIDS meant that the outcomes were different. She began participating in the vibrant group masturbation party scene in the late 1980s, just when radical sex was believed to be dead.

> Beneath the suppressed, grieving façade of the eighties fermented
> a new—or at least updated—sexual revolution.... Word went out all
> over the Bay Area sex community. Nothing like this—multi-gendered
> and omni-persuasional—had ever been tried, at least not within
> memory. It wasn't going to be a jack-off party—women would be
> there. Not a swing party—gay men would be very much in evidence.
> And nobody would fuck—it wasn't allowed. Not a free-wheeling
> seventies-style orgy—those hadn't been run by strict safe-sex rules.
> It wasn't like anything, except maybe the future. It was a new forum
> for radical sex in uncertain times.[43]

Regarding these experiences as "transcendent," Queen became one of the chief organizers of the National Bisexual Conference in 1990. Remembered as the "Bisexuals' Stonewall," the conference concluded with a 150-person party in which many participated in group sex. Queen organized a series of "Jack-and-Jill-Off" parties that drew hundreds to this post-AIDS public sex scene through the mid-to-late 1990s.

Queen's promotion of public sex and her work against bi-phobia—when coupled with the pathbreaking eroticism of Kinney, Sundahl, and Bright—set the stage for an era of unprecedented sexual freedom for queer women. In the 1990s, a new group of lesbians patronized something entirely new and unprecedented in the history of lesbians: the lesbian sex club. Closely resembling the gay sex clubs of the 1970s and early 1980s, these new lesbian ones cultivated a leather aesthetic and S/M play. When Patricia Lake, a reporter for *Off Our Backs*, visited San Francisco's lesbian sex clubs in 1992, she was shocked by what she saw:

> One heavyset butch with shaved punk-head and a spiked collar
> around her neck, chains dangling from her heavy boots, pulled
> the pants down on a small kneeling woman; the butch had a dildo
> strapped on and was putting a condom on it and lubricating it while
> crouching behind the femme, kissing and fondling her a bit and then
> "doing it" to her, while the young woman sucked the plastic dick of
> another woman also in leather, standing above her.[44]

But this was no mere knockoff of the gay sex club of the 1970s. Women created their own variations on the theme of raucous, public sex. Rednour later recalled wearing a "white lace bustier" and "Marilyn-Monroe-white-leather-pumps" while performing gymnastics on a 4 × 4 board above "naked dykes fucking in a plywood labyrinth."[45]

Rednour was an assistant editor at *On Our Backs* at this time; after Lake's article came out, she recalled, "we got a very heavy telephone response." "Lesbian tourists would call our office and say 'Sex clubs? Where do we go?'"[46] From the perspective of some lesbians, there was nothing revolutionary about these sex clubs; they were "disgusting" and "sick."[47] But from the participants' perspective, something more substantial than erotic play was also taking place. "We had finally decided to stop policing each other," Rednour wrote, referring to the politics of her lesbian forerunners, "and start perverting each other." For Phyllis Christopher, a lesbian feminist and professional photographer, the sex parties of the early 1990s were political. "We felt our political work during that era was to promote sexual freedom."

> We were ready to burst free after enduring feminist dogma in
> women's studies groups that put down pornography. And we came of
> age during AIDS, of associating sex with death. We were ready to party
> with our safe sex knowledge, surrounded by women who wanted to
> have a good time rather than talk about serious issues all of the time.[48]

Indeed, although "safe-sex knowledge" prevailed, the lesbian sex radicals of the 1990s also benefited from the reality that AIDS simply did not take the same toll on the lesbian community as on the gay community. Although the SFDPH warned in 1993 that "lesbians and bisexual women report substantial levels of unsafe sexual and drug-using behaviors with male and female partners that may put them at high risk for HIV infection," no lesbian AIDS epidemic ever came.[49] As late as 2006, the CDC reported "no confirmed cases of female-to-female sexual transmission of HIV in the United States."[50]

In Christopher's case, the sex clubs also became the subject of her photographs, part of her body of work, inspired by her lifelong desire to "depict lesbian lives for other lesbians to view, to show a culture that didn't have many images of themselves, that they were beautiful."[51] As Christopher's photographs suggested, the lesbian sex clubs of the early 1990s were just the most dramatic manifestations of a broader expansion in lesbian creativity and erotic entertainment during the period. For example, Rednour met her partner, musician Jackie Strano, at one of Carol Queen's sex clubs. Strano, the lead singer in a dyke band called the Hail Marys, remembered the euphoria of "knowing it was your god given right to seek truth and have pleasure." The couple went on to create their own lesbian pornography company called S.I.R. Video—Sex, Indulgence, and Rocknroll.[52] With the financial support of Nan Kinney and Joani Blank, S.I.R released *Bend over Boyfriend* (1998), which quickly became the best-selling title not only of Fatale Media but at Good Vibrations as well. The couple led workshops on polyamory and jealousy that became legendary in the lesbian community of 1990s San Francisco, and queer writer and pornography producer Tristan Taormino described them as "one of the best known polyamorous couples in San Francisco."[53]

After a major distributor of the magazine declared bankruptcy in the mid-1990s, *On Our Backs* fell on hard financial times. Kinney moved to New Mexico with a new lover and business partner and bought Sundahl's shares of Fatale Media, while Sundahl got married, relocated, and started a new "g-spot ejaculation" education business. Heather Findlay, a graduate of Brown University, bought the magazine out of bankruptcy court. She had irked school administrators in 1986 when she and a friend published *Positions,* a lesbian pornography magazine, in response to *Playboy*'s campaign to recruit Brown women for their "girls of the Ivy League" issue. Though she was fully exposed to antipornography feminism in her women's studies courses, Findlay already recognized that there were "Off Our Backs lesbians" and "On Our Backs lesbians," and that she was emphatically the latter.

Under Findlay's ownership, *On Our Backs* entered a new era of growth. Fully committed to "continuing the important work that Nan and Deborah had been doing," Findlay also sought to professionalize the magazine by expanding its advertising base, expanding subscriptions, and shoring up its finances. During her tenure, subscriptions increased from twelve hundred to five thousand, and the print run increased to fifteen thousand.[54] And more happened than merely the message of *On Our Backs* reaching a greater audience: in the same way that Kinney, Sundahl, and Bright had shattered the taboos of the 1980s, Findlay and her staff shattered one of the last remaining taboos among lesbians: transgenderism. *On Our Backs* was probably the first lesbian magazine to engage the topic of female-to-male transgenders, and to fully embrace their sexuality. And it was certainly the first to publish a photo shoot featuring transgender lesbians. Simultaneously—and in a telling indicator of the impact of the new recognition of queerness as an all-embracing ethos—female-to-male (FTM) transsexuals organized the first international FTM conference in August 1995, drawing 350 participants to the San Francisco Women's Building—a place that had been off-limits even to S/M lesbians in the 1970s.[55]

Of course, not all San Francisco lesbians were erotica enthusiasts, polyamorists, or sex club devotees. But these lesbian sex radicals had an impact on social and sexual mores in the broader lesbian community nonetheless. More mainstream lesbian dance clubs began to feature nude or scantily clad go-go dancers. Fairy Butch, a Good Vibrations employee and sex educator, began hosting a lesbian nightclub featuring lesbian strippers. And Club Q, an erotically charged, monthly lesbian dance club promoted by DJ Page Hodel, operated at several locations throughout the city during the 1990s. Rounding out the awakened lesbian nightlife were more reserved venues like the Lexington—which opened in the Mission in 1997 at the same intersection where Robert Hillsborough had been savagely murdered twenty years earlier—and remained a vibrant spot through the early 2000s.[56] In 2003, *Betty and Pansy's Severe Queer Review of San Francisco* bespoke the diversity of the new lesbian scene:

> In San Francisco there are more kinds of lesbians than you can shake
> a stick at. Some identify as fag boys, some as leather dykes, some as
> old-school bulldaggers, some as high femme, some as super lipstick
> lezzies, and the list goes on and on. In a recent trend, butches are
> coming out as FTMs.[57]

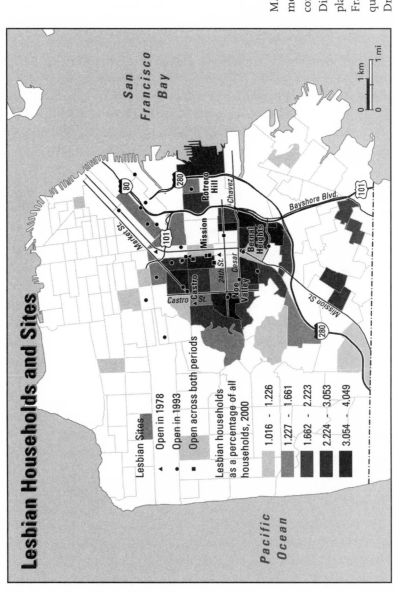

Lesbian Households and Sites

Lesbian Sites

▲ Open in 1978

● Open in 1993

■ Open across both periods

Lesbian households as a percentage of all households, 2000

1.016 - 1.226
1.227 - 1.661
1.662 - 2.223
2.224 - 3.053
3.054 - 4.049

San Francisco Bay

Pacific Ocean

Market St.

Castro

A. Castro St.

Noe Valley

24th St.

Cesar

Mission

Bernal Heights

Potrero Hill

Chavez

Bayshore Blvd.

Mission St.

80

101

280

101

280

0   1 km
0   1 mi

MAP 7. By the 1990s, lesbians moved beyond their historic concentration in the Mission District to reside, shop, and play in broad swathes of San Francisco's southeastern quadrant. Map by David Deis, Dreamline Cartography.

As it had in the 1970s, the shape of lesbian culture in the 1990s had its geographic corollary. The lesbian sex revolutionaries of the 1990s not only expanded social and erotic opportunities for queer women generally but also expanded the geography of lesbian San Francisco. Historically relegated to the Mission District and, by the 1980s, Bernal Heights, many lesbians now turned their attention to other parts of the city. The two best known sex clubs—Klitz-Blitz and Club Snatch—were held at "secret locations" South of Market that were only revealed shortly before the events via telephone. In Bernal Heights, lesbians increasingly gathered around Bernal Books and the bar Wild Side West.[58] Even more dramatic was the expanding residential geography of lesbians in the 1990s. Maintaining a strong presence in the Mission, lesbians also moved to adjacent Noe Valley, South of Market, Bernal Heights, Potrero Hill, Glen Park, the outer Richmond District, Oceanview, the Excelsior, and even Visitacion Valley—Dan White's old neighborhood.

EPILOGUE

Where the Wild Things Still Are

"Going back to California is not like going back to Vermont, or Chicago," Joan Didion wrote in 1965. "Vermont and Chicago are relative constants, against which one measures one's own change. All that is constant about the California of my childhood is the rate at which it disappears."[1] Longtime San Franciscans may be even more inclined than Californians generally to view their home in this way, as a place whose finest hour has passed, where roiling economic forces have crushed the easy eclecticism, bohemianism, and joyful sexual experimentation of the 1960s and 1970s. But nostalgia can be deceptive: the revolution is not over.

Locally, ongoing revolutions in sexual practices and beliefs continue to color daily life. A Japanese-born sex educator leads sold-out classes on bondage and militaristic sex play for San Francisco couples. An enterprising Englishman who owns an outlandish S/M website recently purchased the Moorish-revival San Francisco Armory Building in the Mission District and converted it into a sex dungeon and film set. Until recently, a club called the Power Exchange, billed as an adult play space, hosted countless sexual trysts between men, women, and male-to-female transgenders. Across town in North Beach, the ladies of the Lusty Lady continue to dance for eager patrons, but they now do so in a unionized, worker-owned cooperative, revolutionizing the nature of sex work. And the most recent LGBT Pride Celebrations have drawn well over one million revelers.

More significantly, homosexuals in San Francisco and beyond demand the right to marry, signaling a new phase in their long revolution for full equality. As they had for more than fifty years, lifelong partners Del Martin and Phyllis Lyon again led the charge for homosexual equality, this time as plaintiffs in the California Supreme Court case in which the ban on gay marriage was lifted in May 2008, making California the second state, after Massachusetts, to allow gay marriage. Only minutes after the ruling went into effect on June 16, 2008, Lyon and Martin married at City Hall in a ceremony officiated by Mayor Gavin Newsom. Two months later, Del Martin died, leaving behind her grieving partner of fifty-five years. "I could never imagine a day would come when she wouldn't be by my side. I also never imagined there would be a day that we would actually be able to get married....I am devastated," Lyon wrote shortly after Martin's death, "but I take some solace in knowing we were able to enjoy the ultimate rite of love and commitment before she passed."[2]

Their marriage, and thousands of subsequent marriages of other gays and lesbians in California, reinvigorated California moralists, who quickly set about collecting signatures for an initiative in 2008 to amend the Constitution to eliminate the right of same-sex couples to marry—Proposition 8. All of the more than thirty Assembly members who endorsed the measure were Republicans, and all but one were from rural, suburban, and largely southern parts of the state, demographics consistent with the geocultural divide first evident in the returns for Proposition 16 in 1966, and again for Proposition 6 in 1978. The referendum results revealed a much wider hostility to gay marriage than the endorsements suggested. California voters approved the amendment by a margin of 52.4% to 47.6%—predictably, by much larger margins in the rural and suburban interior. Remarkably, it also passed in generally left-leaning counties like Los Angeles and Sacramento, suggesting that great limits to California's fabled "tolerance" remained.

Even in San Francisco, where almost 69% of the voters rejected the initiative, a close reading of precinct returns revealed that it was still a city of competing moral visions. Voters supported the ban in 54 of the 580 precincts, including parts of Chinatown, Bayview–Hunters Point, and Visitacion Valley. Asians and African Americans, voters over sixty, and voters without college educations generally supported the ban. Catholicism, as it always had, deeply influenced the voters in Visitacion Valley, but so did the highly effective television advertisements that spuriously claimed that failure to pass the ban would result in new requirements that public school children be educated about gay marriage.[3] That hostility to gay marriage still existed in large swathes of

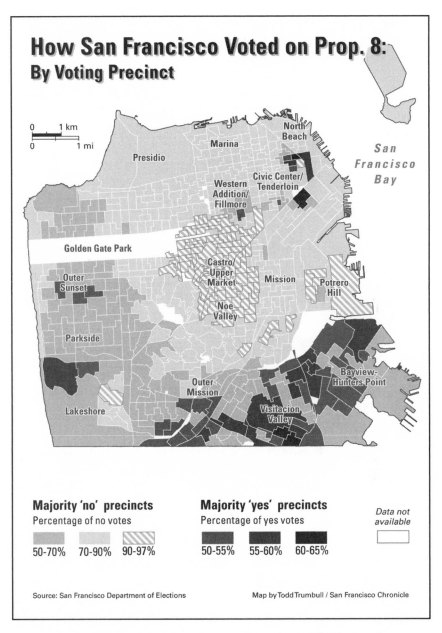

How San Francisco Voted on Prop. 8:
By Voting Precinct

0   1 km
0   1 mi

Presidio

Marina

North Beach

San Francisco Bay

Western Addition/ Fillmore

Civic Center/ Tenderloin

Golden Gate Park

Outer Sunset

Castro/ Upper Market

Mission

Potrero Hill

Noe Valley

Parkside

Outer Mission

Bayview-Hunters Point

Lakeshore

Visitacion Valley

Majority 'no' precincts
Percentage of no votes

50-70%   70-90%   90-97%

Majority 'yes' precincts
Percentage of yes votes

50-55%   55-60%   60-65%

Data not available

Source: San Francisco Department of Elections   Map by Todd Trumbull / San Francisco Chronicle

MAP 8. Map by Todd Trumbull/*San Francisco Chronicle*. Modified by David Deis, Dreamline Cartography.

California and even small pockets of San Francisco in 2008 was a sobering reminder to advocates of gay marriage that their battle for equal rights nationally would be long and hard-fought.

The right to marry is just one front in the current gay revolution. When Governor Pete Wilson signed legislation forbidding discrimination on the basis of sexual orientation in 1992, California joined a handful of states with similar laws, but at the time of this writing, the majority of states still have no such laws. Nor does the historic Civil Rights Act of 1964—the most important law eradicating workplace discrimination in the United States—apply to discrimination on the basis of sexual orientation. In 2003, California joined an even smaller handful of states prohibiting employment discrimination against transgenders. In short, employment discrimination against gays, lesbians, and transgenders is still legal in most of the United States.

If San Francisco's homosexual revolutions now reverberate throughout the nation, the city's recent experience with prostitution may portend national shifts as well. The migration of prostitution from the street to massage parlors and escort services in the 1990s was abetted by transnational immigration flows. As the New San Franciscans have sought commercial sex in massage parlors and through escort services, they have stimulated a growing demand that has been satisfied in part by Chinese, Korean, Vietnamese, Russian, and Mexican human traffickers who entrap unsuspecting women with promises of legitimate employment in the United States and force them into sex work under the threat of violence once they arrive. Given the underground nature of these criminal operations, hard numbers are difficult to come by, but federal agents confiscated more than $2 million in a raid of ten Asian massage parlors in San Francisco in 2005, suggesting that it is a booming business. Even single-family homes in the sleepy Outer Sunset district have been converted to brothels. San Francisco is now just one spot on the global map of an international sex trade that is at times coercive and other times voluntary. It is doubtful that any other American city has been on that map longer, or has experimented with more approaches to protecting the privacy of sex consumers while simultaneously treating prostitutes humanely, than San Francisco. San Francisco's vigorous prosecution of suspected traffickers, for example, may offer critical lessons for other global cities.[4]

San Francisco's early engagement with the "problem" of pornography, particularly the issue of street-front visibility, has also prefigured the nation's. San Francisco's and Detroit's antipornography campaigns in the 1970s—despite their mixed success records—spawned similar campaigns in Los Angeles; Santa Monica; New York; Washington, D.C.; Cleveland; Chicago; and dozens of other American cities. The relevance of those campaigns declined dramatically after the arrival of privately accessible internet pornography in the late 1990s, but here, too, San Francisco's experience shapes the nation's: while the vast majority of internet pornography companies catering to heterosexuals are in southern California, San Francisco became in the early 2000s what the *San Francisco Chronicle* described as the "world headquarters of the gay adult entertainment industry," contributing to the booming high-tech sector that drives the area's economy.[5]

Recent estimates by the California State Board of Equalization demonstrate the enormous fiscal impact of the adult entertainment industry on the economy of California, as well as the profound impact California pornography has on the economy of the United States. According to figures from an industry association, Americans rented 957 million adult DVDs in 2005, "almost all of which were produced in California."[6] Though few reliable figures exist for the total revenue generated by adult entertainment in California, the same association puts it at about $4 billion annually. The geographical reach of the industry is even more remarkable and verifiable, bringing the pornography that was once only available in seedy urban pornography theaters to any home in the nation, even those in bastions of putative morality like Utah County, Utah. A historically conservative county with fewer than four hundred thousand residents, Utah County became the site of a late-1990s obscenity case in which it was revealed that local cable subscribers had ordered at least ten thousand adult videos annually, that a local video store derived 20% of its rental sales from its small adult movie inventory, that the county's sole adult novelty store brought in more than $100,000 annually in sex toy sales, and that the Provo Marriott rented more than three thousand in-room adult videos annually.[7]

More enduring legacies of the sexual revolution are evident in the rising rates of premarital sex and premarital cohabitation in the United States. Between the late 1950s and the early 2000s, the proportion of eighteen-year-olds who had premarital sex rose from 26% to 54%.[8] Similarly, both the practice of, and general societal tolerance for, premarital cohabitation has increased dramatically. More significantly, heterosexual couples have demonstrated an increased commitment to gender equality, mutual sexual fulfillment, and individual freedom since the late 1950s.[9] San Franciscans certainly did not invent these values, but there have been few cities where the proportion of practitioners has been as high, for as long.

"The city," lifelong sex radical Patrick Califia has written, "is a map of the hierarchy of desire, from the valorized to the stigmatized."[10] The topography of that map is highly variegated in San Francisco, where both the flaneur and the tourist can easily detect its contours. But such a map overlays every city, even where the prevalence of heterosexuals seems to render it invisible. Revealing that map of desire in our greatest cities, and locating the deeply contested values and agendas that have informed it, remains one of urban historians' great challenges for the future.

ACKNOWLEDGMENTS

This book could not have been completed without the generous backing of several organizations and dozens of individuals whose support was unconditional and should in no way be interpreted as an endorsement of any of my research or conclusions. Crucial financial support for research, travel, and other costs was provided by: the Whitsett Endowment at California State University, Northridge (CSUN), and its capable manager and History Department Chair, Thomas Maddux; Stella Theodoulou, dean of the College of Social and Behavioral Sciences, CSUN; the National Endowment for the Humanities, which generously provided me with a summer stipend in 2005; the Schlesinger Library at Harvard's Radcliffe Institute for Advanced Study, which awarded me a research fellowship in 2006.

Librarians are indispensable for historians, and I owe a special debt of gratitude to the following librarians, as well as many more not listed: Mary Morganti, California Historical Society; Valerie Rom-Hawkins, UCLA Young Research Library; Berhan Arega, Michael Barrett, Felicia Cousin, and Mary Finley, CSUN Oviatt Library; Greg Kelly, Tim Wilson, Susan Goldstein, Tami Suzuki, and Kenny Lam, San Francisco Public Library; Ellen Shea, Schlesinger Library, Radcliffe Institute for Advanced Studies; Patrick J. Stevens, Carl A. Kroch Library, Cornell University; Terence Kissack, Daniel Bao, Rebecca Kim, and Jacob Richards at the Gay, Lesbian, Bisexual, Transgender Historical Society, San Francisco; Lisa A. Mix and Josue Hurtado, Archives and Special Collections, UCSF Library and Center for Knowledge Management.

The following individuals took time from their busy schedules to share their experiences and memories with me, and the book is much better for it: Joani Blank, Pat Brown, Patrick Califia, Phyllis Christopher, Julian Davis, Sadja Greenwood, Sue Houfek, Espanola Jackson, Marion Jackson, Paul Kantus, Bruce Lamott, Leo Laurence, Laura Lederer, Jimmy Loyce, Ted McIlvenna, Christina Milner-Rose, Jefferson Poland, Shar Rednour, Gayle Rubin, Sam Sloan, Jacqueline Tulsky, Gale Whittington, Nan Kinney, Mother Boats, Deborah Sundahl, Heather Findlay, and several informants who chose to remain anonymous. Others offered invaluable intellectual support by either reading my work or critically engaging me in conversation about parts of it: Talia Bettcher, Peter Boag, Nan Boyd, Bill Deverell, Gary Gates, Jacob Hale, Amyn Kaderali, Terence Kissack, Elizabeth Lobb, Martin Meeker, Becky Nicolaides, Clementine Oliver, Jan Reiff, Susan Stryker, Jack Tilmanny, Allison Varzally, Mark Wild, and the two anonymous reviewers for Oxford University Press.

Photographers Robert Altman, Cathy Cade, Phyllis Christopher, Don Eckert, and Rick Gerharter kindly allowed me to use their magnificent photographs, and Gary Fong and Rick Romagosa at the photo department of the *San Francisco Chronicle* sleuthed masterfully to track down photographs that I knew existed but could never have found on my own. Permission to use the photograph of Carol Doda atop the grand piano was generously furnished by Bill Graham Archives, LLC / Wolfgang's Vault, and Columbia Pictures furnished permission to use the photographic still from *Hardcore*; At the San Francisco Department of Health, Johnson Ojo, Tara Schubert, and Tim Kellogg were extraordinarily generous with their time and data. David Deis of Dreamline Cartography produced all of the maps in this book, with the exception of the Proposition 8 map, which was produced by Todd Trumbull of the *San Francisco Chronicle*. At various stages in the process of writing this book, CSUN graduate students Andrea Palacio, Joe Dixon, and particularly Karen Drohan offered critical research support. Kelly Winkleblack Shea and Susan Mueller provided great administrative support in the history department. An author could not ask for a better editor than Susan Ferber, who helped me refine this book while trusting my instincts. Copyeditor Martha Ramsey was unsparing in her meticulousness and saved me from more than a few technical gaffes. Finally, my father and mother, Henry and Sudie Sides, were my first and best teachers and have been unflagging in their encouragement of my work. My wife Rebecca, to whom this book is dedicated, has been ceaselessly patient and supportive. Little Sarah and Jesse were of absolutely no help at all, and I love them for that.

ABBREVIATIONS AND ARCHIVAL SOURCES

ABC Records of the Alcoholic Beverage Control Board, California State Library, Sacramento.

ACLUNC Records of the American Civil Liberties Union, Northern California Branch, California Historical Society, San Francisco.

AIDS-SFDPH Annual Reports of HIV/AIDS Infection, San Francisco Department of Public Health, 1981–2008.

ARSFPD Annual Reports of the Police Department of the City and County of San Francisco, 1935–1994, San Francisco Public Library.

AUGGR ACT-UP Golden Gate Records, MSS 98–47, Archives and Special Collections, Library and Center for Knowledge Management, University of California, San Francisco.

CDC Centers for Disease Control and Prevention, Atlanta.

COYOTE Records of COYOTE, Schlesinger Library, Radcliffe Institute for Advanced Study, Harvard University.

CTP Charles Thorpe Papers, San Francisco History Center, San Francisco Public Library.

DLP David Lourea Papers, San Francisco History Center, San Francisco Public Library.

EWCSICR East and West of Castro Street Improvement Club Records, Noe Valley Branch Library, San Francisco Public Library.

GLBTHS Gay, Lesbian, Bisexual, Transgender Historical Society, San Francisco.

JFSP John F. "Jack" Shelley Papers, San Francisco History Center, San Francisco Public Library.

JLAP Joseph L. Alioto Papers, San Francisco History Center, San Francisco Public Library.

JMFP James M. Foster Papers, Division of Rare and Manuscript Collections, Carl A. Kroch Library, Cornell University.

JRJP James Rolph, Jr., Papers, North Baker Research Library, California Historical Society, San Francisco.

LAR Lesbian Avengers Records, GLBTHS.

LAT Los Angeles Times.

LMP Phyllis Lyon and Del Martin Papers, GLBTHS.

NSP Nancy Stoller Papers, MSS-2000–6, Archives and Special Collections, Library and Center for Knowledge Management, University of California, San Francisco.

NTAP National Task Force on AIDS Prevention Records, MSS 94–59, Archives and Special Collections, Library and Center for Knowledge Management, University of California, San Francisco.

NYT New York Times.

QSDB Queer Sites Database, GLBTHS.

RAP Randy Alfred Papers, GLBTHS.

SFBOS Records of the San Francisco Board of Supervisors, 1972–1981, City Hall, San Francisco.

SFC San Francisco Chronicle.

SFE San Francisco Examiner.

SFHC San Francisco History Center, San Francisco Public Library.

SFLR Sexual Freedom League Records, Bancroft Library, University of California, Berkeley.

SFWCR San Francisco Women's Centers Records, GLBTHS.

TNSPP Thomas N. Saunders Materials Relating to the History of Planned Parenthood Alameda/San Francisco, 1933–1994, California Historical Society, San Francisco.

WAVPM Records of Women Against Violence in Pornography and the Media, 1977–1983, GLBTHS.

NOTES

INTRODUCTION

1. For alternative and additional accounts of the sexual revolution, see John D'Emilio and Estelle Freedman, *Intimate Matters: A History of Sexuality in America* (New York: Harper & Row, 1988); John Heidenry, *What Wild Ecstasy: The Rise and Fall of the Sexual Revolution* (New York: Simon & Schuster, 1997); Beth Bailey, *Sex in the Heartland* (Cambridge, Mass.: Harvard University Press, 1999); James R. Peterson, *The Century of Sex: Playboy's History of the Sexual Revolution, 1900–1999* (New York: Grove Press, 1999); David Allyn, *Make Love Not War: The Sexual Revolution, An Unfettered History* (Boston: Little, Brown, 2000).

2. Paul Kantus, interview by author, 3 October 2005, San Francisco, CA; Edan Hughes, *Artists in California, 1786–1940* (San Francisco: Hughes, 1989), 377; James P. Woods, Jr., *A Place Where God Lives: St. Paul's Parish, A History 1980–2005* (San Francisco: n.p., 2005), 3; Maitland Zane, "Graffiti Foe Fred Methner Dies at 84," *SFC*, 21 September 1991, C10.

3. On the proposed mental health clinic, see Francis J. Curry to Thomas J. Mellon, 4 December 1970; Fred Methner to Dianne Feinstein, ca. 23 February 1971; Dianne Feinstein to Fred Methner, 2 March 1971; Fred Methner to Dianne Feinstein, 8 March 1971; "Meeting flier," 10 December 1970, EWCSICR. Special thanks to Paul Kantus for making this unprocessed collection available to me.

4. Fred Methner, "Speech before San Francisco Planning, Housing & Development Committee hearing," 7 May 1977, file 239–78, SFBOS.

5. William Murray, "The Porn Capital of America," *NYT*, 3 January 1971, SM8.

6. Bruce Brugmann and Greggar Sletteland, *The Ultimate Highrise: San Francisco's Mad Rush toward the Sky* (San Francisco: San Francisco Bay Guardian, 1971), 30.

7. Herb Caen, *The Best of Herb Caen: 1960–1975* (San Francisco: Chronicle Books, 1991), 70.

8. "1974 General Attitudes and Issues, San Francisco Focus, 1974," 3–4, box 9, folder 459, COYOTE.

9. *Gallup Poll no. 780*, 15–20 May 1969.

10. Todd Gitlin, *The Sixties: Years of Hope, Days of Rage* (New York: Bantam Books, 1993), 202.

11. Throughout the book, I use the term *public space* to refer not only to formally public institutions like public parks and public thoroughfares, but also "quasi-public" places that are privately owned but serve a nonexclusive public, like bars, restaurants, and nightclubs.

12. Although the same issues unfolded simultaneously in New York—and mostly in the Times Square area—they arguably transformed the nature of urban life in New York far less than they did in San Francisco because of the vast size of New York, and the striking geographic, economic, and social distinctions among its far-flung boroughs. Similarly, in Los Angeles, the vast size of the metropolis allowed most Angelenos to avoid discomforting sexual spectacles—concentrated mostly in West Hollywood, North Hollywood, and Hollywood proper—if they chose to do so. To understand the effect of these new sexual spectacles on New York City, see James Traub, *The Devil's Playground: A Century of Pleasure and Profit in Times Square* (New York: Random House, 2004); Timothy J. Gilfoyle, "From Soubrette Row to Show World: The Contested Sexualities of Times Square, 1880–1995," in *Policing Public Sex: Queer Politics and the Future of AIDS Activism*, ed. Glenn Colter et al. (Boston: South End Press, 1996), 263–294.

13. Methner, "Speech."

14. Ronald Reagan came in third place, following actor-comedian Eddie Murphy. Susanna McBee, "Heroes Are Back; Young Americans Tell Why," *U.S. News & World Report*, 22 April 1985, 44.

15. Centers for Disease Control, *HIV/AIDS Surveillance Report* 7(2) (December 1995), 7–8.

16. John D'Emilio, *Sexual Politics, Sexual Communities: The Making of a Homosexual Minority in the United States, 1940–1970* (Chicago: University of Chicago Press, 1983); Timothy J. Gilfoyle, *City of Eros: New York City, Prostitution, and the Commercialization of Sex, 1790–1920* (New York: Norton, 1992); George Chauncey, *Gay New York: Gender, Urban Culture, and the Making the Gay Male Word, 1890–1940* (New York: Basic Books, 1994); Kevin J. Mumford, *Interzones: Black/White Sex Districts in Chicago and New York in the Early Twentieth Century* (New York: Columbia University Press, 1997); Andrea Friedman, *Prurient Interests: Gender, Democracy, and Obscenity in New York City, 1909–1945* (New York: Columbia University Press, 2000); Marc Stein, *City of Sisterly and Brotherly Loves: Lesbian and Gay Philadelphia, 1945–1972* (Chicago: University of Chicago Press, 2000); Mark Wild, "Red Light Kaleidoscope: Prostitution and Ethnoracial Relations in Los Angeles, 1880–1940," *Journal of Urban*

History 28 (September 2002), 720–742; Nan Boyd, *Wide-open Town: A History of Queer San Francisco to 1965* (Berkeley: University of California Press, 2003); Daniel Hurewitz, *Bohemian Los Angeles and the Making of Modern Politics* (Berkeley: University of California Press, 2007).

17. Arnold R. Hirsch, *Making the Second Ghetto: Race and Housing in Chicago, 1940–1960* (New York: Cambridge University Press, 1983); Robert A. Beauregard, *Voices of Decline: The Postwar Fate of US Cities* (Cambridge: Blackwell, 1993); Thomas Sugrue, *The Origins of the Urban Crisis: Race and Inequality in Postwar Detroit* (Princeton: Princeton University Press, 1996); William J. Williams, *When Work Disappears: The World of the New Urban Poor* (New York: Random House, 1996); Kevin M. Kruse, *White Flight: Atlanta and the Making of Modern Conservatism* (Princeton: Princeton University Press, 2005); Matthew D. Lassiter, *The Silent Majority: Suburban Politics in the Sunbelt South* (Princeton: Princeton University Press, 2006).

18. Becky Nicolaides, *My Blue Heaven: Life and Politics in the Working-class Suburbs of Los Angeles* (Chicago: University of Chicago Press, 2002); Robert O. Self and Thomas J. Sugrue, "The Power of Place: Race, Political Economy, and Identity in the Postwar Metropolis," in *A Companion to Post-1945 America*, ed. Jean-Christophe Agnew and Roy Rosenzweig (Oxford: Blackwell, 2002), 20–43. Robert O. Self, *American Babylon: Race and the Struggle for Postwar Oakland* (Princeton: Princeton University Press, 2003); Josh Sides, *L.A. City Limits: African American Los Angeles from the Great Depression to the Present* (Berkeley: University of California Press, 2003); Eric Avila, *Popular Culture in the Age of White Flight: Fear and Fantasy in Suburban Los Angeles* (Berkeley: University of California Press, 2004).

19. Lewis Mumford, "What Is a City?" *The City Reader*, ed. Richard T. LeGates and Frederic Stout (New York: Routledge, 2003), 94.

20. Bryant Simon, "New York Avenue: The Life and Death of Gay Spaces in Atlantic City, New Jersey, 1920–1990," *Journal of Urban History* 28 (March 2002), 301; See also Bryant Simon, *Boardwalk of Dreams: Atlantic City and the Fate of Urban America* (New York: Oxford University Press, 2004).

CHAPTER I

1. Richard V. Hyer, "Bare Flag Revolt," *SFC*, 26 June 1946, 13; "Sally Will Face Uncover Charge Again," *SFC*, 27 June 1946, 13. Rand faced similar charges in Los Angeles that November. "Sally Rand Faces Trial, Engages Lawyer Geisler," *SFC*, 2 November 1946, 5. On the origins of American ideas about French sexuality and sensuality, see Harvey Levenstein, *Seductive Journey: American Tourists in France from Jefferson to the Jazz Age* (Chicago: University of Chicago Press, 1998).

2. Charles W. Dullea, S.J., "A Jesuit Priest in the Service of Higher Education: The University of San Francisco," oral history conducted 1983–1984 by Ruth Teiser, Regional Oral History Office, Bancroft Library, University of California, San Francisco, 6–8; Citizens' Postwar Planning Committee, *Report of the Citizen's Postwar Planning Committee to Mayor Roger D. Lapham* (San Francisco: The Committee, 1945), 4. For a general profile of Lapham, see Charles Raudebaugh, "San Francisco: The Beldam Dozes," in *Our Fair City*, ed. Robert S. Allen (New York: Vanguard Press, 1947):

347–369; on the parking garage, see Leon J. Pinkson, "Union Square Garage Ends Parking Woe," *SFC*, 30 August 1942, 8; Pinkson, "Motor Dealers to Build Quarters, Garages," *SFC*, 3 December 1944, 9.

3. Susan Johnson, *Roaring Camp: The Social World of the California Gold Rush* (New York: Norton, 2000), 170, 278–279.

4. Roger W. Lotchin, *San Francisco, 1846–1856: From Hamlet to City* (Lincoln: University of Nebraska Press, 1979), vii.

5. Oscar Lewis, *San Francisco: Mission to Metropolis* (Berkeley: Howell-North Books, 1966), 144; Alvin Averbach, "San Francisco's South of Market District, 1850–1950: The Emergence of a Skid Row," *California Historical Quarterly* 52 (fall 1973), 197–223; Paul Groth, *Living Downtown: The History of Residential Hotels in the United States* (Berkeley: University of California Press, 1994), 19.

6. Herbert Asbury, *The Barbary Coast: An Informal History of the San Francisco Underworld* (New York: Capricorn Books, 1968 [1933]), 2. Because Asbury does not cite any sources, his work is difficult to verify, but his account of San Francisco is generally consistent with other available evidence from the era.

7. E. S. Capron, *History of California from Its Discovery to the Present Time* (Boston: John P. Jewett, 1854), 146–147; J. D. Borthwick, *Three Years in California* (Edinburgh: W. Blackwood, 1857) 67, 68; B. E. Lloyd, *Lights and Shades in San Francisco* (San Francisco: A. L. Bancroft, 1876), 78, 79.

8. *General Ordinances of the Board of Supervisors of the City and County of San Francisco, December 1, 1915* (San Francisco: Phillips and Van Orden, 1915), 471. For a highly original account of the politics of cross-dressing in late nineteenth-century San Francisco, see Amy Sueyoshi, "Mindful Masquerades: Que(e)rying Japanese Immigrant Dress in Turn-of-the-century San Francisco," *Frontiers* 26 (2005), 67–100; For an account of homosexual activity in nineteenth-century San Francisco, see Susan Stryker and Jim Van Buskirk, *Gay by the Bay: A History of Queer Culture in the San Francisco Bay Area* (San Francisco: Chronicle Books, 1996), 9–13; Nan Alamilla Boyd, *Wide Open Town: A History of Queer San Francisco to 1965* (Berkeley: University of California Press, 2003), 25–28.

9. *San Francisco Call*, 29 January 1907, cited in Asbury, *Barbary Coast*, 262.

10. Though virtually all Chinese prostitutes were described as "slaves" in the vernacular of Gilded Age and Progressive Era reformers, the status of the Chinese prostitute was considerably more complex. As historian Benson Tong has explained, there were various classes of Chinese prostitutes. A small number of them were independent proprietors, while the majority were indentured servants. One particularly odious practice—a function of both economic scarcity and the devaluation of women in China at the time—was the sale of young Chinese girls by their parents to Chinese tongs, which exploited their youth and naiveté, a practice the Ch'ing government not only tolerated but abetted. See Benson Tong, *Unsubmissive Women: Chinese Prostitutes in Nineteenth-century San Francisco* (Norman: University of Oklahoma Press, 1994). On Donaldina Cameron, see Brian Donovan, *White Slave Crusades: Race, Gender, and Anti-vice Activism, 1887–1917* (Urbana: University of Illinois Press, 2006), 110–128; Mildred Crowl Martin, *Chinatown's Angry Angel: The*

Story of Donaldina Cameron (Palo Alto: Pacific Books, 1977); Carol Green Wilson, *Chinatown Quest: The Life Adventures of Donaldina Cameron* (Palo Alto: Stanford University Press, 1931).

11. On the sporadic efforts to restrict vice, see Neil Larry Shumsky and Larry M. Springer, "San Francisco's Zone of Prostitution, 1880–1934," *Journal of Historical Geography* 7 (1981), 71–89; Lotchin, *San Francisco*, 255–258. On Ruef and Schmitz, see Walton Bean, *Boss Ruef's San Francisco: The Story of the Union Labor Party, Big Business, and the Graft Prosecution* (Berkeley: University of California Press, 1968), 46.

12. A. de la Torre to Commissioner-General of Immigration, 7 April 1909, file 52484/9, Records of the Immigration and Naturalization Service, National Archives and Records Administration, Washington, D.C.

13. Neil Larry Shumsky, "Vice Responds to Reform: San Francisco, 1910–1914," *Journal of Urban History* 7 (1980), 31–47.

14. Julius Rosenstirn, *Our Nation's Health Endangered by Poisonous Infection through the Social Malady: The Protective Work of the Municipal Clinic of San Francisco and Its Fight for Existence* (San Francisco, 1913), 7, 10, 11, 43.

15. Ibid., 24.

16. Ibid., 24, 25, 27, 36.

17. Ibid., 56; James Rolph to J. C. Westenberg, 9 August 1913, JRJP, cited in William Issel and Robert Cherny, *San Francisco, 1865–1932: Politics, Power, and Urban Development* (Berkeley: University of California Press, 1986), 108. On religious support for Barbary Coast closure, see H. E. Hatchman to James Rolph, 23 September 1913, 71A, JRJP. J. C. Westenberg to James Rolph, 22 September 1913, 71A, JRJP.

18. Asbury, *Barbary Coast*, 303.

19. *General Laws of California, As Amended and in Force at the Close of the Fortieth Session of the Legislature* (San Francisco: Bender-Moss, 1914), 20–22.

20. Rosenstirn, *Our Nation's Health*, 38.

21. Sally Stanford, *The Lady of the House* (Sausalito, Calif.: Comstock Editions, 1966), 30.

22. Shumsky and Springer, "San Francisco's Zone of Prostitution."

23. Stanford, *Lady of the House*, 32.

24. Ibid., 67.

25. Ibid., 66; "Full Text of Atherton's Graft Report," *SFC*, 17 March 1937, F1–F8; "Rossi Orders Drive against Vice," *SFE*, 24 March 1937, 1.

26. "Officialdom Declares War on Social Diseases," *LAT*, 2 November 1941, 12.

27. "Vice Crackdown: City Moves to Check Army, Navy Disease Rate," *SFC*, 12 August 1942, 3; "Social Problem: City Officials Outline Drive to Curb Prostitution Here," *SFC*, 15 August 1942, 3; Charles W. Dullea, "Law Enforcement and Venereal Disease Control," *San Francisco Police and Peace Officers' Journal*, May 1946, 1, 4, 26.

28. Dullea, "Law Enforcement and Venereal Disease Control," 4.

29. "Special Women's Court in S.F., January 1 to December 31, 1947," box 36, folder 776, ACLUNC.

30. "Special Women's Court, 3-5-45," box 36, folder 777, ACLUNC.

31. Ernest Besig to Dr. J. C. Geiger, 16 January 1945, box 36, folder 776, ACLUNC.

32. Bertram Edises to Ora E. Rhodes, 9 May 1949, box 36, folder 776, ACLUNC.

33. Besig to Geiger, 16 January 1945; Geiger to Besig, 22 January 1945, box 36, folder 776, ACLUNC; Max S. Marshall, *Crusader Undaunted: Dr. J. C. Geiger, Private Physician to the Public* (New York: Macmillan, 1958), 67–74.

34. Edwin James Cooley to Ernest Besig, 21 June 1946. See additional correspondence: Edwin James Cooley to Edmund G. Brown, 30 November 1944; Besig to Cooley, 5 December 1944; Cooley to Besig, 29 April 1946, box 36, folder 776, ACLUNC.

35. Cooley to Besig, 21 June 1946, box 36, folder 776, ACLUNC; Eugene A. Gillis, "Cooperation of Health Officers and Police Departments," *Journal of Venereal Disease Information,* 27 (March 1946), 62–64.

36. "Dullea, Judge in Row over Prostitution," *SFC,* 16 January 1944, 1.

37. California Commission on Organized Crime, *Final Report of the Special Crime Study* (Sacramento: The Commission, 1953), 82–92.

38. See Amanda Littauer, "The B-girl Evil: Bureaucracy, Sexuality, and the Menace of Barroom Vice in Postwar California," *Journal of the History of Sexuality* 12 (April 2003), 173; *Statutes of California, 1953 Regular Session* (Sacramento: California State Printing Office, 1953), 1024; "'Peggy' Reveals Inside Story of Life as a B-Girl," *SFC,* 28 April 1953, 1; Jackson Doyle, "'Compromises' Questioned in B-girl Cases," *SFC,* 11 June 1954, 10. "Two Fined in B-girl Convictions," *SFC,* 16 July 1954, 12.

39. George Dorsey, *Christopher of San Francisco* (New York: Macmillan, 1962), 108.

40. As John Mollenkopf has explained, urban planners habitually "ignored strong elements of community life...to arrive at their pictures of social decay." John H. Mollenkopf, *The Contested City* (Princeton: Princeton University Press, 1983), 174.

41. Mel Scott, *Western Addition District: An Exploration of the Possibilities of Replanning and Rebuilding One of San Francisco's Largest Blighted Districts* (San Francisco: City Planning Commission, 1947), 3.

42. San Francisco Planning and Housing Association, *Blight and Taxes* (San Francisco: Planning and Housing Association, 1947), 7.

43. San Francisco Planning and Housing Association, *Blight and Taxes,* 9.

44. Stanford, *Lady of the House,* 67.

45. Ibid., 180.

46. *Capitol Follies* program [circa 1940], personal collection of Jack Tillmany, San Francisco. For images of the *Capitol Follies,* see Jack Tillmany, *Theatres of San Francisco* (Charleston, S.C.: Arcadia, 2005), 47; Ettore Rella, *A History of Burlesque: A Monograph History of the San Francisco Stage and Its People from 1849 to the Present Day* (San Francisco: Work Projects Administration, Northern California, 1940), 313. Historians have echoed Rella's perspective, arguing that the advent of the striptease robbed burlesque of its earlier satirical and imaginative elements. See, for example, Robert C. Allen, *Horrible Prettiness: Burlesque and American Culture* (Chapel Hill: University of North Carolina Press, 1991); on burlesque generally, see Ann Corio with Joseph DiMona, *This Was Burlesque* (New York: Grosset and Dunlap, 1968),

71–77; Bernard Sobel, *A Pictorial History of Burlesque* (New York: Putnam, 1956); Rachel Shteir, *Striptease: The Untold History of the Girlie Show* (New York: Oxford University Press, 2004); Irving Zeidman, *The American Burlesque Show* (New York: Hawthorn, 1967).

47. Stanford, *Lady of the House*, 31.

48. For a thoroughly illuminating treatment of antiobscenity activism in New York, see Andrea Friedman, *Prurient Interests: Gender, Democracy, and Obscenity in New York City, 1909–1945* (New York: Columbia University, 2000).

49. ARSFPD, 1947–57.

50. Jack Lord, *Where to Sin in San Francisco* (San Francisco: Richard F. Guggenheim, 1953), 79.

51. Lorraine Dong, "The Forbidden City Legacy and Its Chinese American Women," in *Chinese America: History and Perspectives* (San Francisco: Chinese Historical Society of America, 1992), 138.

52. Information on Christopher visit from notes to photograph AAB-1195, SFHC; *Collier's* quoted in Shteir, *Striptease*, 205.

53. First passed in 1872, sec. 311 of the California Penal Code was subtly amended in 1873–1874, and again in 1931. The applicable code in Rand's case was the 1931 revision. See *Statutes of California, 1931* (Sacramento: California State Printing Office, 1931), 1597–1598.

54. Through the 1930s, American judges hearing obscenity cases relied on the definition of obscenity provided in the 1868 English case *Regina v. Hicklin*, in which the chief justice, Sir James Cockburn, wrote that the test of obscenity was "whether the tendency of the matter charged as obscenity is to deprave and corrupt those whose minds are open to such immoral influences, and into whose hands a publication of this sort may fall." The first significant revision to the Hicklin test in the United States occurred in 1934, when in the Second Circuit Court of Appeals review of James Joyce's *Ulysses*, the judge wrote that the "proper test of whether a given book is obscene is its dominant effect." As historians John D'Emilio and Estelle B. Freedman have explained, although lower courts did not always accept the so-called dominant effect doctrine, "the ruling served as a significant precedent allowing judges to evaluate the impact of a work as a whole, rather than isolated passages." John D'Emilio and Estelle B. Freedman, *Intimate Matters: A History of Sexuality in America* (New York: Harper & Row, 1988), 277–279.

55. Richard V. Hyer, "Bare Flag Revolt," *SFC*, 26 June 1946, 13; "Sally Pleads Not Guilty," *SFC*, 28 June 1946, 13; "Sally Argues Graphically for the Judge," *SFC*, 30 June 1946, 6.; John Wesley Noble and Bernard Averbuch, "The Long Blue Nose of the Law," *Playboy* 70 (February 1956), 70. On Ehrlich's other morality cases in the 1940s, see John Wesley Noble and Bernard Averbuch, *Never Plead Guilty: The Story of Jake Ehrlich* (New York: Farrar, Straus, and Cudahy, 1955), 189–204. On Shoemaker's fancy for Rand, see J. W. Ehrlich, *A Life in My Hands: An Autobiography* (New York: Putnam, 1965), 127.

56. "Lili St. Cyr Takes Stand to Defend Performance," *LAT*, 8 December 1951, 3; "Jury Rules Stripping's Art, Free Lili St. Cyr," *LAT*, 12 December 1951, 5. A brief account of St. Cyr's trial appears in the autobiography of her attorney, Jerry Giesler.

See Jerry Giesler, *Hollywood Lawyer: The Jerry Giesler Story* (New York: Permabooks, 1962), 182–186.

57. Dullea, "A Jesuit Priest," 21; D'Emilio and Freedman, *Intimate Matters,* 280.

58. "Minsky Show Ban Vetoed in Newark," *NYT,* 28 April 1953, 32; *Adams Theatre Co. v. John B. Keenan,* 12 N.J. 267 96 A.2d 519 (1953).

59. *Roth v. United States,* 354 U.S. 476 (1957).

60. Christopher Agee, "The Streets of San Francisco: Blacks, Beats, Homosexuals and the San Francisco Police Department, 1950–1968" (University of California Berkeley, History Ph.D. dissertation, 2005), 114–115, 117–118.

61. Jonathan Root, "Burlesque Bows Out," *SFC,* 2 September 1963, 1, 22.

62. Ibid.

63. "Police Used Fancy Science to Trap Inez," *SFC,* 24 October 1952, 1; "Inez, Doctor Arrested in New Abortion Case," *SFC,* 23 October 1952, 1; "Burkett Says Cop Pay-off Tip Ignored," *SFC,* 21 August, 1954, 1. "Famed Abortionist Dies," *SFC,* 29 January 1976, 20.

64. Jerome E. Bates, "The Abortion Mill: An Institutional Study," *Journal of Criminal Law, Criminology, and Police Science* 45(2) (July–August 1954), 161, 163.

65. Thomas N. Saunders, *Planned Parenthood, Alameda/San Francisco, 1929–1994* (San Francisco: Planned Parenthood, 1995), 3, 5.

66. In 1965, sec. 601 was amended to allow public health providers to disseminate information on contraception, but it still forbade "commercially interested" parties from advertising contraceptive devices or abortion services. In 1971, the code was again amended to prohibit the dissemination of information on abortion, while allowing the dissemination of information on contraception. See *Statutes of California, 1937* (Sacramento: California State Printing Office, 1937), 1240; *Statutes of California 1965* (Sacramento: California State Printing Office, 1965), 2389–2390; *Statutes of California, 1971* (Sacramento: California State Printing Office, 1971), 1299.

67. "News Notes," *Birth Control Review,* June 1929, 171.

68. Elisabeth Grew Bacon, "The Booth at the National Conference," *Birth Control Review,* August 1929, 222.

69. "News Notes," *Birth Control Review,* December 1929, 360.

70. "Author Scores Modern Trends," *LAT,* 12 August 1931, 10.

71. Rebecca Whiteman, "Hidden Agendas: The Birth Control Movement in San Francisco," circa 1995, unpublished paper, TNSPP.

72. "Statistics Show Need," *Planned Parenthood Progress,* July 1956, 1, in TNSPP.

73. Thomas Cahill, interview by Paul Gabriel, San Francisco, 28 July 1997, Oral History Project, GLBTHS, 5, 11, 13, 14, 16.

74. On gay communities before the sexual revolution, see Peter Boag, *Same-Sex Affairs: Constructing and Controlling Homosexuality in the Pacific Northwest* (Berkeley: University of California Press, 2003); Nan Boyd, *Wide Open Town: A History of Queer San Francisco to 1965* (Berkeley: University of California Press, 2003) ; George Chauncey, *Gay New York: Gender, Urban Culture, and the Making of the Gay Male*

World, 1890–1940 (New York: Basic Books, 1994); Daniel Hurewitz, *Bohemian Los Angeles and the Making of Modern Politics* (Berkeley: University of California Press, 2007); Marc Stein, *City of Sisterly and Brotherly Loves: Lesbian and Gay Philadelphia, 1945–1972* (Chicago: University of Chicago Press, 2000).

75. Fred Brandt and Andrew Wood, *Fascinating San Francisco* (San Francisco: Chamber of Commerce, 1924), 5.

76. Lou Rand Hogan (writing under the byline "Toto Le Grand"), "The Golden Age of the Queens," *Bay Area Reporter*, October 1974, n.p., vertical files, GLBTHS.

77. On the liberating effects of World War II on homosexuals, see Allan Berube, "Marching to a Different Drummer: Lesbian and Gay GIs in World War II," and John D'Emilio, "Gay Politics and Community in San Francisco Since World War II," in *Hidden from History: Reclaiming the Gay and Lesbian Past*, ed. Martin Bauml Duberman, Martha Vicinus, and George Chauney, Jr. (New York: New American Library, 1989): 383–394, 456–473; John D' Emilio, *Sexual Politics, Sexual Communities: The Making of a Homosexual Minority in the United Sates, 1940–1970* (Chicago: University of Chicago Press, 1983), particularly chap. 2; lesbian bar names come from Boyd, *Wide Open Town*, 69, and QSDB.

78. Boyd, *Wide Open Town*, 61; Sidney Abbott and Barbara Love, *Sappho Was a Right-on Woman: A Liberated View of Lesbianism* (New York: Stein and Day, 1977 [1972]), 71, 73.

79. Chapter 330 of the California Penal Code, commonly known as the Alcoholic Beverage Control Act, was enacted in 1935. See *Statutes of California, Fifty-first Session* (Sacramento: California State Printing Office, 1935), 1123–1153; "Mexico-U.S. Hunt on for Girl's Slayer," *LAT*, 16 November 1949, 1, 3; "Man Held in Sex Killing of Baby, 1½, Near Fresno," *LAT*, 22 November 1949, 22; Subcommittee on Sex Crimes, California Legislature, *Preliminary Report of the Subcommittee on Sex Crimes, California Legislature, 1949 Regular Session* (Sacramento: California State Printing Office, 1949), 28, 72.

80. Henry Evans, *Bohemian San Francisco* (San Francisco: Porpoise Bookshop, 1955), 16; see also Herb Caen, "San Franciscaena," *SFC*, 2 July 1963, 19.

81. See various reports in box 6, files F3718:386, 3718:391, 3718:395; box 7, files 3718:372, 3718:410, ABC.

82. *Stoumen v. Munro*, 219 Cal. App. 2d 302; vagrancy arrest figures based on ARSFPD; William Keller, "Police Abuses Denied by Cahill," *SFC*, 16 November 1958; "Big Sex Raid—Cops Arrest 103," *SFC*, 14 August 1961, 3.

83. Warner Jepson, interview by Paul Gabriel and Philip Hong, San Francisco, 17 August 1995, Oral History Project, GLBTHS, 43–44.

84. Martin Meeker, *Contacts Desired: Gay and Lesbian Communications and Community, 1940s–1970s* (Chicago: University of Chicago Press, 2006), 40–41, 59–62, 1.

85. Del Martin and Phyllis Lyon, *Lesbian/Woman* (Volcano, Calif.: Volcano Press, 1991 [1972]), 223–224.

86. Meeker, *Contacts Desired*, 187.

87. "SIR's Statement of Policy," *Vector*, December 1964, 1. See also "On Getting and Using Power," *Vector*, November 1965, 4, 9–10.

88. Meeker, *Contacts Desired*, 63.

89. Ibid., 62–64.

CHAPTER 2

1. Jonathan Root, "Ten New Arrests: Topless Club Owners Sue Shelley, Cahill," *SFC*, 24 April 1965, 1; "All Topless Cases Will Be Dropped," 11 May 1965, 1; Susan Sward, "Getting Close to Carol Doda," *SFC*, 19 April 1980, 4; Gabrielle Schang, "My Bust Speaks Japanese," *Berkeley Barb*, 6–12 July 1973, 2–3.

2. Nancy J. Peters, "The Beat Generation and San Francisco's Culture of Dissent," in *Reclaiming San Francisco: History, Politics, Culture*, ed. James Brook, Chris Carlsson, and Nancy J. Peters (San Francisco: City Lights Books, 1998), 211. For more on the San Francisco literary renaissance of the 1950s see Michael Davidson, *The San Francisco Renaissance: Poetics and Community in Mid-Century* (New York: Cambridge University Press, 1989); Steven Watson, *The Birth of the Beat Generation: Visionaries, Rebels, and Hipsters, 1944–1960* (New York: Pantheon Books, 1995).

3. Watson, *The Birth of the Beat Generation*, 4; Helen M. Abrahamsen, *A Complete Guide to San Francisco and the Bay Area: Places, Food, Fun* (Palo Alto: Pacific Books, 1954), 53; *Your Guide to San Francisco and Its Nearby Vacationlands* (San Francisco: Californians Inc., 1957), 6. "SF Guide Folders," SFHC.

4. In April 1965, Ray Goman, owner of Goman's Gay 90s restaurant, complained to the Board of Supervisors about the nighttime street crowds in North Beach: "We should break up crowds on the sidewalks.... They look in windows at dancers, nude girls, everything." Mel Wax, "North Beach Chastised Again," *SFC*, 7 April 1965, 1; See also photograph AAB-9665, Historical Photograph Collection, SFHC; Patricia Carson to Board of Supervisors, 17 May 1977, file 239–78, SFBOS.

5. *In re Albert J. Giannini et al. on Habeas Corpus*, Crim no. 11446, Supreme Court of California, 69 Cal 2nd 563; Bill Roddy to Mayor Shelley, 20 October 1965, box 5, folder 3, JFSP.

6. H. Nawy, "The San Francisco Erotic Marketplace," in *Technical Reports of the Commission on Obscenity and Pornography* (Washington, D.C.: U.S. Government Printing Office, 1970), 4:162; Charles R. Gain to Dianne Feinstein, 16 May 1978, file 239–78, SFBOS.

7. Miles Hurwitz, "S.F. Barkers: Doing the Broadway Hustle," *Berkeley Barb*, July 30–August 5, 1976, 10.

8. "North Beach Committee," *SFC*, 31 March 1965, 3; Mel Wax, "North Beach Chastised Once Again"; "Anti-topless Forces Rally in Protest," *SFC*, 22 May 1965, 1.

9. Wax, "North Beach Chastised Once Again."

10. "Shelley Tough on Crime," *SFC*, 24 March 1965, 3.

11. Ron Fimrite, "Daring Daylight Strike by the Topless Raiders," *SFC*, 24 April 1965, 1, 6.

12. "Why the Frowns at North Beach?" *SFC*, 26 March 1965, 36.

13. In 1961, California's obscenity statutes were combined, revised, and renumbered into chapter 2147 of the California State Statutes. The original sec. 311, which dealt with "indecent exposure" and "obscene exhibitions," was renumbered but

not substantively changed. See *California Statutes, 1961* (Sacramento: California State Printing Office, 1961), 4427–4431.

14. *Albert J. Giannini et al. on Habeas Corpus.*

15. "S.F. Faces Massage Cleanup," *SFC*, 25 March 1965, 3.

16. Lisa McGirr, *Suburban Warriors: The Origins of the New American Right* (Princeton: Princeton University Press, 2001), 225–261.

17. *California v. LaRue*, 409 U.S. 109 (1972); "Supreme Court to Rule on Nude Dancers in California Taverns," *LAT*, 20 December 1971, 2; "California Will Act to Clean Up Nude Shows," *LAT*, 6 December 1972, 20.

18. David McCumber, *X Rated: The Mitchell Brothers, a True Story of Sex, Money, and Death* (New York: Simon and Schuster, 1992), 37; Nawy, "The San Francisco Erotic Marketplace," 4:180.

19. McCumber, *X Rated*, 47, 66–67.

20. "Police Report 7/09/1980," box 17, folder 871, COYOTE.

21. McCumber, *X-Rated*, 10.

22. Japanese-language Sutter Cinema advertisement, generously provided by UC Berkeley graduate student Joe Duong, and translated by CSUN graduate student Tomomi Ishihara.

23. David Smollar, "Tourists from Japan Get a Helping Hand," *LAT*, 15 October 1978, G1. Nawy, "The San Francisco Erotic Marketplace," 4:191, 196–198.

24. *Memoirs v. Massachusetts*, 383 U.S. 413 (1966); *Stanley v. Georgia*, 394 U.S. 557 (1969); *Miller v. California*, 413 U.S. 15 (1973). In *Memoirs*, the Court ruled that material had to meet the following criteria for obscenity: first, its dominant theme is prurient; second, it is patently offensive because "it affronts community standards"; and third, it is "utterly without redeeming social value." As legal scholar Donald A. Downs has explained, "only the most explicit material could meet the *Memoirs* test, which shifted emphasis from prurience (*Roth*) to patent offensiveness and the presence or absence of even minimal social value. The minimal social value test, in effect, required the prosecution to prove a negative—always a difficult task." The liberalizing trend continued in 1969, when the Court ruled in *Stanley* that the private possession of legally obscene material was not a crime. In the 1973 *Miller* ruling—which still serves as the benchmark standard for determining obscenity—the Court revised the "social value" criteria articulated in the Fanny Hill case, arguing that material that "lacks serious literary, artistic, political, or scientific value" may be obscene. Again, as Downs explains, "*Miller's* reformulation of the social value test made it less likely that otherwise obscene works would slip over the threshold of protection by the spurious inclusion of minimal social commentary." Donald A. Downs, "Obscenity and Pornography," in *The Oxford Companion to the Supreme Court of the United States*, ed. Kermit L. Hall et al. (New York: Oxford University Press, 1992), 603–604.

25. Eric Schaefer, "Gauging a Revolution: 16 mm Film and the Rise of the Pornographic Feature," *Cinema Journal* 41 (spring 2002), 7–9.

26. "Storefront Boom in Capital; Sex Policy Boosts Grosses," *Independent Film Journal* 21 (January 1971), 5, 30; Nawy, "San Francisco Erotic Marketplace," 4:166.

27. *Gallup Poll no. 780*, 05/15–05/20/1969.

28. San Francisco Committee on Crime, *A Report on Non-victim Crime in San Francisco*, pt. 2, *Sexual Conduct, Gambling, Pornography* (San Francisco: The Committee, 1971), 19.

29. Mike Weiss, *Double Play: The San Francisco City Hall Killings* (Reading, Mass.: Addison-Wesley, 1984), 19, 137.

30. "Facts on Prostitution," box 9, folder 455, COYOTE; Ivan Sharpe, "Open City: Prostitutes Flock to San Francisco," *SFC*, 7 March 1976.

31. Larry Littlejohn et al., "Drugs in the Tenderloin: A Publication of the Central City Target Area Board," January 1967, 15, vertical files, GLBTHS. Monique is a fictious name given to an anonymous interviewee in the Littlejohn report.

32. *Report on Non-victim Crime*, 38.

33. Ella Leffland, "Streetwalker Calls Her Profession 'Fun and Freedom,'" *Sun-Reporter*, 11 June 1966, 3.

34. George Draper, "A Negro 'Ghetto,'" *SFC*, 19 July 1963, 10.

35. Daniel Crowe, *Prophets of Rage: The Black Freedom Struggle in San Francisco, 1945–1969* (New York: Routledge, 2000), 56–61.

36. Warren Hinckle, *Gayslayer! The Story of How Dan White Killed Harvey Milk and George Moscone and Got Away with Murder* (Virginia City, Nev.: Silver Dollar Books, 1985 [1979]), 28.

37. On provincialism and race in the SFPD, as well as the San Francisco Fire Department, see Weiss, *Double Play*, 40–41, 68–70; Gregory Lewis, "Court Lifts Oversight of SFPD," *SFE*, 3 October 1998.

38. "Prostitution Statistics—Women Incarcerated in the S.F. County Jail in 1975," box 9, folder 455, COYOTE.

39. "Who Are the Women Sentenced to San Bruno?" box 9, folder 455, COYOTE.

40. Christina Milner-Rose, telephone interview to author, 1 July 2005.

41. Christina Milner and Richard Milner, *Black Players: The Secret World of Black Pimps* (Boston: Little, Brown, 1972), 160–164.

42. Christopher Agee, "The Streets of San Francisco: Blacks, Beats, Homosexuals and the San Francisco Police Department, 1950–1968" (Ph.D. diss., University of California, Berkeley, 2005), 143–144.

43. William Workman, "A Plan to Harass Prostitute Clients," *SFC*, 9 June 1971, 24.

44. "More Opposition to Haight Theater for 'Boys' Only!" *Haight-Ashbury Independent*, 20 July 1964, 1; "Sordid End to 'Gay' Haight Theater," *SFC*, August 19, 1964, 3.

45. For coverage of the debate in the *San Francisco Chronicle*, see John Calene, "Freeways in Gate Park Opposed by Commission," 11 September 1953, 4; "Big Protest on Park Freeway," 28 April 1964, 1; "Special Muni Fleet for Big Park Rally," 14 May 1964, 1; "Board Unit Rejects Panhandle Route," 15 May 1964, 1. For a secondary account and analysis, see William Issel, "Land Values, Human Values, and the Preservation of the City's Treasured Appearance: Environmentalism, Politics, and the San Francisco Freeway Revolt," *Pacific Historical Review* 68 (November 1999), 611–646.

46. Calculations from: *1940 Census of Population and Housing: Statistics for Census Tracts, San Francisco, CA* (Washington, D.C.: United States Government Printing Office, 1942); *1950 Census of Population, San Francisco–Oakland, Calif.,*

Census Tracts (Washington, D.C.: United States Government Printing Office, 1953); *U.S. Censuses of Population and Housing, 1960, Census Tracts, San Francisco-Oakland, CA* (Washington, D.C.: United States Government Printing office, 1961–1962); *1970 Census of Population and Housing, Census Tracts, PHC(1)-189, San Francisco–Oakland, CA, SMSA* (Washington, D.C.: United States Department of Commerce, 1972) ; *1980 Census of Population and HousingCensus Tracts, PHC80–2-321, San Francisco–Oakland, CA, SMSA,* sec.1; *1980 Census of Population and Housing, Census Tracts, 1980, PHC80–2-321, San Francisco–Oakland, CA, SMSA,* maps; *1980 Census of Population and Housing, Census Tracts, 1980, PHC80–2-321, San Francisco–Oakland, CA, SMSA,* sec. 2 (Washington, D.C.: United States Department of Commerce, 1983). "The Haight–Ashbury" refers to the area bounded by Waller on the South, Fulton on the North, Stanyan on the West, and Steiner on the East. This corresponds to census tracts J13, J14, J15, and J16 in 1940–1960, and census tracts 164, 165, 166, and 167 in 1970–1980.

47. Sherri Cavan, *Hippies of the Haight* (St. Louis, Mo.: New Critics Press, 1972), 45.

48. "New Supervisor for San Francisco," *Haight-Ashbury Independent,* 10 September 1964, 1; "Local Support for No on Prop 14," *Haight-Ashbury Independent,* 24 September 1964, 1; "Western Addition Project…Renewal or Removal?," *Haight-Ashbury Independent,* 1 October 1964, 1; "How the Haight Ashbury Voted," *Haight-Ashbury Independent,* 12 November 1964, 1.

49. "How the Haight Ashbury Voted," 1.

50. Francis J. Rigney and L. Douglas Smith, *The Real Bohemia: A Sociological and Psychological Study of the "Beats"* (New York: Basic Books, 1961), 151–176.

51. Regina Marler, ed., *Queer Beats: How the Beats Turned America on to Sex* (San Francisco: Cleis Press, 2004).

52. Rigney and Smith, *Real Bohemia,* 46–48.

53. Jefferson Poland and Sam Sloan, *Sex Marchers* (Los Angeles: Elysium, 1968), 12–15.

54. Michael Fallon, "New Hip Hangout—The Blue Unicorn," *SFE,* 6 September 1965, 14.

55. Jefferson Poland, "Beatniks So Sexually Conservative," *Berkeley Barb,* 20 May 1966, 6.

56. Jefferson F. Poland, e-mail message to author, 17 April 2008; in the early 1970s, after depositing personal and Sexual Freedom League papers at the Bancroft Library in Berkeley, Jefferson "Fuck" Poland left the San Francisco Bay Area. Clippings and correspondence on the Ft. Funston nude-in are in carton 4, folder 29, SFLR; see also the following *SFC* articles: "Nude Pickets in the Bay," August 22, 1965, 1, 3; "Nude Swim-Ins Switch Tactics," August 23, 1965, 2; "Justice under Wraps," August 24, 1965, 3; "The Naked Revolution," July 22, 1968, 3; See also "Skinny-Dip-In," *Newsweek,* September 6, 1965, 20.

57. "Everything You Always Wanted to Know (But Were Afraid to Ask) about the Psychedelic Venus Church," in *Nelly Heathen* (Berkeley, Calif.: Sensexual Pagan Mediafreaks, 1973) in Historical Society Library Pamphlet Collection, copy courtesy of the Wisconsin Historical Society, University of Wisconsin, Madison.

58. Mother Boats, e-mail message to author, 27 May 2008.

59. Alice Echols, *Scars of Sweet Paradise: The Life and Times of Janis Joplin* (New York: Holt, 1999), 159.

60. Margo Rila, comments at 1999 roundtable, transcribed by Andrea Sharon Dworkin, in "Bisexual Histories in San Francisco in the 1970s and Early 1980s," *Journal of Bisexuality* 1(1) (2001), 91, 92, 93.

61. Ibid.

62. Anonymous interviewee, telephone interview by author, 21 July 2008.

63. Cavan, *Hippies of the Haight*, 47; Michael Fallon, "A New Paradise for Beatniks," *SFE*, 5 September 1965, 5.

64. Michael Fallon, "Bohemia's New Haven," *SFE*, 7 September 1965, 1, 8.

65. Stephen M. Pittel, *The Current Status of the Haight-Ashbury Hippie Community* (San Francisco: Mt. Zion Hospital and Medical Center, September 1968), 4.

66. Cavan, *Hippies of the Haight*, 51–52; "Haight Street Straights Declare War on Hippies," *SFC*, 6 March 1968, 1; "Haight Residents Visit the Mayor," *SFC*, 14 March 1968, 3. "Dropouts with a Mission," *Newsweek*, February 6, 1967, 92.

67. David E. Smith and John Luce, *Love Needs Care: A History of San Francisco's Haight-Ashbury Free Medical Clinic and Its Pioneer Role in Treating Drug-Abuse Problems* (Boston: Little, Brown, 1971), 186. Pittel, *Current Status*, 35.

68. Smith and Luce, *Love Needs Care*, 141–148.

69. California Assembly, Criminal Justice Committee, and California Commission on the Status of Women, *Revising California Laws Relating to Rape: Transcript of the Hearing before the Assembly Criminal Justice Committee and the California Commission on the Status of Women*, Los Angeles, October 18, 1973, 46–47.

70. ARSFPD, 1957–1970.

71. L. H. Whittemore, *Cop! A Closeup of Violence and Tragedy* (New York: Holt, 1969), 236; Dominick Cavallo, *A Fiction of the Past: The Sixties in American History* (New York: St. Martin's Press, 1999), 140.

72. Smith and Luce, *Love Needs Care*, 23; Whittemore, *Cop*, 225.

73. Whittemore, *Cop*, 253.

74. Jerry Cohen, "Savage Mystic Cult Blamed for 5 Tate Murders, 6 Others," *LAT*, December 2, 1969, 1, 3.

75. U.S. House, Committee on Ways and Means, *The Green Book*, 108th Cong., 2nd sess., 2004, Committee Print WMCP: 108–6, M2.

76. Beth Berkov, Maria Cheung, and Mich Taschiro, "Trends in Births and Birth Outcomes for Unmarried Women in California 1966–1985," California Department of Health Services, Health and Welfare Agency, Sacramento, June 1988, 40.

77. *1970 Census Tracts*, 3, 45.

78. Rickie Solinger, *Wake Up Little Susie: Single Pregnancy and Race before Roe v. Wade* (New York: Routledge, 1992), 3, 9.

79. Berkov et al., "Trends in Birth Outcomes," 7.

80. Carolyn Anspacher, "Four Special Schools for 112 Pregnant S.F. Girls," *SFC*, 16 October 1967, 5; "Rash of S.F. Schoolgirl Pregnancies," *SFC*, 20 March 1963, 1.

81. "$10,840 Given to the City for Birth Control," *SFC*, 29 April 1964, 1; "San Francisco Opens First of 5 Birth Clinics," *SFC*, 23 November 1966, 1.

82. Sadja Greenwood, telephone interview by author, 8 June 2006.

83. For specific services and operations of the clinics, see Sadja Goldsmith, "San Francisco's Teen Clinic: Meeting the Sex Education and Birth Control Needs of the Sexually Active Schoolgirl," *Family Planning Perspectives* 1(2) (October 1969), 23–26.

84. "Obstetrician's Poll," 23 November 1966, 32, newspaper clipping, TNSPP.

85. Smith and Luce, *Love Needs Care*, 189.

86. Ibid., 189–191.

87. Joan Didion, *Slouching towards Bethlehem* (New York: Simon and Schuster, 1979 [1968]), 85, 127–128.

CHAPTER 3

1. Paul Kantus, interview by author, 3 October 2005, San Francisco, CA; Charles W. Dullea, "A Jesuit Priest in the Service of Higher Education: The University of San Francisco," oral history conducted 1983–1984 by Ruth Teiser, Regional Oral History Office, Bancroft Library, University of California, Berkeley, 12–13.

2. Jess Stearn, *The Sixth Man* (Garden City, N.Y.: Doubleday, 1961); *The Grapevine* (Garden City, N.Y.: Doubleday, 1964), 283.

3. Paul Welch, "Homosexuality in America," *Life*, 26 June 1964, 66–80. Martin Meeker, *Contacts Desired: Gay and Lesbian Communications and Community, 1940s–1970s* (Chicago: University of Chicago Press, 2006), 189; Jack Fritscher, *Some Dance to Remember: A Novel of Gay Liberation in San Francisco, 1970–1982* (San Francisco: Palm Drive, 1990), 155.

4. "The Conspiracy Revealed," box 18, folder 1, LMP.

5. On the founding of CRH, see box 17, folder 14, LMP. The involvement of clergymen with the issue of homosexuality was certainly not without its opponents. For example, Max Rafferty, a columnist for the *Los Angeles Times*, lambasted the "swinging priests" who "are currently busy renouncing everything their faith has ever stood for and in the process are discarding all canons of decency and ordinary good taste." "In San Francisco," he concluded, "they put on cute little dancing parties for practicing homosexuals." Max Rafferty, "Merchants of Filth Are Mirrors of Our Morals," *LAT*, 26 September 1966, A6.

6. Information on the New Year's Ball comes from the following sources: "The Conspiracy Revealed," and "Statement of the Committee for the Mardi Gras Ball, January 2, 1965," folder 1, box 18, LMP; "Cops Invade Homosexual Benefit Ball," *SFC*, 2 January, 1965; Donovan Bess, "Angry Ministers Rip Police," *SFC*, January 3, 1965. "S.F. Homosexuals: Clerics Blast Cops," *SFC*, September 25, 1965, 1, 4.

7. Del Martin and Phyllis Lyon, *Lesbian/Woman* (Volcano, Calif.: Volcano Press, 1991 [1972]), 239.

8. Judge Leo Friedman chastised the SFPD for its harassment of the guests and instructed a jury to return a not-guilty verdict for the CRH members accused of obstructing justice in their failed attempt to restrict officers' entrance into California Hall. The decision apparently encouraged other local judges to recognize SFPD's needless harassment of homosexuals. See Christopher Agee, "The Streets of San

Francisco: Blacks, Beats, Homosexuals and the San Francisco Police Department, 1950–1968" (Ph.D. diss., University of California, Berkeley, 2005), 271.

9. Del Martin to Dr. Arthur Foster, 11 May 1966, folder b, box 17, LMP.

10. Peter Bart, "War Role Sought for Homosexuals," *NYT*, 17 April 1966, 12; Don Slater to Clay Colwell, 20 April 1966; James R. Turner to Intelligence Unit, ca. April 1966; Del Martin, "Report on Activities of Social Action Committee to the CRH Board," folder b, box 17, LMP.

11. "Homosexuals Protest Draft Exclusion," *Vector*, June 1966, 1, 6; "The Protest...A Qualified Success," *Citizen News*, July 1966, 1; Bob Ross to Members and Friends, 27 May 1966, folder 10, box 19, LMP. Strait was a gay journalist and publisher best known for publishing one of the first gay bar directories, *The Lavender Baedeker* (1963), in the United States. He also published various newspapers, including *LCE* [League of Civil Education] *Citizen's News*, *Citizen's News*, and *Cruise News*. See Meeker, *Contacts Desired*, 207–213.

12. "Deviates Demand the Right to Serve," *SFC*, 22 May 1966, 1B; "Homosexuals Protest Draft Exclusion," *SFC*, 6.

13. Susan Stryker, *Transgender History* (Berkeley: Seal Press, 2008), 65; see also the documentary film *Screaming Queens: The Riot at Compton's Cafeteria* (2005), directed by Victor Silverman and Susan Stryker.

14. Unless otherwise stated, all information on Whittington comes from Gale Chester Whittington, telephone interview by author, 23 April 2006 and 24 May 2006.

15. Jim Kirkman, interview by Jim Duggins, 1995, Oral History Project, GLBTHS, 28–29.

16. Unless otherwise stated, all biographical information on Laurence comes from Leo Laurence, telephone interview by author, 1 June 2006.

17. Leo E. Laurence, "Gay Revolution," *Vector*, April 1969, 11, 25.

18. "Homo Revolt: 'Don't Hide It,'" *Berkeley Barb*, March 28–April 3, 1969, 5, 23.

19. "Gays to Sit," *Berkeley Barb*, 9 May 1969, 12.

20. Pat Brown e-mail message to author, 22 July 2008.

21. "Gay Strike Turns Grim," April 25–May 1, 1969, 7.

22. "Pre-CHF Statements by C. Thorpe," "SF Protests" folder, CTP.

23. Whittington interview; *CHF Newsletter*, 5 June 1969, 93–13, LMP. Subsequently, CHF discovered that Denaro had in fact been fired for stealing, but it scarcely mattered to either CHF or the company. Nor did the mendacious Denaro want his job back. "We just wanted to get people to come out of the closet and stand up for their rights," Whittington recalled.

24. "Press Release, October 31, 1969," "Thorpe Notebook Covers," CTP; "Bad Day for Gay Group," *SFC*, 4 November 1969, 37; Robert Patterson, "The Dreary Revels of S.F. 'Gay Clubs,'" *SFE*, 25 October 1969, 5.

25. Phyllis A. Lyon to Mr. Appleby, 5 August 1970; J. P. Garling, Jr., to Miss Phyllis Lyon, 11 August 1970; "Why Macy's?" leaflet, folder 18, box 21, LMP.

26. On reforms to the Democratic National Committee delegate selection process, see Denis G. Sullivan et al., *The Politics of Representation: The Democratic*

Convention 1972 (New York: St. Martin's Press, 1974). For a short summary of changes, see also "Democratic Reform for '72," *NYT*, 6 May 1970, 42.

27. Randy Shilts, *The Mayor of Castro Street: The Life and Times of Harvey Milk* (New York: St. Martin's Press, 1982), 64.

28. Hebert Gold, "A Walk on San Francisco's Gay Side," *NYT*, 6 November 1977, 17. Rob Waters and Wade Hudson, "The Tenderloin: What Makes a Neighborhood," in *Reclaiming San Francisco: History, Politics, Culture*, ed. James Brook, Chris Carlsson, and Nancy J. Peters (San Francisco: City Lights Books, 1998), 304.

29. John Rechy, *City of Night* (New York: Grove Press, 1984 [1963]), 9, 238.

30. Larry Littlejohn et al., "Drugs in the Tenderloin: A Publication of the Central City Target Area Board," January 1967, 15–17, vertical files, GLBTHS.

31. Ted McIlvenna, interview by author, 20 March 2008, San Francisco, CA.

32. Program for conference "The Young Adult in the Metropolis," 1964, 3, personal collection of Ted McIlvenna, Institute for the Advanced Study of Human Sexuality, San Francisco.

33. Edward Hansen, Mark Forrester, and Fred Bird, *The Tenderloin Ghetto: The Young Reject in Our Society* [alternate subtitle: *Youth and Young Adults in the Tenderloin Area of Downtown San Francisco*] (mimeographed report) (San Francisco: Glide Urban Center, 1966), copy in box 19, folder 15, LMP.

34. The Tenderloin Committee, "Proposal for Confronting the Tenderloin Problem: A Proposal Submitted to the Economic Opportunities Council," box 19, folder 15, LMP.

35. Stryker, *Transgender History*, 76.

36. Susan Stryker, interviewed by Elliot Blackstone, 6 November 1996, San Francisco, CA, GLBTHS, 1–2.

37. Wyatt Buchanan, "Pride Parade Salute for an Unlikely Ally," *SFC*, 23 June 2006, B1.

38. Central City Hospitality House, "Final Report of the Tenderloin Ethnographic Research Project," September 1978, 89–90, vertical files, GLBTHS.

39. For an excellent comparison of the gay populations of other global cities, see David Higgs, ed., *Queer Sites: Gay Urban Histories since 1600* (London: Routledge, 1999).

40. Dennis Conkin, "Polk Street: What Lies Ahead?" *Bay Area Reporter*, 21 June 1990, 63.

41. Ibid., 63.

42. Benjamin Heim Shepard, *White Nights and Ascending Shadows: An Oral History of the AIDS Epidemic* (London: Cassell, 1997), 21.

43. Gayle S. Rubin, "The Miracle Mile: South of Market and Gay Male Leather, 1962–1997," in Brook et al., *Reclaiming San Francisco*, 258.

44. Arthur Fleming, *My Secret San Francisco* (Oakland: Sea Classics Press, 1969), 24.

45. *1970 Census of Population and Housing, Census Tracts, PHC(1)-189, San Francisco–Oakland, CA, SMSA*, 111, 120.

46. "1971 California Scene Map of Polk Street," *California Scene*, May 1971, 27.

47. Regina Elizabeth McQueen, interview by Susan Stryker, 17 July 1997, GLBTHS, 7–8.

48. Kevin Bentley, *Wild Animals I Have Known: Polk Street Diaries and After* (San Francisco: Green Candy Press, 2002), 8, 42.

49. John Rechy, *The Sexual Outlaw: A Documentary* (New York: Grove Press, 1984 [1977]), 47.

50. Rubin, "Miracle Mile," 255; See also Gayle Rubin, "Sites, Settlements, and Urban Sex: Archaeology and the Study of Gay Leathermen in San Francisco, 1955–1995" in Robert A. Schmidt and Barbara L. Voss, eds., *Archaeologies of Sexuality* (London: Routledge, 2000), 62–88; my estimates of South of Market establishments in 1970 comes from "South of Market Street Map," *California Scene*, November 1970, 14; estimates from 1980 come from QSDB.

51. Mark Thompson, "Folsom Street," *Advocate*, 8 July 1982 cited in Rubin, "Miracle Mile," 255; "The Folsom Attitude: Men of South of Market Gathering Places," *Drummer* 37 (1980), 33.

52. Fritscher, *Some Dance to Remember*, 158.

53. "Fire Sweeps 27 Buildings," *SFC*, 11 July 1981, 1.

54. QSDB.

55. Randy Shilts, *And the Band Played On: Politics, People and the AIDS Epidemic* (New York: St. Martin's Press, 1987), 19; Evelyn Hsu and Reginald Smith, "The Big Money in S.F. Gay Bathhouses," *SFC*, 9 April 1984, 1.

56. Shilts, *And the Band Played On*, 58; Larry Kramer, *Faggots* (New York: Plume Fiction, 1987 [1978]). By contrast, historian Allan Bérubé, writing at the height of the epidemic in 1984, tempered this characterization of the bathhouses, arguing that they provided much more than simply sex; they were points of social and business contact, havens from homophobia, and sites of celebration. However, whether one imagines the bathhouse narrowly as Kramer and Shilts did or more expansively as Bérubé did, there is no doubt that the bathhouses hosted an increasingly anonymous, largely depersonalized, and high-volume sex trade. See Allan Bérubé, "The History of Gay Bathhouses," in *Policing Public Sex: Queer Politics and the Future of AIDS Activism*, ed. Dangerous Bedfellows (Boston: South End Press, 1996), 187–220.

57. Selma K. Dritz, oral history conducted by Sally Smith Hughes, 1992 and 1993, in *The AIDS Epidemic in San Francisco: The Medical Response, 1981–1984*, Regional Oral History Office, Bancroft Library, University of California, Berkeley, 1997, 1:17.

58. "The Folsom South of Market Attitude," *Drummer* 37 (1980), 33.

59. Horacio N. Roque Ramírez, "'That's My Place!' Negotiating Racial, Sexual, and Gender Politics in San Francisco's Gay Latino Alliance, 1975–1983," *Journal of the History of Sexuality* 22 (April 2003), 224–258.

60. Mark Thompson, ed., *Long Road to Freedom: The Advocate History of the Gay and Lesbian Movement* (New York: St. Martin's Press, 1994), 212.

61. Here and throughout, I have defined the Castro as the district within the following boundaries: Duboce on the north, Dolores on the east, Twenty-first on the south, and Douglas on the west. This area corresponds to the following census tracts J18, J19, N3, N5, N6 in 1940 and 1950: tracts J18, J19, N3, N5a, N6 in 1960; tracts 169,

170, 203, 205, 206 in 1970 and 1980. *1940 Census of Population and Housing: Statistics for Census Tracts, San Francisco, CA* (Washington, D.C.: United States Government Printing Office, 1942); *1950 Census of Population, San Francisco–Oakland, Calif., Census Tracts* (Washington, D.C.: United States Government Printing Office, 1953); *U.S. Censuses of Population and Housing, 1960, Census Tracts, San Francisco-Oakland, CA* (Washington, D.C.: United States Government Printing office, 1961–1962); *1970 Census of Population and Housing, Census Tracts, PHC(1)-189, San Francisco–Oakland, CA, SMSA* (Washington, D.C.: United States Department of Commerce, 1972) ; *1980 Census of Population and Housing Census Tracts, PHC80–2-321, San Francisco–Oakland, CA, SMSA, sec.1; 1980 Census of Population and Housing, Census Tracts, 1980, PHC80–2-321, San Francisco–Oakland, CA, SMSA*, maps; *1980 Census of Population and Housing, Census Tracts, 1980, PHC80–2-321, San Francisco–Oakland, CA, SMSA*, sec. 2 (Washington, D.C.: United States Department of Commerce, 1983). On Most Holy Redeemer, see Donal Godfrey, " 'Gay and Gray': The History and Significance of the Inclusion of the Gay Community at Most Holy Redeemer Parish, San Francisco" (Ph.D. diss., Church Divinity School of the Pacific, Berkeley, 2003).

62. QSDB; "Map of Upper Market and Upper Miracle Mile Area," *California Scene*, November 1970, 23; Peter Stein *The Castro: A Documentary*, 1997.

63. Peter Groubert and Cleve Jones, interviews, in Shepard, *White Nights and Ascending Shadows*, 19–26.

64. Godfrey, " 'Gay and Gray,' " 14–15, 17.

65. Katie Szymanski, "Twin Peaks: At the Corner of History and Tomorrow," in *Out in the Castro: Desire, Promise, Activism* (San Francisco: Leyland, 2002), 104–105; Jaguar information from anonymous interview with author.

66. Richard Rodriguez, *Days of Obligation: An Argument with My Mexican Father* (New York: Viking, 1992), 31–32.

67. Figures based on analysis of *1940 Census of Population and Housing: 1940 Census of Population and Housing: Statistics for Census Tracts, San Francisco, CA* (Washington, D.C.: United States Government Printing Office, 1942); *1950 Census of Population, San Francisco–Oakland, Calif., Census Tracts* (Washington, D.C.: United States Government Printing Office, 1953); *U.S. Censuses of Population and Housing, 1960, Census Tracts, San Francisco–Oakland, CA* (Washington, D.C.: United States Government Printing Office, 1961–1962); *1970 Census of Population and Housing, Census Tracts, PHC(1)-189, San Francisco–Oakland, CA, SMSA* (Washington, D.C.: United States Department of Commerce, 1972); *1980 Census of Population and Housing Census Tracts, PHC80–2-321, San Francisco–Oakland, CA, SMSA*, sec.1; *1980 Census of Population and Housing, Census Tracts, 1980, PHC80–2-321, San Francisco–Oakland, CA, SMSA*, maps; *1980 Census of Population and Housing, Census Tracts, 1980, PHC80–2-321, San Francisco–Oakland, CA, SMSA*, sec. 2 (Washington, D.C.: United States Department of Commerce, 1983).

68. Shilts, *Mayor of Castro Street*, 27, 33.

69. Ibid., 171.

70. Sidney Abbott and Barbara Love, *Sappho Was a Right-on Woman: A Liberated View of Lesbianism* (New York: Stein and Day, 1977 [1972]), 13.

71. Challenging the notion that the antipornography stance and the valorization of feminine sexuality were essential positions of radical feminism, Echols created the alternate category of cultural feminism at the Scholar and the Feminist Conference, Barnard College, April 24, 1982. "I believe that what we have come to identify as radical feminism represents such a fundamental departure from its roots that it requires renaming. To this end, I will refer to this more recent strain of feminism as cultural feminism, because it equates women's liberation with the nurturance of a female counterculture which it is hoped will supersede the dominant culture"; "The Taming of the ID: Feminist Sexual Politics, 1968–1983," in Alice Echols, *Shaky Ground: The '6os and Its Aftershocks* (New York: Columbia University Press, 2002), 110. This idea is developed more fully in Alice Echols, *Daring to be Bad: Radical Feminism in America, 1967–1975* (Minneapolis: University of Minnesota Press, 1989.

72. QSDB.

73. Sue-Ellen Case, "Making Butch: An Historical Memoir of the 1970s," in *Butch/Femme: Inside Lesbian Gender*, ed. Sally R. Munt and Cherry Smyth (London: Cassell, 1998), 37.

74. For a nuanced and rich account of Joplin's time in the Haight-Ashbury, see Alice Echols, *Scars of Sweet Paradise: The Life and Times of Janis Joplin* (New York: Holt, 1999). For a tacky tell-all account of Caserta's sexual relationship with Joplin, see Peggy Caserta as told to Dan Knapp, *Going Down with Janice* (Secaucus, N.J.: Lyle Stuart, 1973).

75. For the absence of lesbianism in the San Francisco women's movement, see Pamela Allen, *Free Space: A Perspective on the Small Group in Women's Liberation* (Washington, N.J.: Times Change Press, 1970).

76. Marcia M. Gallo, *Different Daughters: A History of DOB and the Rise of the Lesbian Rights Movement* (New York: Carroll and Graf, 2006), 175.

77. Del Martin, "If That's All There Is," *Motive* 32(1) (1972), 45–46, first published in *Advocate*, October 28–November 10, 1970, 74.

78. Elizabeth Sullivan, "Carol Seajay, Old Wives Tales, and the Feminist Bookstore Network," in *Shaping San Francisco*, CD-ROM, 2nd ed. (San Francisco: Shaping San Francisco Collective, June 2000).

79. Ibid.

80. Tomás Francisco Sandoval, Jr., "Mission Stories, Mission Lives: The Making of San Francisco's Latino Identity, 1945–1970" (Ph.D. diss., University of California, Berkeley, 2002), 105–106, 111–112.

81. See Juan Felipe Herrera, "Riffs on Mission District *Raza* Writers," in Brook et al., *Reclaiming San Francisco*, 217–230.

82. Manuel Castells and Karen Murphy, "Cultural Identity and Urban Structure: The Spatial Organization of San Francisco's Gay Community," in *Urban Policy under Capitalism*, ed. Norman I. Fainstein and Susan S. Fainstein (Beverly Hills: Sage, 1982), 257–258.

83. In 1970–1980, the two Mission Census Tracts (tracts 207 and 210) that received the most newcomers and had the highest proportion of single women also witnessed an increase in median income. But this increase in median income

occurred at a rate slower than the citywide increase in median income, and both tracts 207 and 210 had higher median incomes in 1960, before the lesbian migration.

84. Warren Hinckle, *Gayslayer! The Story of How Dan White Killed Harvey Milk and George Moscone and Got Away with Murder* (Virginia City, Nev.: Silver Dollar Books, 1985 [1979]), 72.

85. RB, "Urban Genocide," *Foghorn*, November 1980, n.p., clipping, The ONE National Gay & Lesbian Archives, Los Angeles.

86. Larry Carlson, "The Gay Rental," *Vector*, April 1968, 16–17.

87. Correspondence: Complaints, box 1, Old Wives' Tales Bookstore Records, GLBTHS (housed at SFHC). This file is replete with examples of the store's staff patiently responding to what appear to be largely unfair accusations of intolerance.

88. ARSFPD, 1973–1983.

89. Charlotte Bunch, "Lesbians in Revolt," *The Furies: Lesbian/Feminist Monthly* 1 (January 1972), 8–9, cited in Deborah Wolf, *The Lesbian Community* (Berkeley: University of California Press, 1979), 69.

90. Robin Morgan, *Going Too Far: The Personal Chronicle of a Feminist* (New York: Random House, 1977), 181.

91. Ibid., 171, 182.

92. Echols, *Daring to Be Bad*, 219–220.

93. Martin and Lyon, *Lesbian/Woman*, 63–64; in 1973, Martin and Lyon published an abbreviated follow-up booklet in which they continued to argue that dildos were "rarely used by Lesbians." "The turn-on for a Lesbian," they wrote, "is her woman partner, not a male substitute whether by role play or device." Del Martin and Phyllis Lyon, *Lesbian Love and Liberation: The Yes Book of Sex* (San Francisco: Multi Media Resource Center, 1973), n.p.

94. Patrick Califia, e-mail message to author, 22 July 2008.

95. Ibid.; Pat Califia, "A Personal View of the History of the Lesbian S/M Community and Movement in San Francisco," in *Coming to Power: Writings and Graphics on Lesbian S/M*, ed. Members of Samois (Boston: Alyson, 1982), 244.

96. Gayle Rubin, 19 July 2008. Rubin, "Samois," in *Encyclopedia of Lesbian, Gay, Bisexual and Transgender History in America*, ed. Marc Stein (New York: Scribner's, 2003).

97. Robin Ruth Linden et al., *Against Sadomasochism: A Radical Feminist Analysis* (East Palo Alto, Calif.: Frog in the Well, 1982), 2–3; Hostility to S/M at the Michigan Womyn's Music Festival has been documented elsewhere. See Rebecca Dawn Kaplan, "Sex, Lies, and Heteropatriarchy: The S/M Debates at the Michigan Womyn's Music Festival," in *The Second Coming: A Leatherdyke Reader*, ed. Pat Califia and Robin Sweeney (Los Angeles: Alyson, 1996), 123–130.

98. Carole Altman, "San Francisco's Bisexual Center," n.p., DLP.

99. Naomi Tucker, "Bay Area Bisexual History: An Interview with David Lourea," in *Bisexual Politics: Theories, Queries, and Visions*, ed. Tucker (New York: Harrington Park Press, 1995), 50.

100. Derek Fung, "Trailblazing in the Seventies: Maggi Rubenstein," *Anything That Moves* (winter 1996), 34–36; Jay P. Paul, "San Francisco's Bisexual Center and the Emergence of a Bisexual Movement," in *Bisexualities: The Ideology and Practice*

of Sexual Contact with Both Men and Women, ed. Erwin J. Haeberle et al. (New York: Continuum, 1998), 133, 134, 135.

101. Ann Forfreedom, "Lesbos Arise!" *Lesbian Tide*, March 1973, 5.

102. Janice G. Raymond, *The Transsexual Empire: The Making of the She-Male* (Boston: Beacon Press, 1979), 104.

103. Beth Elliott, "Bisexuality: The Best Thing That Ever Happened to Lesbian Feminism?" in *Bi Any Other Name: Bisexual People Speak Out*, ed. Loraine Hutchins and Lani Kaahumanu (New York: Alyson Books, 1994), 327.

104. Joani Blank, *My Playbook for Women about Sex* (San Francisco: Joani Blank, 1975), 1.

105. In Members of Samois, *Coming to Power*, 212–213.

CHAPTER 4

1. See tour guide books, SFHC, San Francisco Public Library. Quotation from *A Factful and Colorful Guide to San Francisco* (San Francisco: Smith News, ca. 1959), 8; Fred Brandt and Andrew Wood, *Fascinating San Francisco* (San Francisco: Chamber of Commerce, 1924), 40.

2. Fred Robbins, *Facts and Fancies of the Tour thru Golden Gate Park, Sightseeing, Automobile or Walking* (San Francisco: F. S. Robbins, 1916), 1.

3. On the planning of Golden Gate Park, see Terence Young, *Building San Francisco's Parks, 1850–1930* (Baltimore: Johns Hopkins University Press, 2004); on McLaren see Tom G. Aikman, *Boss Gardener: The Life and Times of John McLaren* (San Francisco: Lexikos, 1988), 68–69. See Raymond Clary, *The Making of Golden Gate Park, 1906–1950* (San Francisco: Don't Call It Frisco Press, 1987), and *The Making of Golden Gate Park: The Early Years, 1865–1906* (San Francisco: California Living Books, 1980). While most accounts credit McLaren with ridding the park of the "Keep Off the Grass" signs, the *San Francisco Chronicle* in 1929 credited 1880s park commissioner Frank M. Pixley, who reportedly convinced McLaren that the signs should be burned. "Grass Row Recalls Pixley Removed Last 'Keep Off' Sign," *SFC*, 4 December 1929, 17.

4. The editors of the *Los Angeles Times* appear to have delighted in reporting crime in Golden Gate Park, the sort of park their home city sorely lacked. See "A Murder in Golden Gate Park," 10 April 1886, 1; "A Ghastly 'Find' near Golden Gate Park," 13 March 1888, 4; "Two Suicides," 2 November 1889, 1; "Epidemic of Suicides," 17 June 1898, 4; "Two Suicides," 10 September 1899, A3; "Murder or Suicide?" 4 February 1900, I–3; "Golden Gate Park Suicide," 20 April 1903, 3; "Shoots Himself in Park," 28 September 1906, I–7; "Bank Clerk's Body Found," 6 June 1910, I–1; "Identifies Body," 22 July 1910, II–7; "Suicide Is Identified as Missing Musician," 6 May 1914, II–8; "Nurse Identifies San Francisco Mystery Killer," 27 July 1921, 12; "Find Woman Strangled in Bay City," 10 October 1921, 11; "Strangler Kills Girl," 14 May 1934, 3.

5. "'Dull Day' at the Park, a Mere 15,000 Visitors," *SFC*, 14 December 1936, 7.

6. Katherine Wilson, *Golden Gate: The Park of a Thousand Vistas* (Caldwell, ID: Caxton Printers, 1950), 47.

7. Clary, *Making of Golden Gate Park*, 39, 50.

8. Alma Whitaker, "Love-making a la Mode," *LAT*, 24 April 1927, L7.

9. Untitled article, *San Francisco News*, n.d., cited in Clary, *Making of Golden Gate Park*, 161.

10. New Chalet Thronged on Opening Day," *SFC*, 1 June 1925, 3; "New Beach Chalet Opened to Public," *SFC*, 31 May 1925, 4; "Beach Chalet near Readiness," *SFC*, 19 December 1924, 8.

11. "Lewd Show Raid Sets Off a Furor," *SFC*, 12 May 1952, 1, 9.

12. *Sexual Deviation Research: Report of Karl M. Bowman* (Sacramento: California State Assembly, 1952), 22, 29; *Final Report on California Sexual Deviation Research, March 1954* (Sacramento: California State Assembly, 1954), 119.

13. "Homos Invade S.F.," *Truth*, 11 July 1949, 1, 5.

14. California State Legislature, *Statutes and Amendment to the California Penal Code, 1955* (Sacramento: California State Printing Office, 1955), chap. 35, 477; chap. 169, 638.

15. Thomas Cahill, interview by Paul Gabriel, San Francisco, 28 July 1997, Oral History Project, GLBTHS, 110.

16. California State Legislature, *Statutes and Amendments 1961* (Sacramento: California State Printing Office, 1961), chap. 560, 1672.

17. "S.F. Man Admits Assault on Nurse," *SFC*, 3 August 1957, 1; "Rapist Leads Police to His Torture Kit," *SFC*, 4 August 1957, 1; "Sadist Indicted," *SFC*, 6 August 1957, 1; "Sadist Tells of Attack on Child, 9," *SFC*, 7 August 1957, 1; "Sadist Case Delayed for Mental Test," *SFC*, 22 August 1957, 36; "Bakkerud in Court, Plea Delayed Again," *SFC*, 28 August 1957, 5; "Bakkerud Insane, Says New Report," *SFC*, 18 September 1957, 12; "Judge Rules Today on Rapist's Sanity," *SFC*, 20 September 1957, 32; "Rapist Bakkerud Transferred to Atascadero," *SFC*, 1 October 1957, 26; "Torture-rapist Hangs Himself," *SFC*, 19 July 1967, 2.

18. "Fight against Vandalism: Restrictions on Use of Golden Gate Park Urged," *SFC*, 23 December 1953, 4.

19. "The Gathering of the Tribes," *Oracle*, January 1967, 2.

20. Charles Perry, *The Haight-Ashbury: A History* (New York: Random House, 1984), 126, 120.

21. Todd Gitlin, *The Sixties: Years of Hope, Days of Rage* (New York: Bantam Books, 1993), 210.

22. Jefferson Poland and Sam Sloan, *Sex Marchers* (Los Angeles: Elysium, 1968), 86; Helen Swick Perry, "The Human Be-In," in *"Takin' It to the Streets": A Sixties Reader*, ed. Alexander Bloom and Wini Breines (New York: Oxford University Press, 1995), 315.

23. Thomas Cahill interview, 70–75.

24. "Minutes, 9 May 1968," in uncatalogued records of the San Francisco Recreation and Park Commission Records, McLaren Lodge, San Francisco, CA. "The Park Called an Evil Jungle," *SFC*, 5 October 1968, 3.

25. Clary, *Making of Golden Gate Park*, 181.

26. "Hippies Accused of Park Vandalism," *SFC*, 12 April 1968, 3.

27. Perry, *Haight-Ashbury*, 211.

28. "Is Speedway Through?" *Berkeley Barb*, April 4–10, 1969, 13.

29. "Mayor Says Hippies Have Right in Park," *SFC*, 13 April 1968, 12; "Mayor Will Walk on the 'Wild Side," *SFC*, 15 May 1968, 1, 18; "The Mayor's Futile Stroll in the Park," *SFC*, 20 May 1968, 4; "Mayor Can't Find Sin," *SFC*, 21 May 1968, 3.

30. "Still Something Special," *San Francisco Sunday Examiner and Chronicle*, 2 June 1968, 24.

31. Jerry Gillam, "Dymally Breaks Tie, Senate OK's Sex Measure," *LAT*, 2 May 1975, B1.

32. "SFPD Initial Incident Report, Wed 09/22/76," box 1, folder 5, JMFP.

33. Eric Jay, "The Real Issue in the Hinson Affair," *Washington. D.C. Blade*, 20 February 1981, A19.

34. Bill Soiffer, "Gay Sex in Park Disturbs Buena Vista Neighbors," *SFC*, 27 April 1985, 4.

35. "Police Suspect Gay-haters in Series of Stab Murders," *Advocate*, 14 August 1974, 8.

36. Sara Rimer, "At Russian River, Gay Campers Find They Are Not Alone," *NYT*, 16 August 2002, F1.

37. For a highly original look at gays and lesbians in rural areas, see Scott Herring, "Out of the Closets, into the Woods: RFD, Country Women, and the Post-Stonewall Emergence of Queer Anti-Urbanism," *American Quarterly* 59(2) (2007), 341–372.

CHAPTER 5

1. Randy Shilts, *The Mayor of Castro Street: The Life and Times of Harvey Milk* (New York: St. Martin's Press, 1982), 162.

2. Bill Roddy to Mayor Shelley, 20 October 1965; William C. Roddy to Mr. Peter Trimble, 2 March 1966; John F. Shelley to Thomas J. Cahill, 18 November 1965; Roddy to Shelley, 16 November 1965; Cahill to Shelley, 17 November 1965, JFSP, box 5, folder 34.

3. "Official Drafts a Tougher Law on Street Vice," *SFC*, 10 August 1968, 2; J. Campbell Bruce, "Cahill's Stand on Prostitution Hit," *SFC*, 21 August 1968, 5. "First Male Prostitutes Jailed in S.F.," *SFC*, 13 December 1968, 2; "S.F. Cops Pinch Male Hustlers for First Time," *Advocate*, January 1969, 3.

4. "Biography," in "Finding Aid," JLAP.

5. For an extensive account of Alioto's involvement with downtown redevelopment, see Chester Hartman with Sarah Carnochan, *City for Sale: The Transformation of San Francisco* (Berkeley: University of California Press, 2002).

6. Dianne Feinstein to Thomas M. O'Connor, 4 December 1970; Thomas M. O'Connor to John A. DeLuca, 18 December 1970; O'Connor to Feinstein, 18 December 1970, box 5, folder 38, JLAP.

7. William Murray, "The Porn Capital of America," *NYT*, 3 January 1971, SM8.

8. David McCumber, *X-Rated: The Mitchell Brothers: A True Story of Sex, Money, and Death* (New York: Simon and Schuster, 1992), 40; "Dianne Smites Smut 'For

Gays,'" *Berkeley Barb*, 21–27 May 1971, 6; "Dianne Feinstein: A Brave New Mayor," *Ladies' Home Journal* 96 (March 1979), 164.

9. Daryl Lembke, "Alioto Tries for Tough Look in Mayoral Race," *LAT*, 28 October 1971, A21; "Major S.F. Mayoral Hopefuls Push Law and Order Positions," 30 October 1971, *LAT*, B9.

10. San Francisco Committee on Crime, *A Report on Non-victim Crime in San Francisco*, pt. 1, *Basic Principles, Public Drunkenness*, pt. 2, *Sexual Conduct, Gambling, Pornography* (San Francisco: The Committee, June 1971), 2.

11. Ibid., pt. 2, 38.

12. Ibid., pt. 1, 10.

13. Ibid., pt. 1, 4–5.

14. Dale Champion, "City Is Urged to Loosen Up on Sin," *SFC*, 4 June 1971, 1, 4.

15. In 1977, Feinstein pushed through an additional law that forbade the portrayal of sexual acts or organs at establishments with city entertainment permits. "Sexy Sign Law Is Approved," *SFC*, 14 February 1977, 13.

16. Philip Hager, " 'Everybody's Favorite City' Has Many Residents Worried," *LAT*, 30 March 1975, 3.

17. Moscone campaign flier, box 10, folder 74, JMFP.

18. James Foster, typed notes, "An Attitude toward Gay People," box 1, folder 8, JMFP.

19. Ibid.

20. City and County of San Francisco, Department of Elections, "Historical Voter Turnout," www.sfgov.org/site/elections; immediately following the election, allegations surfaced that Peoples Temple leader and Moscone supporter Jim Jones—who would infamously go on to orchestrate a mass suicide in Jonestown, Guyana, in November 1978—had abetted voter fraud by importing non-residents from neighboring cities to vote for Moscone. About fifty persons were, in fact, later convicted of voter fraud in the election, but none of them were members of the Peoples Temple, nor were they numerous enough to have put Moscone over the top. See Evan Maxwell and Doyle McManus, "State Investigates Alleged Voting Fraud by Temple," *LAT*, 20 December 1978, B28; John M. Crewdson, "Ex-aide Links Threats and Violence to Jones Advisor," *LAT*, 22 December 1978, A20.

21. Susan Sward, "Moscone's Time Was Anything but Quiet," *SFC*, 26 November 1998, A1.

22. Susan Sward, "Joseph Freitas Jr.: 1939–2006," *SFC*, 19 April 2006, B5.

23. Susan Sward, "Richard Hongisto: 1936–2004," *SFC*, 5 November 2004, A1.

24. "Minutes: Tenderloin Citizens Committee," 13 December 1976, box 1, folder 62, COYOTE.

25. Priscilla Alexander, "Working on Prostitution," July 1983, typescript, box 1, folder 32, COYOTE.

26. Hotel Employers Association of San Francisco to Dianne Feinstein, 11 May 1977, file 239–78, SFBOS.

27. Ibid.

28. "Sgt. Robert Spotswood interviewing Margo St. James," box 9, folder 458, COYOTE.

29. Alexander, "Working on Prostitution," 6; see also Margo St. James to Chief Charles Gain, 8 December 1976, box 1, folder 62, COYOTE.

30. ARSFPD, 1970–1973.

31. "Deadly Streets of the City," *SFC*, 5 December 1976, 5.

32. Margo St. James e-mail message to author, 11 November 2008.

33. Jerry Carroll, "Crackdown on S.F. Prostitution," *SFC*, 28 December 1976, 1, 20.

34. Francis Ward, "Detroit's Zoning Law Helps Clean Up Sex Shop District," *LAT*, 18 July 1977, A7.

35. Salvatore M. Giorlandino, "The Origin, Development, and Decline of Boston's Adult Entertainment District: The Combat Zone" (master's thesis, Massachusetts Institute of Technology, 1986), 22–27, 39, 40–41.

36. On Feinstein and feminism, see Kirsten Amundsen, "Dianne Feinstein: Now That Was a Mayor!" in *Women Leaders in Contemporary U.S. Politics,* ed. Frank P. Le Veness and Jane P. Sweeney (Boulder, Colo.: Rienner, 1987), 30–31.

37. See, for example, Andrea Dworkin, "Pornography and Grief," speech presented at First Feminist Conference on Pornography, San Francisco (just prior to the November 1978 march on Broadway); see also Dworkin, "Against the Male Flood: Censorship, Pornography, and Equality," in *Letters from a War Zone* (New York: Lawrence Hill, 1993).

38. Ezekiel Green, "Taking Back the Night," *San Francisco Sunday Examiner and Chronicle,* 11 February 1979, 19.

39. See Laura Lederer to Dianne Feinstein, 27 July 1997, 2 August 1977; Feinstein to Lederer, 4 August 1977, box 1, Correspondence—Administrative Files, WAVPM. In 1980, Lederer also edited a collection of essays on women and pornography. See Laura Lederer, *Take Back the Night* (New York: Morrow, 1980).

40. *Young v. American Mini Theaters Inc.,* 427 U.S. 50 (1976); on the Supreme Court and obscenity, see Richard F. Hixson, *Pornography and the Justices: The Supreme Court and the Intractable Obscenity Problem* (Carbondale: Southern Illinois University Press, 1996).

41. Marjorie Montelius to Board of Supervisors, 16 October 1978; James C. Fabris to Planning, Housing and Development Committee, 16 May 1978, file 239–78, SFBOS.

42. Maitland Zane, "Feinstein Proposes New Anti-porno Law," *SFC,* 19 January 1977, 2.

43. "Statement of Arthur Brunwasser," 21 November 1978, file 239–78, SFBOS.

44. Tom Benet, "Neighbors Object to Porno Zone," *SFC,* 18 May 1977, 5. Peter Tamaras was an influential supervisor who served two terms as president of the Board of Supervisors in the 1960s (see chapter 2, section entitled "Barbary Coast Redux").

45. "Plan for S.F. 'Porno Zone' Is Dropped," *SFC,* 2 August 1977, 4.

46. Ivan Sharpe and Malcolm Glover, "Gay Community Reacts: 'Afraid, but Strong,'" *SFE,* 24 June 1977, 3.

47. Details of the murder here and throughout are from Randy H. Alfred, notebooks labeled "People v. Cordova," RAP Collection, GLBTHS. Randy H. Alfred was a freelance journalist and radio talk show host who attended the trials

and copiously documented the proceedings; see also Bill Sievert, "The Killing of Mr. Greenjeans," *Mother Jones*, September–October 1977, 39–48.

48. For contemporary accounts drawing this connection see William Moore, "Stirring Tribute to Slain Gay," *SFC*, 28 June 1977, 1; Sharpe and Glover, "Gay Community Reacts," 1, 3; Sievert, "Killing of Mr. Greenjeans," 42–43. For historical accounts emphasizing this connection, see Shilts, *Mayor of Castro Street*, 153–168; John Loughery, *The Other Side of Silence: Men's Lives and Gay Identities: A Twentieth-century History* (New York: Holt, 1998), 397–398.

49. For background on Anita Bryant and the Dade County ordinance, see "Miami Area Aides Uphold Homosexual Rights Law," *NYT*, 20 April 1977, 16; B. Drummond Ayers, Jr., "Miami Debate over Rights of Homosexuals Directs Wide Attention to a National Issue," *NYT*, 10 May 1977, 18; B. Drummond Ayers, "Miami Votes 2 to 1 to Repeal Law Barring Bias against Homosexuals," *NYT*, 8 June 1977, 1. "Anita Bryant's Crusade," *Newsweek*, April 11, 1977, 39–40; "Battle over Gay Rights," *Newsweek*, June 6, 1977, 16–22; "Miami Vote: Tide Turning against Homosexuals?" *US News and World Report*, June 20, 1977, 46; "Voting against Gay Rights," *Time*, May 22, 1978, 21–22; "Why the Tide Is Turning against Homosexuals," *US News & World Report*, June 5, 1978, 29.

50. Shilts, *Mayor of Castro Street*, 154.

51. Anita Bryant, *The Anita Bryant Story: The Survival of Our Nation's Families and the Threat of Militant Homosexuality* (Old Tappan, N.J.: Revel, 1977), 85.

52. "Briggs Says Gays Have 'Taken' City," *NewsWest*, 23 June–7 July 1977, 4.

53. "Your Rights as a Parent and a Taxpayer Are under Attack," leaflet, box 1, folder 2, JMFP.

54. Grace Lichtenstein, "Laws Aiding Homosexuals Face Rising Opposition around the Nation," *NYT*, 27 April 1978, A1; "More Cities Face Battles over Homosexual Rights," *NYT*, 28 May 1978, 36.

55. Bryant, *Anita Bryant Story*, 17, 37, 38, 42, 87.

56. Sharpe and Glover, "Gay Community Reacts," *SFE*, 24 June 1977, 1, 3. Randy Alfred, "Freitas Throws a Curve," *San Francisco Sentinel*, 25 August 1977, 8; "Four Youths Held in 'Faggot' Slaying," *San Francisco Sentinel*, 30 June 1977, 1, 12.

57. Martin Duberman, *Left Out: The Politics of Exclusion. Essays, 1964–1999* (New York: Basic Books, 1999), 320; Nora Gallagher, Francis Moriarty and Randy Shilts, "Second Gay Murder Trial: New Facts?" *New West Intelligencer*, 30 January 1978, 6; Randy Alfred, "The Border of Light and Darkness," 20 June 1978, typescript, 9–11, Robert Hillsborough folder, RAP.

58. Tim Speck, "Come Prepared," *Coming Up!* January 1982.

59. Sievert, "Killing of Mr. Greenjeans," 39–40.

60. Sharpe and Glover, "Gay Community Reacts," *SFE*, 24 June 1977, 1, 3.

61. "Big Reward for Clue to Killers," *SFE*, 24 June 1977, 3; Wayne King, "Coast City to Curb Assaults by Gangs," *NYT*, 27 November 1980, A28.

62. "Gay Migration into Black Neighborhoods," *SFC*, 1 September 1979, 5.

63. Horacio N. Roque Ramírez, " 'That's *My* Place!' Negotiating Racial, Sexual, and Gender Politics in San Francisco's Gay Latino Alliance, 1975–1983," *Journal of the History of Sexuality* 22 (April 2003), 224–258.

64. "GALA on District 6 Race," *Sentinel*, 20 October 1977, 5.

65. Sievert, "Killing of Mr. Greenjeans," 46.

66. "KSAN Transcript, 11/30/77," typescript, RAP.

67. Ibid.

68. "Police Press Hunt for Slayers of Gay," *SFC*, 23 June 1977.

69. Charles Lee Morris, "D.A. Plea-bargains Murder Suspects," *San Francisco Sentinel*, 25 August 1977, 1, 5.

70. Alfred, "Freitas Throws a Curve," 8.

71. Sharpe and Glover, "Gay Community Reacts," 1.

72. Ibid.; Phil Bronstein, "Muggings: Gay-Latino Confrontations or No?" *SFE*, 11 November 1980, B1.

73. King, "Coast City to Curb Assaults by Gangs," A28.

74. For a thorough treatment of Dan White and the assassinations, see Mike Weiss, *Double Play: The San Francisco City Hall Killings* (Reading, Mass.: Addison-Wesley, 1984).

75. Warren Hinckle, *Gayslayer! The Story of How Dan White Killed Harvey Milk and George Moscone and Got Away with Murder* (Virginia City, Nev.: Silver Dollar Books, 1985), 16, 27.

76. Weiss, *Double Play*, 276–278; Mike Weiss, "Trial and Error," *Rolling Stone* 12 (July 1979), 47–49.

77. Lydia Shectman, "Off-duty Cops, Lesbians Tangle in Bar Brawl," *San Francisco Sentinel*, 6 April 1979, 1, 15.

78. "Who Are Sue and Shirley?" box 20, Milo Guthrie Papers, Special Collections Library, Duke University.

79. SFPD, "Police Incident Report, March 5, 1980"; SFWC flyer "Fire at the Women's Building"; *San Francisco Women's Centers Newsletter*, October 8, 1980, 1, box 20, folder 4, SFWCR.

80. "The (Im)moral Majority," *Alice Reports*, March 1981, 1–2; "Investigating the 'Moral Majority,'" *San Francisco Women's Centers Newsletter*, June 1981, 1, 3; John J. O'Connor, "Olympics Harbinger and Specials for a Fund Drive," *NYT*, 24 June 1983, C25; "'Christian' Leaders Launch 'Moral War' on Homosexuals," *Advocate*, 19 March 1981, 9; Cliff O'Neill, "San Francisco Leads Nation in Violence against Gays," *Bay Area Reporter*, 14 June 1990, 18.

81. Joyce Haber, "Movies Spotlight Sexual Deviates," *LAT*, 16 April 1968, C8.

82. Nathaniel Rich, *San Francisco Noir: The City in Film Noir from 1940 to the Present* (New York: Little Bookroom, 2005), 9–10.

83. See, for example, Nicholas Christopher, *Somewhere in the Night: Film Noir and the American City* (New York: Free Press, 1997); James Naremore, *More than Night: Film Noir in Its Contexts* (Berkeley: University of California Press, 1998), 35–36, 44–45. See Raymond Durgnat, "Paint It Black: The Family Tree of the Film Noir," and Karen Hollinger, "Film Noir, Voice-over, and the Femme Fatale," in *Film Noir Reader*, ed. Alain Silver and James Ursini (New York: Limelight Editions, 2005), 37–52, 243–260.

84. Robert Joseph, "Tapping S.F.'s Film Potential," *LAT*, 30 April 1967, C16; Gerald Nachman, "Coast's Bay Area Is a Lure for Filmmakers," *NYT*, 12 August 1971, 28.

85. J. Hobberman, *The Dream Life: Movies, Media, and the Mythology of the Sixties* (New York: New Press, 2003), 326.

86. Stuart M. Kaminsky, *Don Siegel: Director* (New York: Curtis Books, 1974), 281.

87. Pauline Kael, "Saint Cop," *New Yorker*, 15 January 1972, 78, 79; see also Roger Greenspun, "'Dirty Harry' and His Devotion to Duty," *NYT*, 23 December 1971, 20.

88. Daniel O'Brien, *Clint Eastwood: Film-Maker* (London: B. T. Batsford, 1996), 112.

89. Herb Caen, "It Takes All Kinds," *SFC*, 4 April 1974, 35.

90. Anthony Ray to Donald Scott, 18 January 1973, box 3, folder 37, JLAP.

91. "Committee Will Boost S.F. as Film-making Site," *LAT*, 30 July 1968, F10. On *Magnum Force* income see Robert Daley to John DeLuca, 4 August 1973, box 3, folder 37, JLAP. On Film Production Office activities generally, see box 3, folders 36 and 37, JLAP.

92. A. H. Weiler, "Film: Effective *Laughing Policeman*," *NYT*, 21 December 1973, 46.

93. Mark Thompson, ed., *Long Road to Freedom: The Advocate History of the Gay and Lesbian Movement* (New York: St. Martin's Press, 1994), 110.

94. "Protestors Call the Film *Cruising* Antihomosexual," *NYT*, 26 June 1979, B7; Les Ledbetter, "1000 in 'Village' Renew Protest against Movie on Homosexuals," *NYT*, 27 June 1979, B2; "Protest Continues on Film *Cruising*," *NYT*, 28 July 1979, 21; Fred Ferretti, "Filming of *Cruising* Goes More Calmly," *NYT*, 7 August 1979, C7; Clarke Taylor, "Gay Drama Offscreen on *Cruising*," *LAT*, 19 August 1979, N32; "Hundreds Gather in New Protest over Filming of Movie *Cruising*," *NYT*, 21 August 1979, D16.

95. William Carlsen, "Gays Picket at the Pyramid," *SFC*, 2 February 1980, 2; Ronald D. Moskowitz, "City Officials Pan *Cruising* after Screening," *SFC*, 14 February 1980, 18; Ronald D. Moskowitz, "Mayor Tried to Block *Cruising*," *SFC*, 15 February 1980.

CHAPTER 6

1. Selma K. Dritz, oral history conducted by Sally Smith Hughes, 1992 and 1993, in *The AIDS Epidemic in San Francisco: The Medical Response, 1981–1984*, Regional Oral History Office, Bancroft Library, University of California, Berkeley, 1997, 1:2–3.

2. Ibid., 7–8.

3. Selma K. Dritz, "Medical Aspects of Homosexuality," *New England Journal of Medicine* 302(8) (February 1980), 463–464.

4. Edward K. Markell et al., "Intestinal Parasitic Infections in Homosexual Men at a San Francisco Health Fair," *Western Journal of Medicine* 139(2) (August 1983), 177–178.

5. Randy Shilts, *And the Band Played On: Politics, People and the AIDS Epidemic* (New York: St. Martin's Press, 1987), 40.

6. Ibid.

7. M. S. Gottlieb et al., "Pneumocystis Pneumonia—Los Angeles," *Morbidity and Mortality Weekly Report*, 5 June 1981, 250–252.

8. Accounts of the AIDS crisis in San Francisco and the Castro in particular include Randy Shilts, *And the Band Played On;* Jim Mitulski, "The Castro Is a Sacred

Place," in *Out in the Castro: Desire, Promise, Activism,* ed. Winston Leyland (San Francisco: Leyland, 2002); Benjamin Shephard, *White Nights and Ascending Shadows: An Oral History of the San Francisco AIDS Epidemic* (London: Cassell, 1997).

9. Mervyn Silverman, oral history conducted by Sally Smith Hughes, 1992 and 1993, in *AIDS Epidemic in San Francisco,* 1:107–108.

10. Research and Decisions Corporation, *Designing an Effective AIDS Prevention Campaign Strategy for San Francisco: Results from the First Probability Sample of an Urban Gay Male Community* (San Francisco: Research and Decisions Corporation, 1984), 3, 116.

11. Leon McKusick et al., "AIDS and Sexual Behavior Reported by Gay Men in San Francisco," *American Journal of Public Health* 75(5) (May 1985), 493–496; Thomas J. Coates et al., *Changes in Sexual Behavior of Homosexual and Bisexual Men since the Beginning of the AIDS Epidemic* (San Francisco: Center for AIDS Prevention Studies, University of California, March 1988), 15.

12. David Lourea, "Safer Sex South of Market," 12 April 1990, box 1, DLP.

13. McKusick et al., "AIDS and Sexual Behavior," 493.

14. Mervyn Silverman, oral history in *AIDS Epidemic in San Francisco,* 1:133.

15. Dritz, oral history in *AIDS Epidemic in San Francisco,* 1:46–47.

16. David M. Cole, "Proposal to Ban Sex in Baths Gets Most Support in S.F. Poll," *Sunday Examiner Chronicle,* 8 April 1984, A1.

17. Jim Higgins, "The Bath House Gang," *San Francisco Policeman,* April 1984, 20.

18. Shilts, *And the Band Played On,* 443, 445. See also Paul Lorch, "Behavioral Modification for Sexers," *Bay Area Reporter,* 24 May 1984, 6.

19. "Bath Ass'n Pledges 'War Chest' for SF Clubs," *Bay Area Reporter,* 24 May 1984, 10.

20. Shilts, *And the Band Played On,* 304.

21. Mervyn Silverman, *AIDS Epidemic in San Francisco,* 106.

22. George Bush to David Werdegar, 16 October 1985, box 12, folder 29, JMFP.

23. "The Death of Leather," *San Francisco Focus,* November 1985, 17.

24. San Francisco AIDS Foundation to Human Rights Commission, 19 September 1989, folder entitled "San Francisco Human Rights Commission," Buzz Bense records, GLBTHS.

25. Kevin J. Jackson, "AIDS-induced Landscape Change: The Castro from 1980 to 2001" (masters thesis, San Francisco State University, 2002), 52.

26. Isadore Barmash, "Store Sales Lagging on Castro St.," *NYT,* 29 December 1984, 29.

27. Polly Ross Hughes, "Fear in the Castro: AIDS May Affect Insurance Rates," *SFC,* 24 April 1986, 3.

28. Robert Lindsey, "Where Homosexuals Found a Haven, There's No Haven from AIDS," *NYT,* 15 July 1987, A16.

29. Fritscher, *Some Dance to Remember,* 527.

30. Randy Shilts, "All Quiet in the Castro," *SFC,* 13 August 1986, 16.

31. Michelle Cochrane, *When AIDS Began: San Francisco and the Making of an Epidemic* (New York: Routledge, 2003), 14, 26, 56.

32. Randy Shilts, "S.F. Hookers Who Made History," *SFC*, 27 August 1987, 4. Unable to diagnose the children in 1978 and 1979, doctors froze their blood and only later recognized their ailment as AIDS.

33. Randy Shilts, "Prostitute Is Off the Streets," *SFC*, 8 January 1985, 5.

34. Gloria Lockett, interview, 14 February 1993, box 5, folder 35, NSP.

35. Lori Olszewski, "Former Hookers Help Their Own," *SFC*, 4 April 1988, D5; for a description of CAL-PEP activities, see Priscilla Alexander, *Prostitutes Prevent AIDS: A Manual for Health Educators* (San Francisco: California Prostitutes Education Project, 1988); on the bureaucratic history of CAL-PEP, see Nancy E. Stoller, *Lessons from the Damned: Queers, Whores, and Junkies Respond to AIDS* (New York: Routledge, 1998), 86–96.

36. Centers for Disease Control, *AIDS Weekly Surveillance Report—United States AIDS Activity*, 31 December 1984, 1; Centers for Disease Control, *HIV/AIDS Surveillance Report*, December 1994, 10.

37. "Antibody to Human Immunodeficiency Virus in Female Prostitutes," *San Francisco Epidemiologic Bulletin* 3(4) (April 1987), 14.

38. Susan Sward, "Needle Drug Users an 'AIDS Powder Keg,'" *SFC*, 25 August 1986, 1.

39. "Update: Acquired Immunodeficiency Syndrome—The Tenderloin, San Francisco," *San Francisco Epidemiologic Bulletin* 4(9) (September 1988), 35–36.

40. Kristen Clements-Nolle et al., "HIV Prevention and Health Service Needs in the Transgender Community of San Francisco," in *Transgender and HIV: Risks, Prevention, and Care*, ed. Walter Bockting and Sheila Kirk (New York: Haworth Press, 2001), 69–89.

41. ACLU AIDS Project, *Epidemic of Fear: A Survey of AIDS Discrimination in the 1980s and Policy Recommendations for the 1990s* (New York: American Civil Liberties Union, 1990), 1, 28, 29.

42. Dudley Clendinen, "AIDS Spreads Pain and Fear among Ill and Healthy Alike," *NYT*, 17 June 1983, A1.

43. Dennis Conkin to David Werdegar, 1 November 1988, box 12, folder 54, JMFP.

44. "Statement by G. Warren Kleinmaier," 31 October 1988, box/folder 12.54; Valerie C. Gilmore to David Werdegar, 10 November 1988, box 12, folder 54, JMFP.

45. Description of available health services comes from "Report to David Werdegar, Director of Health from the Committee for Non-acute Services for Persons with AIDS, 8 December 1988," box 5, folder 5, JMFP; Maitland Zane, "S.F.'s First Live-in Hospice Opens," *SFC*, 3 March 1987, 2.

46. Don Pharaoh, "Transamerica Awards Grant to Residence Program," *Eclipse: The Shanti Project Newsletter*, winter 1989, 11.

47. San Francisco Human Rights Commission, "Report on Sexual Orientation and AIDS discrimination, FY 1986–1987," box 12, folder 54, JMFP.

48. "Proposal for a Hotel Program for Homeless People with AIDS or ARC," box 5, folder 2, JMFP; San Francisco AIDS Office, *San Francisco AIDS Housing Plan Update: Executive Summary* (San Francisco: San Francisco AIDS Office, 1998), 3.

49. Randy Shilts, "Shocking AIDS Rate in Studies of Homeless," *SFC*, 6 June 1989, A8; J. A. Hahn et al., "HIV Seroconversion among the Homeless and Marginally Housed in San Francisco: A Ten-year Study," *Journal of Acquired Immune Deficiency Syndrome* 37(5) (December 2004), 1616–1619.

50. Ilene Lelchuk, "S.F.'s Homeless Legacy: Two Decades of Failure," *SFC*, 7 September 2003, A1.

51. Jennifer McIntyre and Alissa Riker, *Report: From Beyond Shelter to Behind Bars* (San Francisco: Center on Juvenile and Criminal Justice, 1993), 3; San Francisco Board of Supervisors, Budget Analyst, *Matrix Program Costs* (San Francisco: Board of Supervisors, 1993).

52. "The Mayor's War on the Poor Is a War on People with AIDS," leaflet, box 1, folder 1, AUGGR.

53. Lou Cannon, *President Reagan: The Role of a Lifetime* (New York: Simon and Schuster, 1991); William Martin, *With God on Our Side: The Rise of the Religious Right in America* (New York: Broadway Books, 1996); Randy Shilts, *And the Band Played On.*

54. Shilts, *And the Band Played On*, 596.

55. Martin, *With God on Our Side*, 241.

56. Cannon, *President Reagan*, 815–819.

57. Martin, *With God on Our Side*, 241–242.

58. Patrick J. Buchanan, "AIDS Disease: It's Nature Striking Back," *New York Post*, 24 May 1983, 31.

59. Martin, *With God on Our Side*, 242–243.

60. Buchanan, "AIDS Disease," 31.

61. Martin, *With God on Our Side*, 248.

62. Ibid.

63. Victor F. Zonana, "75 Groups Denounce AIDS Initiative as Threat to Prevention, Care," *LAT*, 30 July, 1988, 15; Lori Olszewski, "Some Doctors Vow to Destroy Records if AIDS Measure Passes," *SFC*, 1 October 1988, A2.

64. Larry Kramer, "The FDA's Callous Response to AIDS," *NYT*, 23 March 1987, A1.

65. Douglas Crimp, *AIDS Demographics* (Seattle: Bay Press, 1990), 28.

66. Playwright and gay activist Larry Kramer is often credited with raising the first alarms about AIDS among gays, and with founding ACT-UP in 1987. Larry Kramer's early publications on AIDS are compiled in his book *Reports from the Holocaust: The Making of an AIDS Activist* (New York: St. Martin's Press, 1989 [1981]).

67. Josh Gamson, "Silence, Death, and the Invisible Enemy: AIDS Activism and Social Movement 'Newness,'" *Social Problems* 36 (October 1989), 354, 356.

68. L. A. Chung, "The AIDS Vigil—S.F. Sufferers Rediscover Hope," *SFC*, 12 December 1985, 6.

69. Ibid.

70. Maitland Zane, "Federal Official Says AIDS Vigil Is a 'Blight,'" *SFC*, 9 December 1986, 2.

71. The vigil ended abruptly in December 1995 when a powerful storm leveled the remaining tents. But participants cited lack of interest in AIDS as the main cause of the vigil's demise. One of the last residents told a *San Francisco Chronicle* reporter:

"even ACT UP doesn't act up anymore." See *SFC*: "2 Vagrants Arrested at AIDS Protest," 4 November 1985, 20; "Vigil of Suffering and Hope," 12 December 1985, 1; "AIDS Vigil in S.F. Passes the One-year Mark," 5 November 1986, 11; Steve Massey, "Police Move against AIDS Vigil," 10 June 1989, A2; "AIDS Vigil at U.N. Plaza Folds Its Tent," 18 December 1995, A1.

72. Peter S. Arno and his colleagues demonstrated the vast difference in AIDS care in San Francisco and New York, largely due to the influence of the Office of Gay and Lesbian Health in the San Francisco Department of Health: Peter S. Arno et al., "Local Policy Responses to the AIDS Epidemic: New York and San Francisco," *New York State Journal of Medicine* 87 (May 1987), 264–271. Care in San Francisco was not only superior but actually cheaper, largely because of the role of nonprofits. See Peter S. Arno, "The Nonprofit Sector's Response to the AIDS Epidemic: Community-based Services in San Francisco," *Public Health* 76 (November 1986), 1325–1330.

73. Rick DelVecchio, "Chief Jordan's Explanation of Castro Sweep," *SFC*, 14 December 1989, A4.

74. Rick DelVecchio, "500 Protestors Block Market Street Traffic," *SFC*, 23 June 1990, A11.

75. "AIDS in Racial and Ethnic Minorities—San Francisco," *San Francisco Epidemiologic Bulletin*, September 1986, 1.

76. Ibid.

77. Cochrane, *When AIDS Began*, 72–74.

78. DiClemente et al., "Minorities and AIDS: Knowledge, Attitudes, and Misconceptions among Black and Latino Adolescents," *American Journal of Public Health* 78(1) (January 1988), 55–57.

79. Cathy J. Cohen, *The Boundaries of Blackness: AIDS and the Breakdown of Black Politics* (Chicago: University of Chicago Press, 1999), 249.

80. Meryle Weinstein, "Add AIDS to the List: AIDS Prevention in the Black Community" (master's thesis, San Francisco State University, 1991), 101.

81. AIDS-SFDPH, 1981–2008.

82. Ibid.

83. Benjamin P. Bowser, "Bayview–Hunter's Point: San Francisco's Black Ghetto Revisited," *Urban Anthropology* 17 (1988), 383, 384.

84. Mitchell S. Ratner, ed., *Crack Pipe as Pimp: An Ethnographic Investigation of Sex-for-crack Exchanges* (New York: Lexington Books, 1993), 2. See also Harvey W. Feldman et al., "Street Status and the Sex-for-crack Scene in San Francisco," in Ratner, *Crack Pipe as Pimp*, 133–158.

85. Bowser, "Bayview-Hunter's Point," 389.

86. Perry Lang, "Urban League Urged to Take More Active Role in AIDS War," *SFC*, 23 July 1986, 2.

87. Weinstein, "Add AIDS to the List," 100–102.

88. Mindy Fullilove, "Teens Rap about Drugs, STDs, and AIDS," *Multicultural Inquiry and Research on AIDS*, spring 1987, 1.

89. Reggie Williams to David Werdegar, 20 May 1986, box 1, folder 28, NTAP.

90. Paul Volberding to David Werdegar, 9 June 1986, box 1, folder 12, NTAP.

91. Reggie Williams, "Mission Statement," typescript box 1, folder 1, NTAP.

92. Reggie Williams, "Target Population," typescript box 1, folder 2, NTAP.

93. "Reggie Williams, Renowned S.F. AIDS Activist," *SFC*, 15 February 1999, A17.

94. "AIDS Knowledge and Attitudes of Black Americans," *NCHS Advancedata*, 30 March 1989, 1–2.

95. AIDS-SFDPH, 1981–2008.

96. San Francisco Department of Public Health, *San Francisco Sexually Transmitted Disease Annual Summary, 1998* (San Francisco: San Francisco Department of Public Health, September 1999), 19–20.

97. Mindy Thompson Fullilove et al., "Black Women and AIDS Prevention: A View towards Understanding Gender Rules," *Journal of Sex Research* 27(1) (February 1990), 53, 62.

CHAPTER 7

1. Bill Gordon, "Committee OKs Beach Chalet Restaurant," *SFC*, 2 December 1988, A10; Paul Liberatore, "How Ocean Beach Became a Wasteland," *SFC*, 29 July 1985, 4.

2. Edward J. Fitzpatrick, letter to the editor, *SFC*, 25 November 1996, A18.

3. "A Kiss Is Still a Kiss," *Dykespeak*, May 1995, 16.

4. Dick Walker and Bay Area Study Group, "The Playground of US Capitalism? The Political Economy of the San Francisco Bay Area in the 1980s," in *Fire in the Hearth: The Radical Politics of Place in America*, ed. Mike Davis et al. (New York: Verso, 1990), 8, 12.

5. Ibid., 12.

6. James Haas, "Exploring the Southeast: San Francisco's Last Frontier," *San Francisco Business* 22(10) (October 1987), 16.

7. Marissa Piesman and Marilee Hartley, *The Yuppie Handbook: The State-of-the-art Manual for Young Urban Professionals* (New York: Long Shadow Books, 1984), 12.

8. Alice Kahn, "Yuppie!" *Express*, 10 June 1983, 1, 6–7.

9. Sue Houfek e-mail message to author, 13 March 2008; for news coverage of the event see Sylvia Rubin, "Yupping the Night Away," *SFC*, 4 February 1985, 14.

10. Walker et al., "Playground of US Capitalism," 14.

11. Gerald D. Adams, "Department Stores in S.F. Hit Big Time," *SFC*, 11 September 1988, 1.

12. U.S. Bureau of the Census, *Census 2000 Summary File 3, Sample Data*, http://factfinder.census.gov, tables P24, PCT64I, PCT64D, PCT64H.

13. Ibid., table PCT74A.

14. Edward E. Leamer, "Bubble Trouble? Your Home Has a P/E Ration Too," June 2002, *UCLA Anderson Forecast Report*, June 2002, 5; Leamer, "Update, June 2, 2003: Bubble Trouble? Your Home Has a P/E Ratio Too," *UCLA Anderson Forecast Report*, 2003, 2; *San Francisco Housing DataBoook* (Emeryville, Calif.: Bay Area Economics, 2002), 68.

15. See James Brook, Chris Carlsson, and Nancy Peters, eds., *Reclaiming San Francisco: History, Politics, Culture* (San Francisco: City Lights Books, 1997); Rebecca

Solnit, *Hollow City: The Siege of San Francisco and the Crisis of American Urbanism* (London: Verso, 2000).

16. In order to determine the changing uses of sites of public sexuality in San Francisco, I created a list of sites, drawing on two sources of data. The first was a list of sex businesses submitted to Dianne Feinstein by police chief Charles Gain on 16 May 1978, "List of Adult Businesses, 1978," file 239–78, SFBOS, which contains the names and addresses of sixty-three sex businesses in San Francisco, including pornography stores and theaters, strip clubs, and encounter parlors. My second data source was the QSDB, a database of sites relevant to queer history in San Francisco that Willie Walker (1949–2004), a cofounder of GLBTHS, meticulously compiled during his devoted service as an archivist at the GLBTHS Library in 1985–2000. In combining the QSDB data with Gain's list, I selected only the QSDB sites that were extant in 1978, and to account for business turnover, I further restricted my list to the QSDB sites that were extant in 1978 and open between 1976 and 1980. There was an additional step; copiously detailed and well-cited as it is, one must use the QSDB with caution, as it casts a very wide net. Sites are listed regardless of when they became queer-identified; for example, a bar that opened in 1936 and only became queer-identified one year before its closing in 1968 will be listed as a queer site. In addition, the QSDB employs very liberal criteria for queerness: it lists virtually any site that was referenced in any queer periodical at any time as a queer site, even if it predominantly catered to heterosexuals. So careful cross-referencing was required to determine accurately the timing and extent of a site's queerness. I vetted numerous sites that did not meet my stricter criteria for queerness; restaurants were not included; and I did not include sites that were only briefly queer-identified or did not have closely to do with sex (bookstores, mainstream movie theaters, and markets with gay clientele, etc.). My final group from the QSDB consisted of forty-two gay, bisexual, lesbian, and transgender bars, public and private sex clubs, and porno theaters. These were combined with Gain's sixty-three to make up my final list of 105 sex sites. In May 2008, I documented every site's current usage on the basis of field observations.

17. "Tenderloin Merchants Seek Bigger Anti-crime Effort," *SFC*, 16 January 1985, 5; "Ramada Renaissance: S.F. Hotel Changing Name," *SFC*, 12 April 1989, C6; David Tuller, "Influx of Chinese Capital Expected," *SFC*, 6 June 1989, C1; Kyle Heger, "Checking into San Francisco: How the City's Hotels Market Themselves," *San Francisco Business* 23(10) (October 1988), 18.

18. Julian Davis, telephone interview with author, 14 May 2008; Tenderloin Neighborhood Development Corporation, *TNDC Strategic Plan: 2008–2012* (San Francisco: Tenderloin Neighborhood Development Corporation, 2008).

19. Elizabeth Bernstein, *Temporarily Yours: Intimacy, Authenticity, and the Commerce of Sex* (Chicago: University of Chicago Press, 2007), 30.

20. The perception of the relative "cleanliness" of massage parlors may have been illusory, as the available evidence on San Francisco massage parlor workers suggests: see Tooru Nemoto et al., "Social Factors Related to Risk for Violence and Sexually Transmitted Infections/HIV among Asian Massage Parlor Workers in San Francisco," *AIDS and Behavior* 8(4) (December 2004), 475–483; Tooru Nemoto et al., "HIV Risk among Asian Women Working at Massage Parlors in San Francisco,"

AIDS Education and Prevention 15(3) (2003), 245–255; Sheri D. Weiser et al., "Gender-specific Correlates of Sex Trade among Homeless and Marginally Housed Individuals in San Francisco," *Journal of Urban Health* 83(3) (2006), 736–740.

21. The San Francisco Department of Public Health generously furnished me with complete lists of licensed massage parlors in business in the years 1995, 2004, 2005, and 2008.

22. Leslie Fulbright, "Polk Gulch Cleanup Angers Some," *SFC,* 12 October 2005, B1.

23. Joseph Plaster, "The Death of Polk Street," *San Francisco Bay Guardian,* 29 August 2007, 1.

24. Wade Randlett, "Lawless Legacy Could Mug Supervisor at the Ballot Box," *San Francisco Business Times,* 27 October 2006, 1.

25. Fullbright, "Polk Gulch Cleanup Angers Some," B1.

26. Letters to the editor, *SFC,* 14 October 2005, B8.

27. My calculations are based on 1990 and 2000 block group data from Census tracts 111, 120, and 122. Source of original data: U.S. Bureau of the Census, *1990 Summary Tape File 1 (STF 1); 1990 Summary Tape File 3 (STF 3)—Sample data; Census 2000 Summary File 1 (SF1); Census 2000 Summary File 3 (SF 3);* http://factfinder. census.gov.

28. Sam Whiting, "A 'Fancy, Schmancy' Strip Joint," *SFC,* 3 August 1993, E3.

29. Jonathan Curiel, "Gloves Are Off on Broadway," *SFC,* 28 March 2000, A1.

30. John Koopman, "Hustler Club's Naked Truth," *SFC,* 11 March 2002, B1; Susan Sward et al., "Porn King Moves into North Beach," *SFC,* 13 August 1997, A1.

31. Flynt later fired back in the pages of *Hustler,* bestowing on Diana Russell the title of "Asshole of the Month" in February 2005; see also Jennie Ruby and Karla Mantilla, "With Feminist Pressure, Progressives Rethink Alliances with *Hustler,*" *Off Our Backs* 35 (July–August 2005), 13.

32. Koopman, "Hustler Club's Naked Truth," B1.

33. Shar Rednour, "A Decade of Lesbian Sex," unpublished manuscript, personal collection of Phyllis Christopher, Newcastle, England.

34. U.S. Bureau of the Census, *Census 2000 Summary File 3, Sample Data,* http://factfinder.census.gov, tract 205, http://factfinder.census.gov, tables P53, P77, H60, H63, H85.

35. As Alexandra Chasin has noted, this materialism was abetted by a frenetic rush among marketers to tap into the "dream market" of gays and lesbians. Alexandra Chasin, *Selling Out: The Gay and Lesbian Movement Goes to Market* (New York: St. Martin's Press, 2000).

36. Nan Kinney, telephone interview by author, 10 June 2008; Deborah Sundahl, telephone interview by author, 11 June 2008; Jill Nagle, "First Ladies of Feminist Porn: A Conversation with Candida Royalle and Debi Sundahl," in *Whores and Other Feminists,* ed. Nagle (New York: Routledge, 1997), 158–159, 160.

37. Susie Bright e-mail message to author, 29 September 2008.

38. "Year of the Lustful Lesbian," *On Our Backs* (summer 1984), 4.

39. Nagle, *Whores and Other Feminists,* 159–160.

40. "From the Desk of the Publishers," *On Our Backs* (September–October 1989), 4.

41. Dawn Atkins, "Introduction: Beauteous and Brave," introduction to *Bisexual Women in the Twenty-first Century*, ed. Atkins (Philadelphia: Haworth Press, 2003), 4.

42. Carol Queen, *Real Live Nude Girl: Chronicles of Sex-Positive Culture* (San Francisco: Cleis Press, 1997), 23.

43. Ibid., 68.

44. Patricia Lake, "Women's Sex Clubs: Dousing the Emotional Spark?" *Off Our Backs* 22 (April 1992), 16.

45. Rednour, "Decade of Lesbian Sex."

46. Roxie, "Sister Act: The Ups and Downs of Lesbian Sex Clubs," *Advocate*, 12 January 1993, 63–64.

47. Lake, "Women's Sex Clubs," 16.

48. Phyllis Christopher e-mail message to author, 4 May 2008.

49. City and County of San Francisco Department of Public Health AIDS News and Information, *Two New Surveys Show That Lesbians and Bisexual Women Are at High Risk for HIV Infection*, 19 October 1993, 1, folder entitled "Center for Disease Control," San Francisco Lesbian Avengers records, GLBTHS.

50. Centers for Disease Control and Prevention, *HIV/AIDS among Women Who Have Sex with Women* (Atlanta: Centers for Disease Control, June 2006), 1. Of the 246,461 women reported as HIV-infected in the United States up to December 2004, 534 reported that they had only had sex with women; of these 534, 91% had other risk factors, "typically injection drug use." In the remaining cases, "other risk factors were later identified."

51. Phyllis Christopher, "Sextrospective: A Decade with San Francisco's Sexiest Lesbians," unpublished manuscript, personal collection of Phyllis Christopher, Newcastle, England.

52. Tristan Taormino, "Dyke Porn Moguls," *On Our Backs* (June–July 2000), 30–31.

53. Ibid., 30–31.

54. Heather Findlay, telephone interview with author, 18 June 2008.

55. Henry S. Rubin, "Report on the First FTM Conference of the Americas: A Vision of Community," *Journal of Gay, Lesbian, and Bisexual Identity* 1 (1996), 171–177.

56. Betty Pearl and Pansy, *Betty and Pansy's Severe Queer Review of San Francisco* (San Francisco: Cleis Press, 2003), 137.

57. Ibid., 126.

58. On the founding of Bernal Books, see Shelley Bindon, "Pepper and Her Babies: How Does Rachel Do It?" *Lambda Book Report*, December 1999, 6–8.

EPILOGUE

1. Joan Didion, *Slouching towards Bethlehem* (New York: Simon and Schuster, 1979 [1968]), 176.

2. Rachel Gordon, "A Lifetime of Lesbian Activism," *SFC*, 28 August 2008, A1.

3. Heather Knight, "Some Areas of S.F. Voted to Ban Same-sex Marriage," *SFC*, 14 November 2008, A1.

4. Meredith May, "Sex Trafficking: San Francisco Is a Major Center for International Crime Networks That Smuggle and Enslave," *SFC*, 6 October 2006, A1.

5. Wyatt Buchanan, "San Francisco—Surprise!—Has Surpassed Los Angeles as the Capital of the Gay Adult Entertainment Industry," *SFC*, 23 Feb 2007, E1.

6. Free Speech Coalition, *Adult Entertainment in America: A State of the Industry Report* (Canoga Park, Calif.: Free Speech Coalition, 2006), 4; "State Board of Equalization Staff Legislative Bill Analysis, AB 1551," www.boe.ca.gov.

7. Free Speech Coalition, Adult Entertainment in America, 9; Timothy Egan, "Technology Sent Wall Street into Market for Pornography," *NYT*, 23 October 2000, A1.

8. Lawrence B. Finer, "Trends in Premarital Sex in the United States, 1954–2003," *Public Health Reports* 122 (January–February 2007), 76.

9. Arland Thornton and Linda Young DeMarco, "Four Decades of Trends in Attitudes toward Family Issues in the United States: The 1960s through the 1990s," *Journal of Marriage and the Family* 63 (November 2001), 1009–1037.

10. Patrick Califia, *Public Sex: The Culture of Radical Sex* (San Francisco: Cleis Press, 2000), 216.

INDEX